*Sport in
History*

Sport in History

The Making of Modern Sporting History

Edited by Richard Cashman
and Michael McKernan

University of Queensland Press

© University of Queensland Press, St. Lucia, Queensland, 1979

Typeset by Press Etching Pty. Ltd., Brisbane

Printed and bound by Southwood Press Pty Ltd, Sydney

Distributed in the United Kingdom, Europe, the Middle East,
Africa, and the Caribbean by Prentice-Hall International,
International Book Distributors Ltd., 66 Wood Lane End, Hemel
Hempstead, Herts., England

National Library of Australia
Cataloguing-in-Publication data

Sport in history.

ISBN 0 7022 1355 1
ISBN 0 7022 1356 X Paperback.

I. Sports—social aspect—Congresses. II. Sports—
History—Congresses. 1. Cashman, Richard
Ian, 1940–, ed. 2. McKernan, Michael
Matthew, 1945–, joint ed.

301.57

Contents

Acknowledgments

The editors gratefully acknowledge the assistance of the University of New South Wales, particularly Professor F. K. Crowley, Dean of the Faculty of Arts, in subsidizing this book.

List of Contributors

Barry Andrews teaches Australian literature at the Royal Military College, Duntroon. He has edited Price Warung's *Tales of the Convict System* (St Lucia: University of Queensland Press, 1975) and has written *Price Warung (WilliamAstley)* (Boston: Twayne, 1976) and is currently working on a bibliography of Australian literature in the nineteenth century.

Richard Broome teaches history at La Trobe University. He is currently working on a study of Aboriginal boxers.

Richard Cashman teaches South Asian history at the University of New South Wales. He is the author of *The Myth of "Lokamanya": Tilak and Mass Politics in Maharashtra* (Berkeley: University of California Press; 1975) and is currently working on aspects of leisure in traditional and modern India.

Chris Cunneen is a research fellow working on the *Australian Dictionary of Biography*.

Braham Dabscheck teaches industrial relations at the University of New South Wales and has published a number of articles on sport and industrial relations. He is currently working on the Australian system of industrial relations.

Jim Fitzpatrick is a research student at the Australian National University and is working on the role of the bicycle in rural Australia.

K. S. Inglis holds the Sir Keith Hancock Chair of History at the Australian National University. His publications include *The Australian Colonists* (Melbourne: Melbourne University Press; 1974) conceived as the first in a series of volumes about Australia from the first days of British settlement to the present.

Helen King taught European history at the University of New South Wales. She is continuing research on women and sport in Australia.

Michael McKernan teaches Australian history at the University of New South Wales. He is working on a history of the Australian people during the war 1914-1918.

W. F. Mandle is Head of the School of Liberal Studies, Canberra College of Advanced Education. He has published *Winners Can Laugh: Sport and Society* (Ringwood, Vic.: Penguin, 1974) and several articles on the meaning of sport in modern society.

M. N. Pearson teaches Asian history at the University of New South Wales. He has published *Merchants and Rulers in Gujarat* (Berkeley, University of California Press, 1976) and is currently working on the social history of Muslim India.

Peter Shergold teaches economic history at the University of New South Wales and has published articles on American labour history. He is now working on a study of the Australian wine industry.

Brian Stoddart teaches history at the Western Australian Institute of Technology. He is currently working on the bodyline tour of 1932–33 and its broader implications.

Jurgen Tampke teaches Modern European history at the University of New South Wales. His publications include *The Ruhr and Revolution* (Canberra, Australian National University Press, 1979); he is currently working on German labour history.

Ian Turner taught Australian history at Monash University. He worked extensively on the history of the labour movement in Australia and was writing a book on the social history of football in Melbourne. He died in December 1978.

Ian Tyrrell teaches American history at the University of New South Wales. He is currently preparing a manuscript on the history of temperance in the United States, 1800–1860, and researching mass spectator sport in the United States.

Wray Vamplew teaches economic history at the Flinders University of South Australia. He has published *The Turf* (London: Allen Lane, 1976) and several other books and continues his work on the history of horse-racing.

Preface

The essays in this book began as papers delivered at a conference of historians and representatives of other disciplines, held at the University of New South Wales in July 1977. The participants were conscious that they were entering a new field of Australian historical endeavour in seeking to explain "the making of sporting traditions", for it is unusual, to say the least, for a large number of academics to spend three days in the formal discussion of sport. The contributors hoped to demonstrate that the analysis of moments in the histories of individual sports, or an examination of the long-term evolution or collapse of a tradition, offer rewarding insights to the social historian. They were also convinced that the study of sport would be more than a "service industry" to provide a secondary viewpoint for the general historian. The analysis of particular moments in sport, such as the breakdown of traditional conventions and customs that occurred during bodyline cricket tour, or of the birth of a form of sporting endeavour or of a particularly momentous contest will offer insights into aspects of history that cannot be supplied from other sources. The papers presented to the conference so well fulfilled these aims and expectations that it was determined to publish them, to share them with a wider audience. This book is the result.

The book falls into four major divisions. The first six chapters examine the relationship between sport and society, and, particularly in the chapters by Michael McKernan, Helen King, Jurgen Tampke and W. F. Mandle, the relationship between sport and politics. These chapters also consider the growth of a division between "amateur" and "professional" sport, the conditions for the emergence of mass spectator sport, and the use of sport in literature. Then follow four chapters devoted to particular moments or periods in the development or decline of cricket. Cricket, supremely important in Australia and England, helped bolster feelings of national pride and assisted in shaping national identity. Richard Cashman, concentrating on cricket in India, enables the reader to make a comparative judgement about the place of sport in different societies. In the third section of the book, four contributors devote attention to various branches of football, examining in turn the emergence of the home-grown Australian version and an imported English game, the professionalization of English soccer, and the passion for football in New Zealand which inhibited discussion of questions of race relations. In the final section, attention turns to individual sports as against team sports, in which gambling emerges as an important consideration. Jim Fitzpatrick and Richard Broome emphasize the struggle for self-mastery which sport can involve, while Wray Vamplew discusses the conditions which brought about the popularization of horse-racing in Britain.

While acknowledging the serious nature of our study, historians of sport must guard against justifying its professional content by divorcing themselves from the primary object of their study: men and women at play. The contributors to this book have found a ready co-operation and interest among the devotees of sport and the sporting journalists who have accumulated considerable relevant data. We hope that this book will appeal to both the specialist historian and the general reader and that it may stimulate further interest in what we have found an exciting area of study.

Richard Cashman
Michael McKernan

MICHAEL McKERNAN

Sport, War and Society: Australia 1914-18

The Australian male, it is alleged, is addicted to sport, whether as player, spectator, gambler, or bar-breasting expert. Sport is the Australian national religion: Australians are a race of "sports". While such generalizations were as commonplace in late-nineteenth-century commentaries about Australia as in current analyses of Australian society, it is likely that they constantly over-simplify a complex situation. An analysis of the debate about the role of sport in Australian indicates that there was a division between the "professional" view of sport and the "amateur" view. The pressure of the First World War, which heightened and clarified many of the emerging conflicts in Australian society, brought these divisions about the meaning and purpose of sport into sharp focus. In the amateur account sport had meaning in so far as it taught the young such values as loyalty, determination, unselfishness and the team spirit. Sport was a preparation for something higher, something more important, usually "life". The amateur view was expressed most frequently and most forcefully by those who may be termed the middle-class opinion-makers, for example, headmasters of the Great Public Schools, leading clergymen, and editorialists in the prestigious newspapers. The professional view of sport was more pragmatic. Sport meant entertainment and pleasure, an exciting break from the monotony of urban work; as such, sport needed no further or more serious justification. In this account, gambling heightened the excitement derived from sport and allowed the spectator to test his expertise and judgement in the hope of overcoming, at least temporarily, the tyranny of wage slavery.

Most of the adherents of the professional view of sport were to be found among the Australian working class, while the amateur view prevailed in the middle class. During the war these two great classes moved further apart, divided by the fundamental question of the priority Australians should give to the defence of the Empire. The two views of sport emerged as an important element in this conflict:

those who subscribed to the amateur view demanded the abandonment of sport in wartime because it distracted the nation from its commitment to the Empire, while those who held to the professional view insisted that sport continue, in order to provide some relief from constant contemplation of the horrors of war. This dispute about the meaning and place of sport in Australian life generated such heat because the opponents were divided largely along class lines, so that the debate about sport became an aspect of a larger conflict. However, the debate throws considerable light on the role of sport within Australia and allows us to test generalizations that have stood unchallenged for a long time. While many of the issues in this debate may be trivial in themselves, when seen in the total context they allow the social historian a much fuller understanding of Australian society.

The news of the outbreak of the European conflict caught most Australians off their guard: their ignorance of the situation and their innocent assessment of the might of the Empire led to absurdly complacent predictions about the outcome of the war. The *Pastoral Review*'s sports commentator, "Fife and Drum", commented on the news of war but concluded: "Next month, if all be going well with the Empire, we will talk horse again with a light heart." Many of the sporting bodies made "patriotic gestures" which seemed to reflect this spirit, both the Australian Jockey Club and the Victoria Racing Club discussed cancelling their meetings but decided instead to hand over a portion of the profits to the patriotic funds. The Victorian Football League determined to impose a "patriotic surcharge" by increasing admission prices by 50 per cent, but when attendance declined sharply it became apparent that the League had seriously misjudged the public's mood; the surcharge was abandoned. However, the patriotism of one VFL club was readily apparent. St Kilda's colours — red, gold, and black — were identical with those of Germany. Lest there be any confusion, St Kilda players completed the season with large union jacks pinned to the front of their jumpers.[1]

During August, attendances at sporting fixtures held up well, but as it became apparent that the war would last longer than a week or a month some spectators began to abandon organized sport, although attendance figures indicated that this voluntary restraint was far from universal. Thus while the total numbers at the four VFL final games declined by half when compared with 1913 figures, in Sydney the rugby league finals drew very large crowds. The rising star on the Australian boxing scene, Maitland's Les Darcy, attracted "a vast crowd" and "half Sydney's police force" when he fought Fritz

Holland at the Rushcutter's Bay Stadium, while over the four days of the VRC's Spring Carnival attendance fell by fifty-two thousand compared with 1913; even the Melbourne Cup attracted eighteen thousand fewer patrons.[2]

In keeping with the amateur view that sport was a preparation for something higher, Australian commentators began to suggest that sportsmen had a special role to play in time of war, beyond donating their services to raise funds. From the beginning it was expected that sportsmen would be among the first to enlist, presumably because of their youth and physical condition, but also because sport had prepared them so well for the task. As "Fife and Drum" put it: "We will show that the 'mudded oaf' and 'flannelled fool' has learned his lesson from his games, and that he can catch hold of the bit, and lay down to it, when called upon for real work."[3] By the end of 1914, therefore, the expectation had emerged that the sporting community had a particular role in relation to the war: if eligible, sportsmen should enlist; otherwise they might continue to play their games only to the extent that they did not interfere with the Empire's higher business. On the other hand, another section of the community had shown that they expected sport to continue and would resist attempts to place a heavier burden on sportsmen than on other sections of the community.

The news of the Australian engagement at the Dardanelles and the consequent casualty lists which now became a regular feature in the newspapers generated demands that the expectations about enlistment be realized. "Fife and Drum" reported that while in England the sporting community had responded nobly with, for example, almost an entire county cricket team enlisting, in Australia comparatively few prominent sportsmen had entered the training camps. This reaction led him to reflect on the purpose and meaning of sport:

> What is the good of games if they do not provide a training ground for the sterner battles in our lives. If they do not give us men whose hands they have taught to war and their fingers to fight, then it would be better that we blotted them out from our daily lives altogether, and instituted some system whereby men of war, and with the spirit of Britons, and with the aptitude for war fostered within them, would leap at the call of bugles.

Despite such expectations, in 1914 and in the early part of 1915 sporting fixtures had continued as normal. The Victorian Cricket Association conducted a full round of club competitions and inter-state games, and the president, Donald Mackinnon, later to become director-general of recruiting in Australia, reported one of the most successful years ever. Indeed, he wrote, "But for the gloom that has been cast on the civilised world in consequence of the devastating war . . . the dominant note of this report would be one of joy and general satisfaction." The highlight of the season was the Victorian victory in the Sheffield Shield competition, but Mackinnon also reported that the competition for the club premiership had been keen and that attendances at the various matches were large. J. H. Clayton, the president of the New South Wales Cricket Association, while not wishing to disparage Victoria's achievement, found nevertheless that "the unfortunate war . . . rendered an enthusiastic preparation for the cricket campaign quite out of the question". This may have been so, but in the same report Mr Clayton found it necessary to issue a special appeal to cricketers to enlist and instructed the clubs "to make their annual meetings Recruiting Meetings". By the time of the publication of this report in July 1915 there was an awareness that it was not enough to expect sportsmen to do their duty; they must be actively encouraged to take their part in the war.[5]

As the recruiting movement developed, recruiters became increasingly concerned that sporting programmes hindered their efforts. This may sound fanciful until it is realized that many recruiters had generated the extraordinary notion that every eligible man ought to enlist. So intense was their concern for the Empire and the Australian troops at Gallipoli that they seemed prepared to accept few excuses from eligibles. In this sense it was possible to speak of the "failure" of the recruiting campaign even though 21,698 recruits enlisted from Victoria alone in July 1915.[6]

Recruiters displayed particular bad temper in relation to crowds at sporting events because they consisted largely of young males with apparently no purposeful occupation. Thus the Reverend J. L. Rentoul contrasted the heroes at Gallipoli with the youths at Melbourne football, and he branded the man who, though free to enlist, preferred football as a 'loon, a coward and dastard''. This approach apparently received official sanction when a recruiting poster appeared entitled "Will They Never Come?"; "they" were pictured as a portion of the crowd behind the goals at the Melbourne Cricket Ground. *Sport,* a Melbourne paper, alleged that the poster had prejudiced footballers and spectators against the recruiting movement; they resented what they saw as a "class distinction" directed only against football.[7]

As the frustrations of the recruiters grew, a campaign developed to curtail or even to abandon mass spectator sport. One of the leaders of this campaign was L. A. Adamson, headmaster of Wesley College, one of Melbourne's leading private boys' schools. Adamson explained to his boys that "from its athletic and its moral side the British love of games [had] proved a magnificent asset to the Empire" and that such was the usefulness of sport they might justifiably continue to play. In the wider community, however, sport should be assessed from one standard only, namely whether it hindered or assisted recruiting. Adamson alleged that any patriotic German in Melbourne would pay to help sustain spectator sport because it so obviously interfered with the recruiting movement; therefore, the loyal Australian should try to put down sport. In his address, Adamson made a clear distinction between amateur and professional sport, as if money had corrupted the noble instincts of sportsmen and was incompatible with true sporting ideals and aims. He contrasted South Yarra, the 1914 premiers of the Amateur Football Association, eighteen of whose players had enlisted, with the League clubs whose enlistment figures were not nearly as impressive. Adamson concluded with the statement that no Wesley boy could remain true to the Public Schools' ideal and attend professional football matches. His statement aroused considerable public comment and was supported enthusiastically by the editorialists of Melbourne's daily papers, although those papers perhaps inconsistently retained their concentration on football in the sports pages. However, at least in 1915 the traditionally anti-wowser Sydney *Bulletin* rejected such views: "there's an hour for mourning and an hour for tears, but there's also an hour for bucking up and belting despondency to leg."[8]

The allegation of class bias in the campaign against the continuance of sport derived from the fact that while the commentators and newspaper editorialists bemoaned the playing of football they directed few if any barbs against horse-racing. The committees of the racing clubs comprised almost exclusively the wealthy members of society. Ostensibly the distinction of the treatment of the various sports depended on the utility of each; football served no useful purpose while horse-racing, its supporters alleged, stimulated one of the nation's most important industries, the rearing of horseflesh. "Fife and Drum" argued that racing encouraged breeders to make sacrifices, to experiment in the hope of producing ever better horses. This, he further argued, was essential war work because even as late as August 1917 he was saying "that the nation which comes out on top in the end is that one which possesses the best horse supply". Such exaggerations may perhaps have harmed the defence of racing, but at least racing's supporters could base their argument on utility, which, as we have seen, was a major part of the amateur justification of sport. Supporters of racing also alleged that the sport was a significant employer of labour and that to abandon racing would increase unemployment. This argument succeeded only in so far as participants in other sports who were paid for their services were not regarded as "workers". The case for the continuance of racing made no allowance for spectators at racecourses, as "Fife and Drum" further observed: "Those able-bodied men who frequent our suburban courses should be compelled to go into training . . . The courses, I am proud to say, will be pleased to see their backs."[9]

On the argument of utility, therefore, the organizations controlling football in Australia found themselves very much on the defensive in 1915, and in the face of a sustained campaign several of them decided to curtail the football season. In Sydney the Rugby Union, traditionally a bastion of the amateur view, was virtually forced to abandon its programme because many of the players had enlisted. The Victorian Football Association's decision to curtail its programme is harder to understand. The VFA, formed in 1877, was the senior football body in Victoria, but, following a split in 1897 as a result of which the stronger clubs formed the Victorian Football League, there was intense rivalry between the two bodies with the VFL gradually gaining the edge. Until 1915 the VFA was at least a competitor with the VFL, although its image was more middle class than the League's, whose principal clubs drew their support from Collingwood, Richmond, Fitzroy, and Carlton, which were largely working-class suburbs. Because of the competition between the two bodies for popular support, the VFA's decision to cease playing, although consistent with middle-class patriotism, was self-sacrificial in the extreme. The decision was carried unanimously, however, at a meeting of the VFA on 14 July 1915, during the height of the Victorian recruiting campaign. Perhaps the VFA hoped that the League would be forced to follow its patriotic lead.[10]

The League met on 21 July to consider its position. There were two delegates from each club and they voted in accordance with their club's instructions. While it may be dangerous to assume that a club located in a respectable middle-class area would adopt the ethos of that area, it is interesting that Essendon and the four south of the Yarra clubs supported a motion for curtailment, while the north of the Yarra clubs, traditionally the working class area of Melbourne, voted to continue playing. The motion to abandon games was carried ten votes to eight, but as it failed to secure the necessary three-quarters majority was not implemented. Delegates in favour of continuation argued that the forty thousand patrons who had attended matches on the previous Saturday had demonstrated that they wished the game to go on.[11]

In Sydney the Rugby League, which also drew its support from predominantly working-class areas, showed no inclination to abandon its programme. An additional incentive to continue was the fear by officials that, as their organization was quite recent, another body might try to take their place should they stop their games. It was alleged that there were two syndicates waiting on the sidelines to take control of the sport from the Rugby League, so any suggestion to abandon the season must have been viewed as virtual suicide by the officials concerned.[12]

Although the press campaign against sport concentrated on football, boxing received some attention too. Boxing supporters attracted heavily adverse criticism when they shouted down W. A. Holman, the Labor premier of New South Wales, who had attempted to make a recruiting speech before a championship fight between Les Darcy and America's Eddie McGoorty. The press denounced what it saw as a lack of patriotism on the part of the sixteen thousand strong crowd, and the *Sydney Morning Herald* reported with approval the comments of a Presbyterian minister, the Reverend David Brandt, who called on the government to prohibit "prize-fighting" and "to compel people [who attended such fixtures] to train for the defence of the Empire". One Sydney newspaper, the *Sportsman,* defended the boxing crowd, claiming that they rejected Holman the politician, not Holman the recruiter, and that the premier had been unnecessarily provocative when he threatened to introduce conscription to force the "young loafers" in the audience to do their duty. On the Saturday before the Holman fiasco the stadium crowd had enthusiastically supported a recruiting exhibition and had given a warm welcome to wounded men returned from the Dardanelles; the *Sportsman* may have been correct: the boxing crowds supported recruiting but rejected the hectoring and abuse of would-be recruiters.[13]

Despite early calls for compulsory government curtailment of sporting programmes, restrictions continued to be decided voluntarily by the various controlling bodies. As the 1915–16 cricket season approached, the officials of the game in the various states attracted the fire that had hitherto been directed at footballers and boxers. Although the Victorians protested, an early decision was made against playing interstate cricket, and by October both the NSWCA and the VCA had determined against sponsoring inter-club competitions: only social games would be permitted. In New

South Wales these supposedly patriotic decisions could not have been taken lightly, because cricket there was in a far from healthy state and pessimists believed the survival of the game to be in jeopardy. In the year to 30 June 1914 the Association recorded a loss of £501 19s 11d, its third successive loss. During the following season, affected by the early months of the war, the Association lost a further £835. Even before these large losses had been recorded the Association had set up a committee to examine ways of making cricket more attractive to the public. Although confident that a game that had survived two hundred years was unlikely to die out, especially as "cricket in itself is [so] deeply rooted in the life of the Britisher", nevertheless the committee discussed various proposals, including the introduction of the eight-ball over which was recommended. Committee members noted perceptively that the game depended as much as any other on a dominant personality to draw the crowds in; they sighed for another cricketer in the mould of M. A. Noble. *Bulletin* correspondents fell in with the spirit of the committee's exercise and suggested that it should be compulsory for a batsman to score at least once each over or that two overs in a row should be bowled from each and to eliminate the time wasted as fieldsmen changed positions! These exercises were evidence of the despondency that hung over cricket in New South Wales. In such circumstances the Association showed a daring commitment to the Empire's cause by virtually suspending the game throughout the state. The Sydney *Sportsman* warned that the decision would give baseball a big advantage as that sport, far from prominent in New South Wales as yet, was under little public pressure to stop its activities. Cricket, "already in a comatose condition", as the *Sportsman* warned, "could be killed off by its friends."[14]

By the end of 1915 voluntary action had led to a severely depleted sports programme. A list of sports affected included rugby union, polo, and the annual Sydney gymkhana, interstate and inter-club hockey, amateur athletics in New South Wales and Victoria, and interstate tennis, cricket, and rowing. At club level it is difficult to gauge how much sport was abandoned or how typical was the action of the Sydney Swimming Club, which announced that it would restrict its competitors to the under-twenty-ones and the over-forties. Indeed, even in those organizations which determined to continue to play sport there were some spectacular club failures. For example, in July the *Bulletin* announced that the bottom had fallen out of the Bendigo Football League when Rochester disbanded because of the enlistment of several players followed by the enlistment of thirteen members of the Bendigo City Club. In the north of

Victoria the entire Wodonga team, undefeated to that point, marched to the training camp and enlisted to a man. In general the country seems to have subscribed more wholeheartedly to the amateur view of sport than did the city, although it is beyond the scope of this chapter to analyse the difference closely.[15]

The advocates of the voluntary abandonment of sport did not have it all their own way, however. In Perth when the West Australian Football League decided on 5 August 1915 to curtail its season on 21 August, two of the clubs, Perth and East Perth, decided to test the legality of the decision in the Supreme Court. The League declined to contest the action when it came for decision before the chief justice because, as the president said, "the members of the executive had not felt inclined to leave their occupations to go squabbling in the Law Courts over such a petty matter as a game of football". The season subsequently continued as arranged, and football continued to be played in Perth throughout the war years.[16]

When the South Australian Football League announced that it would abandon its 1916 programme and hold no further matches until the end of the war there was a ground swell of public opinion that demanded that some football be played. The lead came from the Port Adelaide League and Association clubs; clubs, again, based on a solidly working-class district. These clubs amalgamated to form the Port Adelaide Limited Patriotic Football Club, the first club in the proposed Patriotic Football Association which hoped to take over from the SAFL. Significantly after a preliminary meeting at a Port Adelaide hotel subsequent meetings took place in the Adelaide Trades Hall. The PFA loomed as a threat to the existence of the SAFL, which countered with lengthy statements about the necessity of its own patriotic action and drew support from the Labor premier, Crawford Vaughan; the South Australian Cricket Association, which refused use of the Adelaide Oval, the premier ground in South Australia; and the Port Adelaide Corporation, which also withheld the use of the oval under its control. Although other councils rejected the PFA's applications for ovals, sufficient grounds were found to enable a start to the season on 13 May with six clubs: West Adelaide, Norwood, West Torrens, Prospect, Port Adelaide, and Railway. About forty former League footballers had agreed to play. Because Adelaide's leading paper, the *Advertiser,* all but ignored the PFA, it has been difficult to follow its history closely. There were three thousand spectators when Port Adelaide met West Adelaide, and the game was of a high standard, marred only by the condition of the ground, the South Park Lands. Port Adelaide defeated West Torrens for the premiership, thereby justifying the club's initial enthusiasm for some competition. The PFA arranged matches in 1917, but interest appears to have been limited.[17]

The South Australian episode demonstrated that voluntary restrictions had all but reached their limit and that, despite the wishes of many commentators, some sports would persist in distracting apparently unthinking Australians from the realities of war. Press opinion hardened against football. The *Bulletin*, a recent convert to the cause, noted: "War and football are rivals, and there is no room for both of them . . . Every footballer is a possible soldier, so the winter game will have no excuse this year for showing itself in public." In February the VFL drew editorial wrath upon itself when delegates decided to press on with the game. As a concession, however, the League determined that the game would be conducted on strictly amateur lines so that no one could say that a player refused to enlist because he would thus suffer financially.

The decision recalled Adamson's statement that sporting bodies that paid players were behaving exactly as would a patriotic German in Australia. The decision also illustrates the ambivalence towards professional sport in Australia and the strength of the amateur view that real sportsmen played for the love of the game and not for any financial rewards. But the VFL was a semi-professional body and monetary considerations were extremely important. Consider the plight of the Carlton Football Club, which owed its bank £1,650, guaranteed by the officers of the club. Not surprisingly the bank was demanding that the debt be reduced, and if football had been abandoned Carlton would have had no opportunity to do so; its officers would have faced bankruptcy. Such pressures were overlooked by the more affluent clubs. South Melbourne, for example, had assets of £1,750 with no liabilities; South could clearly take decisions independent of financial pressures.

Only weeks before the opening of the 1916 season the clubs that in July 1915 had voted to suspend football unilaterally withdrew from the 1916 programme, leaving four clubs, Carlton, Collingwood, Fitzroy, and Richmond with a dilemma: should they follow suit or attempt to struggle on alone? The situation was extremely dangerous for the health of football in the Australian Rules capital. At the next League meeting a Fitzroy delegate moved that the clubs that had withdrawn from the competition should also be asked to withdraw from the League. Should this motion have succeeded the way would have been clear for the four remaining clubs in the League to invite sympathetic VFA clubs to join them, which would have completely restructured Melbourne's football world. What was intended as a patriotic gesture by the affluent, middle-class VFL clubs, Melbourne, Essendon, South Melbourne, St Kilda, and Geelong, could easily have resulted in their demise. Despite considerable bad feeling, the four playing clubs met in private and decided to allow the others to continue to sit on the League. That body then sent a letter to the press justifying its decision to keep on playing. The League argued that despite the distressing times "some degree of harmless and healthful recreation is both necessary and beneficial to everyone". They pointed out that the majority of the League's spectators were ineligible to enlist, and in this way sought to counter the argument about the swarms of eligibles lounging around the goal-posts.

The League delegates also stressed that the games would provide pleasure and exercise for onlookers and would raise money for the patriotic funds and that few of the players were eligibles. The statement ended on a querulous note: why was football singled out for attack and other sports ignored? The delegates raised the question, but could provide no answer. The answer may be twofold. Certainly by 1916 football was one of the few large branches of sport to continue to attract mass public support; most other types of sport had voluntarily closed or restricted themselves. Football was recognizably professional and working class, without the alleged "utility" or "national concern" of racing. As the opinion makers in Australia began to arrogate patriotism exclusively to the bosom of their own class to deny that the Australian worker was instinctively patriotic, they looked with disfavour on his recreations, implying that while such recreations might be innocent amongst a class that recognized its higher duty, they were definitely dangerous among people blinded to that duty.[19]

So the VFL struggled on with what must have been the least interesting programme in its till then relatively short history. As there were twelve rounds in the season, each club played the others three times before the finals began, in which of course each club was guaranteed a place. The walkout by the five clubs naturally affected attendance and interest in football and had wider ramifications too. The newspaper *Sport,* which in 1914 had been a weekly principally devoted to football news, became in 1916 a monthly which printed virtually an identical sheet, month after month. Their lament at the end of June may be taken as an epitaph for the sorry 1916 season: "What's the matter with the public? They are not attending in such numbers as were seen at the beginning of the season. It seems as if they are getting weary of seeing the same old teams so often in opposition at the same old grounds. Anyhow the teams which are playing are not to blame." Part of the justification for playing in 1916 was that the players would accept no payment and the profits would be devoted to the patriotic funds. The Carlton balance-sheet, when published, mocked both these contentions. Although receipts totalled £885, there were no profits to be handed over. In the spirit of "shamateurism" there were several entries which may have been simply disguised match payments. Thus £99 went towards re-couping the losses players suffered by being absent from work, £45 was devoted to players' travelling expenses, and £57 to injured players. The interest on the club's debt consumed £70 of receipts.[20]

The Sydney Rugby League withstood the uncertainties that racked Melbourne football, perhaps because officials perceived the possibility of collapse to be greater. Nevertheless, while the game continued officials poured out explanations seeking to allay charges of disloyalty. They claimed that most of Sydney's first-grade footballers were married and therefore "ineligible" for service. Even so, the press cast slurs on the unmarried men, and it was therefore a shock to find that in the September 1916 conscription call-up three-quarters of the unmarried footballers secured rejection certificates. This showed, to the officials of the Rugby League at least, "that it was not football that was keeping them from lending a hand". The League also joined in one of the favourite patriotic pastimes of churches, clubs, schools, and other institutions by publishing lists of members who had enlisted. Thus Glebe showed that seven of the 1915 first-grade side were in the ranks, while Easts had twenty-eight players from all three grades in the AIF and Annandale had thirty-one. With such publicity the League hoped to soften public opinion towards the continuance of football.[21]

Alone among all the football codes in Australia, rugby league probably survived unscathed because the patriots' campaign against it was deflected in Sydney by a virulent campaign against boxing. The calls for the abandonment of boxing which had followed Holman's humiliation had failed, and Sydney boxing continued to draw large crowds three times a week. In July 1916 representatives of the Council for Civic and Moral Advancement, a Protestant inter-denominational body, led a deputation to the New South Wales chief secretary, George Black, to argue "the case against the stadium in war-time". Included in the deputation were Archbishop Wright, Bishop Stone-Wigg, Sir Thomas Anderson Stuart, the Reverend Professor Ronald Macintyre, and several other church-men and Liberal politicians. By speaking almost exclusively of "prize fighting" in place of the more usual "boxing" the men of the deputation showed their antagonism to a sport which, they implied, was dominated by money. Wright claimed to speak on behalf of the relatives of the dead whom he supposed found the continuance of sport an indication of the community's apathy towards their sacrifice and suffering. Stuart had observed the queues that formed outside the Stadium at least two hours before the start of proceedings and believed that a large proportion of patrons were "hefty young men apparently militarily fit". Macintyre, who was also president of the State Recruiting Committee, complained that the "prize-fighting business" was a moral nuisance and that "everyone was aware that the Stadium crowd contributed very few recruits in this national crisis". George Black promised to place the matter before cabinet.[22]

As there were fewer boxers than footballers, the press could more easily investigate the private circumstances of the boxers to show eligibility and therefore disloyalty. The antagonisms expressed so forthrightly by the Council for Civic and Moral Advancement fell squarely on Les Darcy, the most prominent Australian boxer, who was constantly asked when he planned to enlist. Rumours and mis-understandings flew about. A report that Darcy had enlisted was amended: he had tried to enlist but his mother refused the permission Les needed as a minor. In August, his manager, Snowy Baker, announced that Darcy had signed up for three more fights after which he would be barred from the Stadium until he had presented himself at a recruiting depot. This minor form of economic conscription was consistent with previous displays of Snowy Baker's patriotism by proxy. Darcy was the scapegoat to Council and press opinion; if boxing was unpatriotic, why did Baker not close down the Stadium entirely? Such pressures apparently un-nerved Darcy; on the eve of his twenty-first birthday, which was also the eve of the first conscription referendum, he took flight to America, illegally without a passport. The press campaign of vilification increased accordingly, only the Sydney *Sportsman* daring to suggest that Darcy be given a fair trial under the law rather than be singled out for special treatment. It was Darcy's fate never to undergo that trial or indeed any other; unable to secure any fights in America, he died, some said of pneumonia, others said of a broken heart. In death he became a symbol of the class conflict generated in Australia under the pressure of war. His Catholicism added to these tensions in a period of remarkable sectarian bitterness. The *Sportsman* believed he had been 'martyred, aye crucified, on the cross of paltry personal spleen and disappointed greed of Australians who dare to call themselves sports' . His body was returned to Maitland via Sydney and its progress became the occasion of demonstrations by those who had triumphed in the defeat of conscription but who felt, nevertheless, alienated by the middle-class patriots. In his funeral panegyric, Father Coady announced that Darcy "was a martyr to truth. His life was offered as a holocaust on the altar of prejudice, of jealousy and of avarice."[23]

In this heightened, passionate atmosphere the opponents of sport realized that exhortation and editorials were now futile weapons against the apparent indifference of the sportsmen; calls for government restrictions became increasingly common. Various win-the-war leagues and other patriotic bodies forwarded resolutions to the federal government, such as this from Ballina: "That as attendance at Race Meetings and Stadiums is detrimental to the Recruiting movement which should enlist the serious attention of the manhood of the Commonwealth the Defence Authorities be petitioned to close such meetings during the continuance of the War." An early reply from the Prime Minister's Department stated that it was "not considered that the prohibition of the [boxing] matches referred to would be followed by any beneficial effect on recruiting". Gradually this belief changed, perhaps because so many organizations and individuals argued the contrary position. A Sydney citizen suggested that if bars, race-courses, and stadiums were closed ten thousand policemen would be available immediately for service in France and that as the police were popular with youth each would attract four or five boys to go with him, the addition to the AIF being, therefore, sixty thousand men. In South Australia all mass spectator sport had been abandoned except horse-racing, which prompted an Adelaide minister to write that the continuance of horse racing was "attracting large numbers of youths and others, who otherwise would be at the ovals and engaged in manly exercises, to places where they are confronted with dangerous temptations". The corollary was that the government must abolish racing as well. A member of the Tasmanian Legislative Council suggested that no man be admitted to a racecourse, theatre, or picture-show unless he was in uniform or "wearing a badge denoting that he is exempt from military or naval service". Such repressive measures implied a large measure of contempt for the sporting community: a minister of religion summarized feelings when he wrote of the "cold-footed slackers at the Stadiums and racecourses: They are selfish, soulless degenerates, who were not fit to blacken the boots of the brave men in the trenches".[24]

The prime minister, W. M. Hughes, believing that he needed to placate this section of public opinion during the May 1917 federal election campaign, announced that his government would introduce controls on sport. When parliament reassembled in July after

Hughes's resounding victory, the governor-general declared: "My advisers consider that action should be taken to curtail sport meetings throughout the Commonwealth, in order to concentrate the minds of the people on the more serious aspect of the war." The government then waited until September before taking action, which meant that it was not forced to move against football, the major spectator sport, in Sydney, Melbourne, or Perth. Would any government have dared to prohibit football finals in Melbourne, especially as in 1917 the VFL had returned to near full strength? Eventually the government announced that horse-racing would be restricted, particularly on weekdays, and that only one boxing programme would be permitted in each state per fortnight. All other sports were believed to have made appropriate voluntary restrictions. Editorialists in the metropolitan press supported the government's action. The *Sydney Morning Herald* was particularly pleased to see action taken against boxing, a sport it believed "which serve[d] no useful purpose at any time"; it thus introduced the amateur notion that sport needed justification beyond itself and must create some good. The writer further showed an unease with the role of sport in Australia, stating that: "the love of sport and ease and luxury was laying deadly hold of us and sapping the national character". His hope that Australians would think "less of sport in future and more of the serious things of life" showed why the restrictions were thought to be important. Indeed, support for these restrictions followed the pattern of other wartime victories against the recreations of the common man. In the case of the early closing of hotels, the "reform" was first urged as a necessary war measure to promote economy and enlistment; once introduced it was discovered to have a general benefit beyond wartime conditions, and advocates soon suggested that it be retained even after the war was over. Where temperance workers had failed to influence the community in pre-war Australia, their cause succeeded when they worked on heightened wartime emotions. Similarly, in the campaign against sport a dissatisfaction with the dominance of sport had emerged which in pre-war Australia had gained no hearing.[25]

Apart from demonstrating the antagonisms some Australians directed towards the prevalence of sport in society, the restrictions seemed to have little other effect. Certainly their introduction did not lead to an increase in the number of recruits offering for service; in fact, numbers continued to be low throughout 1917 and 1918. Paradoxically, boxing, which had suffered a slump following the death of Darcy, experienced another boom. Instead of leaving the Stadium in darkness on the "non-boxing" nights, the promoters offered a vaudeville programme with a few rounds of boxing thrown in as part of the entertainment. Possibly Captain Gallagher and Co. (sharpshooters extraordinary, including Little Edith the child wonder shot), Ford and Perrin (expert dancers and comedians), and the Fredo boys (balancers, acrobats, and instrumentalists at the one time) were surprised to find themselves in the boxing ring, but they were tremendously popular. The youths and other eligibles who had flocked to sport at the Stadium were as much captivated by vaudeville. The supporters of the professional view of sport had made a valid point: the sporting public looked on sport as a form of entertainment and if denied it would seek their enjoyment elsewhere. Few of the opinion makers had accepted sport as another form of entertainment; they had elevated it and had thus misunderstood its grip on the Australian people.[26]

The antagonism that the restriction of sport occasioned derived principally from accusations of class bias. John Wren, the Melbourne sports entrepreneur who owned pony tracks in Brisbane and Melbourne, complained that the government discriminated against his courses which attracted a working-class clientele, as against the socially prestigious racing clubs. He alleged that although Brisbane racing was to have been reduced by half, the state commandant had allotted one of his courses, Kedron Park, six meetings in place of the scheduled fifty-six, and another course, Goodna, had been closed altogether.

Wren asked how owners and trainers could possibly make money on six meetings to July 1918. Three of his other courses, whose meetings had been reduced voluntarily to thirty-eight, now were further reduced to eighteen. Wren showed that the Queensland Turf Club had had twenty-four meetings reduced to eighteen; not, he argued, an equal sacrifice. An employee at one of Wren's Melbourne pony tracks supported his employer: "We that have permitted our flesh and blood to enter the battle resent the mouthings and feel the sting of the propagandists, leisured and dimpled who offer and suggest prohibition in regard to all things but those directly affecting themselves."[27]

From the opposite end of the social spectrum a former Liberal premier of New South Wales, Sir Joseph Carruthers further demonstrated the class nature of the controversy about sport; he supported the contention that the government's interference with sport had increased working-class antipathy and was therefore harming the recruiting movement. He alleged that "instead of helping recruiting, the Federal intervention with racing, damaged it". Indeed, "the keen resentment felt . . . caused many people to cool down in their [recruiting] efforts; especially whilst the Rev. Professor Macintyre was at the head of State Recruiting, more so as he had openly stated that if left to him he would deal severely with the matter.''

As senior vice-president of the National Association in New South Wales, Carruthers felt he must also enumerate the political risks involved in interfering with sport: ''We have the liquor trade against us; we also have the Irish Catholics with few exceptions; we have the trade unions, very largely; and we are making bitter enemies of the Sporting fraternity except for a favoured few. This latter class is more numerous than you imagine. Moreover it includes tens of thousands who are just as loyal as you or I.'' It was this last point that the ''parsons, politicians and newspaper proprietors'' were not prepared to concede. Their view of loyalty demanded that a man be so totally involved in the Empire's cause as to forgo all other concerns. The restrictions on sport remained in force until the end of the war, although there were no moves made against the 1918 football season which in Sydney and Melbourne was played much as before the war.[28]

By 1917, therefore, many middle-class Australians seemed to believe that a devotion to sport indicated an antipathy or indifference to the real issues of the day. But as the sporting bodies were so eager to demonstrate, thousands of participants in the games that attracted mass public interest had enlisted in the AIF. Despite impressive figures such as those of the VCA, which claimed 2,854 of its players were in the ranks, or the South Melbourne Football Club, from which twelve regular players, eight former players, and between seven hundred and eight hundred members had enlisted, so long as some sportsmen continued to play their games, the myth remained that sportsmen were failing to do their duty. For this reason the recruiters had directed specific appeals to sportsmen, and in particular it became popular to recruit ''sportsmen's units'' in which the incentive was to ''train together, play together and fight together''. Apparently recruiters believed that these units attracted particular prestige, but in retrospect the campaign looked like one more gimmick in a recruiting drive which, as the years wore on, became increasingly gimmicky. Thus during one campaign returned men marched through the suburbs in their sports outfits, and, as we have seen, recruiting rallies constantly interrupted sporting fixtures. At one such rally a Mrs Velentine A. Spence appealed to Sydney sportsmen:

> . . . a nation of sportsmen. We must all be sportsmen now for the sake of our future sport, and for the sake of the men. All are sportsmen, in

the truest sense of the word, who have made the great sacrifice that the freedom of the world may be maintained. Sport has more than justified itself so far in the great struggle. It must be so until the end. The rallying cry for next Friday's appeal is "Be a Sportsman". No man who, being fit and able to serve his country, remains at home sheltering behind the heroism of his fellow men, has any right to claim the title which, more than any other, the Briton is proud of. This is the crucial test of sporting instincts.

Here again, neatly expressed, was the amateur view that sport must have some utility, some meaning. While, in a sense, bemoaning what they understood to be Australia's obsession with sport, commentators believed they would work on that obsession in the interests of recruiting.[29]

Such attempts to use the Australian's interest in sport did not succeed because they were based on a misunderstanding of the commitment to sport. The amateur commitment was perhaps greater because sport was given a higher function than that of mere entertainment. Sport taught its participants lessons about life and prepared them for life; it encouraged the development of the virtues that had made the Empire great and that would help Australia to take its full share of responsibility towards the Empire in the future. Thus winning or losing were not as important as the game itself, an attitude that was endangered when money and professionalism entered the sports arena. Such attitudes seem to have baffled the working-class devotees of sport, who took a much more pragmatic approach. Sport was seen more as pleasure and entertainment and in a sense, therefore, was not taken nearly as seriously. To suggest that a few hours spent watching a football match induced apathy or indifference to higher struggles or duties seemed silly. Money could interfere with sport if it led to rigged results but otherwise was accepted as stimulating ever better programmes. Under the pressure of war, these differences emerged far more clearly than they had done in pre-war Australian society, and, on the whole, the amateur view prevailed as fixture after fixture was cancelled. Upon the resumption of peace, sporting programmes quickly returned to normal; even the gloomy predictions about cricket proved baseless, as a Test series against England easily refilled empty coffers. The differences that had briefly surfaced were swept aside in the rush to promote sport, although the subsequent history of sport in Australia bore witness to their persistence. Perhaps only recently, under the pressure of fully professional sport throughout the world, have these differences become less important on the Australian sporting scene.

NOTES

The author gratefully acknowledges the assistance of an Australian War Memorial Grant which allowed him to undertake the research on which this chapter is based.

1. *Pastoral Review*, 15 August 1914, p.738. "Fife and Drum" was Dr W. H. Lang, who in 1915 was appointed handicapper for the Victorian Amateur Turf Club. The VFL's surcharge is discussed in *Sport*, 11 September 1914, which shows that 40,178 people attended the first semi-final in 1913 compared with 24,853 in 1914.
2. Figures drawn from *Sport*, 2 October 1914; Sydney *Sportsman*, 9 September 1914, 16 September 1914, and 11 November 1914.
3. *Pastoral Review*, 15 August 1914, p.783
4. *Pastoral Review*, 16 February 1915.
5. Victorian Cricket Association, *Annual Report for Season 1914—15*, p.7; New South Wales Cricket Association, *Annual Report Balance Sheet Record of Matches Season 1914—15*, p.8.
6. See Michael McKernan, "The Australian Churches in the Great War: Attitudes and Activities of the Major Churches" (PhD. thesis, Australian National University, 1975). chap. 5, "The Failure of Recruiting".
7. *Argus*, 6 July 1915; *Sport*, 9 July 1915.
8. *Wesley College Chronicle*, May 1915; *Bulletin*, 6 May 1915.
9. *Pastoral Review*, 16 June 1916, p.543; 16 August 1917, p.775; 16 June 1916, p.543.
10. The *Bulletin*, 29 April 1915, gave details of some Rugby enlistments: thirty-three Manly players had enlisted, while East Sydney and Annandale with thirty-one volunteers each were next on the long list. For the VFA's decison see the *Age*, 15 July 1915.
11. *Age*, 22 July 1915.
12. *Sportsman*, 5 May 1915.
13. *Daily Telegraph*, 2 August 1915; *Sydney Morning Herald*, 2 August 1915; *Sportsman*, 4 August 1915 and 28 July 1915.
14. New South Wales Cricket Association, *Annual Report Balance Sheet Record of Matches Season 1913—14*, pp.24—25, and ibid., *Season 1914—15*, pp.38—39, and for the committee's report, p.10; *Bulletin*, 15 April 1915 and 29 April 1915; *Sportsman*, 29 September 1915.
15. *Bulletin*, 30 December 1915, 15 July 1915, 5 August 1915.
16. *West Australian*, 9 August 1915 and 12 August 1915. The teams who sued were lying fifth and sixth respectively on the competition table, both only one game behind fourth place. If the season had been curtailed neither team would have been eligible to play in the finals.
17. *Advertiser*, 3—8 April 1916; 21 April 1916; 22 May 1916; 21 August 1916; 30 April 1917.
18. *Bulletin*, 27 January 1916; *Sporting Judge*, 12 February 1916; *Bulletin*, 2 March 1916.
19. *Sporting Judge*, 18 March 1916 and 25 March 1916.
20. *Sport*,, 30 June 1916; *Bulletin*, 26 April 1917.
21. *Sportsman*, 23 March 1916, 4 April 1917, 29 March 1916.
22. Council for Civic and Moral Advancement, *The Case Against "The Stadium" in War Time* (Sydney, 1916), pp.1—4.
23. *Sportsman*, 30 August 1916, 22 November 1916, 30 May 1917, 20 June 1917, and 4 July 1917.

24. These letters, resolutions, and replies are to be found in the file "Sport, Restrictions on", in Prime Minister's Department, Correspondence File, A2, 1918/1151, Australian Archives, Canberra.
25. *Argus,* 28 march 1917; Commonwealth of Australia, *Parliamentary Debates,* vol.82, 11 July 1917, p.8; *Sydney Morning Herald,* 13 September 1917, 15 September 1917.
26. Ernest Scott, *Australia During the War,* vol.11 of *The Official History of Australia in the War of 1914—1918* (Sydney: Angus and Robertson, 1936), appendix 3, p.809; *Sportsman,* 1 December 1917.
27. This correspondence is also contained in the file "Sport, Restrictions on".
28. This correspondence is also contained in the file "Sport, Restrictions on".
29. *Sporting Judge,* 23 September 1916, 26 February 1916; *Sunday Morning Herald,* 11 July 1917, 24 July 1917.

PETER R. SHERGOLD

The Growth of American Spectator Sport: A Technological Perspective

The impact of the technological environment upon the extent and nature of leisure activities has generally been given little attention by historians of sport. It is, of course, widely accepted that other variables avowedly responsible for the growth of sport are intrinsically related to technology. Industrialization implies a technological revolution, with innovation and adaptation progressively improving productive efficiency, stimulating the mass production of standardized goods, capital growth, market specialization, and the division of labour. The technological advances associated with this process have generated long-term gains in *per capita* material welfare, while concurrent changes in the mode of production have increased workplace alienation.

However, there exist few studies of sport which take the technological environment as their basis. The major exception is the work of John R. Betts. In a pioneering article published in 1953, Betts suggested that the rise of sport in America "had been achieved in great part through the steamboat, the railroad, the telegraph, the penny press, the electric light, the streetcar, the camera, the bicycle, the automobile, and the mass production of sporting goods".[1] The paper proved a significant contribution to a very sparse literature, correctly playing down the role of individuals in sport history and stressing "the increasingly close relationship of technology and social change".

Yet in retrospect Betts's work, while imaginative and suggestive, ultimately frustrates the reader. The chronological limits established, 1850-1900, not only exclude twentieth-century technological advances, which have fundamentally transformed American sport, but suggest the difficulty of generalization. Although nineteenth-century communications technology — the telegraph and newspaper — aroused public interest in sport, post-1900 innovations — the radio and television — have had a more ambiguous effect. There are surprising sins of omission, most notably the total absence of comment on construction technology and its impact upon stadium facilities. A clear distinction is never drawn between active and passive involvement in sport, which confuses and distorts analysis. While the statement that "all sports were encouraged by the improved transportation of the post-bellum era" is undoubtedly true, it merely hides the complex role of transport innovation in altering the relative importance of participant and spectator sports and in changing the comparative appeal of the variety of sports available. A similar weakness mars discussion of advances in the mass production of sports equipment or of developments in electric lighting. Sport is rarely placed within the context of alternative recreational pursuits. Thus the motion picture is seen exclusively as a major factor "in spreading the gospel of sport" rather than as a potential threat.[2] Finally, the relationship of technological advance to other independent variables — most notably, the growth of discretionary time — is not pursued, which thereby weakens analysis.

These criticisms should not distort the fact that this present study owes much to its predecessor. The aim is to revive Betts's thesis and to elaborate and refine his analytic framework in order to improve its potential as a basis for historical synthesis.

In early nineteenth-century America, accommodation at major sporting events — primarily horse-racing and boxing bouts — developed as a means to exact payment for the leisure services offered. Barrier fences were built to exclude non-payers and to differentiate various sections of the audience. Buildings remained rudimentary: seats, perhaps; concessionary stalls; and stands for those willing to pay extra for a superior vantage position. As spectator interest in sporting activity grew, and as contests became more regular, so building requirements rose. A reciprocal relationship evolved between the technological imperatives of stadium construction and the increased commercialization of sport. Entrepreneurs required superior stadium facilities in order to increase the sale of viewing privileges and thereby maximize return from their investment in professional sport, while the resultant outlay on building and rise in fixed costs — maintenance, capital depreciation, and ground rental — demanded that additional revenue be received from spectators.

Stadiums, however, could only be as effective in providing spectator access as construction technology allowed. Major innovations came in the late nineteenth century. Development of Bessemer and open-hearth furnaces and the introduction of superior rolling and slitting mills enabled mass production of steel shapes. At the same time, substantial advances were occurring in cement and concrete technology. Steel beams and girders, combined with reinforced concrete floors, transformed construction techniques. For the first time it was possible to envisage large numbers of spectators efficiently accommodated in gigantic, structurally safe, fireproof stands; and of grounds, freed from topographical constraints, able to exploit sites most conveniently located to high-density population areas.

The major deterrent to increased employment of the new construction technology was the inability of sporting enterprises to accumulate the substantial capital funds required. Even after the formation of the National League in 1876, baseball was still "regarded as a diversion by most investors",[3] and stadiums remained primitive: in general, spectator accommodation consisted of wooden stands of low strength, subject to continuous decay and posing a constant fire hazard. Nevertheless, such rudimentary ground facilities represented, in aggregate, a large capital expenditure. Few major baseball clubs, even those situated in large urban centres, felt able to write off in one fell swoop this hard-gained investment; nor were they in a position to attract sufficient private risk capital to exploit the new construction methods.

Meanwhile professional gridiron football, which emerged in the mining and mill towns of Ohio and Pennsylvania in the late nineteenth century, remained a localized — if fiercely fought — sporting activity. It was only college football that was able to tap sufficient alumni funds to place the latter-day gladiators in arenas of a scale of which the Romans (or Greeks) could have felt justifiably proud.[4]

The building costs demanded and crowd capacities permitted by the steel and concrete technology did not represent a rational economic decision even for the universities. The huge edifices which arose to grace campuses, massive stadiums of gargantuan proportions and questionable taste, were grossly underused.[5] College stadiums were status symbols, not commercial propositions: extravagent consumption rather than calculated investment. To a large extent they provided "investors" with a merely psychic income.[6]

Nevertheless, college stadiums quickly demonstrated the *functional* efficiency of steel and concrete construction. In the building boom of the 1920s many more universities, together with a substantial number of municipal authorities, incorporated the new construction technology into the erection of stadiums. More importantly, sporting entrepreneurs now found themselves able to attract sufficient capital to expand access facilities for professional sports. Initially they were able to exploit the growth of enthusiastic local team-identification at the grass-roots level. Far more significantly entrepreneurs were able to attract corporate investment. Transfer of corporate profits into sporting concerns was stimulated both by civic pride and business acumen: it identified industrial enterprises with the regional community, stimulated the local economy, and provided an acceptable outlet for workers' leisure. In more recent years it has also enabled concerns to achieve substantial advertising advantages.[8]

The growth of interest in professional gridiron in the mid-1920s, as Americans eagerly followed the exploits of the Galloping Ghost, Red Grange, stimulated the erection of football bowls. At the same time most major league baseball teams were enabled — indeed pressured — to improve spectator facilities. The masterpiece of the era was constructed in New York City. By 1923 sufficient capital had been attracted to erect a triple-deck stadium from which a maximum eighty-five thousand spectators were able to watch the Yankees in action. Aimed to provide a home for the professional baseball team, economic considerations dictated that it be used for a wide variety of other sporting activity: there was a four-hundred yard cinder track for athletics, space for football, facilities for staging championship prize fights, and — by deft handling of coconut matting — an arena for urban rodeos.[9]

The new steel stands enlarged the capacity of stadiums, while improved spectator comfort and facilities such as electronic score-boards,effective public address systems, and unimpaired field vision attracted more spectators to them.[10] However, profitability was not merely a matter of getting more revenue from an increasing number of spectators. Entrepreneurs were also able to increase revenue by exploiting the new construction technology itself. Steel beams and reinforced concrete flooring freed grandstands from the constraint of building on a solid tiered foundation, and it was soon realized that the roofed enclosure created beneath the stand could be functionally employed, "a logical and businesslike proposition making most possible use of the capital invested in the structure":[11] it was an area that could house concessionary stalls, which complemented revenue received from the sale of viewing privileges and helped to meet the large fixed costs involved in stadium ownership.

Construction technology made up only half the access environment. The development of a transportation network was of vital significance in bringing potential spectators effectively closer to sporting events. As early as 1877, the year after winning the Pennant, the Chicago White Stockings introduced steam cars to replace horse cars on the transit run out to their park.[12] Electric streetcars were inaugurated in the late 1880s, revolutionizing intra-urban travel. By the early 1890s, with the change from direct to alternating current, power transmission became more effective, car motor efficiency was improved, and maintenance costs were reduced; thereafter, electric vehicles swiftly replaced horse-drawn vehicles in American cities and, together with the construction of elevated railroads and/or subways, reduced urban travel time. Steam railways offered spectators the possibility of inter-urban movement, although the large distances frequently involved in American travel militated against the emergence of the sporting excursions which became so important in Britain.

The relation between transport companies and sports entrepreneurs was two-way. The former were well aware of the commercial advantages in securing the patronage of sports spectators and offered discount travel to team supporters, afforded cheap or free facilities to professional participants (in return for reciprocal publicity), leased grounds, and in some instances actually presented spectator sports.[13] In turn, sport promoters realized the necessity for efficient transportation access to stadiums and showed an increasing concern to make the stadium a nodal point for the surrounding transportation network.

Early twentieth-century development of the internal combustion engine substantially altered the access environment. From an extravagent plaything automobiles rapidly emerged as a challenge to existing modes of transport. Patronage on street railways reached a zenith in 1922, after which motor buses carried an increasing share of the public transit market. More significantly, the car emerged as a private means of travel which reduced consumer dependence on public transport facilities and consequently imposed new demands upon sporting stadiums. *Per capita* automobile registration rose from 0.01 in 1910 to 0.15 in 1920 and 0.37 in 1930. At that date it was believed that 50 per cent of sports spectators arrived by car and that it was necessary to provide one acre of parking space per three thousand crowd capacity. By 1960, with *per capita* car registration at 0.70, stadium planners believed that "a good rule of thumb" was to allow one car for every three spectators, a thousand spaces — or approximately 3.4 acres — per three thousand crowd.[14]

The enlarged proportion of ground space that has had to be devoted to the provision of parking, and the increased pressure that private travel has placed upon access routes to stadia, together with the residential decline of most American inner-city areas, have forced many sporting teams to relocate in suburban areas where parking is both ample and safe. Indeed it can be argued that the second major wave of stadium construction (in the 1960s) has been as much determined by the technological imperatives of transportation innovation as by the obsolescence of viewing facilities built in the preceding wave (in the 1920s): that development, combined with the geographical redistribution of population in the United States which has brought new growth areas into the franchise-system of American professional sport.

The automobile has not only transformed consumer access to spectator sport: a wider range of sports has been placed within reach of Americans. Indeed, motor sports have themselves become a leading sector of the professional sports scene. More than that, the family car, together with the airplane, pose a threat to the very existence of spectator sport. The new speed and freedom of mobility offered by technological advances in transportation, coupled with increased discretionary income and time, have offered Americans a wider range of alternative leisure pursuits. Participant sport, be it swimming or skiing, boating or bowling, golf or fishing, has become more readily available; and non-sport recreation activities such as touring, hiking, and camping have proved increasingly popular as vacation enterprises. By the early 1960s it was estimated that over 40 per cent of Americans travelled over five hundred miles by car for their annual holiday. At the same time, outer-city recreational attractions have become accessible as one-day or weekend trips, a trend readily discernible in the marked increase in attendance at national parks and monuments.[15]

In short, transportation innovations have increased ease of access to spectator sport, thereby stimulating its growth, but they have also widened the variety of competing recreational options. As we shall see again, the impact of technological advances on the sports industry is ambiguous. Short-term benefits are often matched by long-term costs.

It is frequently contended that the reduction in hours spent at the workplace has increased discretionary time resources and thereby advanced interest in recreational activities, including sport. Various estimates have been made, all of which indicate that within the American economy leisure time has increased over the last century. Daily hours at the workplace have declined substantially. Average weekly hours in manufacturing fell from 60 in 1890 to 56.6 in 1910, a decline of 5.7 per cent: in the next twenty years there occurred a further 13.3 per cent decrease; and in the following two decades, hours were reduced by 11.5 per cent. Equally important, weekends have been extended, and paid vacation periods have increased. In recent years, working hours have been relatively stable, but employees have been given greater flexibility in selecting work time.[16] They have also been given the opportunity to retire from the wage-earning community at an earlier age than before, and, within constraints imposed by limited pension provisions, to pursue recreational activities on a full-time basis.

Yet the quantity of leisure is not the sum remaining when hours of paid work, together with necessary time expenditure on sleeping, eating, and other items of daily routine are deducted from a weekly or annual total. What is needed, and what has sadly been ignored, is some measure of *effective* leisure. In other words, time is not conceptually homogeneous: its value as leisure is measured most significantly by its relationship to the recreational opportunities available. In part this is determined by the discretionary income available to, and educational/cultural training of, the individual leisure-holder.[17] It is also a function of the technological environment.

Reduction in travel time to sporting events has clearly increased the amount of effective leisure available to Americans, even in situations in which working hours have remained stationary. In other ways too, technological innovation has increased leisure by easing direct access to spectator sport. Two important examples can readily be suggested.

First, through most of America's history, attendance at sporting fixtures has been confined to the daylight hours. Even in the late nineteenth century, evening leisure facilities were limited. The rapid introduction of gas lighting to private residences from the 1880s increased possibilities for household recreation, but opportunities outside the home were few: attendance at lectures or libraries, the occasional theatre or concert trip, and, most important in the years following 1900, visits to the local nickelodeon and movie house. Spectator sport remained a daytime activity. However, advances in electric lighting meant that sport could vie for evening leisure time.

From the late nineteenth century there were attempts to floodlight team sports, but such attempts were fraught with technical difficulties. The major problem was to generate sufficient area lighting without causing a glare that would impair either the player's performance or the spectator's vision, and without excessive use of supporting posts interfering with the view or mobility of the crowd. In consequence, evening events remained infrequent well into the twentieth century. In general, night usage of stadiums was confined to the presentation of massed spectaculars, in which light shortcomings could actually heighten dramatic appeal, or for the staging of boxing contests, in which a very small area had to be brilliantly lit. It was not until the 1930s that earlier difficulties were overcome by the erection of light batteries sited on tall scaffolding at the perimeter of grounds. In 1935 Franklin Delano Roosevelt pulled a switch at Crosley Field, Cincinnati, and instantly 363 lights, set on eight giant towers, blazed into action: below the Reds nudged the Phillies 2-1 before 20,400 excited spectators.[18] The age of major league night baseball had arrived. Effective leisure, at least in terms of sports presentations, had been increased. At the same time a direct stimulus was given to sport, for mean attendances at evening ball games have been consistently higher than at afternoon contests.

Second, attendance at sporting fixtures has generally been adversely affected by inclement weather. In some instances, conditions are too poor for the scheduled event to take place; more frequently, spectators are deterred from attendance. To the extent that weather variabilities can be nullified, attendance at sports meetings can be increased. No longer need leisure choice be reduced by rain, snow, wind or drought. Over the last fifty years there have been continuous improvements in the efficiency of field drainage and in covered-stand facilities. Far more important have been attempts to exclude weather effectively from the sports arena. Madison Square Garden provided a covered stadium suitable for New York sporting contests as early as 1890, and in 1928 Chicago built an auditorium capable of seating twenty-one thousand. Yet even in these large indoor stadiums, space imperatives promoted those sports which required the least amount of room. It seems fair to argue that the technological constraints imposed upon the erection of enclosed arenas have helped to promote professional spectator sports in which movement of players and "ball" is most limited: basketball, from its inception in 1895; ice-hockey; and boxing and wrestling.

However, a number of exciting and far-reaching technological developments have occurred since the Second World War. Just as steel and reinforced concrete created new opportunities for early twentieth-century stadium builders, so recent innovations in flexible steel cables and aerospace plastics have opened up the possibility of major technological advances. The American engineer Lev Zetlin pioneered cable technology in the mid-1950s. By 1965 the Houston Astrodome was completed, a stadium able to accommodate sixty-six thousand spectators completely enclosed —

and air-conditioned — beneath a transparent plastic dome borne on a steel lattice frame. Although the cost was enormous — $31.6 million — similar arenas were planned. Philadelphia and Kansas City, for example, drew up blueprints for stadiums which would incorporate domed roofs that could be opened.[19] Thus new technology has indicated its potential to roof vast arenas capable of providing adequate facilities for the more wide-ranging, space-consuming sports.

Not only baseball and football have been affected. Other popular sports have realized the possibility of increasing spectator attendance by presenting contests in indoor stadiums in which constraints of weather or natural light can be eliminated. As early as 1923, tennis had gained sufficient popular support to warrant the erection of a twenty-two-thousand-seat outdoor concrete arena at Forest Hills, New Jersey. The site remains at the centre of the American tennis circuit, the venue of the United States Open and headquarters of the Lawn Tennis Association, but increasingly professional tennis is played within comfortable indoor stadiums, on artificial, low-maintenance courts.[20] Indoor field and track events have expanded as larger, covered arenas allow year-round competition. Only golf and horse-racing remain outside the gamut of major American professional sports that can be staged adequately in the indoor environment which construction technology now allows.

In short, technological advances can increase effective leisure by furthering recreational opportunities available in any set amount of discretionary time. This effect has been intensified in the area of contemporary spectator sport by its avowedly "peculiar economics", and by the alleged uniqueness of the commodity it produces. Two competing firms (teams), functioning within a rigidly oligopolistic framework (the league), conjointly supply a service (viewing privileges) which can either be consumed directly or at a spatial/temporal distance from the place/moment at which they are produced.[21] The rapid development of twentieth-century media technology has eased the means by which spectators can gain *indirect* access to games, has furthered the share of revenue derived from indirect sales, and has thereby had a profound effect upon the growth of American commmercial sport.

Technological advances have made it increasingly easy to share the excitement of a sporting event without attending the site at which it takes place. In the nineteenth century two developments occurred of major significance for the growth of spectator sports: the invention of the electric telegraph, and the introduction of new methods of paper production and printing which made possible the circulation of cheap newspapers. The former is usually associated with journalistic attempts to report the Mexican War of 1845, the latter with "yellow press" responsibility for the outbreak of the Spanish-American War of 1898. But in each instance, news of victory and defeat on the sporting field was as important to media usage as were the latest dispatches from the Rio Grande or Cuba.

By 1852 more than twenty-three thousand miles of telegraph wires straddled the American continent, helping not only to create a more. unified domestic and capital market but also to establish national interest in sporting events. Already many American newspapers, employing the new collective agencies such as Associated Press, published a column dedicated to the "latest by telegraph", and this collection of miscellania increasingly incorporated sporting information.[22] By the 1870s home-town supporters could read of the successful road trip of the Cincinnati Red Stockings or Chicago White Stockings within hours of the games' completion.

The "global village" of contemporary world affairs had its basis in the introduction of trans-oceanic cables in the second half of the nineteenth century. Again, the transmission of sports news became a major function of the international telegraphs. A considerable share of the revenue gained from the successful Atlantic telegraph (laid in 1866) was received from newspapers and journals willing to pay as much as a pound a word for sporting news. Indeed, by 1867 the *New York Herald* had only twice paid eight hundred pounds for dispatches: the first, to record the King of Prussia's speech after war with Austria; the second, to provide readers with a blow-by-blow description of the boxing match between Mace and Goss. The *Herald's* priorities were generally accepted. When, in 1888, William I lay dead in Berlin, the *New York Sun's* principal European correspondent, Arthur Brisbane, was concerned not with the future of the continuent but with the aftermath of the Sullivan/Mitchell fight in Chantilly.[23]

Clearly, editors were convinced that the latest telegraphic news on sporting events, be they baseball, boxing bouts, positions in the Admiral's Cup yachting series, or results on the racetracks, helped sell newspapers. In 1909 Associated Press were prompted to inaugurate a special summer afternoon sports service, and by 1925 baseball coverage "necessitated the use of ten thousand miles of leased wire for this purpose alone". There can be little doubt that the barrage of world-wide sporting news presented to readers intensified interest in such contests and stimulated spectator attendance at events within the United States.

In the meantime, newspaper readership had soared. On the supply side, production costs were significantly lowered. The introduction of low-quality machine-made paper reduced the cost of newsprint from fifteen cents a pound in 1867 to twelve cents a pound in 1872, to six cents a pound in 1879. Input costs declined further in the 1880s as wood pulp replaced rags, esparto grass, and plant cellulose as a source of paper manufacture: by 1888 newsprint cost only four cents a pound, and by 1900 it had reached a price nadir of less than two cents a pound. [24]

Concurrently a revolution took place in typesetting. In 1887, it has been claimed, "typesetting was essentialy the same art as in the sixteenth century". The rapid introduction of linotyping transformed this static technology. From the mid-1880s newspapers employed matrix-cutting machines able to cast entire lines of type, which to a considerable extent superseded expensive .hand compositing. The Mergenthaler linotype, which had a predominant influence over the industry, allowed type to be set at between four and five times the speed of hand composition. [25] Output costs were further reduced by the development of a more efficient distribution system and by the increased revenues which resulted from the rapid growth of corporate advertising. Costs to the ultimate consumer were substantially reduced. On the demand side, advances in leisure time, increases in *per capita* income, and improved literacy helped to stimulate sales.

Intensive competition, borne of the desire of newspaper producers to gain monopolistic positions within fast-growing regional markets, beckoned publishers and editors toward including more news of popular concern. Human interest stories — shootings and suicides, scandal and sport — stole an increasing share of column inches from the machinations of business, diplomatic intrigue, political policy, and war. The *New York Sun* had published its first sporting story, an account of the fierce seventy-two minute fight between Williamson and Phelan at Hoboken Field in June 1835, in order to condemn interest in such brutal events. However, between 1868 and 1897, when the paper was under the stimulating editorship of Charles Dana, boxing (and a wide variety of other sports) were given an ever-larger share of column space. [26]

By early this century most of the significant developments in sporting journalism had been suggested. Reporters on the *New York Sun* devised a grid system by which they could record detailed accounts of boxing contests, a technique applicable to many other sports; the *New York World* introduced a "sporting editor" in 1883, to have control over a special staff division; the two *Sunday*

Mercurys, produced in New York and Philadelphia, led the way in emphasizing the importance of sports news to the weekend press; the *New York Evening Sun* and *Pittsburgh Press* inaugurated special "sporting editions" as a means of making use of necessary capital investment in emergency presses; and the *New York Times* established a precedent in 1910 when it hired a sports celebrity and "expert", John L. Sullivan, to write a guest column on the Jeffries-Johnson fight.[27]

Circulation was further boosted, and interest in spectator sports intensified, by the application of photo-engraving to newspaper production. In the 1850s, illustrations required wood-block line drawings to be made and zinc cuts produced. In the 1860s the faster chalk plate method was introduced, by which newspaper artists merely had to sketch on a thin layer of chalk coated over metal. However, the 1870s established the feasibility of replacing such drawings with reproduced photographs. Halftoned photo-engraving, printed on stereotype or electrotype presses, was inaugurated by the *New York Herald* in 1893, and by 1900 most large dailies contained arrays of photographic illustrations. The selected copy of the photographic journalist was as significant in capturing the atmosphere of sporting contests as the detailed match report that accompanied it. Perhaps more so — after a decade of apparently ineffectual editorial criticism of gridiron violence, presidential intervention was finally aroused in 1905 after Theodore Roosevelt put down his newspaper in horror at the photograph of the bloody, battered face of lineman Bob Maxwell, who was shown leaving the field after a particularly gory Swarthmore-Penn fixture.[28]

Developments reached their logical conclusion in 1919 when the *New York Daily News* was founded by McCormick and Pattison of the *Chicago Tribune*. It was America's first tabloid, and its dedication to news photography was symbolized by the camera motif on the front page and further demonstrated by its pioneering role in transmitting telephotos by radio in 1924. Circulation, after a slow start, rose rapidly, and by the 1950s it possessed the highest daily circulation in the United States.[29] Its back-page sports-action photographs had done much to make sports figures household heroes and to bring their exploits, on and off the field, into the everyday lives of busy New Yorkers.

By the early twentieth century, then, newspaper technology allowed Americans indirect access to the excitement of sports action. An outlay of a few cents and a few minutes of quiet relaxation enabled tired workers to savour the atmosphere of a dozen different sporting events that had recently been staged in a wide variety of locales. Yet the pre-eminence of the newspaper in sports presentation was swiftly to be challenged by new advances in media technology.

In 1905, in Pittsburgh, after decades of innovation in Kineto-scopes, Mutoscopes, and Veriscopes, the first nickelodeon opened. It proved an immediate success, and within a few years motion picture theatres were, at least in aggregate, big business. They were generally small, cheaply furnished, and dangerously flammable, and their flickering darkness was a refuted haven for every conceivable vice and disease, but movies swiftly attracted the allegiance of workers. For a mere nickel they could enjoy thirty minutes of astonishing entertainment in the hours after work.[30]

The new medium was a competitor with spectator sport for leisure dollars: it was at least a potential substitute. But in catering to popular desire to witness major sporting events, in providing film sequences of contests that people would have been unable to view directly, and by confining footage to the moments of most excitement and tension, film increased interest in spectator sport. As feature motion pictures increased in length, so the newsreel became an integral component of an extended — and correspondingly dearer — theatre programme. Within that segment, sport almost invariably comprised a major sequence: it was, film distributors unanimously agreed, newsworthy.[31]

Both written and filmed news employed a technology suitable to recording sporting events that had taken place in the near past. The rapid development of American radio broadcasting in the 1920s was something quite different. For the first time it became possible to gain indirect access to sports events while they were actually occurring. It is difficult now to imagine the collective excitement of July 1921 as an estimated three hundred thousand New Yorkers listened enthralled to station WJY's description of the Dempsey-Carpentier fight from Jersey City.[32] The first official broadcasting licence had not yet been issued by the Department of Commerce. Receivers were still rudimentary, frequently the engineering handiwork of the listener. Broadcast techniques were equally primitive, information was relayed by telephone, instantly typed, and then read over the air. Yet the thrill of the transmission was no less.

By 1925, power transmission had vastly improved, cheap dependable mass-produced receivers were readily available, and "remotes" (that is, live broadcasts from outside the station) had become commonplace. In excess of $400 million was invested in receiving apparatus, four million sets were in use, and the estimated radio audience exceeded ten million. Now it was possible to savour — indirectly — the actions in a sporting contest as they happened. Radio announcers emerged capable of imparting the tensions in the stadium to the home audience. Some were too successful. Graham McNamee's vivid description of the Dempsey-Tunney prize fight in late 1928 was said to have caused twelve listeners to die from heart attack.[33]

The new media technology to some extent supplanted the old. Many newspapers were worried by the threat to their sporting "extras". "Fight fans no longer call up their newspapers for the latest news," reported one analyst in 1925. "They listen in at their own or their friends' radio sets." It was also suggested that radio posed a danger to attendance at sports, although majority opinion seems to have derided such a hypothesis. Most agreed with a contemporary sociologist who claimed that access to sports through radio broadcast did not satisfy man's desire to congregate with other persons in the mutual enjoyment of games, and that in terms of social psychology radio technology was deficient. Indeed, it was generally believed that radio broadcasts bolstered attendance by stimulating the desire of listeners, especially former spectators, to witness live matches. Yet a more careful social survey undertaken in 1932, while in broad agreement with these conclusions, added a qualifying rider that was to prove of major significance in respect of later technology. Radio, it was claimed, emphasized big matches and star athletes to the detriment of minor league sports contests. Local spectator sport often palled in comparison with broadcast features.[34]

The reason for the decline in popularity of the radio was, of course, the rapid advance made in visual broadcasting and the consequent expansion in the ownership of television sets in America after the Second World War. In 1946 only eight thousand households possessed television sets, compared with thirty-four million radios: by 1970 sixty million families owned televisions, almost equal with the sixty-two million with radios.[35] If any one piece of technology was to be selected as the single most important determinant of the development of spectator sport in the last century, it would be difficult not to choose the television. It has provided Americans with an opportunity to view sporting action play-by-play within the confines and comfort of their own home, but in so doing it has begun to transform the nature of American spectator sport.

Television networks have to pay for sports coverage, and in recent years sports promoters have become increasingly dependent on the sale of broadcast rights. Between 1952 and 1972 the share of major league baseball revenues received from concessions remained stable at about 10 per cent, the proportion derived from stadium attendance fell from 67 to 54 per cent, while the income from radio and television rights increased from 13 to 25 per cent. In major league football the leap in broadcast sales was even greater: from 9 per cent of total club revenue in 1952 to 36 per cent in 1972.[36] It is certain that the statistics from ice-hockey and basketball would reveal a similar picture.

In part the increased dependence of professional sports upon television sales reflects an increase in time allotted to sport by stations. In the same twenty-year period, for example, the proportion of network weekend programming devoted to sport increased from zero to 32 per cent. By then the World Series could attract sixty-three million viewers, the Super Bowl sixty-five million.[37] Equally significant has been the vast increase in broadcast fees that sport can command. Competing channels, viewing sports spectaculars as "leader" items with which to attract patronage and recognizing that television commercials during professional football games can now be sold at more than $200,000 a minute, have proved ever more willing to pay immense sums for television rights. The trend was presaged in 1961 when Congress legislated that the National Football League could sell its entire sports "package" to a single network buyer. The initial agreement the League struck with the CBS network guaranteed the League $10.2 million for a two-year period, assuring each team of $300,000 annually or in excess of two-thirds average team payroll. This total soon soared. By 1970 each NFL club received about $1.5 million in television money alone. Baseball was not far behind. By 1972 the lowest annual revenue from independently negotiated radio-television rights was the $600,000 paid to the Milwaukee Brewers: the highest, the $1.8 million received by the Los Angeles Dodgers.[38]

The growing importance of television to spectator sport has given the medium substantial control over its development. That a given technology can determine the nature of sporting activity is not new. Innovations in equipment technology have not only improved athletic performance (the introduction of the glass-fibre pole for pole-vaulting being the most obvious instance), but have also altered ground requirements (the rubber-wound gutta-percha ball, for example, necessitating the lengthening of golf courses). However, the impact of television upon sports presentations is of a different order. Here it is not the technology *per se* that is the determining force, but the tight programme schedules demanded of the media. Sports that do not readily confine themselves to predictable time limits are unsuitable for neat time slotting and are likely to lose access to television. In order to alleviate such difficulties, the "sudden death" play-off has been introduced to golf tournaments; the "tie break" and "professional set" to championship tennis. It may not necessarily be in the best interest of the sport, the spectator, or the player, but as John Newcombe pragmatically concluded with regard to the altered tennis rules: "If the fans like it and it helps us get tennis on the big television networks, then we should all be for it . . . That's where our money comes from."[39]

Far more important for the long-term growth of spectator sport has been the impact of television coverage upon direct attendance. It is far less demanding both of time and money (given initial capital outlay) to watch sport presented in one's living-room than to journey to the stadium at which the match is being played. To some extent this effect is countered by the difficulty of sharing the crowd emotion without actually being there, by institutional restraints upon the live broadcast of home games in local areas, and by the increased sports interest aroused in the television audience, which might be translated into actual attendance. But such countervailing pressures are ineffective outside of the major urban centres. Attendances at minor league contests in direct competition with televised major league clashes have dropped precipitously. As a result aggregate crowds at spectator sports have fallen.[40]

However, it is not only minor league sport that faces a future threat. Television revenues have certainly provided short-term benefits to spectator sports. It is unlikely that the American Football League would have survived had it not been for the five-year, $11 million contract signed with the ABC network in 1960.[41] Yet the long-term picture reveals a different, and more threatening, complexion.

It may well be that television presents a false picture of sports action, an image which, by over-emphasizing play skills and crowd tension in a particular contest, effectively depreciates the "real thing". Again this aspect of media technology is not new. Newspapers, wishing to hold reader interest, built sensationalism into sport contests, a tendency that was intensified by the willingness of sports promoters to pay for good pre-match publicity. The methods of Tex Rickard in the 1920s epitomize this situation: in 1921, for instance, he bribed reporters handsomely in order to increase interest in, and gate receipts at, the boxing bout between Jack Dempsey and the fading French light-heavyweight Carpentier.[42]

Similarly, films often distorted sporting reality. Even from the earliest days a variety of faking techniques were used. Fraudulent and unauthorized recreations of important fights were staged, using extras to impersonate figures who were but names to the gullible audience. In other instances fights were filmed which, as with so much professional wrestling today, had both the verdict and the time of conclusion pre-arranged. Indeed, the film that "appears to have the dubious distinction of being the first fake news film ever produced" was a fight starring heavyweight champion James J. Corbett.[43] The film was timed to exactly six one-minute rounds, with Corbett's opponent, Peter Courtney, agreeing to be "knocked out" in the dying seconds of the contest.

Radio, too, "recreated" sporting commentaries for its believing listeners. Most successful were the baseball commentaries of Gordon McLendon on the Liberty Broadcasting System in the early 1950s. Information came to the studio on ticker tape, and was recreated into a game by the skilful — but often extravagent — announcer. McLendon went further than most contemporaries in creating atmosphere: he trained his engineers to manipulate sound effects so as to impersonate crowd noise, bat hitting ball, the shouts of food and beer vendors, and even public address announcements presented in the correct regional accent. His commentaries were, in retrospect, too successful. Organized baseball, fearful of McLendon's affect upon attendances, placed increasing restrictions upon his recreations, severely disrupted the service, and forced the network into bankruptcy.[44]

By contrast, the danger from television is far more subtle. Its most devastating effects stem from continued technological innovation. The introduction of colour transmission, use of wide-angle and telephoto lenses, and the development of instant slow-motion replays, "falsifies" reality by presenting a game that cannot be witnessed by the crowd spectator. No videotaped action replays are presented at the stadium — nor, for that matter, glimpses into the private sanctity of dressing rooms, pre- and post-match interviews with the participants, or the continuous commentary of knowledgable observers. Media technology has for the first time reached a stage at which indirect access to professional sport may not only be more convenient but also more rewarding than direct attendance. These developments are accentuated by the tendency to produce "edited highlights" which emphasize the moments of greatest skill and excitement and eliminate the periods of lesser interest which the crowd spectator has to tolerate, and by devoting almost exclusive attention to the major matches and athletic superstars, thereby depreciating the quality of "lower" level, non-televised sports contests.

Meanwhile, the need to attract television presentation has imposed heavy new capital requirements upon sports promoters. Colour transmission, to chose but one instance, required a considerable outlay for superior lighting capability.[45] At the same time the attempt to stimulate direct attendance at sports meetings in competition with an increasing range of alternative recreational possibilities necessitates the provision of superior seating, stadium heating and air-conditioning, convenient parking facilities, and so forth. These demands, combined with growing operational costs and with the vastly improved indirect access allowed by media technology, may result in a "TV sport" as distinct from its spectator heritage as is "TV theatre" from its stage antecedents. While the national television audience will soar, the minority who continue regularly to attend local matches will diminish. Individual sports will either have to adapt to the tight programme schedules and necessary commercial breaks of networks or see their position as spectator sports challenged. Other sports, at present unsuited to a mass audience, may find one through television. Golf has become a majoi *spectator* sport via the new media; squash could well follow suit.

As any historian knows, extrapolation from previous trends is a hazardous process. Yet developments in the technological environment suggest that the future of spectator sport may lie in its ability to capture a television audience. The stadiums, at least those surviving, will become little more than studios; the professional athletes, entertainment celebrities; and the contests an arrangement between sports owners, players, and media entrepreneurs. One can envisage baseball played on washable astroturf, beneath an air-conditioned dome, in the deathly quiet of a deserted arena: only the distant echo of sporting action, the hushed commentary of the announcer and, dispersed in countless homes around the United States, a vast television audience. Such a conclusion might appear more science fiction than reasoned analysis. Yet the historical precedent already exists. On the afternoon of 24 December 1976, at Yonkers, New York, an unusual trotting meeting was held. Races were staged at the remarkable rate of one every ten minutes, and only off-course betting was allowed. The reason was that not a single spectator was present. It was the first "TV meeting"; a sporting contest recorded by camera and played into households later that same evening.[46] It is at least probable that the same technique will be applied to other spectator sports. The electronic age has surely arrived.

NOTES

1. John Rickards Betts, "The Technological Revolution and the Rise of Sport, 1850—1900, *Mississippi Valley Historical Review* 40 (1953): 232; for a more detailed analysis see Bett's doctoral thesis, "Organized Sport in Industrial America" (Columbia University, 1951).
2. The quotations selected are from Betts, "Technological Revolution", pp.256, 237, and 250.
3. David Quentin Voigt, "Cash and Glory: The Commercialization of Major League Baseball as a Sports Spectacular, 1865—1892" (Ph.D. thesis, Syracuse University, 1962), p.104.
4. Harvard built a fifty-thousand-seat stadium in 1909 for $330,000; Princeton spend $300,000 on its arena in 1914; and in the same year the Yale Bowl was constructed to accommodate sixty-one thousand spectators at a cost of $400,000. See *American Architect* 117 (1920): 807.
5. Howard Dwight Smith, "Report on a Trip to Princeton, College of City of New York, Yale and Harvard for the Purpose of Inspecting Stadia at Those Universities", *American Architect* 118 (1920): 161.
6. The infrequent use of college stadia was partly determined by the nature of American spectator sport. The country's two best-loved team sports, baseball and football, require such different field requirements that neither can be comfortably housed in a stadium designed to meet the specific requirements of the other. This fact also deterred substantial capital investment in professional leagues. While the bowl is ideally suited to gridiron, providing a maximum number of good visibility seats and, *ipso facto*, maximum seat rentals, it is singularly unsuited to the field dimensions required by baseball.
7. See, for example, the willing response of residents of the small Wisconsin town of Green Bay in buying "shares" in their professional football team, the Packers, in the 1920s: Nicholas Mason, *Football! The Story of All the World's Football Games* (London: Temple Smith, 1976), p.172.
8. In 1953, to take a famous instance, Annheuser-Busch Inc. puchased the baseball team St. Louis Cardinals for $3.75 million in order to keep the side in the city. But other reasons than local pride were at play. With the help of considerable radio advertising during Cardinal games, Busch, maker of Budweiser beers, increased territory sales by 17 per cent in the following year and accelerated the collapse of small breweries in the area: see USA, Congress, Senate, Subcommittee of the Committee on the Judiciary, *Subjecting Baseball Clubs to the Antitrust Laws,* "Hearings", 1954, pp.18, 102, and 116.
9. Roi L. Morin, "Stadia", *American Architect* 124 (1923): 412—16.
10. On these developments see Harold E. Seymour, *Baseball: The Golden Age* (New York: Oxford University Press, 1971), pp.57—59.
11. *American Architect,* 118 (1920): 617.
12. Betts, "Technological Revolution", pp.233—34, provides a succinct account of the impact of the steamboat and railroad in stimulating "the rise of the turf and outdoor games" in ante-bellum America. See also Voigt, "Cash and Glory", p.173.
13. Ownership of a sports team was generally considered an economic liability. Henry W. Blake and Walter Jackson, *Electric Railway Transportation* (New York: McGraw-Hill, 1917), p.297, note that while "a few companies have ventured to add to their burdens the ownership of a professional baseball team", it needed to "be clearly understood that few minor leagues made money". They added: "An occasional subsidy may not be out of place, but to be the owner is almost as bad as to be the umpire." For an account of the

Canadian scene, see Ian F. Jobling, "Urbanization and Sport in Canada, 1867–1900", in *Canadian Sports: Sociological Perspectives*, ed. Richard S. Gruneau and John A. Albinson (New York: Addison-Westley, 1976), pp.65–67.

14. Statistics on population, the extent of street railway patronage, and automobile registrations may be perused most readily in *Historical Statistics of the United States*, Bicentennial edn. (Washington, DC: Department of Commerce, 1975), series A91–104, Q148–162, Q264–273 (hereafter referred to as *Historical Statistics*). See also Myron W. Serby, *The Stadium: A Treatise on the Design of Stadiums and Their Equipment* (New York: American Institute of Steel Construction, 1930), pp.8–9; Herman J. Penn, *Encyclopaedic Guide to Planning and Establishing an Auditorium, Arena, Coliseum or Multi-Purpose Building* (Greenville, South Carolina: Penn-Fleming, 1963), p.225. Estimated space per car, including driveways, of 150 sq.ft.

15. US, *Action for Outdoor Recreation for America* (Washington, DC: Outdoor Recreation Resources Review Commission, 1964), p. 10; for a good analysis of alternative recreational pursuits stimulated by increased car ownership, see Marion Clawson and Jack L. Knetsch, *Economics of Outdoor Recreation* (Baltimore: Johns Hopkins University Press, 1966).

16. *Historical Statistics*, series D765–778, D802–810; John D. Owen, "Workweeks and Leisure: An Analysis of Trends, 1948–75", *Monthly Labor Review* 99 (1976): 3–8.

17. George Soule, in "The Economics of Leisure", *Annals of the American Academy of Political and Social Science* 313 (1957): 20, tackles this problem from a somewhat different angle: "In depression, the labor force is unable to sell all the time it wants to devote to earning money; idleness is enforced by the lack of demand for workers. Since this idleness is not the result of voluntary choice, it does not fit the concept of leisure; it is a deprivation, not a privilege."

18. *New York Times*, 26 May 1935.

19. For details of these developments, see "Scalloped Prestressed Dome from Prestressed Elements", *American Concrete Institute Journal* 63 (1966): 313–23; "Suspension Roof Frees Arena from Column Obstructions", *Architectural Record* 135 (1964): 185; "Unusual Dome Awaits Baseball Season in Houston", *Civil Engineering* 35 (1965): 63–65; "Retractable Stadium Dome Wins Architectural Award", *Modern Metals* 23 (1967): 54–56; "Welded Steel Frames World's Largest Clear-Span Domed Stadium", *Welding Engineer* 49 (1964): 54–57; and a selection of articles in *Engineering News-Record:* "Record-Span Dome Rooofs Air-Conditioned Stadium", 172 (1964): 26–28; "Mets' Dome Won't Hide Fly Balls", 174 (1965): 20; "Elliptical Dish Sets Record for Cable-Supported Roofs", 174 (1965): 66–68; and "Cantilevered Stands Carry Around Arena's Long-Span Roof", 173 (1964):26–27.

20. Will Grimsley, *Tennis: Its History, People and Events* (Englewood Cliffs, NJ: Prentice-Hall, 1971), pp.208–9.

21. Only one facet of "peculiarity" is emphasized here. For more refined analyses, see Walter C. Neale, "The Peculiar Economics of Professional Sports", *Quarterly Journal of Economics* 77 (1964): 1–14; J. C. H. Jones, "The Economics of the National Hockey League", *Canadian Journal of Economics* 2 (1969): 1–20; Michael S. Canes, "The Economics of Professional Sports" (Ph.D. thesis, University of California at Los Angeles, 1970).

22. Robert Luther Thompson, *Wiring a Continent: the History of the Telegraph Industry in the United States, 1832-1866* (Princeton, NJ: Princeton University Press, 1947), pp.217-39 and 241.

23. Edward B. Bright, *The Electric Telegraph* (London: Walton and Maberly, 1867),

p.247; Frank M. O'Brien, *The Story of the Sun: New York, 1833-1918* (New York: Appleton, 1918), p.391.

24. Alfred McClung Lee, *The Daily Newspaper in America: The Evolution of a Social Instrument* (New York: Macmillan, 1947), pp.530, 742-45.

25. George E. Barnett, *Chapters on Machinery and Labor* (Carbondale, Ill.: Southern Illinois University Press, 1969), p.3. This article was originally published in *Yale Review*, 1904.

26. O'Brien, *Story of the Sun*, pp.58, 391-93.

27. Ibid., p.285; Lee, *The Daily Newspaper*, pp.396 and 629; Elmer Davis, *History of the New York Times, 1851-1921* (New York: New York Times, 1921), p.301; James Melvin Lee, *History of American Journalism* (Cambridge, Mass.: Garden City, 1917), p.379-82.

28. Lee, *The Daily Newspaper*, pp.129-31; Frank G. Menke, *The Encyclopedia of Sport*, 4th ed. (New York: Barnes, 1969), pp.371-72.

29. Jacques Kayser, *One Week's News: Comparative Study of Seventeen Major Dailies for a Seven-Day Period* (UNESCO, 1953), p.41.

30. Eugene Le Moyne Connelly, "The First Motion Picture Theatre", *Western Pennsylvania Historical Magazine* 23 (1940): 1-10.

31. For a good account of the film newsreel and its devotion to sporting items, see Raymond Fielding, *The American Newsreel, 1911-1967* (Norman, Okla: Oklahoma University Press, 1972).

32. Lawrence W. Lichty and Malachi C. Topping, *American Broadcasting: A Source Book on the History of Radio and Television* (New York: Hastings, 1975), p.295.

33. Hiram, L. Jome, *Economics of the Radio Industry* (Chicago: Shaw, 1925), p.220; "Excitement Causes Twelve Fight Fans to Drop Dead During Tense Description", *Radio Digest*, November 1927, p.19.

34. Jome, *Economics of the Radio Industry*, p.274; Marshall D. Beuick, "The Limited Social Effect of Radio Broadcasting", *American Journal of Sociology* 33 (1927): 615. For a second opinion see "Big Radio Audience Follows Grid Games", *Radio Digest*, October 1927, p.8: "No question about it. Radio has been the salvation of many a waning sport in the past few years . . . "; W. F. Ogburn and S. C. Gilfillan, *Recent Social Trends in the United States* (New York: Houghton Mifflin, 1933), pp.148-65.

35. *Historical Statistics*, series R93-105.

36. Henry G. Demmert, *The Economics of Professional Team Sports* (Lexington, Mass.: Heath, 1973), p.13.

37. Lichty and Topping, *American Broadcasting*, p.438; John T. Talamini and Charles H. Page, eds., *Sport and Society: An Anthology* (Boston: Little, Brown, 1973), p.5.

38. Demmert, *Professional Team Sports*, p. 20; Joseph Durso, *The All American Dollar: The Big Business of Sports* (Boston: Houghton Mifflin, 1971), esp. pp.1-24.

39. Quoted in Grimsley, *Tennis*, p.30.

40. Analysis has indicated the existence of an inverse linear correlation between the number of television sets in America and total baseball attendance: see George Miller, "A Study of the Economics of Professional Spectator Sports" (Ph.D. thesis, Claremont Graduate School, 1965), pp.227-28.

41. Ibid., p.214.

42. Lee, *The Daily Newspaper*, p.463.

43. Fielding, *The American Newsreel*, p.10.

44. David T. MacFarland, "The Liberty Broadcasting System" in Lichty and Topping, *American Broadcasting*, pp.188-90.

45. "Coliseum Lighting for Color T. V.", *The American City* 83 (1968): 126;

"Sports Stadiums Face Relighting for Better Color T. V. Reception", *Electrical World* 168 (1967): 58; "Sports Stadiums Gearing for Color T. V. Coverage", *Electrical World* 169 (1968): 41.
46. *Harness Horse*, February 1977.

BARRY ANDREWS

The Willow Tree and the Laurel: Australian Sport and Australian Literature

> Ho Statesmen, Patriots, Bards make way!
> Your fame has sunk to zero:
> For Victor Trumper is today
> Our one Australian hero . . . .
> Is there not, haply, in the land
> Some native-born Murillo
> To paint, in colours rich and grand,
> This Wielder of the Willow?
> Nay, rather let a statue be
> Erected his renown to,
> That future citizens might see
> The gods their sires bowed down to.
> Evoe Trumper! As for me
> It all ends with the moral
> That fame grows on the Willow Tree
> And no more on the laurel.[1]

Not that Victor Daley was the first to notice; when he wrote at the turn of the century, the Australian passion for sport — both playing and watching — was already a cliche.[2] In 1882 Henry Gyles Turner noted: "The energy with which our hearty manhood cultivates cricket, boating, yachting, football, horseracing, hunting, coursing, and kindred developments of athleticism has excited the admiring surprise of our English and foreign visitors."[3] He might have been thinking of Anthony Trollope's observation in 1873 that sport was a national necessity with Australians no less than with Englishmen, but R. E. N. Twopeny in 1883 was even more emphatic: Australia was the most sporting country in the world. Since then many other English and foreign visitors have commented on the passion, among them the novelist Mark Twain and the organist Thomas Wood (who provides a marvellous description of a memorable night, his first in Australia, spent at the trots).[4] The comments of these — often bemused — observers are echoed by the indigenous journalists who in the last decade have turned to analysing Australia and Australians: thus Donald Horne ("for many Australians, playing or

watching sport gives life one of its principal meanings"), Craig
McGregor (sport "occupies a central position in Australian popular
culture"), and, most notably, Keith Dunstan, who moved from
wowsers and knockers to show that "sport is a national obsession".[5]

The indicators of the passion are well-documented:[6] the way
Australians have been moved by the deaths of prominent sporting
personalities (Harry Searle, Tommy Corrigan, Les Darcy, Archie
Jackson, Phar Lap);[7] the attention given to sport by the media (the
ubiquitous racing broadcast began with the crystal set);[8] the fact that
politicians have found an interest in sport useful to their careers; the
ritual of Cup Day ("the great annual day of sacrifice", according to
Twain);[9] the popularity polls of prominent people (sportsmen
invariably do well); and the football jokes (witness Sydney in the
early 1960s, when underneath a notice board proclaiming "Jesus is
Coming" a wag scribbled, "If he does Parramatta will buy him."
The Melbourne equivalent has the sign ask: "What would you do if
God came to Hawthorn?", the wag writing "Move Peter Hudson to
centre-half forward" and the people of Hawthorn asking "Who's
God?"). The causes of the passion are equally well documented.
Some writers have pointed to geography (the climate), others to
economics (the affluence of the inhabitants of the lucky country),
still others to the evidence of history. Thus Australians became
interested because sport was democratized very early, it gave them a
chance to express their national identity, it became a substitute for
religion, it offered them a harmless and socially acceptable outlet for
the aggressive instincts of a country untroubled by civil war.[10]

The passion, it must be emphasized, is not unique to Australians:
there are Liverpool and Manchester equivalents of the Peter
Hudson story, Richard Nixon has barracked for the Washington
Redskins as publicly as Sir Robert Menzies has supported Carlton.[11]
Nor have all Australians approved of the passion. As early as 1834
John Dunmore Lang thumped out a warning against the evils of
racing, which led men from the racecourse towards drink and
crime,[12] and in the 1870s John Stanley James, "The Vagabond",
anticipated the protests of modern journalists by reporting that
Melbourne footballers trooped from the field bloodied and bruised
and that referees wore brass knuckles to establish their authority.[13]
If Lang objected to the spiritual dangers and James to the physical
violence of some sports, the cultural consequences of the games
revolution were categorized in pungent terms by James Francis
Hogan, an ironic surname for one of the first anti-ockers. For Hogan
the native Australian of 1880 was distinguished by his "inordinate
love of field-sports" and his "grievous dislike of mental effort".

The two went side by side, for "this excessive indulgence in physical pleasures" was "at the expense of mental cultivation. . . . To deify muscle, and degrade the mind, is a proceeding that does not augur well for the future."[14] Hogan might be said to have inaugurated the Max Harris-Ronald Conway tradition. Certainly both Harris and Conway have made scathing attacks on the Great Australian Stupor, one of their major targets being the anti-intellectualism of the cultural barbarians who deify the sportsman from their vantage point on the Hill.

It was against the deification of one Victor, Trumper, that another Victor, Daley, protested — and Daley was neither the first not the last Australian writer to use his art as a weapon. Joseph Furphy had already predicted, through Tom Collins, an Australian future in which " 'sport' will seem folly that would disgrace an idiot"; his disappointment at what A. D. Hope was to say of Australians fifty years later can only be imagined:

Now all the Austral scene,
Race-track, pub, football-ground, poker machine —
Pleasing enough to these Yahoos, perhaps,
To whom all books are made with bets, poor chaps!
Whose height of learning is, at most, the claim
To read a jockey's or a horse's name.[15]

Yet it is inaccurate to draw too sharp a contrast between literature and sport in Australia. They are married, to begin with, in the pseudonym of one of Australian literature's most famous sons, Arthur Hoey Davis, who took the "Steele" from the English essayist and the "Rudd", as a contraction of "rudder", from the vocabulary of his favourite sport of rowing.[16] And Davis wasn't the only Australian writer who loved or played sport: A. B. Paterson rarely missed a meeting at Randwick for over twenty years,[17] Henry Handel Richardson won tennis tournaments in Leipzig, Arthur Bayldon billed himself as the champion backstroke swimmer of the world. (Similarly, Ron Haddrick, the actor, played cricket for South Australia in the 1940s. The connection between sport and the theatre, particularly before the First World War, deserves at least one thesis.)[18] Given, indeed, the social context of literature, the social environment to which in some measure all creative writers respond,[19] it is hardly surprising that in Australian literature we find documentation of the significance of sport for Australians, even some evidence of Australian literature celebrating sport. In this survey of the way sport has been presented in Australian literature it is to the documentation and the celebration, as well as to the criticism, that we must turn.

First the documentation, although it must be admitted that just as a passion for sport is not unique to Australians, so the use of sport by creative writers is not confined to Australian literature. There are analogies between life and sport in classical literature, in the Bible, in Elizabethan and Jacobean drama, and, most abundantly, in Victorian literature. For one critic, indeed, the phrase "a straight bat and a modest mind" epitomized the English character in the late nineteenth century, the synthesis between cricket and morality able to be demonstrated by reference not only to didactic novels such as *Baxter's Second Innings* but also to the use of cricket and other sports by Dickens, Trollope, and particularly Meredith.[20] So, too, with Henry Kingsley, who crosses the bridge between Victorian and Australian literature: Frank Maberly in *The Recollections of Geoffry Hamlyn* is a perfect — perhaps too perfect — muscular Christian. The best runner, cricketer, and scholar of his day at Eton, he is disappointed — "how pursy a fellow gets mewed up in town!" — when he just fails to run the four miles from the Buller Arms to Drumston village in twenty minutes. When the governess Miss Thornton wonders whether such violent exercise might bring on palpitations, Maberly insists that "a man at five-and-twenty should be able and willing to run four miles, a parson above all others, as a protest against effeminacy".[21]

Maberly's *mens sana in corpore sano* ethic informs Australian sporting literature, particularly before the First World War; Kingsley's technique of using sport as metaphor or symbol is still employed, particularly by contemporary dramatists and short story writers. The Cup, for example, is one of the rituals of Alexander Buzo's *The Front-Room Boys,*[22] while another traditional sport, boxing, is an important symbol in Angelo Loukakis's superb story of migrant alienation, "The Boxer and the Grocer" in which the success of the visiting Greek boxer mirrors the failure of his host, a long-term Greek migrant.[23] A similar technique is employed in Robert Colvin's "All Pipes and Pharkas"[24] in which the fluctuation in the Wimbledon singles final being broadcast over the bar-room television mirrors the fluctuating relationship of the chief characters in the story, and in Finola Moorhead's "Squash"[25] and David Williamson's *Jugglers Three,* which use sports more recently acquired by Australians. In "Squash" the sexual game becomes part of the sporting game: the "abrupt sportswoman", confident with a racket in her hand but emotionally insecure off the court, wins one of those games against her floppy male opponent but loses the other. (A. D. Hope is more explicit on the sport of sex: the contestants in his satiric allegory "Sportsfield"[26] include the Bedroom Harriers and the Golden Girls!) In *Juggers Three* the motif is table tennis: the swing of the emotional pendulum is dramatized in the movement back and forth of the ping-pong ball. At the end of the play the married couple Graham and Keren are playing table tennis and arguing as the lights go down, which leaves open, as Brian Kiernan has suggested, the final resolution of their conflict.[27]

These several writers seldom register approval (or disapproval) of sport; yet in their deliberate *use* of sport they document its significance for Australians. And to the list of works in which sport is used as metaphor or symbol can be added a much longer one in which there are incidental sporting references. The list encompasses the work of surrealists as well as social realists, visionaries as well as humourists; David Ireland's *The Glass Canoe* as well as Katharine Susannah Prichard's *Working Bullocks* and David Martin's *The Young Wife,* Patrick White's *Riders in the Chariot,* and Thomas Keneally's *Bring Larks and Heroes* as well as Norman Lindsay's *The Cousin from Fiji.* Thus a soccer match between ethnic Melbourne teams is described in *The Young Wife,* thus the wowserism of Sarah in *The Cousin from Fiji* emerges in her report of the secret activities of Cecelia's flighty daughter, Elva:

> "Good heavens where does she spend her evenings I beg and pray?"
> "At the *oval*," said Sarah in awful tones.
> "The oval?"blinked Cecelia, unable to visualize what sink of infamy that might be.
> "The oval. Among low bicyclists. Watching them train," said Sarah, separating the procedures of that infamy.[28]

Now it must be emphasized that the sporting reference is incidental — several pages in *The Young Wife* and *The Cousin from Fiji,* a paragraph or two in *Bring Larks and Heroes,* a phrase in *Riders in the Chariot* — yet the point remains. There is ubiquitous evidence that sport has infiltrated Australian literature.

And yet for all that, it is the "sporting writers", the writers who take sport as their *subject,* who provide the obvious evidence. The category includes, arguably, all Australian journalists who have written on sport, whether for the specialist organs such as *Bell's Life in Victoria,* the Sydney *Referee* and *Australian Cricket,* or for general newspapers which cover sport, as is the case with virtually every Australian newspaper from the 1850s to the present day.[29] But if the category takes into account creative literature — fiction, verse, drama — rather than reportage, then the first sporting writer of major significance is Nat Gould.[30]

Gould (who also raises the vexed question of what constitutes an

"Australian" author)[31] moved from sports reporting into fiction by
way of the racing serial *With the Tide,* written for the Sydney *Referee.*
It began, "Nobody knew exactly who or what Jack Marston was",
least of all its author, as Gould admitted.[32] But he got it finished,
spinning it out as long as possible to gain time to resolve Jack
Marston's fortunes and to gain the benefit of the payment by the
line offered by his editor. Published in 1891 as *The Double Event,* it
was made into a play, was a phenomenal success on both stage and
bookstall, and won Gould wide recognition. Thereafter he churned
out about 130 readable, exciting, and immensely popular novels,
mostly about the turf — and other sports — and in many of which he
drew on his Australian experiences for his settings. There is no
complete Gould collection in Australia, but *Bred in the Bush* might
serve as a typical example of his plots.[33] The title refers not only to
racing but also to the heroine of the novel, Essie Holt, an up-country
Queensland girl of good character if a little rough round the edges,
who is allowed by her widower father to train several horses selected
from those running wild on the property; like Essie, they are bred in
the bush. The horses show potential as racehorses and are
eventually taken to Brisbane, where, despite the prying eyes of
opposition trainers and corrupt bookmakers, one of them wins the
Brisbane Cup. Essie forms a romantic attachment with the young
stud owner Alan Rolt, whom she marries at the end of the novel, to
live as happily ever after as her father (who marries Rolt's elder
sister) and her two assistants from the property (who become
respectively, a successful trainer in the city and a successful coach
driver).

Gould is seldom regarded as a significant Australian writer. His
novels are often melodramatic (crime and mystery are blended with
sport) and invariably sentimental, most clearly so in his presentation
of the world of the colonial and English aristocrats, a circle to which,
as the successful son of a tea merchant, Gould aspired.[34] But he
knew racing and he could tell a story, particularly when he followed
his own advice: "write about men and things you have met and
seen; take your characters from the busy world, and your scenes
from Nature."[35] His significance, however, depends less on any
critical consensus about his work than on his popularity, a popularity
(some of his novels are still in print) that stems from the interest of
his audience in sport. Gould, moreover, inaugurated the Australian
sporting novel. His lineal descendant was Arthur Wright, the most
prolific of the New South Wales Bookstall novelists, who was
advertised as "The Australian Nat Gould" and reached a wide
public with a similar amalgam of crime, mystery and romance,

spread across a range of society but moulded out of a sporting base; his first novel, like Gould's, was serialized in the *Referee* and later dramatized.[36] The tradition continues in the racing whodunits of the Englishman Dick Francis and in four Australian novels of the last decade: Robert Bennett's *The Big Ruck* (in which the promise suggested by the cover blurb — "bedposts or goal posts — he was Australia's top scorer" is confirmed in such lines as "She reached for a switch and turned on a heater, and then their bodies fused"), Hugh Atkinson's *The Games,* Alan O'Toole's *The Coach from the City,* and Christopher Nixon's *The Tour.*[37] Like Gould's fictions, they are novels intended for a popular audience, exploiting the interest of that audience in sport.

If the 1890s produced Nat Gould, it was also the decade in which flourished the bush ballad, an expression of the cultural chauvinism fostered, so the legend goes, by the *Bulletin.* The cult of the stockwhip had its critics even then, however; one of them, R. H. Croll, satirized the prevalent themes of Australian poetry in a quatrain submitted to the *Bookfellow* in 1899:

> Whaler, damper, swag and nose-bag, Johnny Cakes and billy tea,
> Murrumburrah, Meremendicoowoke, Youlgarbudgeree,
> Cattle-duffers, bold bushrangers, diggers, drovers, bush race-courses,
> And on all the other pages horses, horses, horses, horses.[88t338]

Some of the horses, as the third line makes clear, were racehorses, particularly in the poems of "Banjo" Paterson. Paterson wrote of other sports (for example, in "The Geebung Polo Club" and "Saltbush Bill's Second Fight") but his life-long interest in racing is reflected in his numerous poems and prose sketches — and a novel — that deal directly with the subject.[39] Many deal with the seamier side of racing: "How the Favourite Beat Us," for example. As the narrator tells it, he'd come down to the city to back his horse,

> But found she was favourite all of a rush;
> The folk just did pour on to lay six to four on,
> And several bookies were killed in the crush.

Although his horse is a certainty, the owner, full of chagrin at the short odds, decides to have it "pulled" and arranges with the jockey:

> You watch as you're cantering down by the stand;
> I'll wait where that toff is and give you the office,
> You're only to win if I lift up my hand.

But his well-laid plans come unstuck, for when the jockey looks over during the preliminaries the owner is brushing a mosquito from his face. His horse wins by the inevitable furlong and the owner is left to point the moral:

> 'Twas true, by St Peter; that cursed "muskeeter"
> Had broke me so broke that I hadn't a brown;
> And you'll find the best course is when dealing with horses
> To win when you're able, and *keep your hands down.*[40]

Similarly well-laid plans come unstuck elsewhere in Paterson's racing verses. But what might be emphasized at this point is not the morality of "How the Favourite Beat Us" but that it is a tall story, a "yarn" told about his sport by a boozer in a bar. For the tall story didn't die out with Paterson: it became a significant part of Australian popular literature, with comic exaggeration, a rural setting and a sporting subject as major ingredients. Among the rest of Paterson's verse, "The Geebung Polo Club" and "Father Riley's Horse" spring immediately to mind; among the work of his contemporaries, Lawson's "The Grog-an'-Grumble Steeplechase" (a parody of Paterson), J. W. Kevin's "The Judge's Decision", and Thomas Spencer's famous "How McDougall Topped the Score".[41]

And again, as with the descendants of Gould, the tradition lives on. It forms the basis of the humour of the *Australasian Post,* but resides not only there. It lives on in a more sophisticated way in Lennie Lower's "Bradman and the Burglar", in David Forrest's "That Barambah Mob", in Xavier Herbert's "Rocky the Rig", in Athol Mulley and Frank Hardy's *The Needy and the Greedy,* and in some of Hardy's Billy Borker yarns (see particularly "The Greatest Slanter in the History of the Racing Game").[42] But the best exponent writing fiction is surely Dal Stivens, in a memorable series of sketches — "The Linguist", "The Lovesick Racehorse", "The Miraculous Cricket Bat", "The Batting Wizard from the City", "When Trumper Went to Billabong," and my own favourite (with "That Barambah Mob"), "Indians Have Special Eyesight," sometimes known as "The Man Who Bowled Victor Trumper".[43] Within the tradition can also be placed three recent plays: Alan Hopgood's *And the Big Men Fly* and two pieces of alternative theatre, Stephen Mastare's *Phar Lap, "It's Cingalese for Lightning, Y'know"* and Jack Hibberd's *The Les Darcy Show.* The placement can be justified by reference to the authors themselves. Hopgood has insisted that *And the Big Men Fly* is no more than a dramatic "tall story", a yarn about Australian rules full of farce and jokes.[44] (The best one for this New South Welshman is the scout for the VFL club having his camera confiscated at Albury because he's been taking photos of fruit flies!) Mastare has said: "Phar Lap first intruded into my life in a barber shop via the *Australasian Post* in 1958, and since that time has been a constant stranger whom the writing of this play has made familiar."[45] Hibberd, finally, sees *The Les Darcy Show*

> as part of a series of plays on popular Australian characters, mythic
> figures if you like . . . .
> None of these plays stoop to psychological explanation . . . . They
> strive to work emblematically through scenic action and extroversion,
> an agglutination of facts, fibs, images, songs, occasions, jokes, straight
> lefts, and inexplicable distemper. At the very least, they hopefully
> operate as *good dramatic yarns.*[46]

So Paterson, like Gould, is a central figure in a literary tradition in
which, at the very least, sport plays a significant part. Both traditions
are popular ones; both, moreover, *celebrate* sport (and perhaps also,
as commentators are beginning to notice, the place of sport in the
male ethos). The satire of Stivens and Forrest and the corruption of
racing described by Gould, Paterson, and Wright must be conceded,
yet even then Stivens and Forrest express a love of sport and for
Paterson no less than for Gould the racecourse remains "the
gathering-place of the worshippers of speed and beauty".[47] As for
Hibberd, *The Les Darcy Show* is as much a toast to Darcy as *A Toast
to Melba* is to that mythic figure. The last line of the play is precisely
that, as the actors drink "To Les Darcy!" and then carry him
triumphantly from the theatre.[48]

Yet *The Les Darcy Show* (together with Mastare's *Phar Lap*) can
also be seen as part of a third literary tradition in which sport is
celebrated: the occasional writing on the subject. The tradition
probably originated in the 1840s and 1850s with the literary forecasts
compiled for the journals — such as *Bell's Life in Victoria* — which
gave extensive coverage to racing. In the 1850s the predictions
were often cryptic — for example, a writer employing an "Irish"
idiom published his thoughts concerning the Melbourne Turf
Club's meeting in March 1857, and readers had to discover the tips
camouflaged amidst such comic misspellings as "guiness" for
"guineas".[49] A decade later Adam Lindsay Gordon was writing
ballads before the Melbourne Cup in which he predicted how the
race would be run. In 1866, after several breathtaking verses, he had
Tim Whiffler triumph by a neck; the margin was accurate but the
winner was The Barb. In 1867 he predicted the Barb to repeat his
triumph unextended; again the margin was accurate but this time
Tim Whiffler triumphed.[50] Although Gordon retired from the
journal soon after, *Bell's Life in Victoria* continued to publish verse
predictions, and their lead was taken up by others, including, in the
1890s, the *Bulletin*. (Phantom broadcasts can still be heard in bars
and over radio stations in the days preceding the Cup.) Under the

umbrella of the "literary forecast" can also be included, perhaps, those hymns of hope, the team songs. Thus Ian Chappell's 1972 Australians predicted,

> We'll play on through the English rain
> And bring the Ashes back again;[51]

Thus Parramatta supporters predict, to "Click Go the Shears",
> And when we see the other side
> Slowly start to yield
> We lift our voices to the sky
> And glorify the Eels.[52]

The team is also celebrated in the occasional verse written *after* the event. For example, in 1882, *Punch* employed a technique common in occasional writing of adapting or parodying well-known rhymes and tunes to report on the success of the Australians against the MCC at Lords, when W. G. was dismissed second ball in each innings:

> The Australians came down like a wolf on the fold,
> The Marylebone cracks for a trifle were bowled,
> Our Grace before dinner was very soon done,
> And Grace after dinner did not get a run.[53]

But more often it is the individual hero whose triumph or tragedy has provided the occasion for poets, songwriters, and publicists. It is a moot point whether the triumph or the tragedy has provided the greater inspiration, but there are numerous specimens of each *genre*. As examples of the former can be cited tributes to boxers, cricketers, athletes, cyclists, and racehorses. As examples of the latter can be cited the lamentations over the deaths of Harry Searle, Tommy Corrigan, Les Darcy, and of course Phar Lap. Most of the verse is a combination of the execrable and the excruciating; the best is probably Paterson's tribute to Corrigan:

> When any slip means sudden death — with wife and child to keep —
> It needs some nerve to draw the whip and flog him at the leap —
> But Corrigan would ride them out, by danger undismayed,
> He never flinched at fence or wall, he never was afraid;
> With easy seat and nerve of steel, light hand and smiling face,
> He held the rushing horses back, and made the sluggards race.[54]

Paterson was concerned less with telling how Corrigan died than in emphasizing his courage and skill; and in its subordination of narrative to analysis his poem is typical of the occasional writing on sport. With defeat or death the analysis became a post-mortem. After the 1882 test which gave birth to the Ashes, *Punch* was warm in its congratulations to the Australians but perplexed as to the reason:

> Well done, Cornstalks, you whipt us
> Fair and square.
> Was it luck that tript us?
> Was it scare?
> Kangaroo land's "Demon" or our own
> Want of devil, coolness, nerve, backbone?[55]

Australian writers were in no doubt, however, about what had happened to Les Darcy and Phar Lap; they had been both "got at", like Young Griffo before them. The folk belief that Darcy had been poisoned emerged as one of the major explanations for Phar Lap's sudden death:

> They forced Phar Lap to do too much,
> That much we know quite well,
> What caused his death when in his prime,
> The future yet may tell.
>
> He closed his eyes in Yankee-land
> Of every evil thing;
> And there Les Darcy passed away,
> A champion of the ring.[56]

Both heroes probably died of natural causes. In any case, Darcy was vilified by some before he left Australia and Phar Lap shot at before the 1930 cup, yet by their deaths their heroism was reaffirmed; the Darcy and Phar Lap poems are celebrations as well as lamentations, as much the former as is the literature of triumph. And among the virtues celebrated are skill, greatness, courage, honesty, consummate superiority, reliability, contribution to national prestige, charm, and above all (if Marjorie Jackson though not all the equine heroes are excluded) manliness, a virtue emphasized in Mr Laurence Campbell's recitation at the complimentary dinner to Cecil Healy on his return from the Athens Olympic Games:

> You are beaten to earth. Well, well, what is that?
> Come up with a smiling face;
> It's nothing against you to fall down flat,
> But to lie there, that's a disgrace,
> And the harder you're hit, why the harder you'll bounce;

Be proud of your blackened eye!
It isn't the fact that you're licked that counts,
It's how did you fight — and why?
And though you be done to the death what then?
If you've battled the best you could,
If you've played your part in this world of men,
Why, the critic will call it good.[57]

The same virtues are celebrated, I would suggest, if not always in
Paterson's racing yarns then in the other poems which confirm his
preoccupation with "horses, horses, horses, horses": away from the
racecourse Tommy Corrigan becomes the Man from Snowy River.
As well, they are the virtues embodied in the heroes of Gould's
sporting novels and, with the exception of *The Big Ruck,* in those of
his descendants. The ethics of Maberly in *The Recollections of Geoffry
Hamlyn,* for example, find expression in Garnett Grayson in Arthur
Wright's *Rung In,* "as fine a specimen of muscular manhood as had
ever graced the ocean beach . . . six feet in his bare feet, broad
shouldered and deep chested, with not a particle of useless tissue on
his well-shaped body".[58] And there are Garnett Graysons
throughout Gould's novels[59] as well as Wright's.

Yet Grayson is a bushman who puts the "city men in the shade
completely". The comparison is interesting in terms of the
Australian Legend, but of more significance is the fact that in
Wright's novels the "sportsmen" from the "trained atmosphere of
the city"[60] dominate the world of racing, boxing, and even football,
a world characteristically infected by corruption and evil. The theme
finds expression also in Marcus Clarke's *Long Odds,* in Mastare's
Phar Lap, in Cecil Mann's "Chicken", and in Gould's novels,
despite his love for "that great and wonderful mass of human
beings who flock to all racecourses".[61] The bookies like Abe Davies
in *Thrown Away* (who has "a Jewish cast of features of the worst
type")[62] are characteristically corrupt, fixing races by bribing jockeys
with a fondness for drink, money, or loose women. A similar
ambivalence informs Rolf Boldrewood's *Robbery Under Arms.*
Jonathon Barnes, the keeper of the grog shanty to which Starlight's
gang periodically repairs, is a "tall, slouching, flash-looking native"
who'd "been a little in the horse-racing line, a little in the prize-
fighting line".[63] Starlight stands in contrast to Barnes no less than to
the vicious bushranger Moran, but for all his insistence on fair play
Starlight is happy to ring Rainbow in at Turon picnic races, using as
his jockey a drunk, Jacob Benton. And Paterson too, though his
treatment is usually comic, is under no illusions about the honesty
of racing when men seek not the pleasure of the sport but the profit.

It must be readily admitted that Paterson, no less than Gould or Wright, emphasizes that crime doesn't pay: the favourite wins in "How the Favourite Beat Us", the jockey narrator gets his just deserts in "A Disqualified Jockey's Story", the Garnett Graysons triumph in Gould and Wright, the moral balance is preserved.[64] But Jim Roberts in Frank Hardy's *The Four-Legged Lottery* is hanged for the murder of a corrupt bookmaker; he is the victim of racing, which in Australia "ceased to be a valiant sport, and became what it is now — a lottery with four-legged tickets".[65] For Hardy, the sport of kings in a capitalist society inevitably involves gambling. As his narrator puts it, gambling is an "expression of the cultural barbarism imposed on the people by our society . . . it will die only when the system that gives rise to it also dies".[66] Hardy's most successful capitalist, John West, profits by the system. In *Power Without Glory* his tentacles entrap boxing, trotting, cycling and football punters as well as the followers of racing.

Hardy admits that racing is not evil in itself; Jim Roberts grows to love the spectacle "for its own sake. The noble, sleek animals striving, the glamour of the atmosphere, the skill of the riders, the contest for supremacy",[67] which are all aspects of racing presented by Gould and Paterson in their more celebratory moods. For other creative writers, however, writers who turn less to racing than to those sports in which man is the central participant, sport is a symptom of other kinds of cultural barbarism, the barbarisms observed and analysed by John Dunmore Lang, the Vagabond, John Francis Hogan, and subsequent commentators.

For Hogan, it will be recalled, the sound mind was not a consequence of the sound body. The two were in competition, comprising a dichotomy against which the intellectual Miss Russell in *A Salute to the Great McCarthy* protests: "The life without thought. The sporting life."[68] The dichotomy emerges again in David Malouf's "At a School Athletics Day" in his image of

a boy as thick as two short planks, who never
will learn to distinguish
between perfect past and past conditional

It emerges also in Patrick White's *Riders in the Chariot,* in the contrast between the visionary Ruth Godbold and her insensitive husband Tom, whose preoccupations in life are, in order, "beer, sex, and the trots". Or, to take two last examples: in Laurie Clancy's "Forrester's First," Forrester is contrasted with Singleton, a "*revoltingly* [my emphasis] healthy young man, who played

football . . . with a top League team" and who organizes
Forrester's first — disastrous — sexual experience; in Alexander
Buzo's *The Roy Murphy Show,* the inarticulate ocker oaf Chicka
Armstrong is devastatingly portrayed.[69]

A point emphasized by Malouf, Clancy, and Buzo is the hero-
worship accorded these sportsmen: the crowd's breath is "caught on
the heels" of the javelin thrower, Singleton has cut a swathe through
the typists, Chicka is making a guest appearance on television for the
fans. Bruce Dawe changes the emphasis to focus less on the heroes
than on the worshippers. For Dawe, indeed, the synthesis of sport
and morality takes on a new meaning in at least one wintry
Australian state, where Australian rules forms the basis of the
"Life-Cycle".[70] As Dawe records it, the cycle begins with the
christening:

> When children are born in Victoria
> they are wrapped in the club-colours, laid in beribboned cots,
> having already begun a lifetime's barracking.
>
> Carn, they cry, Carn . . . feebly at first
> while parents playfully tussle with them
> for possession of a rusk: Ah, he's a little Tiger! (And they are . . .)

Next comes the initiation of the spectator and the confirmation of
the faith: "a voice"

> like the voice of God booms from the stands
> Oohh you bludger and the covenant is sealed.

Thereafter the spectators "behind their team going up the ladder
into Heaven", their lives dominated by the "home-team's
fortunes":

> — the reckless proposal after the one-point win,
> The wedding and honeymoon after the grand-final . . .
>
> They will not grow old as those from more northern States grow old,
> for them it will always be three-quarter time
> with the scores level and the wind advantage in the final term,

And finally, as passion is withered by age, the myths take over:

> and Chicken Smallhorn return like the maize-god
> in a thousand shapes, the dancers changing
>
> But the dance forever the same — the elderly still loyally crying
> Carn . . . Carn . . . (if feebly) unto the very end,

having seen in the six-foot recruit from Eaglehawk their hope of
salvation.

The rich store of biblical imagery here — the wrapping in the
swaddling clothes, the covenant, the promise of salvation, the
references to the "Demons" and the "Saints" — is reinforced by
the echoes of Laurence Binyon and *The Golden Bough.* Together,
the allusions establish the theme of football as ritual and religion, a
theme to which other creative writers have turned, among them
Barry Oakley, J. M. Couper, John Morrison, and George
Johnston.[71] In "Life-Cycle" the satire is gentle; Dawe is enjoying[72]
the human comedy, as also are Couper in "Sydney Cricket Ground
on Judgment Day, a public holiday" and Morrison in "Black Night
in Collingwood", in which the gloom that descends on a Melbourne
suburban household becomes part of the ritual. (The victim, the
housewife who stays at home, is an archetypal sporting wife.)[73] The
human comedy is also enjoyed in relation to sports other than
football. A light satirical tone characterizes several of Paterson's
racing yarns (particularly "A Disqualified Jockey's Story" and
"Father Riley's Horse"); Lower's "Bradman and the Burglar" (in
which the burglar, the policeman, and the family all finish up
engrossed in the radio descriptions of the tests in England);
Lawson's "The Grog-an'-Grumble Steeplechase", Forrest's "That
Barambah Mob" and Stivens's "The Man Who Bowled Victor
Trumper", which laugh at as well as become tall stories; and finally
Peter Porter's "Phar Lap in the Melbourne Museum",[74] in which
Porter, like A. D. Hope, invokes Swift to describe —

the democratic hero full of guile,
Noble, handsome, gentle Houyhnhnm.

But whereas Hope savagely depicts an Australia where the "Yahoos
live in slavery to the horse",[75] Porter concludes:

It is Australian innocence to love
The naturally excessive and be proud
Of a thoroughbred bay gelding who ran fast.

Yet other writers have sounded more sinister resonances — in
pointing, for example, to the stifling and falsifying consequences of
sport. Buzo's Chicka Armstrong and Clancy's Singleton have little
capacity, it seems clear, to develop any kind of whole life; Kevin
Collopy's swimmers in "At the Pool" are denied even the
opportunity:

> Up and down the clockwork swimmers go,
> Heads dipped, feet threshing in a six-beat kick,
> Covered with barnacles from head to toe,
> Young marvels with a skill that makes me sick.[76]

Similarly, the young schoolteacher in E. O. Schlunke's "The Village Hampden"[77] arrives in a small country town in south-western New South Wales (where the Maher Cup dominated life between the wars no less emphatically than Australian Rules still does in Melbourne) and is ostracized when he refuses to play for the local football club in its cup competition. Although the tone of the story is lightened by its development into farce, the club's domination of the town is emphasized by its demands for the total allegiance of Bellugrians, its treatment of the players as a master race, and its pursuit of the schoolteacher when he attempts simply to relax and enjoy himself.

The schoolteacher takes the club on at its own game and wins; he survives the group pressures. The half-caste boxer in Xavier Herbert's "Come on, Murri!",[78] however, is destroyed by them. Matched with his white friend for the district championship, Murri lacks the killer instinct to finish off the opponent over whom he has, through his skill, established authority, and is knocked out himself. In losing the fight he loses face not only in the eyes of his own half-caste society (who have looked to him as a champion of their hopes) but also in the eyes of the whites in the country town. His friendliness has lost him his friends; perplexed by his isolation, he looks to boxing to reassert his place in society. He challenges the champion to a rematch in the billiards saloon where the celebrations are taking place; this is the cause of his death.

The violence of boxing is important in the resolution of Murri's predicament. Similarly, the link between violence and football, against which The Vagabond protested, is confirmed in the work of writers as diverse as W. T. Goodge, Alan Hopgood, and Alexander Buzo. Goodge asks:

> What barks your shins and "busts" your tile
> And rips your pants in festive style.
> What makes the surgeon softly smile?
> Why football![79]

Playful, perhaps; but in *And the Big Men Fly* there are obvious echoes of the "Heil Hitler" salute in the way in which the football officials of East Melbourne salute each other on meeting with a cry of "C'arn the Crows".[80] (Hopgood's stage directions for martial music to accompany the salute reinforces — or at least enforces — the point.) So, too, with Buzo, this time in *Norm and Ahmed*. The violence that eventually erupts in Norm is clearly signposted in his recollections of his sporting past. Ahmed has just said that he has had no time to play sport:

NO TIME FOR SPORT? Jees, that's a sad state of affairs. I always used to find time to play sport when I was a young feller. I used to play football before the war. Rugby League. I played lock. That was my position, lock. Talk about cover defence! I used to hit 'em hard and low, round the knees, down they went. They can't run without legs, can they? That was my philosophy. But I was always a clean player. Ahmed, I never put the boot in. Always played hard and clean, I was a good sportsman, too. Never sold the dump to a mate. I always played fair, but if they ever mucked me about, biff! Send for the cleaners. All over bar the shouting. Know what I mean? I remember one bloke. A real coot. Played prop for Balmain juniors. A long thin streak of pelican shit. He tried to hang one on me at Leichhardt Oval once, so I administered a knuckle sandwich to him. He woke up in Our Lady of Mercy Hospital. Should have known better; I always observed the true spirit of the game.[81]

For Norm, violence is part of "the true spirit of the game"; it is also part of his code of living, as is demonstrated when he bashes Ahmed at the end of the play. The action has perplexed audiences, but it is surely possible to see that Norm's prejudices are "mucked about" by Ahmed's polite friendliness, and so he responds in the same way as he did when "mucked about" at Leichhardt Oval. In *Norm and Ahmed*, then, sport does not offer a harmless and socially acceptable way of releasing aggression. It confirms the validity of that aggression.[82]

As a final example, sinister resonances of all kinds reverberate throughout the best Australian sporting novel, Barry Oakley's *A Salute to the Great McCarthy*,[83] which records the rise and fall of Jack McCarthy, a recruit from the country who comes down to Melbourne to play Australian rules with Kingswood. McCarthy's rapid rise to stardom (he is voted best new player in the League at the end of his first season) is followed by an equally rapid decline. He falls victim to what he comes to call the "Piranha fish" (p. 189), most notably (among those outside the world of football) the PR man Tranter, who gets McCarthy a broken leg and the sack from his job by involving him in a mad advertising stunt; the rich bitch Andrea Miller, who marries him to pass the time; and her father, who when the marriage breaks up has McCarthy's name smeared in the scandal sheets, causing Kingswood to dispense with his services.

After barely two seasons he is back in his home town with only his memories to sustain him, "tipping the scales at 200 pounds, the hair starting to creep back over the scalp, the family redness taking hold" (p. 2). Left with time to kill, he shares the predicament of the ageing champion in Evan Jones's "Boxing On".[84]

Even this brief summary should make it clear that *A Salute to the Great McCarthy* is not just about football. As Oakley himself has stated, it "was meant to have a wider reference than that — it says something about the city and the country, about innocence and experience, loneliness and popularity. . . . McCarthy . . . [is] . . . torn apart by the callousness and the narrowness of the society around him."[85] In chronicling McCarthy's picaresque journey through a moral underworld, Oakley does not confine his satirical attack to the image-makers, the beautiful people, and the wealthy. His iconoclastic net gathers in the intellectuals (Miss Russell), the businessmen (Fortune and Ogg), the wowsers (McCarthy's aunt), even the old and the feeble (her boarders, "Father Dunphy mumbling Latin ejaculations and breaking wind", O'Meara "talking of spelling errors he'd seen outside shops").[86]

But football remains the major target. In his penultimate match for Kingswood, McCarthy is "hit again. By a feeling. Mad! All this is mad! This arbitrary thing we call a game. Mayhem with groundrules to placate the god Mob" (p. 187). It is a succinct summary of the violence documented also by Buzo, the manipulations and pressures documented also by Herbert, the absurd rituals documented also by Dawe and Hope. It is these features which Oakley sees endemic to the game and is concerned to expose throughout his novel.

The theme of violence is announced in McCarthy's first experience of football in high school: "I'm up there in front, high as all hell, when the side of a building collapses on me, and over I roll in the dust" (p. 3). The comic bravura of the language is repeated in the narration of McCarthy's encounters with a succession of fullbacks — including McKeever, "Mac the Knife, a karate chopper who'd caught me in the neck so often I felt like Charles the First" (p. 45), Galvin, "the Miller from the Canterbury Tales" (p. 78), and Rubbo, the labourer from the nearby docks, a "Mr Oddjob without top hat" (p. 117). But the throwaway lines do not deflect our attention from the insistence that these are primitive men — Uhe is "the cromagnon man from the Ruhr, neckless and with the German madness" (p. 180), Whelan the Wrecker has "legs and arms thick with Neanderthal hair" (p. 195). The extensive use of animal imagery underscores the point: Big Norman has a "rhino gallop" (p. 11), Baldy Adams a "hippo wallow" (p. 38), Tucker is a

"Moose" (p. 89), an all-in country brawl means that "the circus animals have gone mad, and in jumps the little tamer, the whip-cracker and whistleblower in white, threatening penalties, cooling the tempers, pushing the big cats apart" (p. 45). Later, in the dressing room before the first VFL match, the Bears, McCarthy's team, make "wild animal noises, snort and paw the ground", and after McCarthy has been felled, Tucker ("one of the greatest animals ever to put on a boot") exchanges "dinosaur blows" with Fred Yates in front of photographers "hopping round like sparrows on the side of the field, cameras going peck-peck" (pp. 88-90).

If these are the players, the spectators are characteristically presented as the Mob, which packs the arena "howling for blood" (p. 86) as if at some gladiatorial contest or primitive rite. At one metropolitan ground the mounted policemen ride around the boundary "to overawe these primitive North Melbourne Aztecs" (p. 118); after the game, McCarthy sees, from the safety of Fred Yates's car, "their wild Heathcliffe faces, foaming with hate" (pp. 119-20). And the sickness infects the whole city: football is a "medieval plague, a hysteria that holds its fever down till the crowds get to the arenas" (p. 87). In contrast, the crowd in Bernard Malamud's baseball novel *The Natural* comprise largely the fringe of society, the "oddballs"[87] — and even then their violence and fickle-ness is tempered by wit and warmth. Baseball at the Knights stadium is less a violent gladiatorial contest than a madcap melodramatic en-tertainment in which players, officials and spectators all play their roles.

Oakley's attack, then, is much more savage than Bruce Dawe's, and he is at his most vehement in his portrait of the manipulators, the officials and coaches who are the high priests of the rites. Most of all, perhaps, the attack is centred on two of McCarthy's coaches, MacGuinness and Twentyman, each of whom is a "mad Moses" (pp. 9, 102) with fascist leanings: MacGuinness pushes back "a dark Hitler forelock with the left hand" (p. 6), Twentyman is turned into "a Himmler" on Saturdays (p. 96) and chants "Horst Wessel songs of victory" (p. 119) after the North Melbourne match. They are also imaged as potters, manipulating players, shaping the mould as a team. But MacGuinness and Twentyman are both failures, seeking compensation through power; and the point is nowhere better made than in the contrast Oakley draws between the moral prescriptions they dispense to their teams and the sickness of their own likes. Twentyman claims to be "trying to do something with you fellows! Make you into MEN!" (p. 103, Oakley's emphasis), yet he abhors the sexual games of the players at the barbecue, and the children

playing football near the Shrine of Remembrance flee in fear from
his madness.

It is against this madness, together with the other evils that
express themselves in football, that McCarthy finally revolts, his
only triumph his escape from the arena at the end of the novel,
"bearing like a severed head the game's central token, the
football".[88] It is a game that is a "performing art" (p. 8), it has a
"ballet quality" (p. 118), it provides McCarthy with a means of self-
expression, a sense of power as he glories in the high mark, reaching
for the stars. But McCarthy is "Orville Wright McCarthy" (p. 91),
an unsteady flyer who recognizes his fragility when looking at
Hargrave's flying machine in the museum. Like his friend
Ackermann, the earth always awaits.

That McCarthy is back in Warwick with both feet on the ground
when he begins his narrative is a measure of his survival; but at what
cost? He's been torn apart in the city, his home town holds few
prospects; the tone of a *A Salute to the Great McCarthy* is at best
sardonic. The question of Oakley's pessimism apart, the use of the
Orville Wright image in relation of football might serve to reinforce
one final point: in that *A Salute to the Great McCarthy* is about
Australian sport, it is also about Australian society. So, too, is David
Williamson's *The Club,* a play about sports politics which began its
run in Melbourne while this chapter was being written. During the
same period, teams representing Sport and Culture took the field in
television's *The Of Show,* and conflict erupted between participants
at an academic conference on sport in Susan Lever's story "A
Sensible Arrangement".[89] It seems likely, then, that Australian
writers, whatever their attitudes, will continue to document the
connection between Australian sport and literature as they explore
the connection between Australian sport and society.

NOTES

1. "Trumper", by Creve Roe (Victor Daley). The poem probably dates from
    *c.*1902, but is not published in any Daley volume; it is quoted in *Six and Out:
    The Legend of Australian and New Zealand Cricket,* ed. Jack Pollard, 4th ed.
    (Sydney: Pollard, 1973), p.121. *Six and Out* is one of several compilations in
    which many of the poems, essays and short stories discussed in this paper are
    accessible; others include Pollard's *Horses and Horsemen* (Sydney: Pollard,
    1974); W. Fearn-Wannan, comp., *Australian Folklore: A Dictionary of Lore,
    Legends and Popular Allusions* (Melbourne: Lansdowne, 1970); H. P. Heseltine,
    ed., *The Penguin Book of Australian Verse* (Harmondsworth, Mddx.: Penguin,
    1972); Douglas Stewart and Nancy Keesing, eds., *Australian Bush Ballads*

(Sydney: Angus and Robertson, 1955); and Ian Turner, comp., *The Australian Dream; a Collection of Anticipations about Australia from Captain Cook to the Present Day* (Melbourne: Sun Books, 1968). Hereafter these compilations are cited only when earlier sources are inaccessible; similarly, recent reprints of the novels discussed are cited only when I have been unable to see the original.

2. Social commentators — and social historians — have tended to beg the question of what constitutes "Australian sport", usually by employing such catch-alls as "sports and pastimes". I have left it to future sociologists rigidly to define Australian sport, but in order to confine the literature under survey within reasonable boundaries, I have accepted as "sports" those activities of which physical exertion, competition between participants, a code of rules, and a recognized tradition are necessary (and important) components. Thus the racing and polo poems of the bush balladists have been considered, but not those dealing with "riding" and "droving"; to take specific examples, Paterson's racing poems have been considered but little of *The Collected Sporting Verse of Will H. Ogilvie* (London: Constable, 1932). For an example of the way sociologists are beginning to separate "sport" from other "activities" (e.g., "play", "leisure", "recreation", "game"), see Harry Edwards, *Sociology of Sport* (Homewood, Ill.: Dorsey Press, 1973), particularly pp.43-61. On this question the comments of Darrel Chapman and Bruce Milligan have been useful; for their suggestions on other aspects of this chapter and its subject I am grateful to Ann Curthoys, John D'Arcy, John Docker, Kevin Fewster, Ken Inglis, Susan McKernan, Michael McKernan, Bill Mandle, Michael Pearson, John Ritchie, John Robertson, Jill Roe, Ken Stewart, Ian Tyrrell, Wray Vamplew, and Bill Wilde.

3. Quoted in Turner, *The Australian Dream*, p.109.

4. Anthony Trollope, *Australia and New Zealand*, 2 vols. (London, 1873); R. E. N. Twopeny, *Town Life in Australia* (London: Elliot Stock, 1883); Mark Twain, *Following the Equator* (Hartford: The American Publishing Company, 1897; Thomas Wood, *Cobbers* (London: Oxford, 1934).

5. Donald Horne, *The Lucky Country*, rev. ed. (Sydney: Angus and Robertson, 1966), p.23; Craig McGregor, *Profile of Australia* (London: Hodder and Stoughton, 1966), p.134; Keith Dunstan, *Sports* (Melbourne: Cassell, 1973), p.xiii.

6. Unless otherwise indicated, the examples in this paragraph are taken from Dunstan, *Sports*, chaps.1-4, 9.

7. See Scott Bennett, *The Clarence Comet: The Career of Henry Searle 1866-89* (Sydney: Sydney University Press, 1973); Raymond Swanwick, *Les Darcy: Australia's Golden Boy of Boxing* (Sydney: Ure Smith, 1965); David Frith, *The Archie Jackson Story* (Beech Hanger, Kent: The *Cricketer*, 1974); Isobel Carter, *Phar Lap: The Story of the Big Horse*, rev. ed. (Melbourne: Lansdowne, 1971).

8. See Clement Semmler, "The Race Callers", *Quadrant* 21 (May 1977): 26-28.

9. Twain, *Following the Equator*, p.161; on the importance of the Melbourne Cup assignment for journalists, see Lorna Ollif, *Andrew Paterson* (New York: Twayne, 1971). p.87.

10. E.g;, see Horne, *The Lucky Country*, p.157; Ronald Conway, *The Great Australian Stupor* (Melbourne: Sun Books, 1971), p.52; W. F. Mangle, "Cricket and Australian Nationalism in the Nineteenth Century", *Journal of the Royal Australian Historical Society* 59, pt.4 (1973): 225-46; the same author's *Winners Can Laugh: Sport and Society* (Ringwood, Vic.: Penguin, 1974), pp.50-51; and "Sport: A Reference Paper;; and H. Gordon, "The Reasons Why", both in *Sport in Australia: Selected Readings in Physical Activity*, ed. T. D. Jaques and G. R. Pavia (Sydney: McGraw-Hill, 1976), pp.73-103.

11. The Manchester equivalent has the United soccer player Dennis Law move to the wing when God comes to Manchester, while in Liverpool (where the joke probably originated) Ian St. John moves to inside-left. On further parallels between the passion in England and Australia, cf. Fearn-Wannan, *Australian Folklore*, p.21, and Michael Parkinson, *Sporting Fever* (London: Stanley Paul, 1974), pp.151-52. On indicators of the American passion see Edwards, *Sociology of Sport*, pp.3-4.

12. Quoted in K. S. Inglis, *The Australian Colonists: An Exploration of Social History 1788-1870* (Carlton: Melbourne University Press, 1974), pp.130-31.

13. John Stanley James, "Manly Sports", *The Vagabond Papers*, 3rd series (Melbourne: George Robertson, 1877), pp.9-22.

14. Quoted in Turner, *The Australian Dream*, pp.134, 136-37.

15. Joseph Furphy, *Such Is Life* (Sydney: Angus and Robertson, 1944 [first published 1903]), p.132; A. D. Hope, *Dunciad Minor: An heroick poem* (Carlton: Melbourne University Press, 1970), p.14. Furphy completed the draft of *Such Is Life* by 1897, so his comment probably preceded Daley's; another famous egalitarian, Lawson, also seems to have disapproved of sport, to judge from the stanza quoted by Dunstan in *Sports*, p.2:

    > In a Land where sport is sacred,
    > Where the Laborer is God,
    > You must pander to the people
    > Make a hero of a clod.

16. Eric Drayton Davis, *The Life and Times of Steele Rudd* (Melbourne: Lansdowne, 1976), pp.55-56.

17. Clement Semmler, *The Banjo of the Bush: The Work, Life and Times of A. B. Paterson* (Melbourne: Lansdowne, 1966), p.200.

18. E. g., George Selth Coppin and Hugh D. McIntosh were both theatrical and sporting entrepreneurs, John L. Sullivan appeared on stage in Sydney in 1891 while still heavyweight champion of the world, and sporting journals such as the *Referee* regularly ran extensive theatre columns.

19. I have been guided on this point by René Wellek and Austin Warren, *Theory of Literature* (London: Jonathan Cape, 1949), chap.9.

20. Coral Lansbury, "A Straight Bat and a Modest Mind", *Victorian Newsletter*, no.49 (1976), pp.9-18; see also the same author's "Sporting Humor in Victorian Literature", *Mosaic* 9, no.4 (1976): 66-75.

21. Henry Kingsley, *The Recollections of Geoffry Hamlyn*, 3 vols. (Cambridge: MacMillan, 1859, 1: 170-74. I am grateful to Susan McKernan for drawing attention to the point that Kingsley may be satirizing Maberly's ethics.

22. Included in *Four Australian Plays* (Harmondsworth, Mddx.: Penguin, 1970).

23. Angelo Loukakis, "The Boxer and the Grocer", *Meanjin Quarterly* 35 (1976): 246-52.

24. Robert Colvin, "All Pipes and Pharkas", *Southerly* 36 (1976): 89-95.

25. Finola Moorhead, "Squash", *Meanjin Quarterly* 33 (1974): 371-75.

26. In *Collected Poems 1930-1970* (Sydney: Angus and Robertson, 1972). Hope's contemporary, Judith Wright, also has written an "allegorical" poem entitled "Sports Field"; see her *Collected Poems 1942-1970* (Sydney; Angus and Robertson, 1971).

27. In *The Coming of Stork-Jugglers Three — What If You Died Tomorrow: Three Plays*, by David Williamson (Sydney: Currency Press, 1974); Kiernan's comment appears in his "The Games People Play: The Development of David Williamson", *Southerly* 35 (1975): 315-29. As is clear from Kiernan's title, the motif of the game is a prominent one in contemporary Australian drama.

28. Norman Lindsay, *The Cousin from Fiji* (Sydney: Angus and Robertson, 1945), p.235.

29. On the literary techniques of the sporting writers of one genetal newspaper, see George Blaikie, *Remember Smith's Weekly?* (Adelaide: Rigby, 1966), chap.9.

30. Sporting literature does not suddenly begin with Gould, but my sample of the early sporting newspapers has yielded little local creative writing: characteristically, an occasional poem such as "The Pigeon Shooters' Glee", *Bell's Life in Sydney*, 5 December 1846, an occasional story such as "How Tom Dunnage Made a Book", *Bell's Life in Victoria* 23, 30 May 1857, and serials reprinted from English journals, such as John Mills's "The Flyers of the Hunt", *Bell's Life in Victoria*, intermittently 1858-59. With the exception of the racing forecasts discussed later in the chapter, it was not until Gould was serialized in the *Referee* in the 1890s that sport became important in the literary columns of the sporting journals; before then, political satire, mystery stories, moral tales, and (cf. n.18) theatrical notices were preferred.

31. On Gould, see particularly the entry in E. Morris Miller, *Australian Literature from Its Beginnings to 1935 . . . Extended to 1938*, 2 vols. (Melbourne: Melbourne University Press, 1940) 1: 444-46; John Welcome, "Nat Gould Novelist of the Turf", *London Magazine*, n.s. 7 (August 1967): 54-59; and W. Farmer Whyte, "Nat Gould's Life Story", *Sporting Globe*, 28 October 1950-17 February 1951. On the question of Gould's "Australianness", so many authors, particularly before 1900, were born outside Australia that any criterion based on birth is clearly inappropriate; my rule of thumb has been to include as "Australian" those authors (e.g. Kingesly and Gould) who spent at least some time as residents of Australia but not those who merely visited the colonies (e.g. Trollope).

32. Nat Gould, *The Magic of Sport: Mainly Autogiographical* (London: John Long, 1909), pp.169-70.

33. The plots of many of Gould's novels are summarized in Miller, *Australian Literature 2*: 649-50.

34. On this point see particularly Welcome, "Nat Gould Novelist of the Turf", pp.58-59.

35. Gould, *The Magic of Sport*, p.201.

36. The reference to Wright as the "Australian Nat Gould" comes from an advertisement in the *Bookfellow*, no.6 (15 September 1921), p.45; his works are listed in Miller, *Australian Literature 2*: 703-4.

37. Robert Bennett, *The Big Ruck* (London: Angus and Robertson, 1975); Hugh Atkinson, *The Games* (London: Cassell, 1967); Alan O'Toole, *The Coach from the City* (Adelaide: Rigby, 1967); and Christopher Nixon, *The Tour* (Sydney: A. H. & A. W. Reed, 1973). *The Big Ruck* was first published and *The Games* (1968) and *The Coach from the City* (1977) republished as popular paperbacks; *The Games* has also been filmed.

38. See Cecil Hadgraft, "It's Not on the Tip of My Tongue", *Southerly* 30 (1970): 65-68.

39. See *The Collected Verse of A. B. Paterson* (Sydney: Angus and Robertson, 1921); *Three Elephant Power and Other Stories* (Sydney: Angus and Robertson, 1921); and *The Shearer's Colt* (Sydney: Angus and Robertson, 1936). *Three Elephant Power and Other Stories* includes "Done for the Double" by "Knott Gold", a satire on Gould, although *The Shearer's Colt* is little different from and no better than many of Gould's novels. Paterson also wrote the unpublished "Racehorses and Racing in Australia", which is decribed in Semmler, *The Banjo of the Bush*, pp.206-15.

40. *The Collected Verse of A. B. Paterson*, pp.85-86.

41. See Colin Roderick, ed., *Henry Lawson: Collected Verse Vol. 1 1885-1900* (Sydney: Angus and Robertson, 1967); Arthur Ferres (J. W. Kevin), *The Free Selector and Other Verses* (Sydney: Websdale, Shoosmith, 1901); Thomas Spencer, *How Mc Dougall Topped the Score and Other Verses* (Sydney: N. S. W. Bookstall Co., 1908).

42. See Pollard, *Six and Out*, pp.191-99, 248; Xavier Herbert, *Larger than Life: Twenty Short Stories* (Sydney: Angus and Robertson, 1963); Frank Hardy, *The Yarns of Billy Borker* (Sydney: A. H. & A. W. Reed, 1965); and Athol Mulley and Frank Hardy, *The Needy and the Greedy* (Canberra: Libra Books, 1973).

43. Pollard's "The Linguist" and "The Lovesick Racehorse" are accessible in Pollard's *Horses and Horsemen*, the other four stories in Stiven's *Selected Stories 1936-1968* (Sydney: Angus and Robertson, 1969).

44. Alan Hopgood, *And the Big Men Fly* (Melbourne: Heinemann Educational Australia, 1969), preface.

45. "Turf Notes" [program notes] for 1977 season, p.4.

46. Jack Hibberd, *Three Popular Plays* (Collingwood: Outback Press, 1976), p.8; my emphasis.

47. Miller, *Australian Literature* 1: 445.

48. Hibberd, *Three Popular Plays*, pp.130-31.

49. *Bell's Life in Victoria*, 21 March 1857.

50. Part of a sequence "Hippodrama; or, Whiffs from the Pipe", published in *Sea Spray and Smoke Drift* (Melbourne: George Robertson, 1867), and again in *Poems of Adam Lindsay Gordon*, ed. Frank Maldon Robb (London: Oxford University Press, 1912); see particularly pp.85-87, 99-101, 376-77.

51. On the making of the song, see Dennis Lillee [and Ian Brayshaw], *Back to the Mark* (Melbourne: Hutchinson, 1974), pp.82-83.

52. *Big League*, 17-23 September 1977, p.24. VFL and English soccer fans have traditionally been the most enthusiastic musical supporters of their teams, although "rugby" songs, which concentrate more on obscenity than on the virtues of particular teams, are an integral part of the sociology of rugby union, and club songs are a recent innovation in the promotion of rugby league.

53. Quoted in Fearn-Wannan, *Australian Folklore*, p.178.

54. *The Collected Verse of A. B. Paterson*, p.265. For other samples see Dunstan, *Sports*, particularly pp.64-66, 71-72, 75, 111-12, 196, 207-8, 264, 295-96; Fearn-Wannan, *Australian Folklore*, pp.170-1, 178, 442-44; Pollard, *Six and Out*, p.93; Ray Robinson, *On Top Down Under: Australia's Cricket Captains* (Sydney: Cassell, 1975), p.92; and the specialist studies listed in 7, above.

55. Quoted in Fearn-Wannan, *Australian Folklore*, p.178.

56. Ibid., p.442.

57. Quoted in [H. Healy, comp.] *Cecil Healy: A Memoir* (Sydney, n.p. 1918), preface.

58. Arthur Wright, *Rung In* (Sydney: N. S. W. Bookstall Co., 1912), p.28.

59. Alan Rolt in *Bred in the Bush* for example, is a typical Gould hero; and even when Gould's protagonists don't measure up to his standard, the standard itself is always explicit. For example, in Gould's *Thrown Away, or Basil Ray's Mistake* (London: Routledge, [1894]), the virtues of the protagonist Ray are clearly shown to be "thrown away" by his weakness.

60. Wright, *Rung In*, pp.21, 28.

61. Gould, *The Magic of Sport*, p.170; Marcus Clarke, *Long Odds* (Melbourne: Classon, Massina, 1869); Cecil Mann, *The River and Other Stories* (Sydney: Dymock's, 1945).

62. Gould, *Thrown Away*, p.207.

63. Rolf Boldrewood, *Robbery Under Arms* (London: Oxford University Press, 1949 [first published 1888]), p.226.

64. Even to the behaviour of the spectators: for Gould, "You cannot beat an Australian crowd at a great cricket match for enthusiasm and good behaviour. They appreciate every point of the game, and acknowledge every bit of good play, no matter which side makes it" (*Thrown Away*, pp.8-9).
65. Frank Hardy, *The Four-Legged Lottery* (London: Laurie, 1958, epigraph.
66. Ibid., p.77.
67. Ibid.
68. Barry Oakley, *A Salute to the Great McCarthy* (Ringwood, Vic.: Penguin, 1970), p.121.
69. David Malouf, *Bicycle and Other Poems* (St. Lucia: University of Queensland Press, 1970), pp.45-46; Patrick White, *Riders in the Chariot* (London: Eyre and Spottiswoode, 1961), p.258; Laurie Clancy, "Forrester's First", *Southerly* 34 (1974): 269-76; Alexander Buzo, *Norm and Ahmed — Rooted — The Roy Murphy Show: Three Plays* (Sydney: Currency, 1973).
70. Bruce Dawe, *An Eye for a Tooth* (Melbourne: Cheshire, 1968), pp.42-43.
71. Hal Colebatch, "Lines written upon hearing that a man had had his ashes buried between the goal-posts of a football ground", *Southerly* 33 (1973): 275. Couper's poem appeared in *Southerly* 35 (1975): 156, and Morrison's story in his *Twenty-Three Stories* (Sydney: Australasian Book Society, 1962); Johnston's comment is quoted in Dunstan, *Sports*, p.237.
72. On this point see John Hainsworth, "Paradoxes in Bruce Dawe's Poetry', *Southerly* 36 (1976): 186-93.
73. See the chapter "The Sporting Wife" in Anne Summers, *Damned Whores and God's Police: The Colonization of Women in Australia* (Ringwood, Vic.: Penguin, 1975).
74. In *Twelve Poets* 1950-1970, ed. Alexander Craig (Brisbane: Jacaranda, 1971), pp.141-42.
75. Hope, *Dunciad Minor*, p.11.
76. Kevin Collopy, "At the Pool", *Southerly* 24 (1964): 205.
77. In *The Village Hampden*, by E. O. Schlunke (Sydney: Angus and Robertson, 1958). On the Maher Cup, see M. V. Shechan, *The Maher Cup Story* (Temora: J. G. Bradley [c.1963]).
78. Herbert, *Larger than Life*, pp.81-91.
79. W. T. Goodge, *Hits! Skits! and Jingles!* (Sydney: Bulletin, 1899), p.175.
80. Hopgood, *And the Big Men Fly*, p.6.
81. Buzo, *Norm and Ahmed*, p.12.
82. Cf. Dunstan, *Sports*, p.32; Mandle, *Winners Can Laugh*, pp.50-51.
83. References to subsequent quotations from the novel are incorporated within the text.
84. In *Understandings: Poems*, by Evan Jones (Carlton: Melbourne University Press, 1967).
85. Barry Oakley, "The Writer in Australia", *Westerly*, no.3 (1975), pp.65-70.
86. On Oakley as a satirist, see Betty L. Watson, "Barry Oakley and the Satiric Mode", *Australian Literary Studies* 7 (1975): 50-63. Oakley's cynicism, and its effects on the "realism" of *A Salute to the Great McCarthy*, are discussed in Robert Burns's review of the novel, *Nation*, 25 July 1970; see also Oakley's reply, *Nation*, 8 August 1970, and Ian Turner's review of the novel, *Overland*, no. 45 (1970), pp.44-45.
87. Bernard Malamud, *The Natural* (Harmondsworth, Mddx.: Penguin, 1967 [first published 1952]); see particularly p.72-73.
88. Oakley, "The Writer in Australia", p.69.
89. Susan Lever, "A Sensible Arrangement", *Canberra Times*, 21 May 1977.

HELEN KING

The Sexual Politics of Sport: an Australian Perspective

A social historian argues that if we are to "form a just estimation of the character of any particular people, it is absolutely necessary to investigate the Sports and Pastimes most generally prevalent among them".[1] The success of Australian women in the sporting arena, especially from the late 1940s to the present day, and the acclaim they have been given show that there has been a strong sporting tradition among women. This tradition, however, has largely gone unnoticed, and their success and the high standards achieved have not been recognized. Anomalies have emerged. Team sportswomen, for example, have been successful as individuals in capturing public attention and yet team sports are relatively ignored. Why do people go to watch a Wimbledon final in such large numbers and yet very few attend a hockey final? Why is it, too, that women have not become involved in the great national pastimes of football, both rugby and Australian rules? An examination of questions such as these will not only develop our knowledge of women and sport but also add to the growing understanding of the place of women in Australian society.

Women's activities in general have been relegated to the far corners of our national consciousness, to be catered for by special magazines and ladies' pages in newspapers; women's activities in sport are no exception. The recent inclusion of Women and Sport articles in the *Age* received this fate; radio and television coverage is not much better. Even the Australian Broadcasting Commission, which aims to provide a comprehensive coverage of sport at all levels (broadcasting rights and finance permitting) has a separate sports programme for women, "Calling all Sportswomen", compered and organized for radio by June Ferguson. It is true that the ABC covers such events as Olympic finals and the like, but these are world events which occur infrequently. If the media (radio, television, magazines, and newspapers) are one of the most powerful influences "dictating" to women how they should use their work and leisure, it is surprising that Australia has produced any sportswomen at all.[2]

This situation is reinforced in the growing field of sports histories. The historical accounts of Australian sport are exclusively male, and women and sport have either been ignored or there is a tendency to equate Australians and sport with Australian men. While historians such as W. F. Mandle have done much to prove the "history of a society's sport can illuminate the history of the whole society", his findings are based on male-dominated sports. For example, his pioneering article on Australian cricket shows the importance of Australian successes against England in overcoming colonial fears of inferiority and degeneracy, which contributed to the development of a sense of nationalism.[3] How can such judgements about nationalism be made if women's contributions are not sought? Such studies will be incomplete until sports histories include reference to women, not only in separate chapters but as an integral part of whatever subject is being examined.

The cultural image of women in Australia and the western world in general has been one of dependence and passivity, with emphasis on their supportive functions. As a result, certain sports have been socially acceptable for women, usually activities emphasizing flexibility and coordination and having aesthetic appeal and which do not require much strength, endurance, and bodily contact. Diving, figure skating, tennis, gymnastics, and equestrian events fit this pattern. When strength has been necessary, as in the last two, it has been compensated by extreme grace, rhythm, and balance. A. J. Coles argues that it is only recently that "physiological fallacies" have been overcome so that women have been allowed to "sweat in endeavouring to improve their skill or fitness".[4] Herein lies the crux of the problem: the sexual politics of sport are defined in Australia by the accepted role of women in society, which is based on a masculine prejudice concerning the "feminine nature" of women, which is to produce and rear children. Women who defy this, who go beyond the boundaries and compete hard in their chosen sport, are punished by being considered oddities, usually seen as courtesy males rather than as women.

Consequently, sportswomen and their commentators dwell on femininity rather than ability. Anne Summers has argued that this stereotype of the feminine nature has meant that women have been excluded at every level and in every recreational activity seen as important in Australian life, by rules, conventions, and attitudes which ensure that those activities remain the domain of men. Furthermore, women have been limited to a "permitted territory" in which to strive for "self realization" at "lower levels in shadowy areas of allowed art forms or in homes and gardens".[5] The implication is that women's activities in sports are inferior: indeed, for some women there is the belief that they do not have the right to pursue their interests.

It is not within the scope of this chapter to deal in detail with the discrimination facing women in sport; this has been examined by Anne Summers, who has also shown how women have been excluded from "men's sports" in participation, culture, and ritual.[6] However, no one has yet explained how this has occurred. The reasons for these views on women and sport lie, I suggest, in the early attitude that the only sports acceptable for women were those concerned with their health, hygiene, and reproductive functions; serious competition was to be avoided and girls were to be kept girls. Such attitudes evolved during the early nineteenth century as industrialization took hold and subtly altered the structure of society and associated attitudes to life.

The effects of the Industrial Revolution, especially on day-to-day life, led to a "sporting revolution" brought about by changing concepts of leisure time, which was reflected in the growth of mass spectator sports such as racing, football and cricket and which encouraged widespread participation in recreational activities. Sport, involving men only as a rule, was also professionally promoted during the nineteenth century and drew large crowds. By the 1850s, therefore, a great interest had evolved in outdoor athletic activities, including, in America, the development of Muscular Christianity movements, which were essentially masculine. Such movements saw physical prowess and sanctity as compatible because sports and physical activity were seen as building morality and good character. This was to have great influence in schools and colleges, where physical culture programmes and athletic competition became more respectable. They were seen as a useful aid in teaching such lessons as leadership, endurance, and playing the game.

Women, however, were not a part of this "sporting revolution". The lesson that sport taught women was how to be a woman. Sport for women was first introduced in schools in a somewhat paradoxical manner. It was feared that higher education for girls would destroy their femininity and reproductive functions; accordingly, during the nineteenth century, exercises were first introduced to cure distortions of the spine and other maladies thought to be the results of study, limited activities such as calisthenics or light gymnastics being taught in schools to rectify these problems. Sport was seen as a tool or mechanism for keeping girls female. Sport in this case had to be "for something" rather than to be enjoyed for its own sake.

By the 1880s ideas had changed somewhat; the belief that study need not cause ill-health was generally accepted, and physical education was seen as a preventive rather than as a curative measure, with the emphasis on the general well-being of the body. Character training came to be considered as one of the aims of physical education, and it was thought that the discipline of formal gymnastics carried into everyday living would give self-control and poise. This was well illustrated in the handbooks of Australian girls' schools of the period. The Methodist Ladies College, Hawthorn, in its prospectus for 1882–95, took great pains to note that the college was situated in Kew, a suburb declared by the registrar-general to be "the healthiest spot in Australia". The school possessed an "excellent gymnasium", and a "perfect system of drill and physical culture" was taught "under Mr Oscar David a scientific gymnastic instructor". Outdoor games "such as tennis and croquet" were "amply provided for". The MLC was "furnished and managed so as to wrap every girl within its walls in refining influences and to develop qualities of order and refinement and womanly grace".

Later, the number and variety of sports offered to pupils were increased owing to changes in the education system and, more importantly, changes in dress. Gym costumes cleared the floor by seven to eight inches in 1866 and were worn over flannel petticoats and "drawers". In the 1890s bloomers and leggings were adopted. Gradually, however, gaiters were discarded and the bloomer suit declined in favour until short trousers, lightweight cotton suits, and dancing costumes were introduced in the early years of the twentieth century, which allowed much greater freedom. Costume, then, mirrored radical changes over the years in the types of sports engaged in; between 1905 and 1910, for instance, basketball and hockey were introduced into girls' schools in New South Wales. By 1915 the newly established Presbyterian Ladies College at Pymble was advertising that a large area of land had been secured so that the fullest scope could be devoted to games and physical training. The aim of the college was to provide a training to enable their girls to take up their position in life "to receive and intelligently assimilate the deeper lessons which life brings *and adorned with the grace and manner which make the charm of refined womanhood*" (my emphasis).[8] The idea underlying this quotation was that to produce womanly grace and beauty, sport acted to prevent girls from suffering the ill effects of higher education and reinforced their femininity. Besides which, as girls were destined to be wives and mothers, sport played only a secondary role in their lives. The chief inspector of the Department of Public Instruction noted that swimming clubs, cricket clubs, and football clubs in schools gave an opportunity for the less intellectual boy in school "to show his prowess on the green sward". Thus "the future defender of his native land is enrolled in the cadet corps, enjoys the physical training derived from his first exercises in the art of war and learns the value of comradeship".[9] For girls, on the other hand, the home was seen to be the sphere of future usefulness: "The current tendency in education recognizes this fact and insists on the intelligent preparation of the girl pupil for home life."[10]

Such views slowed the participation of women in sport and laid the foundations for the sexual politics of sport. Sport for boys was to teach them team spirit, leadership, loyalty, and how to take the initiative in life. Since women were destined only for home life, sport for them could only be seen as of secondary importance, at most a means of keeping physically healthy with the right physiological proportions. As one ladies' page noted: "The modern beauty must be solid and nearly approach the proportions of the heroic age. The present age is an athletic one, and as long as the young women continue their healthy exercises — lawn-tennis, croquet, rowing, riding, vaulting, jumping and turning in the gymnasiums — bright eyes, good complexions and trim, well knit and muscular figures will be found."[11] This kind of attitude to sport for women explains the lack of serious competition in women's sports beyond the acceptable — tennis, riding, and golf — and also explains the absence of reference to women and sport in the popular press beyond fashion and the odd report when the amazing rather than the usual was commented upon.

The Public Schools Amateur Athletic Association organized swimming instructon and sports day for public schools, although the latter usually involved marching displays and exercises *en masse* rather than any serious athletic events. *The Town and Country Journal* reported such a meeting in September 1900, in which boys were offered running races, throwing at wicket competitions, bicycle races, hurdles, and running high jump. Girls were confined to plain and fancy skipping contests, maypole competitions, display dumb-bells, display wands, competitive dumb-bells and competitive maypole: events that avoided any hint of hectic activity and emphasized decorum and grace.[12] At private schools for girls, sports days or inter-school matches were the exception rather than the rule. The MLC Burwood, New South Wales, claimed to have pioneered athletics meetings for girls in 1906 when first attempts at a sports day were made. Although all high jumps and hurdles had to take place within the seclusion of the school, the event caused an interesting reaction: "At first other schools seemed to wonder if it was quite the correct thing to do, by next year some of them followed suit . . . and now [1936] the All-School Sports are a regular fixture."[13]

By 1936, MLC Burwood had full-time tennis coaches, a sports mistress, and regular competitions for all sports. It had taken twenty years for athletics, and nearly seventy years for regular competitions, to be introduced. But even then, contemporary thinkers of the 1930s were asserting that anatomical, physiological, and psychological differences between the sexes were such as to demand entirely different kinds of sports for women: "Competitive sports are alien to the characteristics as well as harmful in relation to the primary task of women's life, maternity."[14] Furthermore, to safeguard girls in athletics their competition had to be free of "emotionalism", free of "intense competition", free of "heart and pelvic strain", and free of "all attempts to imitate boys", according to Mabel Lee who propounded such ideas. Games should be played for the love of the sport and not just to win. Girls had to be treated as separate entities and not as slightly modified patterns of the "boy" type.[15] While games and sport were not withheld from women at this stage, competition was not encouraged. This was reserved for men; women had to maintain ladylike behaviour. While such ideas were on the decline during the 1930s, their currency hampered the development of competitive sports for a great number of women. This is seen in the limited number of athletic meetings organized for women. Internationally, women athletics did not begin until 1921, when the Federation Sportive Feminine International (FSFI) was formed in Paris. A request from this organization to admit women's athletics to the Olympic games was rejected, and the FSFI was forced to organize its own Women's Games until 1925, when the FSFI handed over international control of women's athletics to the Olympic body. Such discrimination tended to lower the incentive for Australian women to compete. Moreover, only three Australian women athletes had been sent to the Olympic Games by 1936, and athletic championships for women at the Australian national level did not begin until 1930, some thirty years after the first national titles for men.[16]

Women golfers, however, did not face such problems and took the lead. Their first national championship was held in Geelong, Victoria, in 1894, and it was so successful that an Australian amateur championship for gentlemen was held at Caulfield, Victoria in the following year. Tennis too, had an early beginning, the first competitions being recorded in Victoria in 1884 for women and 1880 for men. Golf and tennis were definitely "ladies' sports", since they fitted into the cultural image of women, and the competitions held for each of them was a "women's affair", posing no threat to male followers of golf and tennis. But even these more acceptable sports for women were given very little coverage in newspapers beyond the fashion pages; although occasionally articles of an instructive nature appeared on tennis, for the most part sporting events for women were treated as oddities or as objects of humour.[17] Fashion pages went to great lengths to emphasize the need to remain feminine in appearance while indulging in sports: "The close fitting coat and clearly defined waist are very novel and are, to me, far more workmanlike than the loose jackets which have been in vogue for so long. A nattly little waistcoat, plain linen collar and smart tie complete this neat equestrian costume."[18] The same article notes with relief that since the adoption of shorter skirts by women of fashion, the hockey or golf player no longer needed to feel "a species apart". Tailoring was such as to "render the get up of a sports' woman both workmanlike and picturesque".

There was a morbid fascination about reports on the unusual achievements of women in sport, with warnings that "honours are not always to be borne off by the sterner sex" or "it is only a question of time before men are overhauled in the race for premier place". For example, Mrs Elsie Wallanda remained submerged for 4 minutes 42.25 seconds in 1898, and this feat was greeted with the remark: "It seems obvious that womankind is pre-eminently better suited to swimming, for nature has endowed her with greater chest room." While at hockey: "It would required a very smart team of male hockey players to lower the colours of any international ladies hockey side. Men have no longer the desire to handicap themselves by playing with brooms instead of sticks and the like when they oppose a side of ladies."[19]

The only women's sport to receive any regular coverage was cycling, which became very fashionable during the 1890s. It became an acceptable pastime because it was popularized by the wealthy and "fashionable" and unlike horse-riding it was an inexpensive occupation, a pastime that could be followed by many. "Scorcher" of the *Town and Country Journal* reported: "It is wonderful to note how rapidly cycling is coming into favor with men and women all the world over. In France, particularly Paris, it is a perfect craze with the fashionable classes, in Italy everyone who is considered anybody rides (including the King and Queen) . . . and bicycling is at last becoming the fashion in London."[20]

Beverley Kingston suggests that the bicycle had a liberating influence in giving freedom and mobility in the form of exercise:

"the equivalent for the not so well off of the horse riding for wealthy women". Despite this, women were still restricted by fashion and its "hold over the appearance of ladylike behaviour".[21] This is particularly well illustrated by the inaugural journey of the Sydney Ladies Bicycle Club in 1895 which attracted a large crowd gathered in "morbid curiosity" to watch proceedings. According to "Scorcher", most of the gathering were under the impression that the wheelwomen would be attired in full bloomer costume. "They were, however, to be disappointed as the ladies appeared in ordinary female dress. 'The uniform' which was in two colours, blue and grey, gave the wearers a decidedly natty appearance."[22] All along the road the prospect of seeing a large number of ladies on bicycles excited "a deal of amazement and comment".[23]

In spite of the interest of women in this sport, there are no records of organized competitions and races except the picnic race variety. Indeed, two women, Barbara Whitener of Newcastle and Margaret Hill of Dulwich Hill, were banned from racing against male cyclists in their clubs after winning several events.[24] The lack of serious competition was probably due to the "fashionable" nature of the sport for women; bicycling was seen only as a means of exercise. The flippant manner in which women's sports were viewed is illustrated in the following verse from the *Town and Country Journal:*

The Latest Question
"Shall women ride the bicycle?" is the problem of the hour
For women must have problems — 'tis a part of women's dower
"Shall women smoke?" has gone quite out, "shall women vote?" also
But "shall she bike?" 's the point 'bout which just now she wants to
    know,

"She shall" 's the answer I would give; because I would not like
To see the woman I admire perched high upon a bike;
From what I know of woman's will, of what she does and don't,
I'm certain if man says she "shall" she'll tell him that she won't![25]

In the 1890s, therefore, women were circumscribed by costume and custom in their efforts to take up and pursue a desired sport. The popularity of cycling is important not only from the point of view of the development of the sport but also because of the effect it may have had in the changing role of women in society and their breaking into new sports formerly the preserve of men. If bicycling served as the "poor woman's" equivalent to horse-riding, were there sports followed by different classes of women, and were there class differences within individual sports?

The development of women's cricket is interesting on this account, as it helps to answer some the questions posed above. The first recorded women's cricket match took place in Britain in 1745; games in this period were held between women of the villages and attracted large crowds who gambled on the result. Teams were occasionally organized among ladies of fashion but were played in private. According to Netta Rheinberg, the nineteenth century saw a rise in the numbers of "ladies" as opposed to "women" interested in the game. This is associated with the general emancipation of women seen in their involvement with tennis and cycling. Cricket, like tennis, was introduced to girls' schools such as Roedean, Wycombe Abbey, and the Royal School, Bath, all private schools. With this development and activity came the foundation in 1887 of the first women's cricket club, White Heather, which was made up of women of independent means and largely of aristocratic birth. Women who played in the villages had fair knowledge of the game and must have played in teams of an *ad hoc* nature. It was not until the middle-class and aristocratic ladies adopted the sport in the mid nineteenth century that the game became organized. This perhaps explains its social acceptance in the 1890s, when women's cricket matches became less spectacles for amusement and were played with more decorum.[26]

The only professional players to be found were "The Original English Lady Cricketers; (OELC), inaugurated by the English Cricket and Athletic Association in 1890. The Association believed that the growing popularity of cricket played by women could well be turned to commercial profit. A prospectus was issued and published in the leading periodicals of the day: "With the object of providing the suitability of the National Game as a pastime for the fair sex in preference to Lawn Tennis and other less scientific games, the English Cricket and Athletic Association Ltd have organized two complete elevens of female players under the title of 'The Original English Lady Cricketers'." The public was assured that players would be "elegantly and appropriately attired", that every effort would be made to keep the organization "in all respects select and refined", that a matron would accompany each eleven to all engagements, and that members were not permitted to use their own names. The two elevens toured the country, often attracting crowds as large as fifteen thousand. Initially the OELC attracted derogatory remarks: "The public do not for a moment expect to see a ladies team contend on anything like equal terms with men," one newspaper report stated. Despite such views, the OELC did much to make cricket a more acceptable sport for women. "London will have the opportunity during the next few days of seeing how the much discussed professional lady cricketers play the game into which, up to the present year, the sex has only entered on a kind of sufferance."[27]

The OELC players were all specially selected, well coached, and bowled overarm. However, the organization was closed after only two years, and from that time on women's cricket has been strictly amateur in both Australia and England. Consequently, women's cricket does not seem to have suffered from the conflict between amateur and professional players that characterized male cricket, even though teams were fielded from all levels. The lack of controversy about this may be explained by the different nature of competitive sport for women: sports were undertaken for the beneficial effects of the game physically, the particular sport being chosen from the sense of enjoyment that was derived from it; and the game was played for fun, a situation which still exists ("women will always play for the love of the game and there will be no professional female cricketers")[29]

Following the English model, cricket developed rapidly among women in Australia during the nineteenth century. In 1895 the magazine *Cricket* reported: "The new woman is taking up cricket, evidently with the same energy which has characterized her other and more important spheres of life." Women's cricket was officially organized at the turn of the century in Victoria. By 1905 sixteen clubs were actively engaged in competitions, and by the end of the season this had risen to twenty-one clubs, including the Snowflakes, Forget-me-Nots, and Seafoams. Many of the women involved in promoting cricket came from cricketing backgrounds. Nellie Gregory, captain of the Sirocco's team, and her sister Lily, captain of the Fernleas, were sisters of D. W. and S. E. Gregory. Mrs Agnes McDonnell, the first secretary of the Victorian Ladies Cricket Association wrote: "My brothers all played country cricket and my sisters also played, so I just lived in a cricket atmosphere."[30]

The mixture of players also deserves comment. Teams combined women whose views spanned the whole political spectrum, from Ruby Durrant, captain of the Brighton Ladies Club, who was a teacher with strong Labor views, to Agnes Paternoster, who came from an affluent background. Feminists, too, were involved; Vida Goldstein, the radical campaigner for women's rights was president of the Victorian Ladies Cricket Association from 1905 to 1912.[31] A study of the relationship between the development of sport among women and the rise of feminism may explain the sudden attraction to more robust sports in the 1890s and the emancipation of women.

As well, it would be interesting to see if those women who organized the various clubs and associations were involved elsewhere in politics or other activities. An intensive search through old club records and minutes would do much to enlighten us on these issues as well as throw light on women's organizations in the nineteenth and early twentieth centuries; it might be possible to gauge the numbers of women participating in the sport also. From the limited amount of material available it is possible to conjecture that most women who played cricket came from a middle-class background. These women had been taught that sport was a healthy occupation, a break from work, and not a serious matter beyond developing expertise in the chosen field. Consequently, women themselves reinforced the separate nature of their sport in order to preserve their feminine image.

The number of sports being taken up by women in the 1890s was great, ranging from fishing to cricket to big game hunting, and even from the few examples dealt with so far, it is possible to see several patterns emerging of favoured, popular, and permitted sports.[32] Horse-riding and croquet, for instance, were favoured sports. Constant references in ladies' pages suggest that these favoured sports conformed to the current image of women and the notion of ladylike behaviour. They were also sports that could be participated in by members of both sexes and could be seen as an extension of courting procedures. They were pursued with becoming modesty and gentleness in garments quite unsuited to any degree of muscular exertion. Cycling, tennis, and golf were popular sports; they were practised more widely, although purchase of equipment often put them beyond the reach of those for whom money was a consideration. The patronage given such sports by the rich and elite made them popular sports. Cricket, hockey, swimming, and later athletics, for example, were permitted sports. They were more robust and in some cases were sports normally considered the preserve of men. The greater muscular exertion is compensated for by ensuring that separate competition was held between women and not between men and women. Every effort was made to reinforce the femininity of women with close attention to costume. Women involved in "permitted" sports took the activity very seriously, but they remained isolated groups and their efforts did not excite the attention given to men's cricket or football, for example. By taking up "men's sports" such as cricket, these women were transgressing the image of the dependent female; team sports like hockey developed team spirit, loyalty, and leadership, qualities normally reserved for men. While it is true that some male cricketers, for instance, did take an active interest in the development of the women's game, it has never captured the nation's imagination as has men's cricket. This is characteristic of much of women's sport today, it remains a separate entity, seen in the lack of coverage in present-day news media.

Women spectators have also been afflicted with this idea of separation, manifested in what they were permitted to view and in membership of sports clubs and institutions. Here they have often been relegated to auxillary status, only to raise money and cater for sportsmen, or they are only granted associate membership. This may be explained by nineteenth-century ideas of respectability which did not permit "ladies" to watch boxing matches, for example, as the sight of half-naked men and rough language, it was believed, would upset feminine sensitivity. Moreover, since sport played a secondary role in most women's lives, it was thought that they had no interest in viewing sporting fixtures. Most would not have had the time anyway, if the great number of advertisements for recuperative tonics for women in nineteenth century newspapers is any indication. Besides which, race meetings or boxing matches gave men the opportunity to get away from women and families, to be one of the "boys". It was not likely that men would encourage women to attend such functions, beyond special occasions like racing carnivals, where ladies of quality went to be noticed. For others, such affairs have been seen as an opporunity for a day out with "mum and the kids". The assumption that only men wished to take sport seriously has meant that women, in some instances, are prevented from viewing sport from the same central positions as men: the location of the men-only enclosure opposite the winning post at Randwick is one example. Similar restrictions are placed on women's entry to members-only bars at cricket grounds. At less exclusive levels, women these days form a good part of the crowd at football, cricket, and racing events. The question of how and why they have become involved has yet to be explained. At the purely speculative level, general emancipation, national pride, and involvement with sport at the school level may account for the increase in their numbers.

W. F. Mandle has suggested that organized sport as a mass entertainment was a notable feature of the latter part of the nineteenth century, which prompted the rapid development of such team sports as football and cricket.[33] This does not seem to be the case for women, who achieved prominence as individuals rather than in teams and in the favoured and popular sports rather than the permitted (although swimming is an exception). Neither have their sports developed as mass entertainment, except for tennis. This development may be explained in two ways. Sportswomen involved in tennis, riding or golf succeed because they were and are taking part in sports long accepted as "Women's sports", and while they require strength and control, they are aesthetically pleasing to watch. Others such as athletes and swimmers have achieved fame and interest because of their nationalist appeal. Women such as Fanny Durack and Dawn Fraser achieved much publicity and huge followings as a result of their great efforts and success at a national and international level, representing Australia in Olympic and Commonwealth games; they are seen as "golden girls", or as Anne Summers has described it, they are recipients of a "diffused nationalistic gratitude".[34] Sportswomen I consulted agreed that press coverage for successful sportswomen was good and that often female swimmers and athletes stole the limelight from male counterparts. However, compared with coverage given football in New South Wales, where even the lowest grades are reported on a weekly basis, the coverage these women get is slight or of an intermittent nature. Indeed what interest is expressed in their achievements warrants investigation. If cricket can be said to be involved in the development of Australian nationalism in the nineteenth century, then the work of Australian women athletes, swimmers, and tennis players could be said to have performed a similar task in the twentieth century.

What emerges strongly from a survey of the media's treatment of sportswomen is the great desire of sportswomen and sports reporters to assure the public of the femininity of the players. For instance, women Olympic contestants must undergo a sex test. Even in the nineteenth century the femininity of sportswomen was in question; in 1895 the *Indianapolis Journal* reported:

> If the bloomer fad continues to boom
> Ere long the fellow rude
> Can't tell if the vision gliding by
> is a daisy or a dude.[35]

The Australian Town and Country Journal was assuring women in 1905 that the shorter skirts required for sport need no longer make the hockey or golf player feel a "species apart".[36] In 1962, the writer Ken Knox, referring to Dawn Fraser's particularly suitable physique for swimming, emphasized that she was "essentially" a woman even though she "does not have the same sort of curves that have won Jayne Mansfield or Marilyn Monroe such prominence".[37] Moreover, Dawn Fraser asserted that had she been a male swimmer it would have been easier to train and get a better job; people would have "accepted" her more readily.[38]

It would appear that not only have sportswomen battled to be accepted in all sports, but they have been stuck with a masculine image as well. One explanation for this may be a legacy from daring to take up sports hitherto thought to be male preserves, and another is that as a result of their training they do not conform to socially acceptable images of women. The whole pattern is a strange about-face, considering sport was first introduced to maintain the feminine nature of women. The change may well have come when women tried to introduce serious competition into their sports. A dichotomy seems to exist here, though, as sportswomen frequently put their success down to training with men. Ken Knox noted that Dawn Fraser, who trained with men, began to think in men's times. It was not long before she was swimming men's times. Ilsa Konrads and Lorraine Crapp also trained with male swimmers, and Knox concluded that "all women can benefit by training with men".[39]

The implication here is that women have to look beyond the shorter horizons laid down for them if they are to succeed; perhaps the effort involved, the determination, and sacrifices made are those features normally associated with sportsmen and hence the masculine image. The denial of the male image on the part of sportswomen is quite understandable. As Peg McMahon, an *Age* journalist, has argued, "women don't want to be compared with men on the sporting fields; they want to be compared with other women. That's what is relative."[40]

Although the survey of women and sport above shows that a strong sporting tradition existed at the turn of the century, it was in the 1940s and 1950s that Australian women dominated in world swimming and athletics. Shirley Strickland was the first Australian woman to win a place in an Olympic athletic event, coming third in 1948 at the London Games in both the 80 metres hurdles and the 100 metres. She was also a member of the 1948 Olympic 400 metres relay team, which finished second. Majorie Jackson won a record seven Commonwealth games medals in 1950 and 1954, while Betty Cuthbert set world records from 60 metres to 440 yards and came back in 1964 to win the Tokyo Games 400 metres. Australian swimmers have been no less illustrious. Lorraine Crapp, Dawn Fraser, Ilsa Konrads, and Alva Colquhoun gave outstanding performances at Olympic and Commonwealth Games and on tours throughout Europe from 1956 to 1958. According to June Ferguson, the reason for this sudden flourish was the Australian women, unlike most of their counterparts in Europe, did not suffer from the deprivations and chaos of the Second World War; their diets and training were not so badly affected, consequently they were in better form.[41] As mentioned above, the effect of this on the Australian public and the fillip their efforts gave to Australia's international image would be worthy of further research. But the point here is that for these women to have achieved such amazing speeds and their participation in fields normally reserved for men points to some changes in the evolution of sports for women. Changes in clothing and scientific techniques enabling greater mobility are probably the most obvious reasons for this development — but what about changes in attitudes?

Some change may have occurred as a result of two world wars, which highlighted the need for a fit and able nation not only of men to fight but also of women to organize and run industry and essential services. The other impetus to change could be the emphasis placed on sport as a nation-building factor, as illustrated by the totalitarian regimes which emerged in Germany, Italy and the USSR in the 1930s. The effect of such movements could be seen in comments like: "No country can properly promote national physical growth and efficiency except through a government programme of physical culture . . . . It is not necessary to believe in Stalin or Hitler to realize that they are achieving a colossal victory in promoting the physical welfare of their people." The writer cited the number of German victories in the 1936 Munich Games as proof. The conclusions are also interesting: physical efficiency was not a question of self-defence but of national pride and duty. "Physically unfit we cannot expect to exist as a nation, let alone defend our country. Compulsory conscription of motion is one thing, compulsory participation in sports and games of all citizens is another. It is a humanitarian physical welfare ideal before it is a safeguard in national danger."[42]

Were the efforts, then, of women (and men) in the 1940s and 1950s a product of such ideas? Information in government education reports suggests that this might be the case. Decisions were taken in 1937 to proceed with the organization of physical culture in New South Wales on a state-wide basis. "Greater recognition is being given to the national importance of a high standard of physical fitness among peoples and measures for promoting the standard of physical education are being taken by every progressive country," stated the Department of Public Instruction. It saw physical culture as being conceived as training that contributed to good citizenship and sound mental and bodily health. An advisory body was appointed to examine existing conditions and to make recommendations in connection with various aspects of the scheme.[43] By 1954 a teaching diploma of physical education had been established and physical education in schools had grown owing to an increase in grants for equipment. The delay in organization may be put down to the disruption caused by war, but these measures together with the inauguration of the National Fitness Movement by the federal government in 1939 may well have contributed to post-war success and the greater involvement of women. Despite these developments, the overall position of women in sport did not change. National fitness movements might have enabled more women to participate in more sports, but the idea that their sport was more for physical fitness, and perhaps a part of national defence and nation building, remained the same. It did nothing to raise the standing of women's cricket and hockey to the level of great national pastimes with cult figures such as there are in men's sports. This may have something to do with the economics of sport as well; the only sportswomen involved in lucrative occupations are tennis players and golfers, and it is only recently that women have attained financial parity with men in tennis. In spite of the improvement of facilities and the greater emphasis on the benefits of physical education in the 1930s and 1940s, the sexual politics of sport still operate, to be lifted only periodically when women's achievements contribute to the national ethos.

This chapter is an exploratory one which, it is hoped, will raise questions and foster discussion not only on the sexual politics of sport but on sport history itself, especially the need for including women as an integrated part of such studies. It is now possible to try to answer some of the questions posed in the introduction on the nature and development of sport for women in Australia. The politics of sport evolved in the nineteenth century to counteract the harmful effects of the emancipation of women, when sports for women assumed first a curative and then a preventive function to ward off sterility and ill-health, and then to maintain physical well-being. With sport relegated to this level, it was impossible for the efforts of sportswomen to be taken seriously. They were also to be encumbered by unpractical costumes and by customs which decreed that women's role in society was first and foremost as wives and mothers; anything else was of secondary importance. Such concepts were introduced at the school level and were reinforced by society at large in newspapers and journals. Where sports such as bicycling and tennis did become popular, it was due to the patronage of the rich and famous that made the pastime socially acceptable and fashionable to follow. Occasionally, the sport was taken over and organized by the "ladies" of the middle and elite classes, as with cricket. However, serious competition was to be avoided, as it did not conform to ladylike behaviour and the cultural image of women, factors which continued to hamper the development and acceptance of sportswomen in 1920s and 1930s, and hampers their recognition today. It accounts also for the exclusion of women from the more robust games of football, introduced for boys at school and later as a game to be played professionally. These games taught boys leadership, courage, and lessons in life; the lesson in life for girls was how to be a woman. Consequently, professional sportswomen were not to be found. When they did emerge, it was in the favoured and popular sports, and it is only these women who have so far achieved widespread recognition.

It is only on intermittent occasions that sportswomen in Australia attract great attention, when their efforts are associated with the image of Australia at the international level. The great efforts of Australian women in team and other less-well-known sports are ignored in the rush to concentrate upon the efforts of Australian sportsmen. That such sportswomen for the most part remain anonymous is due to the nineteenth-century legacy which saw sport for women as a separate affair of little use beyond physical fitness and a mechanism to maintain the femininity of women. If "a just estimation of the character" of Australians as a whole is to be made, then we must stop equating Australians and sport solely with Australian men; only then will be sexual politics of sport cease to exist.

NOTES

1. Joseph Strutt, *Sports and Pastimes of the People of England* (London: J. White, 1801), quoted by Ian Turner, "A Comment" (on an article by W. F. Mandle, "Games People Played"), *Historical Studies* 15, no.60 (April 1973): 536.
2. D. C. Mercer, "Women", in The Department of Tourism and Recreations's *Leisure — A New Perspective* (Canberra: Australian Government Publishing Service, 1975), p.265.
3. W. F. Mandle, "Cricket and Australian Nationalism in the Nineteenth Century", *Journal of the Royal Australian Historical Society* 59, no.4 (December 1973): 225-46.
4. A. J. Coles, "Sport in Australian Society", in *Leisure — A New Perspective*, p.288.
5. Anne Summers, *Damned Whores and God's Police* (Ringwood, Vic.: Penguin, 1975), p.82.
6. Ibid., chapter 3, "The Sporting Wife".
7. Methodist Ladies College, Hawthorn, *An Ideal College for Girls, Handbook 1882-95*, (n.p., n.d.), p.13.

8. PLC Pymble, *Advance Prospectus* (Sydney, 1915), pp.6-7. For a general discussion see also D. S. Ainsworth, *The History of Physical Education* (New York: A. S. Barnes, 1930).
9. Legislative Assembly of NSW, *Report of the Minister of Public Instruction for the Year 1904* (Sydney, 1905), pp.48-49.
10. Ibid.
11. *The Australian Town and Country Journal* (hereafter referred to as *T & C Journal*), 9 March 1895, p.36.
12. Ibid., 29 September 1900, p.53.
13. MLC Burwood, *Jubilee Souvenir 1886-1936*, p.77-79.
14. S. K. Westman, *Sport Physical Training and Womanhood* (London: Bailliére, 1939), p.ix.
15. Mabel Lee, *The Conduct of Physical Education* (New York: Barnes, 1930), p.439.
16. Jack Pollard, *Ampol's Sporting Records* (Sydney: Pollard, 1973,), pp.115-16.
17. S. J. Baker, *The Pacific Book of Australiana* (Sydney: Angus and Robertson, 1967), p.255; Pollard, *Ampol's Sporting Records*, pp.405-6.
18. *T & C Journal*, 19 April 1905, p.42.
19. Ibid., 23 February 1910, pp.32-33.
20. Ibid., 18 January 1895, p.41.
21. Beverley Kingston, *My Wife, My Daughter, and Poor Mary Ann* (Melbourne: Nelson, 1975), p.127.
22. *T & C Journal*, 29 March 1895, p.44.
23. Ibid.
24. Baker, *Pacific Book of Australiana*, p.255.
25. *T & C Journal*, 2 February 1895, p.34.
26. Rachel Heyhoe Flint and Netta Rheinberg, *Fair Play: The Story of Women's Cricket* (Sydney: Angus and Robertson, 1976), pp.13-28.
27. Ibid, pp.25, 26-27.
28. Women pioneered the technique of overarm bowling in the mid nineteenth century. Christina Willes and Mrs W. Lambert are both said to be responsible for its inception: their skirts were too full to allow underarm bowling.
29. Heyhoe-Flint and Rheinberg, *Fair Play*, p.173.
30. Ibid., pp.91-93.
31. Ibid.
32. A division suggested to the author by Dr Beverley Kingston.
33. W. F. Mandle, "Games People Played: Cricket and Football in England and Victoria in the Late Nineteenth Century", *Historical Studies* 15, no. 60 (April 1973): 511-12.
34. Summers, *Damned Whores*, p.79.
35. *T & C Journal*, 18 January 1895, p.41.
36. Ibid.
37. Ken Knox, *The Dawn of Swimming* (London: Stanley Paul, 1962), p.44.
38. Dawn Fraser, interview with author, Sydney, 28 April 1977.
39. Knox, *The Dawn of Swimming*, p.70.
40. Peg McMahon, "Women and Sport", *Age*, 11 April 1977.
41. June Ferguson, interview with author, Sydney 23 March 1977.
42. D. Warren, "Compulsory Games and Physical Training", *The Home*, 1 April 1937, p.63.
43. Legislative Assembley of NSW, *Report of the Ministers of Public Instruction 1938* (Sydney, 1938), p.2-3.

JURGEN TAMPKE

Politics Only?: Sport in the German Democratic Republic

Several contributors in this book stress the relevance of sport to political development. Michael McKernan, for example, shows how the working class and the middle class, split in their reaction to Australia's involvement in war, further demonstrated that division in their differing conceptions of sport. Richard Cashman discerns how the British in India promoted cricket as part of their grand Imperial strategy, and W. F. Mandle deals with the Irish Republican Brotherhood's attempt to use sport to further their nationalist objective. That sport can take on a highly political character was also shown during the controversial South African Rugby Union tour in 1971. Only a few people today would adhere to the view expounded by the rugby union organizations, the state and federal governments, and most newspapers that "you cannot mix sport and politics". In fact the position taken by the prime minister, Malcolm Fraser, when he declared at the Inter-Parliamentary Union meeting in Canberra in April 1977 that no sporting team selected on a racial basis would be permitted to compete in Australia, showed a complete turn-about from the stand of his predecessor William McMahon in 1971.

On the other hand, sports enthusiasts in Australia would flatly reject any suggestion that they are nothing more than pawns in the world of big power politics. In fact as far as Australia is concerned, none of the authors in this book nor any other responsible writer could make such an outrageous claim. Yet, it is precisely this approach which is put forward bluntly and unquestionably when it comes to dealing with sport in the people's republics of Eastern Europe. It is alleged that Communist sportsmen and sportswomen are not in it for the joy and fun of sport but are "brain-washed sporting automata"[1] who advance the political machinations of their governments. As a study of Eastern European Olympic teams soon reveals that the concept of computerized human sports robots is untenable, this chapter sets out to analyze more clearly the relationship between sport and politics in Eastern Europe and to investigate other causes of their outstanding sport performances. The example chosen is the German Democratic Republic, today the most successful sporting nation in the world.

The German Democratic Republic (GDR), more conventionally known in Australia as East Germany, was in the news a great deal at the time of the 1976 Olympic Games in Montreal. The success of the GDR athletes was outstanding. Coming from a nation whose population is not much bigger than that of Australia, they won forty gold medals, twenty-five silver, and twenty-five bronze; overall they came second only to the Soviet Union, surpassing even the United States. To anyone moderately familiar with international sport, this did not come as a great surprise. There have been outstanding performances by the GDR in sport for about a decade. But to many people in Australia this did come as a shock which was heightened by the fact that the Australian medal tally was unimpressive. As Australia now faced what the West Germans had had to put up with for a long time, and what later annoyed Western Europe and more recently the United States, an explanation for the GDR's international sporting success was sought. The answers given in Australia to explain this success were in line the Western tradition of a decade or so ago. Basically three kinds of explanations have been put forward. The first is best described as the "SOS" approach: "Success or Siberia". In this explanation, top performance is extorted from athletes terrified of the consequence of failure; sport is forced on a reluctant populace by an authoritarian regime. This explanation passed unchallenged in the West until the mid 1960s. The West German government's Handbook on the GDR used such terminology as late as 1967.[2] Even as late as 1972, during the Winter Olympics at Sapporo, the *Bildzeitung,* West Germany's largest circulating daily newspaper, explained the GDR toboggan team's victory over the West Germans, who had been favoured to win the gold medal, in the following manner: "the toboggan racers from the German Democratic Republic are driven to success by brutal training methods. Their super form comes from hellish torments inflicted upon them in the torture chamber of trainer Kohler . . . who . . . chained his men to the toboggan."[3] However, such crude explanations are now less frequent in Europe. The normalization of relations between the two Germanys in the late 1960s and early 1970s and the general spirit of *detente* between East and West which prevailed at that time encouraged a more realistic appraisal of GDR sport. Moreover many Western Sports writers who studied the improving performances of GDR sportsmen and sportswomen could find no evidence to support this case. Today, few journalists who pride themselves on being "informed" would present GDR sport thus.

However, old prejudices often die hard, particularly in Australia. Kevin Newman, the minister responsible for sport in the Fraser government, from whom one might have expected better, explained the GDR success to a "This Day Tonight" reporter on the SOS principle. He alleged that young children who showed any talent were torn away from their parents and set solely to the task of training. An eminent Australian columnist and "man of letters" even more recently espoused this cause: "East Germany has umpteen world champions of all kinds. Who are they? Do they have any identity? Name one of them? Who cares? To watch these mechanical automats is no more inspiring than observing a chess championship between two computers."[4]

The second explanation often given for GDR sports success is more sophisticated. It claims that they have developed the most effective ways to make use of anabolic steroids; that superiority in drugs accounts for their success. Doping has been around for a long time and at times was widely practised at sports events.[5] Only recently there were misgivings in West Germany when some of their Olympic swimmers admitted that they had air blown into their rectums so they could "lie on the water flat as a board".[6] This not only caused the swimmers involved considerable pain but also led to charges that unfair methods were used in the Federal Republic. Of course, the outside observer is in no position to provide evidence that doping does not take place among GDR athletes. But those who claim it does take place have even less evidence. For one thing, controls at all international sports events are very rigid; furthermore, although drug usage is often enough detected, no GDR athlete has ever been found doped. This second explanation, then, like the first one, at least lacks evidence and persuasion.

It is the third explanation given in the West today which is the only one worth looking at, because it does not rely on mere speculative accusations. While acknowledging that the success is the product of an immense effort, the explanation seriously challenges the wisdom of such an effort. The immense financial costs are criticized. These huge costs are sacrificed to achieve the only goal sport in socialist countries is said to have — that is, to spread the glory of the system. And we, a responsible society, cannot throw money away for such dubious political purposes. A *Sydney Morning Herald* editorialist wrote:

It will be unfortunate if Australian competitors' disappointment at their relatively poor Olympic Games showing is allowed to develop into a national inquest, with the inevitable pressure for large Government handouts. Any suggestion of an official Government inquiry, presumably to find out how Australia can keep up with (or preferably surpass) the Joneses of international sport should be knocked on the head. Such an inquiry is the reverse of what is required . . .

. . . Sport . . . should not be made a matter of national prestige, a yardstick by which nations are measured. That can be left to East Germany and Russia (whose athletes are State-financed, State-trained, State-directed). . . . Australia has a fine Olympic record, quite out of proportion to the size of its population; it cannot always expect to do so well.

. . . Governments can help, within limits, by financing better facilities; but it would be better to give up competing at the Games than to try to emulate East German and Russian methods.[7]

It was this kind of explanation which was almost unanimously presented throughout the Australian news media. There were only a few exceptions. While W. F. Mandle, speaking on "PM" one evening during the Games, said that we should overhaul our whole basic attitude to sport and that we should follow some of the GDR's initiatives, and Rod Humphries in four short articles in the *Sydney Morning Herald* gave the GDR a chance to put their side of the story,[8] these were exceptions. The great bulk of comments were in line with the above-quoted editorial.

Before analyzing this approach in detail, two short points need to be made. The first is that it is true that the GDR spends more money on sport than does Australia, but then the Australian sports budget is so small that it would fall short in comparison with most countries. It is not so certain whether the German Democratic Republic spends more money on sport than some other Western countries do. The issue is on what kind of sport is the money spent. In the GDR, for example, most of the money goes into facilities that encourage active participation of the population in sports. In West Germany, equally large sums of money are spent on spectator sports. The sports arenas of the leading West German soccer clubs are huge, modern complexes which offer the visitor all comforts. The average soccer fan approaches his home ground on a six- or eight-lane highway, leaves his car at the parking ground, and enters a fully roofed stadium which offers him not only a comfortable seat but also the services of beer and "Würstchen" (sausage) boys who provide him with necessary refreshments. This is the normal West German stadium of a top soccer side, and if we account for the sums involved in the construction and the maintenance of these sports arenas we are dealing with figures of the magnitude of the GDR sports programme. The point is that there are several ways of spending money on sport, and that the GDR is not necessarily the only big spender.

There is a second fallacy in the assumption that all that is required for international success is the willingness to spend large sums of money. Again the West German example will illustrate this. Since about 1969 both the West German government and industry in the Federal Republic have spent vast sums of money on raising the standards of the top West German athletes. Initially this was intended to ensure that the host's performance in Munich in 1972 was fairly successful. This was an understandable policy, as the amount of money involved in the staging of the 1972 Olympics Games was so huge that there was the fear of a probable backlash should West Germany's own performance be too mediocre. This policy was successful. West Germany did well in Munich, though not nearly as well as their fellow Germans in the east. So both industry and government in the Federal Republic continued to spend large sums on their top athletes — allegedly as much as did the GDR.[9] Nevertheless, despite this large outlay, at the 1976 Olympic Games the GDR again outscored the Federal Republic, this time by as much as four to one. Thus care should be taken with oversimplifications.

How then are we to explain this success. What is the history of sport in East Germany? One of the top priorities for the GDR Government after the division of Germany was made final in the early 1950s was to completely reconstruct the education and health system. This was to be expected with a Communist government in charge. In the old Germany both health care and education had a class bias, so any socialist government would try to remove the inequalities. What made this task especially important was that the GDR inherited some of the least privileged parts of Germany: the heavily proletarianized working-class parts of Germany, East Berlin, Saxony, and Thuringia. Its rural population, too, was poor; most of the land to the east of the river Elbe was until the 1950s still owned by the big land-owners, the Prussian *Junkers*. Part of the GDR programme to provide equality and good standard of health was the construction of sporting facilities on a large scale. In fact, since the early 1950s the GDR budget allowed annually between 1.5 and 1.8 per cent for sport.[10] In 1974 the sports figure was 180 million marks out of a total budget of 108 billion, just under 1.8 per cent of the budget. Almost 80 per cent of this — 141 million marks — went to the construction of further facilities or to the maintenance of existing ones. The result of it all was impressive. In 1974, for example, there were about four thousand gymnasiums, two thousand swimming pools and stadiums, 10 per cent of which were heated indoor pools. There were four hundred ski jumps and fifteen hundred boatsheds and houses. The number of sporting fields amounted to 7,500 (1,000 of which are described as large). The figure for sports halls was given as 224 and for stadiums as 306.[11] It is not easy to estimate the corresponding figures for Australia, as no regular statistics are kept here. Nevertheless, to judge from the small amount of material available, the difference is vast.[12] Although the GDR and Australia have roughtly comparable populations, there would be about three times as many sports fields in the GDR as in Australia, there are roughly twice as many swimming pools, and there are possibly four times as many sports halls and gymnasiums. This is a significant difference.

For a small amount of money[13] a citizen in the GDR can join any sports club he likes,including clubs for such sports as tennis, hunting, yachting, sports which in the old Germany were open only to the privileged section of the community. With facilities like this, it is not surprising that the number of people in the various sporting associations grew steadily. Today, 2.6 million citizens (about one-sixth of the total population) are members of one of these sporting bodies. Altogether it is estimated that about 40 per cent of the total population makes regular use of the facilities.[14] This interest in sport is further fostered by generous work and travel allowances. All active sportsmen and sportswomen, not just the top few, are entitled to training sessions per week during their working hours, and they can travel very cheaply to their place of competition. There are thirty-five basic sports associations in the GDR, all well provided for with instructors and coaches which makes it possible for everyone interested in sport to exercise, be trained, and compete on a regular basis. Adults and young people are encouraged to qualify for the national sports badge, for which more than five million people have competed over recent years. There are also numerous competitions in which large numbers of athletes participate: the Freiburg open-air gymnastic festival; the "Berlin Race", a mass shuttle relay competition; the "Festival Miles" competitions; various "peace bicycle races"; contests to determine the "strongest apprentice" or "the best girl athlete", to name only a few, in addition to the regular local competitions in all fields of sports ranging from soccer to volleyball.

Sport also plays an important part in schools, although not quite as important as is at times alleged. At primary and secondary school, four hours a week are set aside for sport and gymnastics. This amounts to about 10 per cent of the curriculum, the corresponding figures for German and mathematics are 20 per cent each. Hundreds of thousands of youngsters compete in the national youth sports festival, the so-called Spartakiade. The basic idea of the Spartakiade is not unique; it can be compared to local school district sports festivals only on a much larger scale. The Spartakiade is no doubt a paradise for talent spotting. Finally there are special schools for specially gifted and promising children. These special schools are not limited to sport; other special interests, like art and music, are catered for in the same way. All these schools follow the normal curriculum but emphasize their particular field of speciality. Although good sporting performances are necessary for entrance to the sports school, they are not the only prerequisite. Advanced results in non-sport subjects are also required, and a pupil who fails to maintain acceptable academic results loses his place, sports performance notwithstanding.[15]

The bulk of the large sums of money spent on sport in the GDR, then, is spent for the benefit of the whole population and for all age groups; not just the top athletes benefit. The question now is: Why does the government do this? Why all this effort? The answer, according to the GDR government's publication *A New Chapter in the History of German Sport*, is:

> The question of physical culture and sports cannot be one of indifference. . . . If the term "health" is an integral part of the complex theme "human happiness" then the fact that in the era of rapid scientific and technical progress mankind is faced with living and working conditions that demand an increased preparedness of body and mind cannot be overlooked. . . . The principle of giving every citizen the chance of maximum development of body and mind . . . included quite naturally, physical culture. A healthy mode of living, the raising of the standard of health of the whole of the people is, in the last consequence, unthinkable without regular participation in some form of sport.[16]

This may sound rather lofty. Many people in Australia, especially academics, take a condescending view of sport. Still, to many in our society the basis of the hypothesis "sport leads to health leads to happiness" is valid. Most people believe that it is good to feel healthy. They would agree that when the strain and pressure of work is really on, two or three days of bushwalking, for example, does wonders, both for body and mind. And are there not thousands of people in Australia who enjoy the satisfaction of a regular game of squash?

There is also a more pragmatic reason for this sport effort. No doubt the amount the GDR spends on sport pays dividends. As sport doctors in particular tell us, people who play sport are healthier and considerably less likely to fall ill and use the health facilities. Loss of labour power is a particularly vulnerable aspect of the GDR economy because of the small work-force and the considerable shortage of labour. A comprehensive and advanced sports programme as general health insurance is something many people connected with sport in the West have been demanding for a long time. In fact West Germany has for some years now been engaged in a major "keep fit" campaign for all citizens.[17] Thus sport as health insurance should not be too readily dismissed in a discussion of the GDR's sport performance; indeed, it throws doubt on the view so common in the West that the whole sport effort has only the one purpose of glorifying socialism. The bulk of the money spent on sport in the GDR goes to the average sportsman and sportswoman who are unlikely to compete in any international event. On the other hand, the advanced facilities, and the larger number of people participating in sport do provide the basis for the international success, and with this solid groundwork it just takes a little more effort to achieve top international performance.

Before turning to the GDR's international performances, there are two comments on superior performance sport in general that need to be made. The first is that superior performance sport has been criticized for some years now. There is talk that there are threats to the health of the athlete. This debate of course concerns all sporting countries, not only the GDR, although here the medical authorities are renowned for being particularly careful in checking the effect of sport on an athlete's health.[18] Secondly, there is the challenge to the whole Olympic idea. Many criticisms have been made recently of the whole concept of the modern Olympic Games. The huge amount of money involved to stage the Games these days, the creation of showpieces to display the nation's wealth, the general deterioration of the Games to the level of the old Roman "bread and circuses" — all this has been strongly criticized. This whole tendency probably reached its peak with the 1972 Munich Olympic Games, where the total costs came close to a billion dollars, and where many of the facilities built with this money are now standing idle, having been used once for a fortnight only. It is perhaps interesting to note that the cost for the after-game rubbish and general clean-up in Munich amounted to twenty million marks, which is just four million less than the total costs of the 1956 Melbourne Olympics. But this too is again a general criticism, directed against the lavish display and not against the idea of having the top athletes of all nations compete with one another. If a country accepts the concept of having her athletes compete with other nations — and almost all nations do accept this — it then seems only fair enough that these athletes are well supported in their efforts. So in the GDR, in addition to the broad basis for sport which has been outlined above, the top athletes are assisted first by scientific research work into sports performances and secondly by generous leave to allow for training.

The scientific research work is carried out by the German College of Physical Education *(Deutsche Hochschule fur Korperkultur)* in Leipzig, an instruction that caters principally for the education of sports teachers. There are ten thousand sports teachers working in the GDR today who received their education at this sports academy. It is not a closed shop; guest students are welcome, and about 20 per cent of the study places are reserved for students from the Third World. There is also a team of scientists working in Leipzig carrying out studies aimed at raising training methods and performances; for example, they have worked on the construction of rowing boats, skis, bob-sleds, or anything else that helps to improve the performance of their athletes.

As well, the GDR athletes receive very generous treatment as far as training time and preparation are concerned. A top GDR athlete can devote himself to his sport without having to fear financial loss or setbacks in his professional career. This at times leads to claims that they are really not amateurs, and that consequently they should not compete in amateur events. *Staatsamateure* (state amateurs) is the phrase coined. The Swiss-based newspaper *Neue Zuricher Zeitung* in a thorough and informative series of articles on GDR sport concluded that this is not a correct assessment:

> "Fame" in sport does not free the athlete from career obligations or from basic military training; during the sporting career the athlete's career education is continued — though in slow motion, at times under favourable conditions in army or police sports clubs. Thus if the Swiss athletes feel disadvantaged in comparison with their competitors from the east, then they have a case, but terms like "full-professional from the east" or "state amateurs" present a distortion of the situation; the basic difference to the Swiss sport system consists in the fact that in the GDR sport, occupation, and military are coordinated, during as well as after the sporting career. [On the other hand] . . . in Switzerland sport and occupation present themselves often as alternatives.[19]

Privileges enjoyed by the top GDR athletes are also a far cry from the amount of money earned by leading Western professionals. In the latter case we are talking in terms of hundreds of thousands or indeed millions of dollars. When the 1972 United States swimming hero Mark Spitz retired from competitive swimming he became a millionaire. The top GDR swimmer at the 1976 Montreal Olympics, Kornelia Ender, collected twenty thousand marks at the end of her swimming career. Ender is studying to become a veterinary scientist and expects a salary of about twenty thousand marks annually. If we take into consideration that her swimming involvement would set her back at least one year, the twenty thousands marks would just cover her professional losses.

Let us now turn to an evaluation of the political component in GDR sport. In 1974 the *Canadian Journal of History and Physical Education* published an article on this topic written by G. A. Carr of the University of Victoria, British Columbia, which supports the claim that sport in Eastern European countries has only a political purpose.[20] As evidence for this Carr cites quotations from the statutes of the GDR Sports Committee. The author then lists various government departments that control sport in the GDR and goes on to describe how the various sports associations are used for political indoctrination. Carr finally quotes the West German GDR sports authority, Willi Knecht, who speculates that in the GDR as much as one billion marks is spent on sport annually. "The end", it is alleged, "justified the means."[21]

What does this article amount to? It is true that there are several references to sport in the GDR Constitution. There is no secret about this. To quote from one of their government publications:

> Laws were passed in the GDR which guarantee that the state and social organizations responsible, working closely together with active participants,will make physical culture and sport available to everyone. Through the Socialist Constitution of the GDR, the right of all citizens to physical education and the corresponding responsibility of the state and society are made the law of the land. Article 18 of the Constitution proclaims that sports are part of socialist culture and serve the general physical and intellectual development of the people.
> This right is explained in detail in other sections of the Constitution. Article 25, for example, states that the government and society as a whole will encourage sports as a part of the civil rights of every citizen to participation in cultural life. Other articles of the Constitution call for the development of physical education, school and mass sports and tourism in order to preserve health and labour power among the broad masses.[22]

Admittedly this is political, but unless we subscribe to the view that there is no relation between sport and politics in modern society, can we make much of this? Perhaps there are no links, or only a few, between sport and politics in Canada, perhaps in Australia also, but as far as the tense political life of central Europe is concerned the two cannot be taken in isolation. The opening paragraph of the constitution for the West German Sports Federation (Deutscher Sportbund), for example, states that "the DSB is a free federation of the German athletic and sports associations and sports institutions. The seat is in Berlin." Given the controversial status of the former German capital, this is a highly political sentence.

There is also nothing blatantly political in the second claim that the GDR sports associations are subordinated to government institutions. In Australia too there are various departments at federal, state, and municipal level which are in charge of the administration of sport and the distribution of money. Carr does not present any evidence for his statement that sports associations are used for indoctrination. There have been no studies of sports club life in the GDR. The statistical figures for their sports associations show that the largest body is the soccer federation with half a million members. Why are we not to assume that these half a million soccer players are kicking the ball every Sunday or Saturday for the mere fun of it, just as they do in West Germany? The second largest sports organization is angling, and can Carr really allege that the average Upper Thuringian trout-catching fraternity is the centre of large-scale politicking?

Carr also hints at the old "Fuhrerprinzip" in sport — that the GDR are the spiritual heirs of Hitler's totalitarianism,[23] a claim also made in an article in 1973 by Louis Burgener, a French authority on sport.[24] This is a particularly unfortunate statement if only because many of the GDR leading politicians were in concentration camps during Hitler's regime. There was also a more serious effort made in the GDR to clear up the Nazi past than in West Germany.

Most difficult to accept is the final assertion that hundreds of billions of dollars are invested in sport each year because the political end justifies all means. The GDR's impressive economic performance over the last fifteen years has been commented upon favourably not only in Eastern Europe. This economic miracle (their small state is now the tenth largest industrial power in the world) does not really suggest that literally hundreds of billions of dollars are thrown away. After all, the political value of sports success is most questionable. Admittedly there is no doubt that the great international success swells the pride of the people in the GDR, that it gives them a sense of achievement. This again is not confined to the GDR. But as far as the external political value is concerned, if we maintain this argument we attribute a degree of naivety to the GDR which we would feel hurt to be accused of ourselves. There are very few people in the West who believe that communism is better than capitalism because a sportsman from the East jumps three centimetres further than someone from the West. In fact, if anything the political results have been negative. From the time of their earliest success in the West, the GDR sports performance has always been presented in the blunt and oversimplified terms discussed above. The *Neue Zuricher Zeitung* in its more balanced approach quotes that at least sport helped to put the GDR "on the map diplomatically". Even this does not correspond to the country's history,[25] as neither the wave of recognition by developing nations throughout the 1960s nor the real diplomatic breakthrough which followed the normalization of relations between the two Germanys in the early 1970s can be traced back to sports success.

By way of conclusion it should be said that the GDR success does not rely on little children who are torn away from their parents, nor has anyone yet proved that they have developed the "miracle steroid", nor do they throw money away. Instead they are now reaping the benefits of a generation of a well-organized physical education sports and health system. The fact that the GDR at international competitions today can give a proud answer to the question "What is the explanation?" is the product and not the cause of this advanced sports policy. Some Western European nations, notably West Germany, are contemplating now the elevation of sport to a more important position in their social system. This is not brought about by a desire to catch up with their fellow Germans in the East but by a concern about their deteriorating health. If this policy continues, it will probably, after some years, bridge the gap between them and the GDR. But then in times of economic instability it is sport in the Western world that is cut first.

NOTES

1. Max Harris, "Gelding the Lillee", *Australian*, 5 February 1977.
2. Bundesministerium für Innere Angelegenheiten, *SBZ von A bis Z* (Bonn: Deutscher Bundesverlag, 1967), pp. 448-49.
3. Quoted in *Spiegel*, 14 February 1972 (author's translation).
4. Max Harris, *Australian*, 5 February 1977.
5. Note, for example, *Proceedings of the Ninth Annual Conference of the Australian Sports Medicine Federation* (Adelaide, 1972), pp.19-22.
6. *Neues Deutschland*, 7 February 1977 (author's translation).
7. *Sydney Morning Herald*, 27 July 1976.
8. Ibid., 12 August, 17 August, 18 August, 20 August 1976.

9. *Spiegel,* 19 July 1976, pp.90-95.
10. *Statistical Pocket Book of the German Democratic Republic* (1975), pp.101-3.
11. *Informationsheet,* p.2.
12. A chart on various sporting facilities in New South Wales was compiled by Helen Svensson, a Brisbane journalist for a UNESCO report on "Entertainment and Society" in Australia. Her findings are yet to be published. Among other things, her chart lists 1,162 sports fields and 244 public swimming pools.
13. The payments of monthly dues for adults are 1.30 marks, 0.20 marks for children, and 0.80 marks for apprentices, students, and pensioners. *Informationsheet.*
14. Ibid., p.4.
15. *Neue Züricher Zeitung,* 25 March 1977.
16. Joachim Fiebelkorn, *A New Chapter in the History of German Sport* (Dresden: Verlag Zeit im Bild, 1965), p.4.
17. For example, Deutscher Sportbund, *Sport-Freizeit-Arbeit,* 1976.
18. See *Neue Züricher Zeitung,* 31 January 1977.
19. *Neue Züricher Zeitung,* 25 March 1977 (author's translation).
20. G. A. Carr, "The Birth of the German Democratic Republic and the Organisation of East German Sport", *Canadian Journal of History and Physical Education* 7, no. 1 (May 1974): 1-21.
21. Ibid., p.20.
22. *Fun-Health-Fitness,* Panorama, GDR, p.17.
23. Ibid., p.16.
24. Louis Burgener, *Information Historique* 35 (1973): 63.
25. *Neue Züricher Zeitung,* 20 March 1977.

W. F. MANDLE

Sport as Politics: the Gaelic Athletic Association 1884–1916

An article, "A Word About Irish Athletics", appearing in the 11
October 1884 issue of the nationalist weekly paper *United Ireland*
was the direct cause of the formation of the Gaelic Athletic
Association, although there had been some earlier moves to provide
a governing body for Irish Games.[1] The article, written by Michael
Cusack, a Dublin "crammer", himself a Gaelic athlete and a
Fenian, criticized English domination of sport in Ireland and called
for "Irish people to take the management of their games in their
own hands".

. Three weeks later eight men met in Miss Hayes's hotel in
Thurles, Country Tipperary, to found the GAA.[2] It was decided to
invite Parnell, Michael Davitt, and Archbishop Croke of Cashel to
become patrons of the Association. By design or accident these
choices demonstrated accurate recognition of the three most
important streams feeding Irish nationalism of the time: the
parliamentarian Parnell; the old Fenian and recent Land Leaguer
Davitt; and the radical churchman Croke. That all three could be
called upon and expected to work in harness also demonstrated the
apparent harmony prevailing at that time between potentially
conflicting elements. A fourth element, present in force at the
meeting, was not called upon so publicly for support. Three of the
eight who met at Thurles — John Wyse Power, J. K. Bracken, and
F. R. Moloney — were members of the Irish Republican
Brotherhood, which was henceforth to exercise a directing influence
on the Association.[3]

All those invited to become patrons accepted, Croke most
magniloquently in a famous letter that became the creed of the
GAA. Nine years before Douglas Hyde, in founding the Gaelic
League, spoke of the necessity of de-Anglicizing Ireland, Croke and
those who supported the GAA set out their challenge to the social
and cultural oppression that went hand in glove with political and
economic control. Croke noted:

the ugly and irritating fact that we are daily importing from England, not only her manufactured goods, which we cannot help doing, since she has practically strangled our own manufacturing appliances, but together with her fashions, her accents, her vicious literature, her music, her dances and her manifold mannerisms, her games also and her pastimes, to the utter discredit of our own grand national sports, and to the sore humiliation, as I believe, of every genuine son and daughter of the old land.

Ball-playing, hurling, football-kicking, according to Irish rules, casting, leaping in various ways, wrestling, handy-grips, top-pegging, leap-frog, rounders, tip-in-the-hat and all such favourite exercises and amusements, amongst men and boys may now be said to be not only dead and buried, but in several localities to be entirely forgotten and unknown. . . .

If we continue travelling for the next score years in the same direction that we have been going in for some time past, condemning the sports that were practised by our forefathers, effacing our national features as though we were ashamed of them, and putting on, with England's stuffs and broadcloths, her masher habits and such other effeminate follies as she may recommend, we had better at one, and publicly, abjure our nationality, clap hands for joy at the sight of the Union Jack and place "England's bloody red" exultantly above the "green".[4]

This manifesto was a shrewd and important recognition of the way in which a popular culture might be eroded. The GAA wavered only in its years of greatest weakness from a fierce and uncompromising hostility to "foreign" games, expressed most famously in "the Ban" of which we shall have more to say below.

To recognize the cultural importance of games in the 1880s was highly percipient. The games revolution that began in England in the 1870s quite rapidly affected Ireland. An Irish Football Association, modelled on the English FA and using its laws, was founded in 1880; an Irish Football Union to control rugby in Dublin was formed in 1874 and joined with the Belfast organization in 1881; and athletics meetings were run by the English Amateur Athletic Association. Cricket (perhaps wrongly regarded as an alien game) had eight county clubs by 1879, and an Irish Cricket Union was formed about the same time as the GAA.

The GAA had not only to challenge the developing organizational and popular strength of English games; it had to counter the moral and historical overtones that went with the games revolution, over-tones that emphasized the character-building worth of team games and their essential usefulness to, even precondition of, England's imperial mission, something to which Irishmen would be particularly sensitive. To counter this, the GAA from the start took great pains to emphasize the distinctiveness and long history of Irish sports. Irish football was claimed to have separate origins from the Anglo-Saxon versions, hurling was traced back to the days of Cuchulain and vested with legendary grandeur, and Irish athletics were said to be coeval in origin with those of Greece.[5] A popular cultural heritage that could be set against the oppressive English claims was asserted, even to the point of emphasizing that Irish athletics were less concerned with foot-racing than with jumping and weight-throwing. As *United Ireland* put it on 5 September 1885, the GAA's "ideal Ireland was dotted all over with miniature armies of hurlers, bowlers, jumpers, weight-throwers, merry dancers and joyous singers".

Initially the challenge was mounted on the athletics front. Gaelic football was not fully organized for a year or two, hurling and handball and bowling were *sui generis,* but in athletics war was declared almost right away. On 17 January 1885 the GAA announced that after St Patrick's Day no athlete would be allowed to compete at a GAA meeting if he competed elsewhere under other rules — the first Ban, in fact.[6] In response, on 21 February 1885 the Irish Amateur Athletic Association was formed, intended "to quash the GAA".

Far from quashing the GAA, the IAAA, which issued a counter ban to be effective from 1 September 1885, was forced to concede defeat by April 1886. A clash between rival meetings held at Tralee on 17 June 1885 set the pattern. Irishmen, invited by a combination of Fenian and priest "to choose between Irish and foreign laws", turned up fifteen thousand strong to the GAA meeting, while only a few thousand watched that of the IAAA.[7]

All that summer the GAA spread rapidly. The combination of the clergy, the National League, former Land Leaguers, and the Irish Republican Brotherhood irresistible. By mid-July *United Ireland* announced that it could no longer carry reports of all GAA meetings, and Cusack claimed that there were "hundreds" of clubs in existence by August. The movement was unashamedly and aggressively nationalist. The very names of the clubs revealed its nature. There was a host of Young Irelands, there were Emmets, Kickhams, and Erin's Hopes; there were clubs named after Biggar, Davitt, and Parnell; the green flag with the gold harp floated over GAA meetings. Sport was serving a nationalist purpose, as the *Irishman* of 8 November 1884 had forecast: "If any two purposes should go together they ought to be politics and athletics. . . . A political people we must be; the exigencies of our situation force us into perpetual war with England. . . . While fighting the enemy in the bye-ways which are called constitutional, we must maintain a certain degree of readiness to meet our enemy in the field. Our politics being essentially national, so should our athletics."

Elated, perhaps even intoxicated, by the success of the movement they had done so much to create, the IRB moved more openly to control it. In doing so they almost destroyed the GAA, bringing upon it both the hostility of the Church, which in favourable mood had proved so important to its growth, and the close attention of Dublin Castle.[8]

The IRB had already played its part in founding the GAA. In successive annual conventions of the Association the Brotherhood increased its hold. In 1885 an advanced IRB man from Cork, J. E. Kennedy, was added to the executive, and during the year three non-IRB men, including Cusack, left. What is more, in September 1886 the GAA invited John O'Leary, a noted Fenian and at that time president of the Supreme Council of the IRB, to become a fourth patron.[9] Just as the initial choice of Parnell, Davitt, and Croke as patrons reflected the balance of nationalist forces in Ireland at the Association's inception, the addition of O'Leary showed the way the balance was tilting within the GAA after only two years' existence.

The annual convention of 1887 is generally taken as the one where the IRB made its bid to control the GAA. The evidence suggests that from the outset the IRB had a strong influence; by 1885 they were virtually in charge; by 1886 indisputably so. As an IRB leader remarked to a police agent in November 1887, the priests who came to Thurles that month to oppose the IRB were "about a year too late'.[10] In 1886 the president, Maurice Davin, had retained his position, but all four vice-presidents, all three secretaries, the treasurer, the official handicapper, and the records' secretary were members of the IRB. Within three months this new executive, bypassing Davin, banned members of the Royal Irish Constabulary from competing at GAA meetings and made all central executive members *ex officio* voting members of all county committees. Davin resigned, but the executive went ahead with its efforts to centralize power in IRB hands. It banned and boycotted the two great Dublin athletics meetings of the year, declaring that those who opposed the GAA were "a weak minded, dissentient clique, acting under the control of the worst form of the West British element. On the one side [was] INDEPENDENCE; on the other side, TREACHERY."[11] Croke himself was moved to protest, and he offered to mediate in the bubbling disputes about dictation and illegality. He was snubbed. "We do not want one or all of our

patrons as judges," *the Gael* commented. "We want them to remain
in their high and dignified position of honour."[12] The IRB,
conscious that its activities were occasioning opposition — among
others South Tipperary, Limerick, and Wexford were calling for IRB
heads — moved to stack the 1887 convention. Each affiliated club
(there were by now over six hundred) was allowed two delegates.
The IRB created phantom clubs, offered to provide delegates for
clubs who could not afford the expense of sending representatives,
and ascertained which clubs had not sent delegates and filled the
vacancies unasked. On 1 November IRB leaders met "to arrange for
the Thurles Convention . . . and exclude all but IRB men".[13]

But the church was not so easily put aside. It too had its stake in
the GAA: the leading patron was an archbishop, the basic
organizational unit was the parish, and the ordinary priesthood, men
of the soil and the country, loved the Gaelic games for what they
were and for what they could do for the health and morals of their
young parishioners. What the IRB might do to such young men was
to them anathema. The Brotherhood was an oath-bound secret
society, what was more, it was a revolutionary one. Too often the
priests had seen young men go out in futile uprisings, betrayed by
informers, outmatched by the forces against them. They were not
going to allow the GAA to slip so easily and so blatantly into the
hands of this latest nationalist revolutionary society.

Led by a Tipperary priest, Father Scanlan, they took the fight up
to the IRB from the start of the 1887 convention. Overconfident,
the Brotherhood tried to instal P. N. Fitzgerald as chairman. There
followed a free fight, and Scanlan and about two hundred of the
eight hundred present left the hall to set up a rival GAA. Those who
were left beat off by trickery a move to re-elect Davin as president,
then proceeded to stack the executive once again.[14] Elatedly, P. J.
Hoctor telegraphed to the Glasgow IRB leader "Victory all along the
line"; another boasted that "they were proud the priests were put
out . . . the Club was composed of Fenians, and not of rotten
Nationalists and if the priests had left long ago they would have less
trouble in organizing their men".[15]

Vainglory was premature. The IRB might control the centre; it
did not control the country and had now to reckon with a hostile
priesthood, and with Archbishop Croke. Within three weeks of the
convention, nearly 250 clubs registered their dissent and disgust
with what had happened at Thurles. On 30 November the executive
went to its Canossa at the archbishop's palace. They agreed to a
fresh, "Reconstruction", convention on 4 January 1888, again at
Thurles. There, under a new delegate system, only eighteen of the

eighty men who met can definitely be identified as members of the IRB. The elections of officers went against them — Davin became president once again, and only three of sixteen county delegates (a new set of officials designed to counter centralism) were from the IRB. Once again a choice of patron symbolized the new conformation. William O'Brien, the nationalist ally of Parnell, was invited to become the fifth patron of the GAA. Defeat for the IRB was only temporary. P. N. Fitzgerald, present at the Reconstruction Convention, had at one stage foreshadowed "that though they might be beaten, still, perhaps in twelve months or two years they might rise again".[16]

Fitzgerald's more optimistic forecast proved to be the justified one. At the next convention, held in January 1889 at Thurles, there was another walk-out of delegates again led by a priest, Father Sheehy of Limerick. Davin followed, and the IRB once more took over the GAA. As Dublin Castle commented: "We, therefore, have to deal with an Association now clearly given over to the purposes of the Irish-American revolutionary party."[17] This time there was to be no reconciliation with the Church. Already, during 1888, as the IRB sought to mend its fences and increase its influence at the local level, preparatory to once again taking over the GAA at the centre, the clergy, on their guard since the events of November 1887, began to divert their flocks away from the GAA. In the north and in Mayo there were denunciations, in Limerick there were two county boards set up, one led by the IRB man Pat O'Brien, the other by Father Sheehy. In Cork, IRB men on the county board sued a Father O'Connor for slander. He had accused them of being "informers and Castle spies and persons in the pay of the Government".[18]

Now, after January 1889, the Church turned almost wholly against the GAA. Father Sheehy had called for the abandonment of the allegiance to the Central Council, and henceforth the clergy preached against the GAA and sought to persuade clubs not to affiliate with it. The IRB was left in charge of a truncated organization. By the time the November 1889 convention came around, thirteen counties refused to acknowledge the executive and only nine sent delegates. The IRB, in an unwontedly quiet atmosphere, proceeded further to pack the executive.[19]

But they were no longer in control of all Gaelic games. During 1890 the GAA continued to grow, from 777 clubs the previous year to 820, but there were now 191 clubs run by the clergy, and a further 122 unaffiliated with the Association. The IRB still controlled 497 clubs with about forty thousand members, but there was about fourteen thousand now outside that control.[20]

The attitude of the clergy to the GAA throughout the period covered by this chapter is a complex, fascinating, and important one. Initially, the Church was energetic on the Association's behalf. After 1887 it turned against it for what it saw as the best of reasons, the preservation of young men from the dangers of premature rebellion and the wiles of *agents provocateurs*. Then, in 1891, the attitude taken up by the GAA in the Parnell split reinforced the clergy's opposition.

Elements in the GAA declared their support for Parnell even before the parliamentary party split, and when he returned to Ireland on 8 December 1890 he was met by a GAA delegation. As he waged his bitter campaign for support throughout 1891, the GAA largely supported him. This further aroused the ire of the Church, which grew more and more uncompromising in its stand and its rhetoric against Parnell. None who supported him escaped condemnation, and the GAA was no exception.[21]

In Sligo the clergy were instructed to undermine the Association from within as well as to denounce it. In Louth there was "steady resistance" by the priests. In Carlow and in Tipperary the GAA was denounced; in Kilkenny, Queen's County, and Waterford it was boycotted. In Galway and in Mayo there was a concentrated attack on the Association, in Cavan a bitter fight with the IRB. In County Cork one parish priest signalled his victory by entering Mitchelstown "on horseback bringing the youth of his Parish marshalled behind him". It was not only the parish priests who participated in the onslaught. Bishop Gillooly toured Roscommon and Mayo denouncing secret societies "in particular the members of the GAA". The Bishop of Ossory attacked the Association, and the Bishop of Achonry called it "very dangerous" and bade his clergy attend meetings in order to destroy it. The Bishop of Ardagh denounced it in a pastoral letter in April, Archdeacon O'Rorke of Sligo declared that "he would do all he could to wipe out the Gaelic Athletic Association", and the Bishop of Cavan worked to break it up in his diocese throughout the summer.[22]

Other factors operated to diminish the GAA. Fenians such as Davitt, never wholly devoted to Parnell, turned against him, and at GAA meetings in Roscommon, Galway, Kerry, Cork, and Leitrim declared against Parnell. Provincial feeling against Dublin (another continuing element in the GAA's internal politicking) played its part — the president, now P. J. Kelly of Galway, refused to turn up at a meeting in December 1891 because "the Dublin Gaels" desired to "control the Association from there".[23]

Even so, the active hostility of the Church was the greatest single factor in causing the decline of the GAA before and during 1891. It has been argued that the Parnell split maimed much of Irish life: it very nearly killed the GAA. By 1891 the authorities could count only 339 clubs left, 66 of them run by clergy. Membership had fallen to under sixteen thousand. The evidence of the 1891 convention, not held until January 1892, told a worse story. Only six counties sent delegates, and the executive reported only 220 clubs affiliated. Things were to get worse before they got better; in 1893 only three counties — Dublin, Cork, and Kerry — sent delegates. Diminished and debt-ridden, the GAA seemed doomed.

One thing is abundantly clear. The survival, followed by the revival, of the GAA was wholly due to the Irish Republican Brotherhood. It was they who officered the Association throughout the 1890s, then brought about the surge of growth that began about the turn of the century. Throughout the country there were doubtless many persons, both clerical and lay, with an interest in Gaelic games, but it was the IRB alone that was devoted, not entirely selflessly perhaps, to the maintenance of a national organization, however weak, debt-ridden, even pathetic it appeared for many years. At least six of the members of the Central Committee, as it was now called, elected in 1893 were of the IRB, and in 1894 as the Association revived in counties where it had long been dormant, in the eight that held county conventions seven elected presidents who were IRB men. In 1895, with revival well under way, assisted by a public message of support from Croke, the IRB maintained its hold and, what is more, kept the football and hurling championships going, together with the athletics meetings. Admittedly the championships did not attract many teams and ran at least a year behind, but the flag was kept flying, despite the continuing hostility of the Church, apart from Croke, whose support was in any case adversely received by many other churchmen.[24]

The IRB's motives may have been open to question — indeed, Dublin Castle had no doubts at all as to what the Brotherhood was up to — but some credit must be given men such as Frank Dineen, an athlete himself, for a devotion to the Gaelic games themselves.[25] But on balance secret society concerns prevailed, as one episode in the 1890s revival of the GAA showed.

The American wing of the Irish revolutionary movement, Clan na Gael, had split early in the 1890s, partly over personalities, partly over policies. The breakaway group, the Irish National Alliance (or Brotherhood), sought to gain support within the IRB, precipitating a power struggle that necessarily involved the GAA. For about five years, 1896 to 1900, the Association's recovery was virtually at a standstill while its erstwhile and potential leaders, men like Figzgerald, Hoctor, Dineen, and Tobin, fought obscurely to ally the IRB with "the new movement" or to preserve it as "the old IRB". Club and membership figures tell the story. In 1895 the GAA grew rapidly. The number of clubs increased from 173 to 244, the active membership, both "clerical" and "Fenian", from 3,400 to over 4,000. In 1896 this growth continued, to 343 clubs and over 7,500 active members, the increase being almost totally "Fenian". At this point growth halted. In 1898 the figures were 356 and 7,000; in 1899, 303 and 8,100; in 1900, 311 and 7,100. In 1900 the two rival American organizations came to terms. The effect on the GAA was remarkable: 411 clubs and 10,727 active members by the close of 1901.[26]

The almost subservient place of the GAA in the wider context of the Irish nationalist movement was once again demonstrated by the effects of the IRB-INB struggle, just as it had been in the late 1880s and at the time of the Parnell split. The GAA was almost a puppet. Fashioned and controlled by Irish nationalism, it was for a long time at the mercy of what happened to the factional forces who pulled the strings.

Neither Church support, nor the impact of those who did not fear to speak of '98, nor the oft-expressed intention of the revolutionary movement to "work up" the GAA had more than a limited effect by the close of the century. Yet within five years the GAA was on the march again. Its debts that had lingered since the late 1880s were paid off, unprecedentedly large crowds attended its matches, an increasingly discriminatory Ban was vigorously enforced, and parishes and counties where Gaelic games had long languished now had teams and committees. Within ten years the GAA was both prosperous and powerful, and Gaelic football was probably the most popular game in the country. The Association had a headquarters ground, soon to be purchased and renamed Croke Park. By 1914 the GAA could claim to be the single most important institution (outside the Church) in the country, its place in Irish life and Irish nationalism assured.

How had the transformation been achieved? In brief, the old leadership, the Fitzgeralds, the Dineens, the Hoctors, and the Tobins, were swept away. A new wave of nationalists, still of the IRB (now reunited) but younger and more able, equally intense but, on the evidence, more flexible in furthering their purposes, took over. Just as the IRB at large benefited from the coming of such men as Tom Clarke and Bulmer Hobson, the GAA prospered under J. Nowlan of Kilkenny, L. J. O'Toole of Dublin, J. P. O'Sullivan of

Kerry, and J. J. Walsh of Cork. These men were dedicated politicians and revolutionaries: they were also devoted to Gaelic games for their own as well as for nationalism's sake. Under their control the GAA at last began to make contact with the mainstream of the games revolution that was affecting the whole European and imperial world at this time. On the continent, in the United States, in South America, in Australia, New Zealand, South Africa, and India, mass-spectator team games, principally varieties of football, were becoming part of the entertainment industry of capitalist society, an integral part of the social fabric.

At the beginning of the twentieth century the magic of this transformation had left Ireland virtually untouched. The moment when Irish games became genuinely popular, rather than an almost antiquarian exercise in Irishry or an adjunct of revolutionary nationalism, can be almost precisely dated. Between 23 July and 13 October 1905 Kerry and Kildare played three games to decide the 1903 (such were still the arrears) Gaelic football championship. The games were universally agreed to have been the finest, and "the most sensational played" since the inception of the GAA.[31]

So far we have neglected the purely athletic aspects of the GAA, concentrating on its political history. This has been excusable, for it is arguable that until 1905 the GAA was principally a nationalist, indeed an extreme nationalist, organization that played its games and ran its meetings largely as a nationalist exercise. From 1905 onwards the sporting wing of the GAA marches more equally with the political. The nationalist allegiance of its leaders, particularly of the Central Council, is not in doubt, but more and more, as report after report of even the hypersensitive Castle authorities indicates, the GAA grows because of an interest in sport.[32] To attempt to explain why a game becomes popular is to try to answer the riddle of the Sphinx — why rugby in Wales, why gridiron in America, why Australian rules in Melbourne? To attempt the task with regard to Irish games, particularly Gaelic football, we need to retrace our steps a little and look at the development of the style and technique of the game from the start.

In this particular struggle, that of IRB versus INB, athletic considerations took second place to political ones as leading men of the GAA took sides. Dineen, president since 1895, was active on behalf of the INB, so was P. J. Hoctor, so was Pat Tobin of Dublin, the GAA's secretary. J. K. Bracken, one of the founding fathers, cast his lot in with the new movement, lavishly financed as it was from America via Paris and the two Dr Ryans. By the close of 1896 the INB seemed to be in control of a majority of county committees, and at the centre, R. T. Blake, who had succeeded Tobin, was virtually dismissed from his post, ostensibly on grounds of incompetence (shades of Michael Cusack), in reality because he had objected to Dineen's and Tobin's work on behalf of the INB.[27] The equivocal P. N. Fitzgerald was active on the other side, although rumours arose from time to time that he had joined or was about to join the INB. The weight of evidence suggests that he remained loyal to the old IRB (or perhaps to paymasters in the Castle?). Certainly he played a prominent part in helping organize the '98 Centenary Committee, dedicated to celebrating the 1798 Wolfe Tone rebellion.[28] This was very much an IRB affair; thousands of GAA men came to Dublin for the 15 August 1898 march, but the turnout was limited by the fact that the INB, and hence considerable sections of the GAA, were not fully in accord with the organizers. The GAA did not gain as much as it might have expected from so potent a celebratory event; it remained heavily in debt, its football and hurling championships still hopelessly in arrears, its membership virtually static.[29]

The revival that had taken place from 1894 onwards had come to a halt. Not even the declared support of the ageing, semi-retired Croke made much difference beyond an initial impact. Faced with continuing clerical hostility — the Bishop of Kerry denounced the Association in April 1895 for its secret society connections — a deputation stacked with IRB and INB men waited upon Croke, now sixty-two, at Thurles. To the surprise of the deputation, Croke declared that he was "totally unaware" of any secret society connection with the GAA; as far as he knew it was "a purely athletic body and that alone". A few days later the GAA published its new constitution, article 2 of which declared that the Association "shall be strictly non-political and unsectarian. . . . No political questions of any kind shall be raised at any of its meetings." One may be pardoned for suggesting that for much of its future life the GAA was acting in breach of its own constitution.[30]

Neither Church support, nor the impact of those who did not fear to speak of '98, nor the oft-expressed intention of the revolutionary movement to "work up" the GAA had more than a limited effect by the close of the century. Yet within five years the GAA was on the march again. Its debts that had lingered since the late 1880s were paid off, unprecedentedly large crowds attended its matches, an increasingly discriminatory Ban was vigorously enforced, and parishes and counties where Gaelic games had long languished now had teams and committees. Within ten years the GAA was both prosperous and powerful, and Gaelic football was probably the most popular game in the country. The Association had a headquarters ground, soon to be purchased and renamed Croke Park. By 1914 the GAA could claim to be the single most important institution (outside the Church) in the country, its place in Irish life and Irish nationalism assured. How had the transformation been achieved? In brief, the old leadership, the Fitzgeralds, the Dineens, the Hoctors, and the Tobins, were swept away. A new wave of nationalists, still of the IRB (now reunited) but younger and more able, equally intense but, on the evidence, more flexible in furthering their purposes, took over. Just as the IRB at large benefited from the coming of such men as Tom Clarke and Bulmer Hobson, the GAA prospered under J. Nowlan of Kilkenny, L. J. O'Toole of Dublin, J. P. O'Sullivan of Kerry, and J. J. Walsh of Cork. These men were dedicated politicians and revolutionaries: they were also devoted to Gaelic games for their own as well as for nationalism's sake. Under their control the GAA at last began to make contact with the mainstream of the games revolution that was affecting the whole European and imperial world at this time. On the continent, in the United States, in South America, in Australia, New Zealand, South Africa, and India, mass-spectator team games, principally varieties of football, were becoming part of the entertainment industry of capitalist society, an integral part of the social fabric.

At the beginning of the twentieth century the magic of this transformation had left Ireland virtually untouched. The moment when Irish games became genuinely popular, rather than an almost antiquarian exercise in Irishry or an adjunct of revolutionary nationalism, can be almost precisely dated. Between 23 July and 13 October 1905 Kerry and Kildare played three games to decide the 1903 (such were still the arrears) Gaelic football championship. The games were universally agreed to have been the finest, and "the most sensational played" since the inception of the GAA.[31]

So far we have neglected the purely athletic aspects of the GAA, concentrating on its political history. This has been excusable, for it is arguable that until 1905 the GAA was principally a nationalist, indeed an extreme nationalist, organization that played its games and ran its meetings largely as a nationalist exercise. From 1905 onwards the sporting wing of the GAA marches more equally with the political. The nationalist allegiance of its leaders, particularly of the Central Council, is not in doubt, but more and more, as report after report of even the hypersensitive Castle authorities indicates, the GAA grows because of an interest in sport.[32] To attempt to explain why a game becomes popular is to try to answer the riddle of the Sphinx — why rugby in Wales, why gridiron in America, why Australian rules in Melbourne? To attempt the task with regard to Irish games, particularly Gaelic football, we need to retrace our steps a little and look at the development of the style and technique of the game from the start.

Like all the games of football that became codified in the second half of the nineteenth century, Gaelic football had its origins in rough-and-tumble folk football played in previous centuries. The Irish version was called *caid* and involved the customary mauls and brawls in fields or across country. Michael Cusack's codification, owing much to Maurice Davin, was published in 1885. Often accused of being a bastardized amalgam of the already long-codified soccer and rugby games, it is possible that such bastardization as there was occurred deliberately, because Cusack wished to distinguish his game from the other codes. He was particularly anxious to emphasize differences from rugby, regarded, in Dublin at least, as the greater Anglicizing threat.[33] Hence perhaps the strict controls over running with the ball, and the ban on picking it up directly from the ground, also the provision that it might be punched forward. The linear nature of rugby was avoided by an absence of an offside rule (as in Australian rules), and scoring depended solely upon getting the ball into a confined space, not merely across a line. Similarly, the use of the hands, no offside rule, and the provision of "near miss" point posts showed the game to be different from soccer. In its early days Gaelic football was hardly a spectacle of sophisticated elegance. "Follie the ball, man, follie the ball!" was one cry as packs of players surged up and down the field of play, pairs of them being allowed, until 1886, to indulge in individual wrestling bouts, called handigrips, while the rest chased the ball. With time came greater sophistication, aimed at opening up the game, which in turn ensured that spectators might enjoy the contests as much as the players. This has been the crucial factor in the stylistic development of the various football codes as mass entertainment sports.

As early as the 1890s Dublin teams had abandoned the maul, the forearm hit, and the chase in favour of "kick and catch" — a style familiar to all Australian rules followers. To this, Kildare sides added, towards the turn of the century, the overhead forward or lateral hand pass, thus opening the game up and adding to its fluidity at the same time.

The static kick-and-catch technique was further modified by Kerry sides early in the century with the catching player swinging clear, then playing on swiftly. All these developments made Gaelic football a faster, more open, and consequently more exciting and attractive spectator sport. So did successive alterations of the rules that gradually cut the number of players down to fifteen, abolished point posts in favour of an under-and-over-the-bar form of scoring, and by the introduction of "the parallelogram", which cleared the area near goal of "whips" who hung around near the goal-keeper to harass him. Not all innovations in this nationalist game found favour. The Louth and Antrim sides of the early 1910s were criticized for their short ground foot passing, in soccer style, and there were those who rejoiced in their defeat by traditionalist Kerry.[34]

Within the first decade of this century Gaelic football emerged as an attractive game for spectators which began to make such demands upon its players that teams, though strictly amateur, now went in for regular training. Publicity responded to and fostered the changes: sports pages devoted more space to the game; sports papers were founded.[35] Heroes and stars emerged, a folklore of goals scored or missed was built up, a tradition of great games was shaped. The public responded and the GAA grew, both as spectator and participant sport.

Hurling was similarly affected. Its Irish historical tradition was much stronger than football's, especially in areas of the south and west. To some "licensed savagery", to Cusack a great art, hurling was uniquely Irish and celebrated as such.[36] It failed to attain the popularity, nationally and in Dublin, that football achieved, but it benefited from the reduction of the number of players, the narrowing of the scoring area, and from the development of concepts of positional play. To many still the greater of the two Irish codes, hurling suffered as most games using a weapon suffer, even cricket, from the distancing that occurs by its use. Direct hand, foot, head and body contact with the ball has proved to have greater appeal.

Another factor that helped the GAA was its comparative abandonment of interest in athletics. Meetings continued to be held, but the diminishing appeal of regular contests, renewed difficulties with the IAAA, and the increasing concentration by the GAA's leaders upon team sports led to Gaelic athletics falling into decline.

The GAA's new leaders, partly by choice, partly by necessity, found themselves more and more concerned with the adminis-tration of a growing prospering institution. From 1905, income was beginning to run into thousands of pounds.[37] Elaborate and spectacularly successful tournaments such as the Croke Memorial of 1912 – had to be organized. Regular championships, which for most of the GAA's history had run one or two years in arrears and were subject to perpetual dispute, were at last brought into line, were given specified dates for completion, and though still subject to occasional storms, ran smoothly and efficiently. In 1912 the GAA was given the chance to buy its own ground. As a consequence it had to become a limited liability company.[38] Croke Park now needed stands and facilities, groundsmen and officials, hence more money and more management. Institutionalization and respectability (in this respect at least) were now complete. Success had made of the GAA a sports body at last, and a wealthy and popular one. Its success was based to a significant extent upon the appeal of the games it fostered, an appeal that though it might overlap and be linked to nationalism, was just as much the appeal of increasingly attractive games.

But the national purpose was not neglected. At two levels, that of IRB domination of its executive and that of opposition to the Anglo-Saxon games of the garrison, the GAA maintained its nationalism, even, in the case of the Ban, intensified it. That the IRB began, as soon as the dispute with the INB was over, to concentrate on developing the GAA is, on the evidence, incontrovertible. Equally incontrovertible is the fact that the IRB continued to dominate office-holding at both central and local levels. The major difference between the 1900s and the 1880s was that the IRB was dealing with a larger, more popular, and more successful Association, and that it was more circumspect.

Dublin Castle picked up the intentions of the IRB very early. It noted in December 1899: "If any serious attempt is made to re-organize the IRB, it is in the GA Association the earliest indications will be noticed." By July 1900 it noted that "important things were afoot" — the IRB had formed a GAA county board in Kerry under Michael Moynihan and there was activity in many areas, including Wicklow, Galway, Wexford, and King's County. At the annual convention in September 1900 "the extreme party dominated proceedings" and Major Gosselin heard rumours of a great new IRB organization using sporting and literary societies to further its political ends.[39]

By 1901 the scheme was well under way; at least as far as the GAA was concerned, it was receiving "the active support of the extreme members of the IRB who evidently regard[ed] this association as excellent seditious training, as a means of interfering with recruiting for the British Army, and as an organization which [would] swell the ranks of the IRB". Despite the lingering opposition of certain clergy, especially in the North, the GAA grew, and in September 1901 Nowlan became the new president, attending immediately afterwards a secret IRB meeting. By 1902 the Castle was convinced that the GAA was "only a name for a huge Fenian movement".[40] IRB organizers, itinerant like Frank Dorr in the West, or locally static like Stanley in Outh, Keeshan in Tipperary, Cosgrave in Wexford, Keane in Galway, Purcell in Kilkenny, and many others, worked to expand the GAA. The effort was apparently financed from the American Clan na Gael.[41]

By the time the GAA attained prosperity, the IRB had consolidated its hold. Every key official was an IRB man, and the Brotherhood dominated the provincial councils and the majority of county boards. Where moderates tried to hold out, as in Cork, IRB coups, led in that county by J. J. Walsh, ousted them.[42] It is true that in some areas the clergy held high office, as in Leix, Offaly, and Carlow, but this was perhaps as much a measure of the IRB's new-found skill as a representation of the realities of control.

The IRB's circumspection extended to practising swearing-in recruits to the Brotherhood only sparingly. Leading clergymen — Croke's successor Archbishop Fennelly, Archbishop Walsh of Dublin in 1903, and the Bishop of Dovin in 1916 — were induced to praise and support the GAA. The kind of clerical hostility incurred in the 1890s was avoided by moderation in furthering the more extreme ends of the Brotherhood and concentration on fulfilling the role envisaged in article 2 of its amended 1873 constitution, viz.: "The IRB whilst labouring to prepare Ireland for the task of recovering her independence by force of arms, shall confine itself in time of peace to the exercise of moral influences — the cultivation of union and brotherly love amongst Irishmen, the propagation of republican principles and the spreading of a knowledge of the national rights of Ireland."[43] That, and the dilution of influence engendered by the sports-based success of the Association, might blind some to the fact that the IRB was still very much in charge, as much as it had been at any previous time. There was not a man who meant anything in the organization of the GAA who was not of the Brotherhood. Nowlan the president, O'Toole the secretary, O'Sullivan who as auditor helped transform the finances of the IRB, and Walsh of Cork have already been mentioned; it is worth noting that Walsh was sentenced to death (commuted to ten years penal servitude) on 4 May 1916 for his part in the Rising and Nowlan was sent to Wakefield prison on 13 May.[34] Among the six vice-presidents in 1915 – 16 were IRB men J. Keene, J. Whelan, and the very extremist Thomas Kenny of Galway. Other names of IRB men, including Dan Fraher and Michael Crowe, the treasurers, are scattered through lists of officials. That the IRB recruited among the GAA is undoubted — Thomas Ashe, Austin Stack, Diarmud Lynch, and Michael Collins were among those who came to the IRB by way of the GAA, and when first the Irish Volunteers and then the Rising occurred, the IRB knew where its fighting men might be found.

In the 1900s such things lay in the future. The immediate task was to strengthen the GAA and receive a fiercer spirit of cultural nationalism among the Irish people. The most notable public manifestation of this policy was the increasing ferocity of the Ban. The concept of the Ban, had sprung from a desire to prevent any playing of foreign games by Irishmen. A great risk was taken: to penalize whose who chose to play both an Irish and a foreign game was to take the chance that the players would abandon the Irish game. Despite this, the Association went ahead. Within four months of its foundation in January 1885, it had imposed a ban on athletes competing under other rules. In February 1886 it forbade its football and hurling clubs to play against those not abiding by Gaelic rules. In September 1886 persons playing non-Gaelic games were declared ineligible for membership of GAA clubs, a decision that later in the year became rule 12 of the Association. The Ban became more specifically political when it excluded members of the Royal Irish Constabulary from membership in February 1887, although soldiers and sailors still remained eligible. Even the Reconstruction Convention of January 1888 decided to maintain the Ban on the RIC (extending it, reasonably enough, to members of the Dublin Metropolitan Police, but still admitting servicemen).[45]

The desperate straits the Association found itself in during the 1890s were illustrated by the virtual abandonment of the Ban in 1893 as it applied to policemen and in September 1896 as it applied to the playing of other games — on the grounds, significantly enough, that rule 2 of the new 1895 constitution declared the GAA to be "strictly non-political".[46]

In 1899 there were signs that attitudes were again hardening. A London Board decision to refuse affiliation to a Royal Irish Fusiliers club was endorsed on the grounds "that none but men of disreputable character were in the army, and the Irishmen who took the Saxon shilling forfeited his claim to Irish nationality".[47] At the 1900 annual convention, Cusack spoke out against police bands playing at GAA tournaments, and Thomas O'Sullivan made the first of his many fiery speeches on Irish nationalism.

O'Sullivan was a Kerryman of Fenian stock, a member of the IRB, a journalist and an intense nationalist, much in demand for speeches at Manchester Martyrs memorial meetings. The new wave takeover of the GAA in 1901 swept O'Sullivan to power and influence. At the 1901 convention he had one motion passed dissociating the GAA from police sports, and one that called upon the Association "to resist by every means in their power the extension of English pastimes to this country". The following year any member who played "Rugby or Association football, hockey, or any imported game" was rendered liable to suspension, and in 1903 police, soldiers, and sailors were banned from playing Gaelic games. Cork fought hard to keep discretionary power in the hands of the county committees but at the 1906 convention was soundly defeated, whereupon, with some sarcasm, one of its delegates moved that all British government employees, including postmen and schoolteachers, should also be banned. His motion was rejected forty seven to fifteen.[48] Cork made one last bid, in 1908, to declare that the Ban was contrary to the "non-political" rule: it lost seventy to nineteen. By 1910 the Ban was complete, extended even to jail wardens in 1909, and it lasted another sixty years.[49] The GAA was aware of what it was doing; its 1907-8 *Annual* stated that the Ban had "done more to make the name of the English garrison obnoxious to hundreds of young Irishmen than all the speech-making and literature conceivable could possibly effect".[50]

To the Ban, the GAA added a continuing anti-recruiting campaign, from the time of the Boer War onwards, and support for Irish industries. No opportunity was lost to attack West Britishism, or to sneer at soccer and rugby and cricket, or to claim that, for instance, tennis was a Celtic game of great antiquity.[51] The Ban and its concomitant manifestations of nationalism may have had their frenetic, even comic, side, but the Ban was both effective and successful. The GAA took on the social and cultural big battalions of the garrison, supported as they were by the press, and to do it credit, won, largely because the stand taken was, once Cork's objections had been disposed of, so determined. The choice and the penalties were made clear; so were the reasons for them. Those who chose Gaelic games knew what they were committed to, both in terms of sport and in terms of nationalism, not necessarily to the Brotherhood, but certainly to "Irish Ireland".

> Each foreign game, we now disdain
> Golf, cricket, and ping pong
> Rugby and soccer in our midst
> Have flourished far too long
> So true to name, each Irish game
> We'll pride in, and we'll play
> In bold young Ireland — Irish Ireland
> Ireland, boys, hurrah.[52]

The Home Rule crisis of 1912 gave the GAA, at last, a quasi-respectable chance to exchange, as it had long desired, its camans for rifles. The Irish Volunteers, founded in November 1913, were readily supported by the GAA. It refused, on the grounds of its non-political nature, to declare its support officially, although some urged it to do so, but at club and county level the connection was very close, as Dublin Castle anticipated. The *Gaelic Athlete* suggested how the volunteers should be helped: "Teams . . . should be allowed to form companies subject and under the control of the Executive of the Volunteer movement. Both the Executive of the Dublin GAA and the Executive of the Volunteer movement should come to some understanding on this point." On 14 December 1913 it seems that they did. An informal conference took place in Dublin at which it was declared: "It is hoped that Gaels living in districts where Volunteer corps have not yet been inaugurated will take steps to institute a branch of the organization."[53] The response was immediate and widespread. In Limerick the GAA began forming Volunteer branches in December. The Wexford annual convention accepted Nowlan's recommendation that "every member, as an individual" join the Volunteers "to learn to shoot straight". At Tuam the Star Football Club ruled: "Every member . . . shall be a member of the Tuam Volunteer Corps, attend its drills and bear arms in pursuance of its objects".[54] The Galway County Board declared its support, and five Athlone football clubs formed companies of Volunteers; the same thing happened in Derry, Mountmellick, and Rathmolyon. In Cork J.J. Walsh was active on behalf of the Volunteers, so was Roche in Limerick, P. J. Cullinane in West Cork, and the whole GAA in County Waterford.[55]

The GAA's 1914 annual convention refused to commit itself to the Volunteers, but Robert Page's address on their behalf, in which he claimed that they had "everything in common with the GAA" and urged delegates to go back and "earnestly exhort the clubs they represented to organise, and help in the arming and drilling movement", was "received with acclamation".[56]

The majority of GAA members who joined the Volunteers had no doubt as to where their loyalties lay when shortly after the outbreak of war the movement split into the pro-Redmondite National Volunteers (the vast majority) and the Irish Volunteers. Such were the close links between Volunteers and Association that those in the Volunteers who wished to show their allegiance to Redmond decided to form a rival GAA, the National Gaelic Athletic Association, in 1915 in order to gain recruits for their cause.

Many countries came to identify their sport with their national self-images — New Zealanders with their All Blacks, South Africa with their Springboks, Englishmen and Australians with the cricketers, and so on. The sport came first, and though it sprang from and was coloured by the society that nurtured it, that society came only gradually to discern in what ways the particular sport acted as an exemplar of the society's professed national virtues. The case of Ireland and the GAA is subtly different. Irish Nationalists chose to use sport as a vehicle for spreading nationalism, creating and re-creating games in order to further their cause. This is not to say that there was not a long-standing tradition behind Irish games, but, as with the Irish language, the tradition was dormant, and the practice in an advanced state of decay.

The GAA from the start was anti-British and Irish nationalist. Its founders saw in reviving Irish games a method whereby the British might be attacked, initially at the cultural level, although the prospect of physical usefulness to the cause was never far away. The special role of the IRB in the founding and furthering of the Association tended to make of the GAA even less of a purely natural outgrowth of Irish society.

At no stage (apart from some months in 1888) did the IRB relinquish control of the GAA. Thoughout, the majority of its central officials were members of the Brotherhood; throughout, with varying degrees of success, they used the GAA to further their aims. By the 1910s the popularity of the games they fostered had to some extent overtaken the IRB's power to control them, but Nowlan, O'Toole, Crowe, and Fraher maintained their position at the top, and a host of officials throughout the county were also men of the IRB. The GAA provided, as it was always intended to provide, the muscle for the Easter Rising of 1916.

The extent of the GAA's participation in the Rising has received much scattered comment, not least on the part of the authorities. By matching lists of those taking part and those arrested with lists of GAA teams and committees, it may be possible to determine more precisely the Association's involvement. Suffice it to say that it is unlikely that the IRB, which precipitated the Rising, would have neglected to use the influence it had over the GAA, whose own very history was in large part but a preparation for 1916. As one authority has already noted, the model for the Brotherhood's later infiltrations of the Gaelic League, the Volunteer Movement, and Sinn Fein was its infiltration of the GAA. As a case study in the use of a front organization, the history of the GAA warrants attention.

It has further claims to the historian's interest. Conor Cruise

O'Brien many years ago pointed out its place in the history of the Irish national revival, but such is the blind eye that most historians turn to sport and other manifestations of popular culture that no one followed up his hint. Even O'Brien's history of the IRB pays scant attention to one of its greatest success stories; indeed, he can write that by 1916 "after more than half a century of existence, the IRB had achieved no practical result whatever".[57] The power and the nature of the GAA shows this was not so.

Study of the GAA also adds to our knowledge of the nature of the Church's relationship with Irish nationalism. The hostility to the movement that emerged, with what the Church thought were good reasons, so soon after the Association's foundation was succeeded by wary support of its nationalist, if not its revolutionary, aspirations. It is probable that the patronage of the archdiocese of Cashel and the good wishes of Archbishop Walsh of Dublin came more easily to a GAA that in the twentieth century owed its success increasingly to its sporting appeal, but there is some evidence that certain parish priests were, by 1916, not far removed in nationalist fervour from members of the Brotherhood itself.[58] The GAA prospered most readily when the Church stood at its side, and this formed another reason for its growth in the early years of the century.

The study of the GAA might throw light upon other aspects of Irish life before independence. For instance, to what extent was county loyalty engendered by the GAA? It would be ironic if the GAA was a factor, for there was criticism of the irrational English-determined boundaries of the counties. Again, what was the effect of the travel and meeting of Irishmen from far distant areas? The IRB knew its worth, but what of the Kerryman who might not otherwise ever have visited Dublin save on a special GAA cheap excursion train? How influential in developing a sense of difference between "Gael" and "garrison" was the GAA's propaganda and the increasing starkness of its Ban? A cultural effect greater than that of the Gaelic League? What too were the relationships between League and Athletic Association? Many belonged to both; both appealed to similar sentiments, perhaps at different cultural levels.

Professor O'Farrell, in his comments upon this chapter, has indicated other areas of Irish life where questions suggested by the growth of the GAA might be asked. The GAA was intended to be so much a part of the Irish nationalist movement, one might even say part of the Catholic nationalist movement, that it is impossible to separate it out as a purely sporting organization. It is also in-advisable, as this chapter has demonstrated, to neglect study of the

GAA if one wishes fully to understand the full nature of Irish nationalism in the past century.

A NOTE ON SOURCES

It is one of the hazards of secret and semi-secret societies that their histories must often be told from the files of their enemies. The GAA and its mentor the IRB are no exception. I am conscious of the dangers involved in using Castle records for an Irish revolutionary organization, but often there is nothing else. Father Mark Tierney and T. Desmond Williams have both testified to the usefulness and accuracy of police reports in the period, in the *Irish Press* of 21 April 1967n and in *Secret Societies in Ireland* (Dublin: Gill and Macmillan, 1973), p. 5. Where it has been possible to check, in memoirs, or in the jargon of nationalist rhetoric, the attribution of IRB membership has proved to be correct. Unfortunately, after about 1908, police reports grow less useful. Sir Antony MacDonnell, under-secretary from 1901, grew dis-illusioned with the efforts of Crime Branch Special, see PRO CO 904/11 November 1907 and 15 May 1908. His officers seem thereupon to have ceased the meticulous work of previous years. Dr Hazlehurst has also suggested to me that, after 1912, military intelligence files not yet released, or even acknowledged to exist, might contain information that is certainly not in police files proper. In any case, research is hampered by the fact that, through accident or design, many of the records supposed to be in police files, particularly in the PRO, are missing.

NOTES

I am indebted to the Australian Research Grants Committee for its assistance, and to Professor Oliver MacDonagh for advice and encouragement. Barbara Gow assisted in the newspaper research for this paper. A special word of thanks is due to the staff of the State Paper Office, Dublin Castle, who, despite working in difficult conditions are the most helpful I have ever encountered.
The following notes have been edited. Interested readers may consult the full set of references in the author's possession.

1. The first suggestion appears to have come from Maurice Davin in October 1877 (*Irish Sportsman*, 27 October 1877).
2. The eight were Cusack, Maurice Davin, John Wyse Power, John McKay, J. K. Bracken, P. J. Ryan, St. George McCarthy, and F. R. Moloney. Wyse Power was a Dublin journalist and an "extreme" nationalist until the mid-1890s'; see State Paper Office, Dublin Castle (henceforth SPO), Crime Branch Special (henceforth CBS) file 11207/S, and Public Record Office, London (henceforth PRO), CO 904/18/856. McKay was a Cork journalist, soon to leave the Association; see R. Smith, *Decades of Glory* (Dublin: 1966); p.15. Bracken was a prominent IRB man; see SPO CBS 12844/S and Andrew Boyle, *Poor Dear Brendan* (London: Hutchinson, 1974), pp.19-20. Ryan was a young local solicitor, see GAA, *Sixty Glorious Years of the G.A.A.* (Dublin: 1947), p.10. McCarthy was a Royal Irish Constabulary constable from Templemore, Bracken's home town, who not surprisingly took no further part in the Association, see *Sixty Glorious Years*. For Moloney, see SPO CBS 126/S, Return of Advanced IRBs and FBs (Fenian Brothers) who attended Thurles GAA Convention BC (henceforth Return of Advanced IRBs).

3. The Irish Republican Brotherhood, an oath-bound secret society dedicated to the creation by education and revolution of an independent Irish republic, was founded by James Stephens in 1858. For its history, see Leon O'Broin, *Revolutionary Underground* (Dublin: Gill and Macmillan, 1976).
4. Quoted in *Croke of Cashel*, by Mark Tierney (Dublin: Gill and Macmillan, 1976), p.195.
5. *United Ireland*, 19 September 1891, traced Gaelic games back to the third century B. C.
6. *United Ireland*, 24 January 1885.
7. T. S. O'Sullivan Papers, National Library of Ireland (henceforth NLI) MS 15385; *United Ireland*, 30 May, 13 and 27 June 1885.
8. *United Ireland*, 11 July 1885; *Freeman's Journal*, 6 August 1885. The number of clubs is unknown, but there were sixty-eight affiliated clubs by March 1886; my article "The IRB and the Origins of the Gaelic Athletic Association" forthcoming (1978) in *Irish Historical Studies* gives a more detailed account and documentation of episode.
9. *Freeman's Journal*, 30 September 1886.
10. F. B. Dineen was the IRB man, county centre for East Limerick. He was speaking to Constable O'Reilly, whose report is dated 11 November 1887 in SPO CBS 126/S.
11. The quotation is from a cutting from the GAA SPO CBS 126/S. All issues of *The Gael* seem to have disappeared.
12. Quoted in *Story of the G. A. A.* by T. W. O'Sullivan (Dublin: 1916), p.46.
13. *Freeman's Journal*, 10, 17, 24, and 31 October 1887; see accusations regarding non-existent clubs in ibid., 29 November 1887; regarding delegate impersonation, ibid., 17 November 1887; and regarding proxy delegates, ibid., 19 November 1887; Inspector Bourchier to Captain Slacke, 5 December 1887, reporting information from informer "Bendigo" and report of Inspector Jones, 9 December 1887, both in SPO CBS 126/S.
14. Reports of the convention are drawn from *Freeman's Journal*, 10 November 1887, and police reports contained in SPO CBS 126/S.
15. Bourchier to Slacke, 5 December and 14 November 1887, in SPO CBS R6/S.
16. *Freeman's Journal*, 5 January 1888.
17. PRO CO 903/2.
18. For the north, see SPO CBS Secret Societies Reports, Belfast, March, November, and December 1888. For Mayo, see ibid., Western Division, December 1888. For Limerick, see SPO Chief Secretary's Office Registered Papers 1888/12260; *Cork Examiner*, 19 November 1888. 20 and 21 March 1889.
19. *Freeman's Journal*, 23 October and 7 November 1889.
20. These figures are obtained from a conflation of information contained in PRO CO 904/16 and SPO CBS 296/S.
21. *Freeman's Journal* 2, 4, 5, and 8 December 1890 for meetings of clubs and their resolutions in favour of Parnell; the president of the GAA, P. J. Kelly, declared in May that "the Gaels and the Hillside men would stand or fall by Parnell"; see SPO CBS Secret Societies Report, Western, May 1891.
22. SPO CBS Secret Societies Report, Midland, December 1890 and January 1891; for Louth, see SPO CBS 2701/S, for the others SPO CBS 2786/S; for Galway, Mayo, and Cavan, see SPO CBS Secret Societies Report, Western, April and May 1891; and for Cork, ibid., South West, November 1891; for Gilhooly, see ibid., West, May and June 1891; for Ossory, ibid., South East, February 1891; for Achonry, ibid., Midland, January 1891; for Ardagh, O'Rorke, and Cavan, ibid., April, May, and August 1891.

23. F. S. L. Lyons, *The Fall of Parnell* (London: Routledge and Kegan Paul, 1960), pp.78-79; SPO CBS Secret Societies Report, Western, November 1891.

24. SPO Divisional Commissioners Reports (henceforth DCR), Western, April 1895; "a large number of Priests differ with [sic] the Archbishop's opinion".

25. See, e.g., SPO CBS Monthly Report, Western, January and May 1894, South Eastern, October 1892 and April 1893, Home Office Precis on Secret Societies (henceforth HO SS), 1 May 1895, where the statement "the society is to be used as a recruiting ground for the I. R. B." sums up the whole Castle attitude.

26. Figures derived from SPO CBS 26268/S.

27. HO SS, 11 October 1896, reporting that most county officials supported the INB.

28. There is a very full account of the '98 Centenary Movement, to early in 1898, in SPO Intelligence Notes, Miscellaneous Notes B XXVIII, February 1898, pp.1-56. For Fitzgerald, see esp. pp.1, 7-8, 9, 25-28.

29. In 1901 the GAA was still at least £800 in debt, and still owed Davitt £450. The 1901 convention decided that the GAA had "a moral obligation" to pay off all debts, including those incurred before 1894 which had been repudiated in 1895 (O'Sullivan, *Story of the G. A. A.*, pp.148-49). The 1896 championships were not played off until February 1898, and not until 1912 did they come fully into line (*Sport* [Dublin] 13 November 1915).

30. Tierney, *Croke of Caskel*, p.259; SPO CBS 9854/S, and 9888/S; *Cork Examiner*, 22 April 1895; a copy of the 1895 constitution is in SPO CBS 9914/S.

31. O'Sullivan, *Story of the G. A. A.*, p.158; *GAA Annual and County Directory* 1910-11, pp.14-15.

32. SPO, The Inspector General's Monthly Confidential Reports (henceforth MCR) are particularly full of such opinions, of which the following of Kilkenny in July 1905 may serve as fully representative: "The GAA comprises, it might be said, the bone and sinew of the country . . . . It is non-political, and while many of its members are I. R. B. . . . they confine their attention to sport and athletics." See also, e.g., PRO CO 904/11, February 1905.

33. "Carbery" [P. D. Mehigan], *Gaelic Football* (Dublin: 1941), pp.145-51; S. P. O'Ceallaigh, *History of the Limerick G. A. A.* (Tralee: 1937), p.32, for bastardization, see, e.g., John Arlott, *The Oxford Companion to Sport and Games* (London: Oxford University Press, 1975), p.391.

34. *Gaelic Athlete*, 5 July 1913: "It was a battle Gaelic v. Soccer and Rugby tactics, and Gaelic won."

35. *The Champion* was founded in December 1903, but ceased publication early in February 1904 (see SPO HO SS, 15 March 1904). *The Gaelic Athlete* started publication on 6 January 1912 and continued to 15 April 1916. *Sport*, the *Freeman's Journal's* weekly, devoted more and more space to Gaelic games in the 1900s, as did the *Freeman's Journal* itself.

36. SPO CBS Monthly Report, South East, April 1893, *Annual 1907-8*, p.13, where hurling is described as "the nearest approach to warfare consistent with peace", and a game that "gave to the tumultuous spirit of the Gael a zest surpassed only in the rush of battle".

37. O'Sullivan, *Story of the G. A. A.*, p.169, reporting receipts of nearly £3,000.

38. Jones's Road had been bought by Frank Dineen in 1908. He sold it to the GAA after lengthy negotiations in October 1913 for £3,500. In order to obtain a loan, the GAA had to become a limited liability company; see *Gaelic Athlete*, 25 October 1913, 10 January and 18 April 1914.

39. SPO HO SS, 23 December 1899; ibid., 11, 14, 15 May, 2 June, 6 and 11 July, 3 September 1900; ibid., 19 September and 1 November 1900.

40. Ibid., 15 March 1901, 18 March 1902.

41. HO SS, 19 May, 13 and 27 June, 21 November 1902.
42. J. J. Walsh organized the coup in 1909; see J. P. Power, *A Story of Champions* (Cork: 1941), pp.93-95, realizing "the potentialities of the GAA as a training ground for physical force".
43. T. W. Moody and Leon O'Broin, "The I. R. B. Supreme Council 1868-78", *Irish Historical Studies* 19 (1975): 286-332.
44. *Sinn Fein Rebellion Handbook* (Dublin: 1916), pp.55, 74.
45. B. MacLua, *The Steadfast Rule* (Dublin: 1967), pp. 23-29.
46. O'Sullivan, *Story of the G. A. A.*, pp.103, 124-125.
47. Ibid., p.145. He said that the GAA was "essentially a patriotic organisation, having a patriotic mission to fulfil".
48. Ibid., pp.149-58; p.176.
49. MacLua, *The Steadfast Rule*, p.47.
50. *The Gaelic Athletic Annual and County Directory for 1907-8* (Dublin: 1907), p.26.
51. References are innumerable; see, for some good examples, *Gaelic Athlete*, 25 April, 6 May, 6 and 27 June 1914.
52. Ibid., 3 February 1912.
53. *Gaelic Athlete*, 6 and 20 December 1913.
54. PRO CO 904/91, County Inspector's Report, Limerick, December 1913; *Gaelic Athlete*, 17 January 1914; *Irish Volunteer*, 28 March 1914.
55. For Galway, see PRO CO 904/14, March 1914; for Athlone and Derry, *Irish Volunteer*, 18 April 1914; for Mountmellick and Rathmolyon, ibid., 2 May 1914; for Walsh, ibid., 18 april, for Roche, ibid., 23 May, for Cullinane, ibid., 2 May; and for Waterford, PRO CO 904/93, Co. Waterford Report, May 1914.
56. *Gaelic Athlete*, 18 April 1914; *Freeman's Journal*, 13 April 1914.
57. O'Broin, *Revolutionary Underground*, p.140.
58. For examples of clerical activities, see PRO CO 904/97, June 1915, and *Royal Commission on the Rebellion in Ireland, Minutes of Evidence* (Commons Papers 1916, vol.II), pp.23, 30, 77, 86.

BRIAN STODDART

Cricket's Imperial Crisis: the 1932–33 MCC Tour of Australia

On 18 January 1933, during the third test match of the 1932–33 England-Australia cricket series, the Australian Cricket Board of Control dispatched this telegram from Adelaide to the committee of the Marylebone Cricket Club in London:

> Body-line bowling assumed such proportions as to menace best interests of game, making protection of body by batsmen the main consideration, and causing intensely bitter feelings between players, as well as injury. In our opinion it is unsportsmanlike, and unless stopped at once is likely to upset the friendly relations existing between Australia and England.

The remainder of the English tour came close to being cancelled during the next three weeks. Discussions and negotiations were held at the highest political and diplomatic levels in both England and Australia. A fierce debate raged in the press and on radio in both countries. Similarly, bodyline was a major topic of conversation wherever people met in all walks of life. Had the tour been called off, sporting relations between England and Australia would definitely have been damaged. More seriously, the wider imperial links which bound the two countries might also have been affected. One British diplomat, at least, feared that cricket's entry "into the scope of diplomacy" could well have had extremely serious political consequences.[1]

The controversy arose from a new form of bowling attack developed by the English team. It was an adaptation of *leg theory,* which had been practised in England for some years by county bowlers attempting to restrict the high scoring that had become common since the First World War. However, its initial description of *fast leg theory* was replaced by *bodyline* after Australian journalists like Jack Worrall, Hugh Buggy, and Ray Robinson used the word to economize on their cables to England. A fast bowler pitched the ball well short of the batsman on or outside the line of leg stump. When the ball reached the batsman it was travelling towards his chest or head at speeds up to 145 kilometres an hour. Numerous fielders were placed on the leg side so that if the batsman tried to step inside the line of flight and hit the ball he would risk being caught. Most batsmen preferred to duck underneath the delivery or scramble out of its way, but because the ball was bowled so quickly, a number of them were inevitably struck painful blows. The pace of the delivery was both the new feature of and the key to this attack, and the MCC team contained four of the finest fast bowlers of that era. Harold Larwood, Bill Bowes, Bill Voce, and G. O. Allen, the Australian-born amateur, had all finished well towards the top of the 1932 English county averages — Larwood, in fact, topped those averages by taking 203 wickets at an average of 12.9 runs per wicket.[2] There was little respite then, for Australian batsmen confronted by these bowlers and their new methods.

The bodyline controversy has been interpreted hitherto almost entirely within its playing context, with hapless Australian batsmen beset by ruthless English bowlers. There is, of course, considerable validity in that approach, but it does not fully explain the bitterness with which the 1932–33 tour is remembered even now. Two aspects of cricket history suggest that an account based upon the broad context of English and Australian society, and upon the nature of the Anglo-Australian relationship, during the early 1930s will yield a more satisfying explanation.[3]

Firstly, every tour undertaken by England or Australia since 1877, when official test matches began, had been marked by some controversy. During a late nineteenth century match between England and New South Wales, for example, the Sydney crowd invaded the playing field, upset by an umpiring decision against a local player. In 1912 the sensations began even before the Australian team left for England. Almost half the players originally selected refused to tour because the newly formed Board of Control overruled their choice of manager. During the Australian tour of England in 1921, English batsmen were unable to cope with the sheer pace of Macdonald and Gregory, much to the consternation of English crowds who often questioned the legitimacy of the attack.[4] The important point to be made here, however, is that none of these controversies went beyond their sporting contexts; they were purely cricketing issues. Bodyline, on the other hand, spread beyond the sporting arena to create enmity between England and Australia in a variety of social circles: governments, cricket administrators, players, the cricketing public, and the general public. This unprecedented development suggests strongly that non-cricketing conditions contributed to the crisis.[5]

The second aspect of cricket history important here certainly had strong social connotations, especially in the context of the early 1930s. That was cricket's considerable imperial significance. Throughout the British Empire, the game was widely regarded for its role in maintaining imperial unity and keeping good temper between nations. In India, Africa, the West Indies, Australia, New Zealand, even Canada and Hong Kong, cricket symbolized the cultural hegemony of British social values and their successful transfer from generation to generation throughout the Empire. In the imperial vocabulary, "to play cricket" meant more than participation in a mere game; it was the embodiment of British fair play, justice, and sportsmanship. Cricket displayed throughout the Empire the continuity and organization of British social traditions. Changes to the laws of the game, for example, were made only after full reflection upon their possible consequences; and they emanated solely from the MCC, which symbolized British authority in such matters. Cricket's social standards, too, were strictly maintained. The rigid separation of "amateurs" and "professionals", which lasted into the 1960s, was the most spectacular but by no means the only example of this. This social role of cricket was taken especially seriously in the outposts of Empire where "progress" was measured essentially by success in British terms against British standards maintained in British institutions. Sport was as important a yardstick as politics or economics in this measuring process, and cricket was undoubtedly considered the most important form of imperial sports activity.[6]

Viewed in this cultural context, the Australian charge that the English team played in an "unsportsmanlike" manner becomes more than a sporting bubble, for it challenged the imperial tradition that Britain set the standards for civilized social behaviour. The charge was serious enough in its own terms. But it assumed even greater significance because it occurred during the economic depression of the early 1930s when imperial relations generally underwent what was probably their most stringent test ever. That is, events on Australian cricket fields helped confirm a popular impression that accustomed social order and organization was about to be radically transformed. For at the beginning of the MCC tour, cricket was one of the few social institutions in both countries apparently untouched by the all-prevailing social crisis. By the end of the tour however, it was clear that even so strong and traditional a cultural prop as cricket had not escaped the social turmoil. For many people, consequently, a protest against bodyline was a protest against the wider social changes impinging upon their lives.

In England, the press reported the 1932 cricket season as "one of the brightest and most inspiring" in county championship history. Yorkshire won its sixteenth championship, while Sussex won praise for playing cricket "as it should be played by those who love it because it is a game and yet calls for the same strenuous energy and concentration as if it were a business". The widely regarded importance of cricket in encouraging social discipline and normality was implicit in this review and in accounts of the MCC's departure for Australia. A "huge and enthusiastic crowd" saw the players off from St Pancras Station, and all the way to the ship at Tilbury people "assembled at every station, women waved from back gardens, and men stopped working on their allotments". As the *Observer* put it, cricket was not everybody's game, but it was everybody's news. Socially, England seemed its normal self in cricket terms.[7]

But the touring side left an England vastly different from that left by any previous team. The period from September 1932 to January 1933 which coincided almost exactly with the tour programme — marked the depths of the economic depression in Great Britain. At least 25 per cent of the workforce was unemployed, and bankruptcies rose by 12 per cent between 1930 and 1932. The middle classes, for whom cricket was a great passion, felt these figures suggested that the established bases of their social position were breaking up, and that they were consequently vulnerable to pressure from sections of the community normally kept in check. Crimes without violence against property, for example, rose by over 60 per cent between 1930 and 1933. Thieves were created by unemployment, it was argued, and constituted "a great menace than usual to those who are loyal to the laws of social fellowship and 'play the game' — the game of good faith and mutual trust which makes English life the most free from shadows that any race of men have ever lived",[8] In that climate, British authorities acted quickly to curb threats to fair play and social order, qualities maintained so much through discipline in sports generally and cricket particularly.

As the English players sailed for Australia, a Lancashire weavers' union official appeared in court accused of inciting fellow workers to resist strike-breaking attempts by mill officials following a wage dispute. In Birkenhead, near Liverpool, numerous unemployed workers were arrested during widespread rioting. Police considered that the night of looting and stone-throwing was inspired by "Communists" active among the unemployed. "Communists" were also thought responsible for an attack on a newly elected Conservative MP after the declaration of a by-election poll in London. On the Broomhead Moors near Sheffield, gamekeepers employed by local land-owners clashed with members of the Ramblers' Rights Movement who walked on property traditionally administered as part of the Yorkshire county estates. In the midst of this widespread social tension and change, then, it was reassuring for the middle classes to see Herbert Sutcliffe, the Yorkshire professional, going off to Australia with a cricket bat which he promised to get autographed for the son of Lord Harewood of Yorkshire. Cricket, at least, retained its social stability and ordered hierarchy in the midst of otherwise worrying social alterations.[9]

When they landed at Fremantle in Western Australia, the MCC players found themselves in as socially fragile a situation as the one they had left. In Western Australia, an emergency bill to place a special 4½d in the pound tax (to help alleviate the economic crisis raised by the Depression) was being guided through its final parliamentary stages. At least 29 per cent of the national workforce was unemployed, with the figure being as high as 34 per cent in some states. Even those who were employed were feeling the pinch economically, for the fall in real wages far outstripped the decline in retail prices. As in England, there were fears that this economic dislocation was contributing to the breakdown of social order. A Communist Party organizer was on trial in Sydney for having incited unemployed workers to join his organization. There were riots in New South Wales following the implementation of compulsory questionnaires for those seeking unemployment assistance. In Perth, womens' organizations opposed legislation aimed at liberalizing gambling laws. Such liberalization, they argued, might prove momentarily expedient in boosting government revenue, but in the long term it would set an "anti-social and uneconomic" example for future generations. The *West Australian* lamented that the necessity of a city campaign against vandalism demonstrated "the failure of discipline in school and home".[10]

Just as in England, then, an MCC tour was welcomed by many Australians as an assurance that not all traditions and standards had disappeared. It reminded Australians that they were part of a wider social organization in which they had always found comfort, both material and psychological. As one Western Australian politician declared at the MCC's first official reception in Australia: "We look upon these visits as a powerful influence in cementing the bonds of Empire. In that respect they are, I think, second only to the influence of Australian soldiers in the Great War. Australia is part of the British Empire, and its people are of the same stock as those of England."[11]

The tour, in fact, assumed considerable importance in the matter of Empire by taking place at a time when imperial relationships generally, and those between Great Britain and Australia particularly, faced numerous pressures. As in Canada and New Zealand, it was widely believed by Australians that Britain's repudiation of the gold standard had contributed substantially to colonial economic depression. These misgivings were then deepened by Sir Otto Niemeyer's criticisms of the Australian economy, and by the Ottawa Agreement on tariff and trade conditions which was popularly thought to favour Britain rather than her satellites. In Australia, these economic tensions were heightened by changes in the political relationship with Great Britain. The 1931 Statute of Westminster was supposed to have altered Britain's constitutional role in Australia; yet this was followed very shortly by Governor Sir Philip Game's dismissal of J. T. Lang's New South Wales government. All this political and economic disquiet bearing upon the imperial structure was underlined in India, the very heart of the Empire, where widespread unrest was regarded apprehensively by its imperial partners who felt, perhaps, that it symbolized the imminent breakdown of longstanding British sovereignty in many parts of the world.[12]

An interesting feature of the Indian case was that it demonstrated the importance of cricket in its colonial context. When an MCC team to tour India was announced in 1931, Indian cricket authorities complained that they were being sent a second-rate side. The implication was that, just as in politics, India was being treated badly in cricket by the British. Lord Willingdon, viceroy of India and an old English county player, realized that there were potential political dangers in this discontent. Cricket administrators in India came exclusively from the social groups upon whom the British relied for much of their political support in the subcontinent. Willingdon therefore smoothed the matter over diplomatically in the midst of political problems which, on the surface, appeared to be far more pressing than any cricket concerns. Against this general background, then, the MCC tour of Australia took on an even greater imperial significance than usual, and its progress was monitored closely throughout the Empire.[13]

The tour opened in Perth with matches against Western Australia and an invitation team that included Don Bradman.[14] He failed in both innings on a damp wicket, but there was no bodyline bowling involved. The MCC then beat South Australia and Victoria convincingly, again without short-pitched bowling. Bodyline made its first appearance in Melbourne against another invitation team. Bradman fared badly, falling to Harold Larwood in both innings, moving away from the flying deliveries and playing them un-orthodoxly. Australian captain Bill Woodfull, playing more correctly, took the first of many heavy body blows he was to receive in the following weeks. Larwood was rested for the New South Wales match, but Bradman and Jack Fingleton, another test player, still looked most uncomfortable against the short-pitched bowling of left-hander Bill Voce.

In this build-up to the first test in Sydney, the three players who held the key to the bodyline theory and controversy had already emerged. The fortunes and on-field actions of Bradman, Larwood, and Douglas Jardine, the English captain, held widespread public attention for weeks. Music hall songs were even written about the battle in which they were joined.[15] But their personalities were important for more than their cricketing aspects. Each demonstrated to a widely attentive and largely resentful audience of administrators and spectators that in cricket, just as in society generally, important conventions and traditions were undergoing major changes.

Donald George Bradman was born the son of a carpenter in Cootamundra, New South Wales, in 1908 and later moved with his family to Bowral.[16] He scored heavily in local cricket matches from the age of twelve; centuries were regular, double and triple centuries not uncommon. By the age of eighteen he had attracted the attention of the New South Wales selectors, even though he was a country player with no experience on turf wickets. He was given a trial in Sydney, the selectors were impressed, and, through a system of cricket patronage, he entered Sydney grade cricket. During the 1927−28 season he played regularly for New South Wales, scoring a century on debut and finishing with an average of forty-six. A good performance against the touring MCC side in the following season gained him selection for the first test. Australia was ground into sub-mission in that match, and Bradman failed. Dropped for the second test, he was recalled for the third to make 79 and 112, while he scored another century in the fifth test. Another successful domestic season followed, and he was a natural selection for the 1930 tour of England. In that year, at the age of twenty-two, Bradman turned on the most phenomenal scoring feats ever seen in the cricket world. He sustained his form over a whole English summer to score 2,960 runs in all games at an astonishing average of ninety-eight. His test record was even more spectacular: 974 runs in seven innings at an average of 139. Even so, Australia won the series only by two matches to one with two drawn. Bradman clearly made the difference between the sides, and most commentators argue that his success in 1930 marked the real birth of bodyline, as English cricket sought to nullify the genius of the "boy from Bowral".

Because of this success, and at least partly because of the social conditions in which it was achieved, Bradman became a new kind of Australian sports personality. In confounding the view that Australian cricketers were strictly amateurs, he turned sports success to commercial advantage in the midst of general economic distress and, in so doing, challenged the authority and values traditionally possessed by Australian cricket administrators. While on tour in England he wrote a book which was serialised in the press; one-third of his tour bonus was subsequently withheld by the Board of Control, which argued that he had contravened a contract clause that forbade players from writing about matches in which they were involved. This did not diminish Bradman's public popularity. Fingleton recalls how Bradman left the rest of the Australian team in Perth after the 1930 tour to undertake a triumphal overland journey. Some players did not take kindly to this, arguing that Bradman's commercial commitments were so great during the tour that the only time they saw him was when he went out to bat. This commercial image was consolidated late in 1931 when he signed a joint contract with a newspaper, a radio station, and a sports goods organization. At the beginning of the next season the Board of Control told Bradman that he could not play and write, and for a while it seemed that he would not play against Jardine's side. That he did so suggests that cricket's new commerical aspect was a powerful one in an age of economic stress, and that a new state had been reached in player-administrator relationships.[17]

Douglas Robert Jardine marked a similarly new change in the traditional conventions of English captaincy. He was an amateur, like all English captains until the early 1950s, but he was an amateur who looked and played like a professional. This was in direct contrast to the affable, outward-going, "the-game's-the-thing" characters who were his predecessors in Australia, notably A. P. F. Chapman who had captained the 1928–29 team. Jardine was born in Bombay in 1900, and the family name was well known in India. His grandfather had been a judge of the Allahabad High Court in north India, and his uncle was a senior member of the Indian Political Service, which handled British relations with the Indian princely states. Jardine's father was educated at Balliol College, Oxford, played cricket for Oxford University, and became advocate-general of the Bombay presidency after a career at the Bombay bar. Two other Jardines occupied major positions in the Bombay legal profession. Douglas Jardine was an only child, so the sense of tradition and independence created in this colonial climate would have impressed itself upon him. Independence and aloofness were certainly a mark of his character. While at Horris Hill, an English preparatory school with a tradition of good cricket coaching, he was said to have corrected his coach on a technical matter by referring him to a basic coaching manual. Herbert Sutcliffe wrote later that he had spent a lot of time with Jardine during the 1928 – 29 tour, yet knew him as little at the end as he had done at the beginning. Sutcliffe thought Jardine "a queer devil" at that stage, but gradually came to regard him as "one of the greatest men" he ever met.[18]

By the time Jardine went from Winchester to New College Oxford, he was an established player with a string of fine performances to his credit. In 1921 he scored ninety-six not out for Oxford against the Australian touring side before the match was called off early. Some writers have argued that Jardine never forgot the incident, and that thereafter his inherent tough-mindedness became even more pronounced when playing against Australia. He left Oxford with a degree in 1923 and, while playing for Surrey, qualified as a solicitor by 1926. Selected for the 1928 – 29 MCC tour, he discovered Australian crowd behaviour, something to which he never became reconciled and which seemed to strengthen his resolve when playing Australia. He led a team to India in 1931 and was then chosen to lead the team to Australia in 1932 – 33. His leadership experience was limited, but his attitude towards the game clearly impressed the selectors. On hearing that Jardine had been appointed captain of England, an old schoolmaster of his at Winchester is reported to have said, "Well, we shall win the Ashes — but we may lose a Dominion."[19]

Harold Larwood played a crucial role in that prophecy. In the five test matches he bowled 220 overs (so more than any other bowler), took thirty-three wickets (Allen, with twenty-one was the next most successful) at an average of nineteen runs per wicket. Of English bowlers who have toured Australia since Larwood, only Frank Tyson in 1954—55 and John Snow in 1970—71 have approached his record of the 1932—33 tour, a performance that ranks as one of the greatest fast-bowling feats of all time. Larwood was the archetypal English professional fast bowler. Born in Nuncargate, Nottinghamshire, he began his working life in the local coal-mines at the age of fourteen. His cricket was learned initially from his father, who captained the colliery side. An old English player who lived near by thought Larwood showed promise and recommended him to the county authorities. By 1924, when he was still not twenty, Larwood had played for the county, and by 1926 he was playing for England. He toured Australia in 1928 – 29 and enjoyed some success, but in England in 1930 he suffered at the hands of Bradman, as did all English bowlers that year. On his own report, however, Larwood did learn in 1930 that Bradman did not like short-pitched deliveries; between 1930 and 1932 he improved his accuracy so that he could direct such an attack to a carefully placed field. In so doing, he initiated a cricket revolution in which the fast bowler was no longer subservient to batsmen as he had been throughout the 1920s because of the perfect pitches which encouraged very high scoring. Much of the bodyline controversy consequently revolved around what the *Manchester Guardian* called "the contrast between the revolutionary and the classical idea", a clash between old and new conventions of cricket behaviour.[20]

These key figures did not meet in the first test, for Bradman was unable to play because of illness. England won easily, Larwood bowling forty-nine overs in the match to take a total of ten wickets for 124 runs. Only Stan McCabe, who scored 187 not out, played Larwood effectively; all other Australian batsmen succumbed to the bodyline attack. Criticism of the English bowling methods became so vehement that an English newspaper writer accused Australian journalists of inflaming public opinion. The Board of Control was to meet in Melbourne during the second test, and there were reports that the MCC committee would be asked to impose restraints upon its team's tactics.[21]

Jardine and his fellow selectors, however, were so convinced of bodyline's success that they played their four fast bowlers in the Melbourne test and did not carry a slow bowler. The decision seemed vindicated when Bradman was bowled first ball, playing wildly at a bouncer from Bill Bowes. Bowes wrote later that the "crowd was stupefied. Bradman walked off the field amid a silence that would have been a threatrical producer's triumph." But the other Australian batsmen batted on a wicket that was too slow for the English fast bowlers; the Australian bowlers then worked hard and Australia took a first innings lead. Only Bradman played well in Australia's second innings, scoring a magnificent 103 not out in 183 minutes which took Australia to 191. England again fell to the Australian bowlers, and Australia won the match. But this squaring of the series did not ease the tension completely; Larwood was booed on numerous occasions when batsmen were hit. The *Argus* reassured itself and its readers that "cricket is a grand old game, no matter what may have been done to it by those who sublimate it and call the result Test cricket".[22] Changes in the conventions of cricket, and all that they represented, clearly rested uneasily with most of the Australian press and public.

The scene shifted to Adelaide for the third test. Interest was so high that special trains carried three times the normal number of passengers from Melbourne to the South Australian capital, where the Englishmen became unpopular before the match even began. Upset by the behaviour of a youthful crowd at practice sessions, Jardine had the ground closed to spectators. The *Sydney Morning Herald* hoped that such unpleasantness would not prevent the game from being "played in the tradition and the spirit that have made it what it is — the true embodiment of British sport and fairplay".[23]

England batted first and made 341 after being four for 30 at an early stage. Australia began batting on the Satuday afternoon, and "vehement protests followed when Woodfull was hit" over the heart by a lifting delivery from Larwood. Numerous "hostile demonstrations" followed when other batsmen ducked under similar deliveries. Newspaper reports read over the Sunday rest day ensured that a record crowd thronged the Adelaide Oval when play resumed on Monday. The atmosphere, tense from the outset, erupted when Australian wicket-keeper Bert Oldfield glanced a short-pitched ball from his bat into his face. One English observer felt that "if some impetuous member of the crowd had set himself up as leader any number would have followed him over the fence with unimaginable results". Jack Hobbs, one of England's greatest-ever batsmen, who was covering the tour for a London newspaper, said later that he had left the ground worn out by the noise of the crowd in a demonstration which an experienced Australian observer agreed was "remarkably hostile". Police armed with batons and automatic pistols were said to have been sent to the ground for fear of an imminent full-scale disturbance.[24]

Australian crowd behaviour had bothered English touring teams for many years, mainly because Australian spectators shouted advice of all kinds to players during the course of the game. This was very different from the demure atmosphere that generally surrounded English cricket grounds. "Barracking", as it was known, had emerged in Australia at least as early as the 1890s, and one self-confessed exponent of the art estimated that by the 1930s it was practised by at least 70 per cent of Australian cricket watchers. But although barracking alarmed many Englishmen, it contained an element of social control that matched English crowd behaviour. Participation was almost entirely verbal, invasions of the pitch being almost unknown, and apparent ill-feeling rarely outlasted the duration of the game. One spectator in Adelaide, for example, gave vent to his anger with Jardine by shouting during a drinks break, "don't give *him* a drink! Let the bastard die of thirst!" Such emotional outlets perhaps lessened the danger of physical violence breaking out. On an earlier tour, Herbert Sutcliffe endured the jibes of a Brisbane crowd for four days and was then delighted by some well-known barrackers who presented him with tobacco pipes as a memento.[25]

In 1932–33, however, there was a sharper edge to this normally abrasive but relatively ordered crowd participation, and it may be linked to the underlying social and economic conditions. The crowds were bigger than ever before. Record attendances were set on nearly every ground, and a world record for cricket match attendance was set during the Melbourne test. Spectators went to great lengths to be assured of a good vantage point. In Melbourne, for example, the first enthusiasts reached the gates at 5.30 a.m. on the first morning; many people ate breakfast outside the ground, and an hour before the gates opened a twelve-wide queue was over quarter of a mile long. Many of these people were thought to have attended the cricket at least partly to unburden themselves of the wider pressures bearing upon them. One correspondent thought that Australian spectators needed, more than ever before, to identify with a standard of excellence attained by a champion so that they might re-assert some of their general social confidence. Harold Larwood thought that many people were at the grounds in anticipation of an Australian victory which might provide hope and encouragement in the face of unemployment and dole queues. Jack Fingleton explained much of Bradman's public popularity in similar terms; to see Bradman succeed was to see Australia triumph in the face of adversity.[26]

But it is easier to evoke the size and atmosphere of those crowds than to analyse their composition. It is unwise, for example, to assume that they were "middle class' simply because, given the depressed economy, it was relatively costly to attend the matches. People were *prepared* to pay to see the cricket because they thought it would offer them some degree of psychological comfort and a good deal of entertainment. One Melbourne man, though he could "ill-afford" to do so, paid eight shillings for two stand seats so that he might take his wife to the cricket and give her a day's entertainment. People like him paid almost seventy thousand pounds in gate takings at the five tests, and the *Argus* calculated that for admission, transport, and refreshments the Melbourne crowd spent at least forty thousand to watch the second test.[27]

It seems sensible to suggest, then, that the crowds probably reflected fairly closely the general social mix of Australian society. A number of observers confirmed this by drawing social distinctions between people who sat in members' stands and those who watched from the "outer". But the important point here was that both sections reacted angrily to English tactics during the really fiery moments of bodyline, particularly in Adelaide. In a time of Australian stress, there was a degree of social cohesion and identity perhaps unmatched in any other social situation of the time. Nevertheless, the one constant feature of the crowds was their very complexity. By the end of the tour, for example, many people went to see bodyline bowled, were vocally disappointed when it was not produced immediately, and then reacted bitterly when it did make an appearance.[28]

But as England dominated then won the Adelaide test, bodyline spread its effects beyond the playing arena and the crowds to the administrators and politicians who were as much concerned with its underlying social significance and issues as with its purely cricketing aspects. The press reflected something of this trend. One English writer felt that Larwood had made a battlefield of the Adelaide Oval, that the "morality" of his bowling was in question; it was "not cricket" and might have political and economic repercussions. The Times felt that "any breach in the mutual good will and friendliness between the players of the two countries which have survived the ordeal of many a desperate encounter over the period of more than half a century would be a cricketing disaster of the first magnitude".[29] One Australian writer argued that cricket, like the established social order, was being ruined by the "Philistines of a ruthless modern age" for whom sporting encounters were "grim international encounters in which everything is staked upon the prowess of a few chosen champions". Spectators who so "lost their perspective and their sense of humour as to attempt to control the tactics and deflect the fortunes of the game by angry advice", and who "roared continuously from behind the fence", were the sporting equivalents of mobs that roamed both England and Australia.[30] None felt the force of this incipient cricketing and social breakdown more keenly than the game's administrators in Australia and England.

The mixed reaction that greeted the 18 January telegram in Australia reflected the public's divided attitude towards the Board of Control. Since its formal creation in 1912, the Board's short history had been as much marked by federal-states' rights questions as the wider political federation movement which had partly encouraged its appearance. To assert its position, the Board elaborated an authoritarian air which made it unpopular with states' associations and players; the 1912 controversy over the Australian touring team, mentioned earlier, was just the first of many. One cricket-minded

New South Wales politician, for example, painted the Board as an oligarchy which from its inception had assumed powers "incompatible with the prosperity of Australian cricket and players".[31]

The choice of the world *oligarchy* was important for there was a popular view that the Board, besides being politically authoritarian, was socially unrepresentative of Australian cricketers and their communities. The *Bulletin,* for example, felt that bodyline's most distressing feature was that Australians who had "no use for the Board or its works may be mistaken for small-minded people who attach exaggerated importance to cricket matches". The *Bulletin* missed the real point in one way; many Australians, besides members of the Board, *did* attach considerable importance to cricket matches, especially those against England. One Australian cricket writer pointed out shrewdly that "Marylebone, and the spirit of cricket, have probably stood higher in this faraway land than, perhaps, in England".[32] That was because cricket, including its organization and administration, helped determine the progress and place of Australia within the Empire.

For the people who administered Australian cricket, success in running such a British institution as cricket determined their social status as much as success in economic or political spheres. And the importance of that cricket status was increasing rather than diminishing by the early 1930s. The *Australian Cricketer* made the interesting point that before the First World War there had been no need for people to parade their social status by traveling from Melbourne to Adelaide to watch test cricket, unlike the early 1933 situation.[33] An analysis of the Board's membership supports the view that cricket was a major feature of the colonial aristocracy's benchmark. Further, it suggests that the 1932 – 33 crisis resulted at least partly from that group's desire to preserve tradition against commercialism and revolutionary tactics which smacked of the undesirable changes it perceived in society more generally.

In 1932 – 33 there were thirteen men on the Board: three each from New South Wales, Victoria and South Australia; two from Queensland, and one each from Western Australia and Tasmania. These men shared a common social heritage, an above-average education, and a commercial-professional background.[34] One of the New South Wales members, for example, traced his ancestry to an infantry officer of the New SouthWales Regiment who arrived at Sydney in 1792. Similarly, the Western Australian representative descended from families that had been among that state's early colonists. At least half of the Board's members had been educated at prestigious private schools; and many had proceeded to a university education, particularly for the professions — there were at least four lawyers and two medical practitioners among them. There were, besides, two stock exchange members, a pastoral agent, the managing director of a timber company, and a bread company director. Their membership of the Board invariably followed a lengthy spell in state cricket administration, where their positions in some part resulted from their social and occupational status. Few of them had playing experience in first-class cricket. Two examples help demonstrate what cricket meant socially to these people and, indirectly, why bodyline upset them.

Dr Allen William David Robertson, chairman of the Board, exemplified the role of cricket as a medium for upward social mobility. Born in 1867 in Deniliquin, on the Victoria–New South Wales border, where his father ran a general store, he was orphaned at an early age and went to Melbourne in the care of an aunt. He worked first in a warehouse and was then apprenticed to a chemist for whom he worked in a number of Victorian country towns. During his time in the country, Robertson qualified for entrance to the University of Melbourne, where he began studying medicine part-time, eventually graduating at the age of thirty-six. He worked in private practice in Melbourne besides holding various hospital posts. Capitalizing on his professional standing, he formed a business partnership with other doctors and developed property in the heart of Melbourne. The social mobility which augmented this economic success stemmed from his involvement with the University Cricket Club. Robertson was appointed as its president in 1914; five years later he became a Victorian representative on the Board of Control, and he became its chairman in 1930.[35]

William Charles Bull, on the other hand, saw cricket from a more established position in Australian society. His father had been born in Liverpool, New South Wales, about 1840; along with his brothers he was trained for the legal profession in Sydney and, after serving in local government, sat in the New South Wales parliament late in the nineteenth century. His son was born in 1881 and educated at Sydney Grammar before qualifying as a solicitor in 1909 and joining his uncle's law firm. Like his father, he quickly became a prominent member of the New South Wales Cricket Association (which held many of its meetings in his uncle's office), rising through its executive ranks and becoming a New South Wales representative on the Board of Control in 1925.[36]

These men identified solidly with the British and imperial traditions of cricket. In that sense, their telegram to the MCC was as much a plea as a demand for protection of the game and all that it had come to represent socially for them by the 1930s. Incidentally, their views were clearly shared by at least some Australian players. Woodfull himself wrote later that cricket "is of such world renown, and is so finely British, that it rests with all cricketers, and especially, of course, first-class cricketers, to hold its good name dear". It was a measure of the Board's apprehension about general change, then, that its hasty wording of the 18 January telegram accused the English team of "unsportsmanlike" play, a charge that cut at the heart of British sporting and social traditions. A more judicious cable might have won the Board greater sympathy from the MCC, but the imperial cricket authority could not ignore such an accusation from a colonial subordinate. As *The Times* suggested, neither the MCC nor England could tolerate such a charge: "It is inconceivable that a cricketer of Jardine's standing, chosen by the MCC to captain an English side, would ever dream of allowing or ordering the bowlers under his command to practice any system of cricket that, in the time-honoured English phrase, is not cricket.[37] The MCC, a pre-eminent English social institution whose formation predated the foundation of Australia, met the charge with the full weight of its social and political power.

There were, for example, numerous important peers of the realm on the MCC committee, among them Hampden (first title created in 1307), Buccleuch (1663), Dartmouth (1711), Hawke (1776), and Lucan (1795). Then there was Sir Francis Lacey, a lawyer who married into the aristocracy and served as MCC secretary between 1898 and 1926; his knowledge of cricket politics was second to none. Wider politics were also presented. Lord Ullswater was an eminent lawyer who served in parliament between 1883 and 1921, acting as Speaker in the House of Commons for sixteen years. Sir Stanley Jackson had played cricket for Yorkshire, been financial secretary to the War Office in the early 1920s and chairman of the Unionist Party in the mid-1920s before becoming governor of Bengal in 1927, a post he held until 1932 — he was clearly accustomed to dealing with imperial crises of all kinds. Viscount Bridgeman had served as home secretary and first lord of the Admiralty during the 1920s, and had been MCC president in 1931. Sir Knyaston Studd, lord mayor of London in 1928–29, had spent a lifetime in city politics.[38] These last three, along with Lord Lewisham, who was the current MCC president, formed a formidable deputation to the Dominions Office at the height of the crisis.

The MCC committee did not fail those of its supporters who favoured a hard line towards the Australian Board of Control:

We, the Marylebone Cricket Club, deplore your cable message and deprecate the opinion that there has been unsportsmanlike play. We have the fullest confidence in our captain, team and managers, and are convinced that they would do nothing to infringe the laws of cricket or the spirit of the game. We have no evidence that our confidence is misplaced. Much as we regret the accidents to Woodfull and Oldfield, we understand that in neither case was the bowler to blame. If the Board wishes to propose a new law or rule it shall receive our careful consideration in due course. We hope that the situation is not now as serious as your cable appears to indicate, but if it is such as to jeopardise the good relations between England and Australian cricketers, and you consider it desirable to cancel the remainder of the programme, we would consent with great reluctance.[39]

In its political sense, it was a document worthy of Whitehall.

The situation was so fluid by the end of January that the future of the tour was by no means clear. Some sections of the press felt that the Board had been soundly defeated by its imperial master; others that the MCC had been, as the British were generally in political and economic matters, typically condescending towards a member of the Empire worthy of better treatment. The Board of Control met to reconsider the matter. A long discussion produced a more conciliatory telegram which, however, still did not withdraw the word *unsportsmanlike*. By that stage, there were rumours that the Australian prime minister had spoken to his London representative about the crisis.[40] The MCC, alarmed by the charge that it had undermined a tradition of sportsmanship upon which much of the imperial ethos was based, had already sought diplomatic assistance in its dealings with the Board.

In fact, E. T. Crutchley, the British government's representative in Australia, was so concerned by the possible damage being done to imperial relations by the controversy that he took the initiative and asked the MCC managers for their interpretation of it.[41] Their reply, which reached him on 1 February, claimed that the situation had been inflamed unnecessarily by the Board's initial telegram. On the same day he received from the managers a telegram prompted by the Board's second telegram to the MCC committee. Crutchley was asked to use his "influence" and have the word *unsportsmanlike* withdrawn, or the rest of the tour was likely to be cancelled. The British government's representative telephoned J. A. Lyons, the Australian prime minister, whose first comment was: "It looks as though we are leading two opposing armies." Both men viewed the situation very seriously from the imperial angle. The British representative stressed "that the cancellation of the tour would be a very grave thing, for Australia especially, just when feeling was so good". This clearly referred to an improvement in Anglo-Australian relations in wake of the political and economic difficulties of recent years. Lyons telephoned Dr Robertson to convey "the importance of the matter from the national point of view".

Neither side was anxious to yield ground in the bargaining that followed. Lyons, for example, wanted to know what "gesture" the MCC would make in return for the withdrawal of the word *unsportsmanlike*. On the basis of information received from the English management, Crutchley replied that the field placings might possibly be modified. Robertson, too, clearly wanted an assurance about a "gesture", for the prime minister later asked Crutchley for confirmation about the altered field placings. At that point the English management adopted a hard line, declaring that they would not bargain about the withdrawal of the "obnoxious" word. They were clearly seeking an unconditional Australian surrender. At this level, cricket events were only the superficial manifestations of wider social, political, and economic considerations concerning the future status of the imperial relationship. Had negotiations broken down and the tour been cancelled, the popular view would have been that the MCC had contravened those conventions of "fairplay and sportsmanship" upon which much of imperial life was based; consequently, incalculable psychological damage might have been done to Anglo-Australian and wider imperial ties.

It was only on the eve of the fourth test in Brisbane that the crisis was averted. There were reports that the MCC team was virtually on strike and would not play the match unless the offending word was withdrawn by the Board of Control. In London a special MCC sub-committee followed up Crutchley's work by calling on the secretary of state for the dominions, J. H. Thomas, who denied that their visit had any political connotations. They had, he said, merely wanted to use the diplomatic communications system to establish rapid contact with Australian authorities. But the fact that an earlier caller to discuss the cricket situation was the governor of South Australia, Sir Alexander Hore-Ruthven, suggests that the MCC visit was more important than Thomas admitted. The demands made by the MCC throughout this official and non-official activity in England and Australia were met in time to save the fourth test when the Board of Control signalled: "We do not regard the sportsmanship of your team as being in question. . . . We join heartily with you in hoping that the remaining Tests will be played with the traditional good feeling."[42]

England won the fourth test, and the series, and the tour reached a tired end in a situation from which the tension was never really removed. A real crisis had been avoided, but not without cost to the personal feelings of Englishmen and Australians about each other at all levels in society. Crutchley reported that on a visit to his Canberra club at the conclusion of the affair, "Everyone I spoke to with one exception was quite frantically against present practice and the hated word . . . cropped up, with temper, in quite unexpected quarters." In another very different social situation an English-born university student, listening to the radio broadcast of the third test with some friends in Tasmania, supported the MCC players. His friends became so cool towards him, to the point of not speaking, that he packed his bags to leave their home. Only at the last moment did they ask him to stay.[43]

In purely cricketing terms the events of 1932–33 were dramatically stirring; memories of them remain vivid for those involved directly as players and for those who watched. The bodyline tour's importance in cricket history is that it constituted a major stage in the evolution of the game. Short-pitched bowling had appeared before the early 1930s without becoming a cricketing convention. By breaking the tradition that batsmen should be protected from such tactics, bodyline established a new role for fast bowlers. The cricketing and public acceptability of "bouncers" as bowled by Miller and Lindwall, Tyson and Trueman, Hall and Griffiths, Lillee and Thomson, and the rest since the Second World War has derived in many ways from the tactics employed by Harold Larwood and his colleagues. After bodyline, and unlike before it, batsmen could never anticipate with certainty that fast bowlers would invariably pitch the ball up to them.

But cricket history alone does not explain the full significance of the bodyline tour which, more than most sports events, became a matter for widespread public concern and comment. Cricket's imperial significance, the fragility of Anglo-Australian relations, and the social ravages of the economic depression combined to give the on-field events a sharper edge than might normally have been the case. For most people in the early 1930s, life was a series of abnormalities which created uncertainty about the future. In that context, the 1932–33 tour was initially regarded as a reassurance that not all the accustomed traditions of national and imperial life had been upset, and that social change might not be so widespread as feared initially. When the tour turned sour, it was a sure indication that all aspects of life had been altered drastically by the bewildering social, economic, and political changes of the early 1930s.

Reactions to that realization revolved around the relationships exhibited between Englishmen and Australians at all levels in society, manifested in different ways in different circles. The series was an unfriendly one for the English and Australian players; few of them met socially off the field, a rare occurrence in Anglo-Australian cricket. Cricket administrators in both countries pondered the prospect of a future without England-Australia test cricket; each group considered the other primarily responsible for damaging a major imperial cultural institution. Politicians and diplomats, already grappling with difficult issues in dispute between the two countries, wondered how these cricketing developments might further complicate official relations between England and Australia. For the Australian public, seeking assurances of social normality and sporting success to counteract social failure, bodyline bowling was simply one more example of Great Britain adversely effecting Australian life in the early 1930s. Alternatively, the British public generally regarded complaints about the MCC tour as yet another example of Australian social immaturity, a condition that had to be remedied with firm action.

Yet what remains most important, perhaps, is not that Australian and English relationships were threatened by the bodyline controversy, but that they survived it. The friendly receptions given to Harold Larwood when he emigrated to Australia in 1950, and to Douglas Jardine when he re-visited Australia shortly before his death in 1957, serve as at least one testimony to that social and cultural continuity. That the links and continuities survived is a tribute not only to the inherent strength of the traditional Anglo-Australian connection, but also to the international power of cricket as a culturally unifying institution.

NOTES

This study of the bodyline tour will be more fully developed in a later work.

1. The telegram was reproduced in most newspapers of the time and in most books written about the tour. The following books raise the point briefly: Geoffrey Bolton, *Britain's Legacy Overseas* (London: Oxford University Press, 1973), p.109; Fred Alexander, *Australia Since Federation* (Melbourne: Nelson, 1967), pp.91, 127; J. R. Robertson, "1930 -39", in *A New History of Australia*, ed. F. K. Crowley (Melbourne: Heinemann, 1974), p.449; F. K. Crowley, ed., *Modern Australia in Documents* (Melbourne, Wren, 1973), vol.1, p.525. The following are among the more popular accounts of the tour: Ronald Blythe, *The Age of Illusion: England in the Twenties and Thirties* (Harmondsworth, Mddx.: Penguin, 1964), chap. 7; Robert Graves and Alan Hodge, *The Long Weekend* (London: 1961), p.290-91; Egon Kisch, *Australian Landfall* (Melbourne: Macmillan, 1969), final chapter; E. T. Crutchley Diary, 1 February 1933 (extracts from the diary, and from other Crutchley papers mentioned

subsequently, were kindly made available to me by Mr Brooke Crutchley). Brian M. Petrie, "Sport and Politics", in *Sport and Social Order: Contributions to the Sociology of Sport*, ed. Donald W. Ball and John W. Loy (Reading, Mass.: Addison-Wesley, 1975).

2. Space precludes a full discussion of the origins of bodyline, but, as with the tour itself, there are numerous interpretations; some Buggy papers are held by the La Trobe Library in Melbourne, but they contain no references to the tour — though Harold Larwood and Kevin Perkins, *The Larwood Story* (London: Allen, 1965), note that Buggy made a collection of cricket material available to them. The county averages may be seen in *Cricketer*, Spring Annual 1933, p.36.

3. For example, Sir Robert Menzies' foreword and Sir Donald Bradman's introduction to E. W. Swanton, *Swanton in Australia with M. C. C., 1946-1975* (London: Fontana, 1976), pp.12, 16. For a fascinating journalistic attempt to put the Brooklyn Dodgers baseball team of the early 1950s into the context of American society, see Roger Kahn, *The Boys of Summer* (New York: Harper and Row, 1972).

4. Professor Inglis details the incident elsewhere in this volume; see also D. K. Darling, *Test Tussles On and Off the Field* (Hobart: the author, 1970), pp. 58-61; Ronald Mason, *Warwick Armstrong's Australians* (London: Epworth, 1971).

5. Professor Inglis impressed upon me the importance of this point.

6. This subject warrants considerable investigation, but for the purposes of this paper see Lord Hawke, *Recollections and Reminiscences* (London: Williams and Norgate, 1924), and Sir Pelham Warner, *Long Innings* (London: Harrap, 1951). For some colonial perspectives, see C. L. R. James's magnificent *Beyond A Boundary* (London: Hutchinson, 1969); W. F. Mandle, "Cricket and Australian Nationalism in the Nineteenth Century", *Journal of the Royal Historical Society* 59, no.4 (December 1973).

7. Roy Webber, *County Cricket Championship* (London: Phoenix, 1957); *The Times*, 31 August, 19 September 1932; *Observer*, 18 September 1932.

8. Figures calculated from tables 96, 125, and 205, *Statistical Abstracts for the United Kingdom for Each of the Years 1913 and 1923 to 1936* (London: HMSO, 1938). For background to the period, see Derek H. Aldcroft, *The Inter-War Economy: Britain, 1919-1939* (London: Batsford, 1970); T. O. Lloyd, *Empire to Welfare State* (New York: Oxford University Press, 1970); *Observer*, 11 September 1932. For some aspects of social history, see John Stevenson, *Social Conditions in Britain Between the Wars* (Harmondsworth, Mddx.: Penguin, 1977),; Noreen Branson and Margot Heinemann, *Britain in the 1930s* (London: Heinemann, 1973).

9. *Manchester Guardian*, 17 and 19 September 1932; *The Times*, 19 and 20 September 1932. Sutcliffe later led the players' support for Jardine; see Bruce Harris, *Jardine Justified: The Truth About the Ashes* (London: Chapman and Hall, 1933), p.24.

10. *West Australian*, 19-26 October 1932; *Official Yearbook of the Commonwealth of Australia*, 1933 (Canberra, 1933), p.743; ibid., 1936, pp.523-43; G. C. Bolton, *A Fine Country to Starve In* (Perth: University of Western Australia Press, 1972).

11. *West Australian*, 19 October 1932.

12. See Ian M. Drummond, *British Economic Policy and the Empire, 1919-1939* (London: Allen and Unwin, 1972), part I , chap. 3; and especially W. F. Mandle, "Sir Otto Niemeyer: Catalyst of Australia's Depression Debate" in his *Going It Alone: Australian National Identity in the Twentieth Century* (Harmondsworth, Mddx.: Penguin, 1977). Ratification of the statute caused considerable discussion in Australia; for example: Commonwealth of Australia, Parliamentary Debates, vol. 131, 1931, pp.4500-29; for something of

Senate concern over the statute, see Sir Keith Officer Papers, Interview Transcript, series 2, box 7, Australian National Library; Bethia Foott, *Dismissal of a Premier: The Philip Game Papers* (Sydney: Morgan, 1968); A. S. Morrison, "Dominions Office Correspondence on the New South Wales Constitutional Crisis 1930-1932", *Journal of the Royal Australian Historical Society* 6, no. 5 (March 1976). For a general view of the Indian situation at this time, see Judith M. Brown, *Gandhi and Civil Disobedience: The Mahatma in Indian Politics, 1928-34* (Cambridge: Cambridge University Press, 1977); R. J. Moore, *The Crisis of Indian Unity 1917-1940* (Oxford: Oxford University Press, 1974).

13. Walter R. Hammond, *Cricket My World* (London: Stanley Paul, nd[1947?]), p.101; Harry Pichanik wrote from Rhodesia, for example, "You would no doubt be surprised to see how keenly cricket enthusiasts are following the progress of the M. C. C. tour": *Australian Cricketer*, 1 March 1933, p.97.
14. The following two paragraphs are based upon tour book and daily newspaper accounts.
15. Harold Larwood, *Body-Line?* (London: Elkin Mathews and Marrot, 1933), pp.72-73; one England player thought Australian cricketers received more attention than film stars or politicians; R. E. S. Wyatt, *Three Straight Sticks* (London: Stanley Paul, 1951), p.87.
16. Don Bradman, *My Cricketing Life* (London: Stanley Paul nd [1938?]); A. G. Moyes, *Bradman* (Sydney: Angus and Robertson, 1948).
17. J. H. Fingleton, *Cricket Crisis* (Melbourne: Cassell, 1946), p.50; *Bulletin*, 18 January 1933.
18. R. C. Robertson-Glasgow, *46 Not Out* (London: Hollis and Carter, 1948), pp. 104-5; Herbert Sutcliffe, *For England and Yorkshire* (London: Arnold, 1935), p.117.
19. See Sir Pelham Warner, *Lord's 1787-1945* (London: White Lion, 1974), pp.206-7. The selectors' role in the development of bodyline was clearly an important one. T. A. Higson, for example, had a reputation for being tough-minded with an intense will to win; see John Kay, *A History of County Cricket: Lancashire* (London: Sportsman's Book Club, 1974), pp.124-26 Quoted in E. W. Swanton, *Sort of A Cricket Person* (London: Fontana, 1974), p.69. The biographical details for the Jardine family are gathered from *Who's Who?, Who Was Who?*, and *Dictionary of National Biography*. For some of Jardine's attitudes towards cricket, see his *Cricket* (London: Dent, 1936).
20. Larwood and Perkins, *The Larwood Story*; Ronald Mason, *Sing All A Green Willow* (London: Epworth, 1967), pp. 69-75; Larwood, *Body-Line?, pp 15-16*; W. A. Oldfield, *Behind the Wicket: My Cricketing Reminiscences* (London: Hutchinson, 1938), p.199; *Manchester Guardian*, 3 January 1933; A. C. Maclaren, *Cricket Old and New* (London: Longmans Green, 1924), pp.2-5.
21. *Observer*, 18 December 1932. Some English players shared this view; Freddie Brown, *Cricket Musketeer* (London: Kaye, 1954), p.102; *Sydney Morning Herald*, 29 December 1932.
22. Bill Bowes, *Express Deliveries* (London: Stanley Paul, nd [1949?]), pp.106-7; *Argus*, 2 January 1933.
23. Jardine's account appears in his *In Quest of the Ashes* (London: Hutchinson, 1933), p.126, see also Crutchley Diary, 14 January 1933; *Sydney Morning Herald*, 13 January 1933.
24. *The Times*, 16 January 1933; *Argus*, 16, 17 January 1933; *Sydney Morning Herald*, 17 January 1933; Oldfield, *Behind the Wicket*, p.202; Harris, *Jardine Justified*, p.10; Wyatt, *Three Straight Sticks*, p.97; J. B. Hobbs, *The Fight for the Ashes* (London: Harrap, 1933), p.120.
25. W. F. Mandle, "Pommy Bastards and Damned Yankees: Sport and Australian

Nationalism", in *Going It Alone*, R. T. Corrie, *The Barracker at Bay: An Outspoken Reply to Bodyline* (Melbourne: Keating-Wood, 1933), p.5. For an indication of what little has been done on the behaviour of sports crowds, see Michael D. Smith, "Sport and Collective Violence", in Ball and Loy, *Sport and Social Order*, Alan Kippax, *Anti Body-Line* (Sydney: Sydney and Melbourne Publishing Co., 1933), p.45; R. S. Whitington and George Hele, *Bodyline Umpire* (Adelaide: Rigby, 1974), p.155; D. R. Jardine, *In Quest of the Ashes*, p.140; Sutcliffe, *For England and Yorkshire*, pp.41-42.

26. *Manchester Guardian*, 2 January 1933; *Daily Herald*, 2 January 1933; *Argus*, 3 January 1933; *Australian Cricketer*, 1 December 1932; Larwood and Perkins, *The Larwood Story*, p.94; Fingleton, *Cricket Crisis*, p.28.

27. "Disgusted" in *Argus*, 2 January, 1933; Victorian Cricket Association, *Annual Report 1932-33*, p.21; Arthur Mailey, *And Then Came Larwood* (London: Bodley Head, 1933); R. W. E. Wilmot, *Defending the Ashes 1932-1933* (Melbourne: Robertson and Mullens, 1933), p.58; *Argus*, 4 January 1933.

28. For example: Larwood, *Body-Line?*, p.84; Kippax, *Anti Body-Line*, p.27; Wilmot, *Defending the Ashes*, p.255; Mailey, *And Then Came Larwood*, p.105.

29. *Manchester Guardian*, 16 January 1933; *The Times*, 19 January 1933; however Mailey, *And Then Came Larwood*, p.94, denied that there were wider political, social, or economic ramifications to these cricketing events.

30. *Argus*, 21 January 1933; the *Australian Cricketer*, 1 December 1932, argued that this was the age of "Big Cricket".

31. *Sydney Morning Herald*, 20 January 1933; *Argus*, 21 January 1933; *West Australian*, 19 January 1933. For example, see the quarrel between the Melbourne Cricket Club and the New South Wales Cricket Association reported in *Sydney Morning Herald*, 15 May 1906; Wilmot, *Defending the Ashes*, p.58; *Sydney Morning Herald*, 2 January 1933.

32. *Bulletin*, 25 January 1933; *Australian Cricketer*, 1 February 1933.

33. *Australian Cricketer*, 1 March 1933.

34. The following information has been gathered from scattered sources.

35. *Australian Encyclopedia*, 1958 ed., vol. 7, pp.465-66. For some views on sport and social mobility, see: John W. Loy, "The Study of Sport and Social Mobility", in *Sociology of Sport*, ed. G. S. Kenyon (Chicago: Athletic Institute, 1969); Gunter Luschen, "Social Stratification and Social Mobility Among Young Sportsmen", in *Sport, Culture and Society*, ed. J. W. Loy and G. S. Kenyon (London: Macmillan, 1969); Richard S. Gruneau, "Sport, Social Differentiation, and Social Inequality", in Ball and Loy, *Sport and Social Order*.

36. *Who's Who in Australia. Sydney Morning Herald*, 16 and 17 May 1906.

37. W. M. Woodfull, *Cricket* (London: Pitman, 1936), p.2; There were only three board members in Adelaide when the decision was taken to send the telegram; *The Times*, 19 January 1933; C. Stewart Caine, editor of the authoritative *John Wisden's Cricketers' Almanack for 1933*, p.307, used almost exactly the same expression. *Daily Herald*, 19 January 1933, carried a more indignant report.

38. *Who's Who?* and *Who Was Who?*

39. This telegram was widely reported in the daily press. Sydney J. Southerton, editor of *Wisden's* for 1934, noted contentedly that the MCC "never lost their grip of the situation" (P. 332).

40. *Daily Herald*, 24 and 26 January 1933; S. H. D. Rowe (Western Australian member of the Board) in *Sydney Morning Herald*, 25 January 1933; *"The Sporting English?" — From Front Line to Bodyline: A Commentary from a "Man in the Street"* (Sydney: Macquarie Head Press, n.d. [1933?]), pp.23-24. This telegram may be found in the daily press of 1-2 February 1933; *Bulletin*, 1 February 1933.

41. The next two paragraphs are based upon Crutchley Diary for 1, 2, and 4 February 1933; and on Crutchley to P. F. Warner, 2 February 1933; Warner to Crutchley, 6 February 1933; Crutchley to Warner, 10 February 1933.

42. *Daily Herald*, 3 February 1933; *Argus*, 3 February 1933; *The Times*, 3 February 1933; Warner to Crutchley, 6 February 1933; *Manchester Guardian*, 3 February 1933; *Bulletin*, 8 February 1933; J. H. Thomas, *My Story* (London: Hutchinson, 1937), p.293; Swanton, *Sort of A Cricket Person*, p.77. This telegram may be seen in the daily press.

43. See tour book and press accounts. Swanton, *Sort of A Cricket Person*, pp.77-78, and *Wisden's* 1934, pp. 328-31, outline some of bodyline's complications for the 1934 Australian tour of England, which was in doubt for some time. See also Alfred Stirling, *Lord Bruce: The London Years* (Melbourne: Hawthorn, 1974), p.16, for an indication of Australian political reactions in London. Crutchley, to Warner, 10 February 1933; Graham McInnes, *Humping My Bluey* (London: Hamish Hamilton, 1966), pp.142-44.

K. S. INGLIS

Imperial Cricket: Test Matches between Australia and England, 1877–1900

On 13 May 1878, ninety-one years to the day after the first convict settlers of Australia left Portsmouth, eleven Australian colonists landed at Liverpool to play cricket in England.[1] The convicts had taken eight months. The cricketers made the trip home in forty-six days, having travelled by steamship from Melbourne to San Francisco, across the United States by train, and from New York to Liverpool by steamship; their manager, John Conway, who had picked the side, appointed D. W. Gregory captain, and arranged the tour, was there to meet them, having come by the faster and dearer mail steamer route through the Suez Canal.

Eight of the eleven were Australian-born. F. E. Allan and M. Blackham were born in Victoria; Alex Bannerman, H. F. Boyle, T. W. Garrett, D. W. Gregory, W. L. Murdoch, and F. R. Spofforth were born in New South Wales. Charles Bannerman, brother of Alex, was born at Woolwich before his parents emigrated. T. P. Horan was born in Dublin but grew up in Melbourne. G. H. Bailey was born in Ceylon but learned to play cricket in Tasmania. In age they ranged from thirty-two to twenty. Three of them were six feet (183 cm) and over, and their average height was about 178 centimetres. They were all of urban occupations (or all but one if surveying counts as rural): three worked in banks, six were civil servants, one was a solicitor, and one a professional cricketer. The professional cricketer, Charles Bannerman, was in a sense the only member of the party for whom the tour of England was work. The solicitor, Murdoch, was leaving his practice while he travelled (and would go bankrupt the following year). The banks and the colonial governments (in Garrett's case the Supreme Court of New South Wales) thought well enough of the journey to give their men about a year off to play. For that year the players were shareholders in a joint stock enterprise, each putting in fifty pounds and agreeing to take an equal share of whatever money they made. They played a series of matches in Australia and New Zealand to raise the money to get to England. In England they were joined by W. E. Midwinter, a player of English birth and colonial experience who had gone home to be a professional player for Gloucestershire, and who would play with the Australians when the county let him.

They were an unusual sort of Australian in England. Unlike the returned colonists who brought home wealth made out in Australia and deployed it to live as nearly as they could in the manner of English gentlemen and ladies, and unlike the rich squatters and merchants who came over to spend money for a season or two, they were young men of modest means here for a summer of sport in which they hoped to make some money and take it back to the colonies.

Although nobody but Conway (a fellow cricketer and journalist) had picked them, they were described as "an Australian Representative Team", and the canvas bag carrying their equipment was labelled boldly "Australian Eleven". Before leaving their homeland they had been encouraged to see themselves as having a serious national purpose. "They wish to show John Bull", said the *Australasian,* weekly companion to the Melbourne *Argus,* "that we can play cricket here as well as the old folks at home can."[2] The paper added that their visit would reduce ignorance and illusions about Australia and would attract immigrants.

Certainly they found people in the homeland ill-informed about themselves and their society. The only cricketers from Australia who had ever come to England before this team were a party of Aborigines who toured during the summer of 1868, and some people expected that the team of 1878 would also be aborigines. "Whoy, Bill, they beant black at all," an observer of the visitors on their second day ashore, in Nottingham, was said to have remarked; and a player picked to oppose them two weeks later had a friend say to him "I hear you are going to play against the niggers on Monday." The tourists discovered a "general ignorance of Australian geography, very few persons appearing to understand that Sydney, Melbourne, Adelaide, and Brisbane are hundreds of miles apart". By their presence they were educating Englishmen a little. On railway stations and at hotels they noticed that people "looked steadfastly at them, surprised to find them fashioned as they were, and their habits and customs the same".[3]

The antipodeans, for their part, knew so little about England (according to Fred Spofforth's later recollection) that none of them had packed a sweater for the journey, and all shivered in silk shirts during their first game at Trent Bridge.[4] They had been objects of great interest when they arrived in Nottingham by train from Liverpool. A reporter estimated that eight thousand people lined the streets from the railway station to their hotel. Seven thousand were said to have attended the first day of their match against the Nottingham county team and ten thousand the second day, despite cold and rainy weather both days. On the third day the crowd was small because the Australians were so evidently headed for defeat. They lost by an innings and fourteen runs. That evening they were given a dinner by the county cricket club, whose chairman proposed "the Australian Eleven" and predicted in a kindly tone that they would win many matches on English soil.

The Australians arrived unnoticed in London on Friday 24 May, the Queen's birthday, a holiday in their colonies but an ordinary working day here. On Monday 27 May they were to play an eleven of "Marylebone Club and Ground" — that is to say amateurs (or gentlemen) and professionals (or players) invited to represent England's senior cricket club. The MCC was as old as British Australia, having been formed in 1787 and taken the name Marylebone in 1788. It was the acknowledged maker and interpreter of the laws of cricket, and the ground named after its first manager, Thomas Lord, was the centre of the cricketing world. *The Times* judged the side now chosen to oppose the Australians "a well-selected team", and another newspaper thought it "as good a one as could be found to represent London and England, and probably nearly as good as the Club has ever turned out". There were about a thousand people at Lord's when play began on the Monday.

Parties of cricketers from England had visited Australia in the summers of 1861 – 62, 1863 – 64, 1873 – 74 and 1876 – 77. The first, a team of professional players led by H. H. Stephenson of Surrey, was invited out by two immigrants, Spiers and Pond, who ran a catering business in Melbourne, and who made a profit of eleven thousand pounds from this enterprise. The second visit, inspired by the success of the first, was led by the Nottingham professional George Parr, and all the other players were professionals except E. M. Grace, one of four sons of a surgeon and his wife in Bristol who were bringing up their boys to be strenuous part-time cricketers. Parr's men paid their own way and made seven thousand pounds. A younger Grace, W. G. , led out the party of 1873 – 74, and a still younger brother, G. F. Grace, was in the team, which had three other amateurs and seven professionals.

W. G. Grace had transformed the art of batting. In 1871, when twenty-three, he scored nearly three thousand runs in a season at an average of seventy-eight. From then on he was known wherever cricket was played as "the Champion". The Melbourne Cricket Club invited him to bring a team to Australia after that season of

1871, but was daunted at first when the great amateur asked for £1,500 and expenses. Two years later the Melbourne, South Melbourne, and East Melbourne clubs together offered him that sum, agreed amounts for the other amateurs, and £170 and expenses for each of the professionals. The colonial clubs covered their costs easily: in the first game alone, against a team representing Victoria, forty thousand people in three days paid £5,000 to watch.

One of the professionals in W. G. Grace's team, James Lillywhite, took out his own party of professionals three years later. Like all the earlier teams, this one played against odds, eleven from England against a more numerous local side, the number being fixed by an agreed judgement about the weighting likely to provide a fair balance: twenty-two, eighteen, or fifteen. It was never less than fifteen until late in Lillywhite's tour. When fifteen from New South Wales and Victoria defeated the visitors, Lillywhite agreed to a request from the Victorian Cricketers' Association for a meeting on level terms, eleven from England against eleven from Victoria and New South Wales. The encounter in Melbourne on 15, 16, and 17 March 1877 was billed as a "Grand Combination Match".[5] The colonial team won by forty-five runs after Charles Bannerman made 165 in the first innings and Tom Kendall took seven English wickets for fifty-five in the second. In a return match two weeks later the Englishmen won by four wickets. Lillywhite and his partners encouraged their Australian opponents to believe that if they went to play in England they would fare well and make money, and Lillywhite himself acted as their agent in finding teams to play against during the summer of 1878. After so solid a defeat by the first team they met in England, the Australians' prospects for success did not appear great.

Like the game at Trent Bridge, the encounter at Lord's was intended to last three days. It was all over in just less than one. MCC and Ground, batting first, were all out for only thirty-three, to the amazement of a crowd which built up from one thousand to four thousand as the wickets fell. W. G. Grace hit Allan's first ball for four and was caught off the second. Spofforth and Boyle took all the other wickets, Spofforth getting three in successive balls. But then the visitors in turn made only forty-one. In the English team's second innings Grace was bowled for no score by his second ball from Spofforth, who took four more wickets while Boyle took five for three. The home side was out for nineteen, the Australians scored twelve runs for the loss of only Charles Bannerman, and at half past five the game had ended. The crowd that cheered the victors into the pavilion included about four hundred returned and visiting colonists. The 27th of May 1878 was a grand day for the Australian players and their compatriots, and for English cricket. The defeat of Lillywhite's professionals in Melbourne had been an impressive feat, to be sure; but it was another thing again for eleven Australians to overwhelm at Lord's this team of gentlemen and players led by W. G. Grace. "The Colonials", as *The Times* put it next morning, "beat the greatest and most powerful club in the world", and in doing so they began a new epoch in the history of the game.

For the rest of the tour the victors of Lord's were inspected with enthusiastic curiosity wherever they went. The two devastating bowlers attracted most attention, and fine exhibits of colonial man they were: Harry Boyle 183 centimetres high and solidly built, Fred Spofforth, "the demon bowler", as the papers were calling him, 190 centimetres, broad-shouldered, a lean man with long arms, the perfect Cornstalk.

The Australians' first victory was a fine advertisement for the rest of the tour. When they met a team representing Surrey at London's other principal ground, the Oval, the crowd of some twenty thousand on the first day was by far the largest ever assembled there; and when the visitors won by five wickets on the second day, the not-out batsmen Murdoch and Garrett were "rushed by the crowd, and patted on the back all the way to the pavilion". Of nineteen games played on even terms — eleven against eleven — the Australians won ten, lost four and drew five.

John Conway and Dave Gregory and their companions, well rewarded for their investment, sailed back to Australia in triumph. Before the players went back to work at their desks and stools they had one game in Melbourne against an English team which had just arrived for the summer of 1878–79. Lillywhite's team of 1876–77 had called itself "All-England" — a name first used by professionals earlier in the century. The party of 1878–79 were described as "The Gentlemen of England", a title mildly misleading in two ways, for the team lacked the greatest of gentlemen, W. G. Grace, and although it was planned as an entirely amateur enterprise, two professionals, Tom Emmett and George Ulyett of Yorkshire, were added to the group to make up the numbers. The leader was Lord Harris, captain of cricket at Eton eight years earlier, captain now of Kent, the first aristocratic patron of cricket to visit these colonies. He had been born in Trinidad when his father was governor, and was to spend much of his life promoting cricket at home and in the Empire. Lord Harris's eleven lost by ten wickets to Gregory's team. In other matches they defeated Victoria and scored one all in two games against New South Wales.

In 1880 another Australian team set out for England, composed of five men who had made the journey in 1878 and seven who had not. They were sponsored by the New South Wales and Victorian Cricketers' Associations; but in England they were made to feel unwelcome for most of the summer. Why? Gentlemanly historians were to leave the question mysteriously unanswered. The authorized version of the history of cricket, by the MCC chronicler H. S. Altham, notes their difficulty in finding opponents, finds it curious, and gives no hint of its cause. Lord Harris's version, in his autobiography, is tactful to the point of disingenuity. Australian sources, then and later, were less reticent. To J. Henniker Heaton, a colonial writer compiling in 1879 a reference work on Australia, the event that provoked the snubbing of the tourists seemed worth listing at the end of a section on riots which began with the convict rebellion of 1804 at Castle Hill and included the Eureka Stockade.[6]

On Saturday 8 February 1879, the second day of a game between Lord Harris's eleven and an eleven of New South Wales at the Sydney Cricket Ground, thousands of spectators rushed on to the ground in protest against an umpire's decision that W. L. Murdoch was run out. Someone hit Lotd Harris with a whip or a stick, and several other English players were scratched or had clothing torn. Play was abandoned for the day. The *Sydney Morning Herald* of 10 February feared that the episode would "remain a blot upon the colony for some years to come". In mitigation of what had happened, the paper observed that only three thousand, at most, of the ten thousand spectators took an active part in the disorder; and it put some of the blame on one of the English professionals, who "made use of a grossly insulting remark to the crowd about their being nothing but 'sons of convicts' ".

Just before play was due to resume on Monday morning, four public men representing the world of colonial cricket waited on Lord Harris and conveyed profound regret at the outrage, expressing the hope that it would not prevent another English team from visiting these colonies. Lord Harris's reply was courteous but stiff: he thought the event could not easily be forgotten.

It was not. The team Murdoch led to England in 1880 could not get proper teams to play against them, even when they advertised for opponents. Murdoch spoke about the cause of their punishment at a mayoral banquet in Leeds, assuring his hearers that no *cricketer* had been to blame for the fracas in Sydney and declaring that he trusted to English forbearance and fair play. "An Old Etonian" invoked these principles in *The Times,* urging that it was wrong to make the colonial visitors go on suffering. C. W. Alcock, secretary of the

Surrey club, implored Lord Harris (so Harris wrote later), "to help to make things pleasant before they left, and to get up and captain an England Eleven". Lord Harris yielded, and the Australians were granted in the second week of September a game against an eleven of England. *The Times* declared that Lord Harris had shown "a chivalry which must command the respect of our colonial friends as well as that of our own cricketers". Lord Harris judged that "considering the lateness of the season, and that some of the amateurs were on the moors, we got together a very good, and indeed a representative team".[7]

The attendance at the Oval showed that whatever the gentlemen in command of cricket thought, a great many people wanted to see Australians play. The match was watched by twenty-five thousand on the first day, almost as many on the second, and in all, a crowd which *The Times* judged "the largest ever known to have been present at any game of cricket".[8] The Australians had to play without Spofforth, who had broken a finger. W. G. Grace hit 152 in the Englishmen's first-innings score of 420, and although Murdoch made 153 not out in the Australians' second innings, the colonists lost by five wickets.

As a contest the game had gone against them, but as a healing ritual, a burying of the hatchet (a phrase much used) the encounter was gratifying to them and to their countrymen who read the cabled reports of it. The healing was completed by a banquet for the Australians at the Mansion House on 4 October, put on, as the lord mayor of London said, "to do honour to them before their return to the land of their adoption". (Was it a slip, or a felicitous fiction, for the lord mayor to imply that they were of British rather than colonial birth?) Murdoch took the lord mayor's remarks as "a compliment which would be highly appreciated by every person in Australia". He referred to "a little cloud" which had been visible when the team reached England, and which he thanked Lord Harris for dissipating. The English captain said that "that book was closed forever". *The Times* reported cheers. When they had subsided, Lord Harris delivered a sermon on cricket, an art form practised widely now among Englishmen as their Protestantism became ever more secular and their games, as taught and interpreted by schoolmasters, ever more closely identified with their civilization.

To the world in general, said Lord Harris, it might seem strange that the lord mayor of London should thus honour a mere game; but cricket was more than a game: "it was a school of itself, and a grand school too (hear, hear), for it encouraged the good and discouraged the bad qualities of human nature". It required at once a cool head, a steady hand, a sharp eye, and sound judgement: it encouraged self-denial; selfishness, cruelty, and oppression were foreign to it. Two characteristics of cricket he dwelt on above all others. First, purity: there was no inducement to a cricketer but honour. Second, service to the empire: "the game of cricket had done more to draw the Mother Country and the Colonies together than years of beneficial legislation could have done". "Hear, hear," said the company. The significance of the meeting at the Oval had been put into the necessary words by the one man who had the power to do so. The disgrace of Sydney had been erased.[9]

Visits of English teams to Australia and Australian teams to England now became normal events. English teams went out to Australia in 1881–82, 1882–83, 1884–85, 1886–87 and 1887–88. Australian teams went to England in 1882, 1884, 1886, 1888, and 1890; and from 1882 the teams representing the two countries were said to be competing for a prize, the Ashes.

The Australians led by Murdoch in 1882 were generally judged to be a stronger team than the parties of 1880 or 1878. Between mid-May and late August they played twenty-nine games, winning eighteen, losing three, and drawing eight. They showed, said *The Times,* "that thoroughness which gives to most pastimes their greatest charm".[10] At the Oval on Monday 28 August they met a team chosen by Lord Harris and three other gentlemen to be the best that England could raise. *The Times* called this eleven "the England team" and "England", a usage it had not employed before. A writer in *Cricket,* a weekly paper launched that summer just in time to welcome the Australians, reported the players nervous on account of the "important issues at stake": "It was the influence of the title of the match, England against Australia, I believe, that produced the very evident general over-anxiety."[11] More than twenty thousand people attended on the first day.

Murdoch won the toss and batted. The Australians were all out for 63, and England made 101 by the end of the day. On Tuesday, after heavy rain and in front of another twenty thousand spectators, the Australians were all out for 122, leaving England 85 to win. By the time they reached 51 for 2, the match looked to be over. But Spofforth and Boyle bowled maiden after maiden and took wicket after wicket until the last Englishman, Peate, was out when the side still needed 7 runs. For a moment the crowd were stunned. Then they began to applaud, and a knot of Australians in the pavilion went wild with joy as Spofforth was carried in shoulder-high. The Demon had taken 14 wickets for 90 in the match, bowling at the end 11 overs for 2 runs and 4 wickets. As *The Times* saw it, the victory had been a triumphant display of character, of gallantry in adversity, added to that thoroughness which the colonists had displayed all season.[12]

A farewell banquet was given to the Australians at the end of the season in the Criterion Restaurant, Piccadilly, one of the newest and most popular amenities of London. It had been put up in the 1870s by Spiers and Pond, the men who had begun Anglo-Australian cricket by bringing out Stephenson's team in 1861–62. The partners had returned to England, laden with money from that tour, from their Cafe de Paris in Melbourne, and from other enterprises, in time to tender successfully for refreshment rooms along the earliest underground railway line, the Metropolitan, in 1865. They made these rooms the first places in London where families up from the country for the day could dine cleanly, substantially and cheaply. The Criterion complex — restaurant, refreshment buffet, ballroom, private dining-rooms, and theatre all under the same roof — was a more ambitious venture in the same market, by men who had learned in Melbourne that there was profit to be made by an imaginative and egalitarian response to the needs of people with plain tastes and moderate incomes. Colonial visitors could be thoroughly comfortable in Spiers and Pond establishments, and could even feel proud of them. When Mr Punch in 1878 told the Australian cricketers (in an imaginary interview) that all social reforms begin in England, they were shocked. "You dare say that, when you know that Spiers and Pond came from Australia!" All in all, the Criterion Restaurant was a fine place for the visitors of 1882 to be given a feast.[13]

They glowed to the tribute of Sir Henry Barkly, once governor of Victoria, who toasted from the chair "The Australian Cricket Team". He made them sound like a conquering army. "The strict discipline, enormous energy, and indomitable pluck", he declared, "deserved and should receive unstinted praise." Murdoch in response proposed "The Cricketers of England" and "Success to Cricket". The Australian captain was no orator, but he had been improving with practice during the summer, and his confidence may well have been strengthened by his knowing that he was now being hailed as the W. G. Grace of Australia. Sir Henry Barkly's speech provoked from him what George Giffen, the South Australian player making his first tour, judged an "exceedingly neat reply": "I feel very much like your able General, Sir Garnet Wolseley, must feel when he contemplates the result of the Egyptian campaign. He was sent out to do a certain thing — to crush Arabi — and he has done it. I was sent home as captain of an Australian cricket team to beat England, and I am proud to have done it."

Metaphors from warfare were plentiful in newspaper praise of the Australians. "A reader might fancy", observed a writer in *Cricket,* "that a Muscovite XI had beaten their traditional foes" rather than "men just as much national as if they hailed from Cornwall or the Hebrides."*Cricket* thought that in general the press was responding extravagantly to the Australians' victory and their compatriots' defeat: "A victory by 7 runs hardly furnishes a logical deduction that Australian cricket is so much superior to England as to give cause for such a universal wail of decadence." Yet *Cricket* itself, looking for something new to say on Thursday to readers who had been offered full reports of the match in the daily papers of Tuesday and Wednesday, wrote not merely of decadence but of death, in jocular parody of an *in memoriam* notice:

SACRED TO THE MEMORY
OF
ENGLAND'S SUPREMACY IN THE CRICKET FIELD
WHICH EXPIRED
ON THE 29TH DAY OF AUGUST, AT THE OVAL.
"IT'S END WAS PEATE. "[14]

The makers of the *Sporting Times,* also known as *The Pink 'un,* a gossipy weekly for fast gentlemen, had time to see that jest in *Cricket* before their own paper went to press for the week, and Saturday's *Sporting Times* carried a more elaborate *in memoriam* notice which was to give a symbol to the game.

In Affectionate Remembrance
OF
ENGLISH CRICKET
WHICH DIED AT THE OVAL
ON
29TH AUGUST, 1882,
Deeply lamented by a large circle of mourning friends and acquaintances
R. I. P.

N. B. — The body will be cremated and the ashes taken to Australia.[15]

It was a topical fancy. The Cremation Society, founded in 1875, was arousing much controversy, and the first cremation in the modern history of England was to be performed some six weeks after this item was published. The piece was reprinted by other journals in England and Australia, and the conceit took on. In the week Murdoch's team returned home, the *Bulletin* in Sydney wrote of "the revered ashes of English cricket which had been laid on the shelf of the Australian Eleven". Another English team was now in Australia for the summer of 1882–83, eight amateurs and four professionals under the Honourable Ivo Bligh, heir to the Earl of Darnley. In Melbourne, responding to a toast to the team, Bligh said that they had come to beard the kangaroo in his den and to try to recover the Ashes.[16]

Bligh's team played three times against Murdoch's eleven, losing once and winning twice. A group of admiring ladies in Melbourne tried to reify the metaphor by burning a bail used in the third game and presenting the ashes in an urn to the English captain. Bligh took home the urn, and took also one of its donors, Miss Florence Morphy, who became Mrs Bligh and later the Countess of Darnley. After Lord Darnley died she gave the urn to the MCC for safe keeping, where it lodges now in a Memorial Gallery with other relics, incuding the scorebook of the game at the Oval in 1882 in which the scorer's writing grows ever more shaky as he records the fall of England's wickets in the second innings. It became a cherished mystery of the game that the ashes in the urn, though material, were not real. No trophy would ever change hands at the end of a series — one way, perhaps, of symbolizing what Lord Harris affirmed in his sermon of 1880: that a cricketer has no inducement but honour. In 1883 Bligh and his team were not thought to have recaptured the real, i.e. metaphorical, Ashes; for they played and lost a fourth game, arranged afresh late in their tour, against an Australian eleven.

A fourth Australian team, led again by Murdoch, spent the summer of 1884 in England. For the first time in England a series of three representative matches was arranged. They were billed as "Australia v. England". The first, at Manchester, was drawn. The second, at Lord's, England won by an innings. The third, at the Oval, was drawn. The encounters were acquiring the character of an international institution. *Test matches,* some reporters were now calling them.[17] The phrase suggested more than mere play. A match is a contest that may or may not be a game. A test may be an ordeal, a proving, a trial. It was difficult to say exactly what had been proved in the season of 1884, for although the Australians lost one match, they had the better of the two that were drawn. "Through an utterly absurd arrangement", declared a writer in the Melbourne *Argus* of 16 September 1884, "the three representative matches that were to have decided the question of supremacy between the two great cricketing powers were each limited to three days."

The visit of an English team to Australia in 1884–85 did little to settle the question of supremacy. The visitors were all professionals, their tour being a speculation on the part of Shaw, Shrewsbury, and Lillywhite like those of 1876–77 and 1881–82; and a team lacking the leading amateurs could not now seem truly representative of England. Moreover, the Englishmen found that they could not easily get a representative Australian side to play against them. When they challenged Murdoch's team, just back from England, to matches in Melbourne and Sydney, the Australians asked for half the takings. "Such a demand," wrote Shaw, "coming from a team supposed to be amateurs, playing at home, staggered us." "Our visit to Australia", the professionals wrote in their own account of the 1884–85 season, "was essentially a business one", and they were outraged that men with other jobs, and in their own country, should demand an equal share of the takings with men "who had travelled thousands of miles in pursuit of their profession". The Englishmen offered 30 per cent. Most of the Australians refused. Twenty pounds a man for a match? Rejected, wrote Shaw, "with contumely". Finally a match was arranged at Adelaide with Murdoch's eleven on their own terms, the South Australian Cricket Association taking half the risk and paying each team £450. The Englishmen won by eight wickets. For a second match against a combined Australian eleven, at Melbourne, a team was gathered of men who had not been in Murdoch's party. England won by ten wickets. In a third encounter with an Australian eleven, in Sydney, some of Murdoch's men agreed to play, having "come to their senses at last", so it seemed to James Lillywhite. The Australians won by six runs. There were two further international matches, Australia winning the first, in Sydney, and England the second, in Melbourne. Over the whole series the Englishmen won three matches and lost two; but their victories were rendered a little hollow by the refusal of leading colonial players to play against them. Some gave domestic and other personal reasons for staying out, but the Englishmen did not believe them. "The real cause of all this disturbance was money," wrote Lillywhite; "nothing but money!"[18]

Murdoch, Giffen, and others of the 1884 team — seven in all — who refused to play against England except for half the takings, were criticized severely in the Australian press. A movement arose to exclude them from the next team to visit England, and the party chosen to go in 1886 was the least representative so far. It was also the first to be other than a private enterprise of its members, being chosen and sponsored by the Melbourne Cricket Club. It fared badly, losing three times to teams representing England.

In 1886–87 Shaw and Shrewsbury took out another professional party which twice defeated Australian elevens weakened by not having Scott and Bonnor, who had stayed in England after the season of 1886, and Giffen, who declined to play. Twelve months later two English teams arrived simultaneously in Australia, combining once to play (and defeat) an Australian side and otherwise touring separately and competitively. "Probably there was never such a prominent case of folly in connection with cricket," reflected Lord Hawke, captain of the mixed team of amateurs and professionals who had come out at the invitation of the Melbourne Cricket Club. "The cricket rivalries of Melbourne and Sydney were our undoing," wrote Alfred Shaw, entrepreneur of the professional team invited out by the New South Wales Cricket Association. It was a spectacular display of unfederal enterprise on the part of the hosts. In Sydney they had wanted an English team to help celebrate the centenary of British settlement. In Melbourne they had simply wanted an English team. Neither lot consulted the other. There was too much cricket for the paying public, and too little mystique associated with matches against England when the mother country was represented twice over. Both parties lost money.[19]

The fiasco discouraged people in both countries from organizing another tour in a hurry. From 1881 to 1888 there had been an English team in Australia for some part of every year. Nearly four years passed before the next one arrived. In that time the rhythm of Australian visits to England remained as it had been since 1878 — one every two years; but it was touch and go in 1888, and the 1890 tour turned out so dismally that there was talk of suspending the visits for a long time.

By 1888 Spofforth had retired from international cricket and went to live in England that year; Boyle was forty; several of the best players (among them Murdoch) did not go, and there were squabbles among those who did. Thanks largely to the bowling of two newcomers, C. T. B. Turner and J. J. Ferris, the Australians won one of the three matches against sides representing England; but they lost the other two. In 1890 Murdoch, now thirty-six, led a team to England for the first time since 1884. As in 1888 and 1886, the team lacked leading colonial players, including George Giffen, for reasons disputed among players, administrators, and journalists. The team of 1890 played two matches against representative English sides, and lost both. This touring party became the first to lose more games than it won.

The late 1880s were bad years for Anglo-Australian cricket. Two English sides at once, both losing money heavily, then none for years. Giants of the early Australian sides retiring, other champions apparently sulking, no new men emerging to compare with the old heroes except perhaps Turner, spoken of by some as another Spofforth. Talk of "a very pronounced falling off of public support" in the *Australasian* in 1887; letters in the *Sydney Morning Herald* under the heading "The Decline of Cricket" in 1891. What went wrong is difficult to say, as contemporaries were so divided about it, and historians of cricket, being even more whiggish than historians at large, have been disinclined to look hard into the interruption of progress that followed the golden years of 1882–84 in which the Ashes were created and test matches were first written about. The doldrums, H. S. Altham calls the period from the mid-1880s to 1891. Whatever kept Australian cricket becalmed in those years, it was the collision between English professionals and Australians commercials at the end of 1884 that had brought it to a halt.[20]

The wind blew fair again in the Australian summer of 1891–92, thanks to a skilful imperial diplomat, the Earl of Sheffield, who took out at his own expense a team which had W. G. Grace as captain and Alfred Shaw as manager. As Lord Sheffield and Dr Grace were both compared sometimes with John Bull, the team was England incarnate. The earls of Sheffield exemplified what envious foreigners said about the capacity of the English aristocracy to survive: the first earl had been patron of Edward Gibbon, and now the third was patron of W. G. Grace: Altham calls him the Maecenas of cricketers. He has been in the diplomatic service, and then in the House of Commons as a Conservative. Since 1884 his private cricket ground at Sheffield Park, in Sussex, had been the place where Australian teams began their tours, playing against an eleven of England raised by their host. He had been active in the Volunteer movement and would later promote the Territorials. He was virtually lifelong president of the Sussex County Cricket Club, and he resolved now to invigorate imperial cricket.

"Everything was done on a princely scale," wrote Alfred Shaw, "from the fee of the captain downwards." The urge to see the forty-three year-old Grace contributed to immense crowds and takings, which enabled Lord Sheffield to recover fourteen thousand of the sixteen thousand pounds the visit cost him. Of three five-day matches between team representing England and Australia, the local side won the first two and lost the third. Winning the second match meant for Australians winning a series for the first time since 1882. The outcome of "the second great test match", as the *Sydney Morning Herald* called it, was uncertain until the last day, when England, needing 227, were dismissed by Turner and Giffen for 156. "For a time", reported the *Herald*, "the spectators rushed about as though demented, such hand-shaking, such congratulations, such cheering and waving of hats, canes, and umbrellas." Kangaroos in cartoons rejoiced over defeated lions.[21]

Lord Sheffield's best service to the imperial cause was to take home a losing team. "Twelve months ago", said the *Age* in a tribute to him at the end of the season, "the suggestion of such a marvellous revival in the grand old game being probable or even possible would have been laughed to scorn." His achievement was commemorated in a trophy paid for out of money he had left behind for the advancement of cricket in the colonies. The Australasian Cricket Council, a federal body formed in 1892 and representing cricket associations in Victoria, New South Wales, and South Australia, commissioned a shield, to be competed for each year by teams from the three colonies. It showed a batsman and a bowler beside a plate depicting the Sheffield Park cricket ground; it bore the arms of the Earl and the kangaroo and emu of Australia, the whole surmounted by a statue of Victory. The Australians named it the Sheffield Shield.[22]

An eleven under the auspices of the Australasian Cricket Council and led by John Blackham, who had been Australia's wicket-keeper since 1877, visited England in 1893, losing one match against England and drawing two. A. E. Stoddart was captain of an English team which went to Australia in 1894–95 for a series that unrolled perfectly: two all and one to play when a hundred thousand people in five days attended the Melbourne ground and saw England win by six wickets. From 1890 to 1899 Australian teams went to England every three years. In 1896 there was a new hero among the amateurs of England, the Indian prince Ranjitsinhji, and there was a new problem posed by the professionals, five of whom expressed the mounting confidence of their trade by putting an industrial demand to the Surrey club, which was choosing the team for the third and decisive test match at the Oval: twenty pounds for the match instead of ten pounds, or no play. Three gave in, two stayed on strike, and England won the series.

Stoddart led out another touring side in 1897–98. The visitors suffered badly in the unusually great heat of that Australian summer, and had other misfortunes including injuries and illness. Australia, wrote Ranjitsinhji in a vivid book about the tour, had "easily repossessed itself of the ashes of English cricket from the latest invading team". The Australians kept the Ashes in England in 1899, when Joe Darling was captain and Victor Trumper made his first tour. "Mr Darling's eleven of 1899", *The Times* declared in a leading article at the end of the season, "is the best that has ever come from the Antipodes." It was good for the cause of imperial cricket that the last Australian team to visit the old country in the colonial era should win, so that the mythical Ashes were in their country when it became a commonwealth.[23]

Why did so many people in Australia play and watch cricket, and why were their best players so good that they could compete on even terms with the best of England, when the motherland had about ten times as many people? Such questions were asked with relish between 1800 and 1900.

There is no sure way to measure the popularity of nineteenth-century pastimes. It depends on what counts as evidence, and some of the evidence cannot be counted. The most popular sporting event in the continent as measured by the numbers of people attending it was the Melbourne Cup. The crowd of a hundred thousand at Flemington in 1880 (when the population of Melbourne was less than three hundred thousand) was larger than gathered at any other sporting occasion in nineteenth-century Australia, and perhaps at any non-sporting occasion too. It may well be that horse-racing was more talked about than any other sport, and that more bets were placed on horse-races than on any other sporting contest (though sculling may for a time have challenged horse-racing on that score). But if we are looking only at games, a category which in ordinary usage excludes horse-racing, cricket comes first. "Cricket is now the premier game of the people of Britain," said the author of a survey of pastimes in 1886, "as it is unquestionably the most popular game of the colonists of Australia." How many men and boys played it compared with other games, including all the varieties of football, we shall never know. Richard Twopeny supposed in 1883 that cricket must take first place in his catalogue of Australian sports, "because all ages and all classes are interested in it, and not to be interested in it amounts almost to a social crime".[24] Figures of attendance at games where people paid to watch are patchy, but solid enough to tell us that intercolonial and international cricket matches regularly attracted larger crowds than most football matches. Apart from the people attending, large crowds gathered outside the offices of newspapers and sports stores while cricket matches were on elsewhere in the same city, or in another colony, or on the other side of the world, to see the latest scores put up as they came in by telephone or telegraph. The hundred thousand people who attended the last test match in Melbourne in 1895, over five days, made up the largest crowd so far to watch a game of cricket; and the thirty-six thousand who went to the Sydney Cricket Ground for the first day of the fifth test in 1898 were the largest crowd to attend a cricket match on a single day.

Twopeny noted that the popularity of football was more local than that of cricket. "But in Melbourne", he wrote, "I think it is more intense."[25] Attendances at football finals in Melbourne, according to newspaper reports, were eight thousand in 1880 and twenty thousand in 1900; and in Sydney, attendance at the final in 1900 was six thousand. Such intercolonial contests as there were in football could attract crowds comparable with those at test matches. Thirty thousand people saw a game in Melbourne between Victoria and South Australia in 1890. That was a larger crowd than had yet gathered at any cricket match on a single day. If all Australians had played the same sort of football, the game might well have become in these years more popular than cricket; but we might as well speculate about what would have happened if all their railway lines had been of the same gauge.

Some of the people attending international and intercolonial cricket matches were there to see celebrities. Spofforth and Murdoch, Boyle and Gregory, later Darling and Trumper; Shaw and Hornby, Stoddard and Ranjitsinhji; above all, Grace: these men drew spectators in Australia as Sarah Bernhardt (touring Australia in the year of Grace's second visit) drew theatre audiences. International cricketers were described by the *Australasian* in 1880 as "theatrical stars". In England and Australia, cricket became in the later nineteenth century a popular entertainment. *The Times* noticed among the record crowd of twenty thousand at the Oval on 28 August 1882 a sort of spectator not hitherto attracted to cricket grounds: "Many of the general public even who do not as a rule take much interest in cricket have concerned themselves about this match." There is grist for social historians in a remark by the actor Oscar Asche about his father, a Norwegian immigrant in Melbourne, attending the international match in March 1877: "He knew nothing about cricket, but he went because his pals went." Crowds at sporting events were being enlarged now by urges and opportunities new to the common man: to see famous performers one had read about in the papers and heard talked about at work or in the pub; to be part of a crowd enjoying a quantity of leisure not before conceded to working pople. The new forces were as well represented in Australia as anywhere in the world. Young W. S. Jevons, watching the Grand National Cricket Match at Sydney in January 1857 between teams from Victoria and New South Wales, calculated that over the three days of play, nearly a quarter of the population had attended for some part of the time, "and the business of the town", he wrote to his brother at home, "was quite interrupted. I take this to be a sign, not of laziness, but that the people are so well to do as to be able to spare more holy days and really to enjoy themselves more than the people of other countries."[26]

Cricket flourished here as nowhere else outside England. "In no other country and in no other of our colonies has cricket thrived as it has done in Australia," declared *The Times* on 7 September 1880. Why it was not thought to have thrived quite so well in other societies formed by emigration from England is a question I shall not try to answer here. Leaving aside the place of cricket in the United States and Canada, New Zealand, and South Africa, why did so many people in Australia play and watch the game?

To begin with, Australians played or watched whatever games were transported from home. Emigrants after 1850 were coming from an England in which outdoor games had a new popularity and social purpose, to a land rich in the social and climatic conditions favourable to such games. When colonial men and boys began to play football, there was not yet, and there never would be, one single code followed at home which could be the model out here, and before anybody thought much about games as activities in which nations or sub-nations were represented by teams, people in New South Wales and Victoria had committed themselves to different codes of football, rather as people in adjoining valleys of New Guinea committed themselves to different languages. The rules of cricket, on the other hand, were codified by the MCC four months after the first fleet reached New South Wales, in good time to make sure that the game was played everywhere in the continent exactly as at home, and that it could become for Australians, as football never could, a national and international game.

As Mandle has shown, Australian cricket was transformed after 1860 by players who had learned the game lately in England and by the visits of English sides. Spofforth looked back on the tour of 1873–74 as having stirred up a national interest in cricket among Australian colonists. "Hitherto it had been learning," he wrote in 1892; "within a very little while it was to teach."[27] The Australians' victories of 1877, 1878, and 1882 provoked people in both countries to marvel and wonder; and although cricketers were not thought to be great readers of books — Grace was famous for reading almost nothing outside his set of *Wisden* — nobody trying to explain success or failure in the late nineteenth century could escape entirely the influence of that tradition of speculation about evolution which culminated in *The Origin of Species*.

The Australian victors at Lord's in 1878 were celebrated in England for being "all of our own flesh and blood", as an imperialist paper put it; "and we welcome their prowess cheerfully as a proof that the old stock is not degenerating in those far-off lands". Interpreting the result of that game in terms of imperial genetics became a commonplace in the burgeoning popular literature of cricket. "That day, as I and others have repeatedly stated," wrote C. F. Pardon, of *Bell's Life,* in 1884, "marked the birth of the Australian colonies as a cricketing community. . . . we did not know how remarkably proficient the descendants of Englishmen had become under the glorious climate of the greater England below the line." Lord Harris believed that the climate gave Australians "an immense advantage", not only by letting them play for more of the year, but by making them better throwers and bowlers. "The Australian aborigines were . . . great throwers, and the Caucasian in the Antipodes has acquired through the effect of climate a like elasticity of the throwing and bowling muscles."[28]

Nat Gould pointed to the open spaces in Australian towns: "The many parks and recreation grounds in the large cities afford the youngsters every opportunity to indulge in cricket." The great all-rounder George Giffen, born in Adelaide in 1859, recalled scampering off to the parklands of that city after school to play with a rubber ball and a stick, with a kerosene tin or nail-can or tree for a wicket. Those parklands were gifts offered by nature and society to many more lads in Australia than in England. If Giffen's father had remained a carpenter in England instead of emigrating, George may never have had a chance to play cricket; out here he was like "the vast majority of Australian boys", Giffen reflected, in taking to cricket "almost before the days of pot-hooks and hangers had ceased". Richard Twopeny perceived the difference in 1883: "There is no class too poor to play, as at home."[29] The difference in overall populations may have been misleading. Given the climate, the parklands and paddocks, the public holidays and Saturday half-holidays, and differences between the schools and other institutions of the two societies, there may well have been as many boys and young men playing cricket among Australia's four million people in 1900 as among Great Britain's nearly forty millions.

Moreover, English tours of Australia meant more to the host population than Australian tours of England. Greater crowds attended test matches in Melbourne and Sydney than in London or Manchester, though charges for admission were higher in Australia and though neither colonial city had as many people as Manchester. The largest attendance at a cricket match in England in the nineteenth century was not at a test match but at a match between the county teams of Nottingham and Surrey at the Oval in 1892, when 63,763 paying patrons and an uncounted number of members attended over three days. Twopeny observed that the encounters with England made cricket surge in popularity. "The success of the first Australian Eleven bred cricketers by the thousand," he wrote in 1883. "If that eleven was picked out of, say, 10,000 men and boys playing cricket, the present has been chosen from 20,000, and by 1890 the eleven will be chosen from 100,000."[30] As a colonial-based imperial patriot, Twopeny risked the prophecy that "from 1890 onwards, the cricket championship [would], except through occasional bad-luck, become permanently resident in Australia". He underestimated not only the bad luck but the capacity of English society to produce champions from among its leisured gentlemen and semi-gentlemen and its professional players. But Twopeny was right in seeing that it was the international encounters that did most for the game at large among Australians.

When the very first English team landed from the *Great Britain* in 1861 the *Argus* noticed strain as well as delight in the air of Melbourne, as if "some tremendous crisis was at hand", or some trial which was "to make or mar us for ever" was approaching. Rachel Henning, writing to her brother-in-law in England, thought it "a most audacious thing of the colonists to challenge the finest players in the world, and to imagine that they could teach their respected Grandmother". The victory of Stephenson's eleven over the Victorian eighteen "ought to take down the colonial 'bounce' a little," she thought. We do not know what she thought when another Victorian eighteen beat an English eleven in 1874. *The Time*'s correspondent resident in Victoria reported after that win: "Our unexpected success delighted all patriotic colonists, though many lamented the intolerable 'blowing' which would follow it. There had not been much to complain of yet in that respect." The *Australasian* noticed, however, "some certainly very straight-up-and-down blowing".[31] Blowing was a colonial word and habit which Trollope had just explored in his book on Australia and New Zealand, with a gentle wit which nevertheless gave much offence to its touchy objects. There was much blowing after the victory of eleven colonists over eleven Englishmen at Melbourne in 1877. The *Australasian* published verses headed "The Brazen Trumpet", which ended:

Now, Ant'ny Trollope,
Say we can wallop
The whole of creation at blowing,
But take back your sneer —
My word, now! Look here!
D'ye think it's for nothing we're crowing?

Melbourne Punch offered its own rhymed account of the match:

> Then rose a shout Australian
> That echoed to the main,
> "Twas confident, not 'blowing'.
> "Again we'll do the same!"[32]

Australians could be proud not only of their players but of the amenities created for play, delighting in the amazement of Englishmen at colonial cricket grounds, blowing as the Victorian government blew in the official catalogue of the Colonial and Indian Exhibition of 1886: "There are no more perfect arrangements of the kind in the world than those of the Melbourne Cricket Ground." Conversely, Australians could be proud when they saw how modest were the appointments of English grounds, even Lord's, which struck the tourists of 1878 as "scarcely equal to the Melbourne Cricket Club". In the motherland they could savour, too, how poorly informed the English spectator was about the state of play, lacking the encyclopaedic scoreboards they took for granted at home. They were made aware how much more equality colonists enjoyed when they saw how little was done to give people in the shilling enclosure a view of the game, compared with the slopes and mounds of Australia. "In the old country", Nat Gould wrote after a decade in the colonies, "there is far too much catering for the priviliged few at the expense of the many." Australians, he thought, would not put up with the conditions he recalled at English grounds.[33] If only Spiers and Pond had been put in charge of them!

Australians made heroes of their victors. When Harry Boyle from Bendigo bowled W. G. Grace at Melbourne in 1873, "about 1,500 Bendigo men, who had come because Boyle was their champion, went fairly mad and cooeed with true Australian fervour". When the team of 1878 returned home to Sydney, Spofforth noticed that "the old motto, 'Advance Australia' seemed to span every corner. . . . We were the heroes of the hour." The sculler Edward Trickett had enjoyed such a welcome a year earlier, when twenty-five thousand people cheered him into Sydney after he had won in London what was described as the championship of the world. Genial English praise of these achievements was transcribed at length for the pleasure of readers in Australia. "She has beaten the mother country on the Thames, and now she beats England at Lord's. At the present rate we shall have nothing left of our long-boasted athletic performance."[34] It was a novel experience for colonists to know that they were being noticed in England. The year 1877 was the beginning of a long period in which Australians realized with mixed feelings that the names of their sporting champions were familiar to many people in the motherland who knew nothing either of their national leaders or of any Australian achievement except in sport.

Nearly all the cricketers who represented Australia at cricket against England were native-born colonists, and the few who were not were sometimes given Australian birthplaces in patriotic popular celebration. Currency v. Sterling, Natives v. Englishmen (or v. the rest of the world), the Colonies v. England — these had long been common ways of dividing players into teams for cricket and other games, and there was a tradition of banter about the genetic, moral, or other significance of the outcome. Before the tourists of 1878 left for England, the *Australasian* declared that they wished "to prove at Lord's and the Oval and other grounds in England that the colonials are worthy descendants of the good old stock from which they have come". Mandle, who quotes this passage, shows how ardently the early Australian wins in England were interpreted in the colonies as having provided reassurance that "the manly qualities of the parent stock flourish as vigorously in these distant colonies as in the mother country", as offering proof "to the millions of our friends at home that the climate of Australia had no enervating influence on the Anglo-Saxon race". As we have seen, the point was made also by observers in England; but out in the colonies it was made in tones of exhilaration and relief for which there was no place in metropolitan responses. Mandle detects also a less overt feeling that achievement on the cricket field refuted suspicions in England and fears in Australia that colonists were weakened physically or morally as a people by the convict element in their parentage — suspicions and fears to which the fracas at Sydney in February 1879 may well have contributed for a time.[35]

Mandle writes that after the victories of 1877 and 1878, "the laudation of Australian cricketers and Australia's national identification with them was settled". He then quotes a writer twenty years later, in 1897, who discerned in Australians a passion for cricket "intensified by an unfilial yearning on the part of young Australia to triumphantly thrash the mother country".[36] It is an eloquent passage, but I think it invites a little more analysis. The journal in which it appeared was itself a thoroughly imperial artefact, being the colonial edition of the *Review of Reviews*, founded at home in 1890 by W. T. Stead, an ardent imperialist who was also maker of the *Pall Mall Gazette*. "An unfilial yearning," the writer says. "Unfilial" seems to me to strike the jocular note common in journalism relating cricket to the world off the field. Is the yearning to thrash a parent so unfilial? A mother, perhaps: but to thrash, say, John Bull? A son who wants to go on for ever competing with his father is surely less unfilial, less adventurous, less radical, than one who leaves home.

An anti-imperial nationalism might have disposed Australians not to play cricket at all. So intense a devotion to the most English of games was a sign of how spontaneously and profoundly Australians embraced the culture of the motherland. The nationalism of cricket was all of a piece with the sentiment of the Australian Natives' Association; and even an ardent ANA man could think a little wistfully of the Americans' capacity for creating sports of their own, while "the only out-of-door recreations which have firmly established themselves throughout Australia", as W. H. Sowden said in 1892, "are the English cricket, the English football, and the equally national amusements of aquatics and horse-racing". As if in apology for the natives' lack of inventiveness, Sowden suggested that climate had more than British patriotism to do with it; but then he went on — despite, as he said, Trollope's advice not to blow: "John Bull, jun., has taken up the traditional old manly games of John Bull, sen., and has fairly beaten his father at them." Any imperial federationist in Sowden's audience of 1892 could have been deeply reassured by that image.[37]

There were people in Australia indifferent to cricket, among them the great old Anglo-Australian Sir Henry Parkes, who grew up in Birmingham too early and too poor to be touched by the game and was a middle-aged colonist before the missionaries of the mid-century propagated it in his adopted land. There was perhaps a little Irish-Australian dislike of the Englishness of colonial recreations in James Hogan's distaste for the "inordinate love of field-sports" out here. But the ideology that inspired the Gaelic Athletic Association in Ireland — "our politics being essentially national, so should our athletics" — does not appear to have been embraced by many Irish Australians. The sons of Irish immigrants played cricket as other Australian boys did: Herbert Moran recalled being sent to see Stoddart's team of 1894–95, and for Stoddart's next visit Australia's wicket-keeper was James Joseph Kelly.[38] The makers of the *Bulletin*, though surly from time to time about their compatriots' attachment to the "Anglo-Colonial" encounters, and though they could make the visit of an English team the occasion for fiery rhetoric about the nastiness of English society, evidently thought too well of the game ever to attack it; whether from a prudent concern for circulation or a relish for the game itself, the *Bulletin* carried a good deal of straight reporting about cricket, including test matches.

The *Bulletin* declared after the victories of 1897–98: "This ruthless rout of English cricket will do — and has done — more to enhance the cause of Australian nationality than could ever be achieved by miles of erudite essays and impassioned appeal."[39] The paper may well have been right. Certainly the Australian cricket teams helped the cause of federation: the emu and kangaroo on their caps and blazers (as on the Sheffield Shield) were an emblematic advertisement for the coming Commonwealth. But Lord Harris may have been right, too, when he said that cricket "had done more to draw the Mother Country and the Colonies together than years of beneficial legislation could have done". It had long been an object of imperial policy to encourage a sense of Australian nationality such as would move the inhabitants of these colonies to form a federation. If an English defeat at cricket enhanced that cause, it could be celebrated as earnestly in the Colonial Office as in the *Bulletin* office.

The principal cricket grounds of Australia, though improvements on their models, were as English as the cathedrals. They reminded people from home of Lord's or Old Trafford; Adelaide's ground, like Surrey's, was called Oval. The pitches were made of Australian soil planted with English grass. The ambition of B. J. Wardell, secretary of the Melbourne Cricket Club from 1878 to 1911, was to make Australia's MCC the counterpart of England's. The comings and goings of touring teams were occasions for affirming imperial solidarity. The Australians played at Lord's and were feted by lords, and the explanation that Lord's was really named after Thomas became itself a pleasing ritual. Lord Sheffield received them lavishly. Lord Harris and Lord Hawke gave them hospitality. The Prince of Wales watched them play, and met the 1896 team at Sheffield Park. Lord Carrington took the 1899 team, and the visiting New South Wales Lancers, to the Empire Theatre. After the games came the speeches. The team of 1878 were given a grand banquet by those Australians in London who were the mainstay of the Royal Colonial Institute. The Duke of Manchester, presiding, confessed himself "disgracefully ignorant of the game of cricket" but full of admiration for "the pluck and spirit which have induced the Australian cricketers to come half-way round the world to play an old English game on the soil of Old England". He was cheered by the company; and so was Hugh Childers, the returned colonist from Victoria who had been in Gladstone's ministry, when he spoke of the connection between imperial and colonial prosperity, and again when he said: "Whether in the field, on the racecourse, or in the cricket field, Englishmen were Englishmen all the world over", and yet again when he said: "We could not better describe a good Englishman than by saying he makes a good cricketer."[40]

For the rest of the century it was the custom for such sentiments to be expressed in speeches about cricket at both ends of the empire. At Sydney's new Hotel Australia in 1891, Lord Sheffield jested about whether the real credit for discovering Australia was due to Captain Cook or to cricket; and at the same hotel in 1898 George Reid as premier, replying to Edmund Barton's toast, "wound up", Ranjitsinhji reported, with "a grand eulogy for the game". Retired governors were frequent guests at the banquets in England, and working governors attended them in Australia. "These international games", said Lord Brassey at Melbourne in 1898, "tend to engage the attention of both England and Australia towards each other, and hence a close relationship of good feeling and brotherhood results." Observers closer to the colonial earth than governors also saw the test matches as enhancing the solidarity of empire. Nat Gould perceived them in the context of an imperial culture embracing other kinds of play: "The visits of Australian cricketers, scullers, and athletes to England certainly strengthen these ties, as also do the visits of an English Eleven, or prominent actors and actresses, to Australia."[41]

From time to time there were incidents that momentarily strained the connection, as when Grace accused an umpire of unfairness at Sydney in 1892, and when crowds heckled and hooted at test matches in 1897–98 in a manner that some of the Englishmen believed ought somehow to be stopped. These moments of conflict invite the historian's attention: it is, I think, a significant fact that among the English players the most vehement in deploring the Australian habit of "barracking" — troubled by it as an expression of disorder, sensing in it a threat to civilization — was the Indian Ranjitsinhji. But not until the season of 1932–33 was the boundary between play and non-play crossed as dangerously as when the Sydney ground was invaded in 1879. The frictions of 1880 to 1900 were easily contained and quickly forgotten.

The language of warfare was often used of test matches; but the language was a pretence, a reassuring joke. Playing the game of cricket might be a physical and moral preparation for the battlefield, as for less awful arenas of life; but a game it remained. The captains of Australia and England were not opposing generals except for those few hours with bat and ball in which their armies obeyed the laws of cricket proclaimed by the MCC. Off the field they were friendly acquaintances, fellow-subjects of the queen, British kinsmen. Spofforth and Murdoch settled to live in England as happily as any other returned colonists.

At both ends of the Empire the word *cricket* was coming to be used by the end of the century as a moral metaphor at large, a synonym for honourable dealing with other men off the field as well as on: the *Oxford English Dictionary* has an example from 1900 in its definitions of this most untranslatable of English words. Only Englishmen, it was said, really understood its meaning. Women were thought to have an imperfect grasp of what cricket was about. Foreigners were reassuringly ignorant of it. In 1899 colonials and Englishmen enjoyed telling each other a story in which Kruger quakes with fright as the news that a contingent of Australian soldiers is on the way to South Africa: "And I hear that Eleven of them have defeated all England!"[42]

Alfred Shaw, publishing his memoirs near the end of the war in South Africa, looked back over his quarter-century of cricket and wrote: "If we did ever so little to bring Englishmen and their Colonial brethren more closely together than they were before; if we played but an insignificant part in sowing the seed of that magnificent display of patriotic sentiment, seen in the closing year of the nineteenth century, we are more than satisfied." I think Shaw was right to believe that imperial cricket did play some part in making the climate of sentiment in which sixteen thousand men went from Australia to fight for England in South Africa. Two great wars later John Curtin said at Lord's: "Australians will always fight for those 22 yards. Lord's and its traditions belong to Australia just as much as to England."[43]

"TEST MATCHES": A NOTE ON USAGE

The earliest recorded use I know is from the first English tour, of which W. J. Hammersley's *Victorian Cricketers' Guide* (Melbourne: Sands and Kenny, 1862) said: "Of the thirteen matches, five only can be termed 'test matches', the three played at Melbourne and the two played at Sydney."[44] Nobody else appears to have taken up Hammersley's usage. These five matches were between eleven visitors and eighteen local players, and posterity did not accept *test match* as an appropriate name for so lopsided an encounter. A match could not be a test match unless each side fielded the same number of players, and unless the teams were agreed to be fairly well representative of their constituencies. Nobody appears to have thought at the time of calling the first eleven-a-side game at Melbourne in 1877 a test match; but from that year on, journalists writing about the now frequent meetings between English and

Australian sides were evidently feeling for words to capture the special character of these encounters. The *Age* in 1878 wrote of "the first four great matches" — meaning eleven-a-side games against teams at least representative of countries. The *Times* wrote of the 1880 tour that "at one time it seemed probable that the Australians would be permitted to return without having *tested* [my emphasis] their ability against the cricketing strength of England", and C. F. Pardon, looking back on the summer four years later recalled the feeling of relief "that the colonial players could at last measure their strength with the most famous of our picked men". The game at the Oval in 1882 was for sporting papers "the great match between England and Australia" (*Cricket*), "the big cricket match" (*Sporting Times*).[45]

The earliest use I know of *test match* apart from Hammersley's in 1862 is in an Australian newspaper of 1883, and for the next ten years I think Australian usage is more widespread than English. In a pursuit of the origins of the term undertaken by contributors to the scholarly journal *Cricket Quarterly,* the first example spotted so far (apart from Hammersley's) is from the *Sydney Morning Herald* of 3 January 1883 on Bligh's team: "the first of the great test matches". The Melbourne *Argus* used it in a review of the 1884 series on 16 September 1884, and a London correspondent of the Sydney *Daily Telegraph* wrote of "the three test matches" in a dispatch published on 20 September 1884. C. F. Pardon, editor of the sporting paper *Bell's Life,* also wrote of "the three test matches" at a time when he could not have seen either of those Australian papers.[46] Evidently the phrase had a fair currency in England that summer. W. F. Mandle has found it used that year in Boyle's and Scott's *Australian Cricketers' Guide,* where the game at Manchester is described as "the first of the International test matches". Mandle notes another use for that series, in *John Lillywhite's Cricketers' Companion* of 1885: "three test matches between England and Australia". James Lillywhite uses *test match* in 1885 retrospectively, of games played in England by the Australian tourists of 1884, 1882, and 1880.[47]

In these examples from 1883–85, the English usages are all from the sporting press, while the Australian usages are from a sporting publication and from general daily newspapers. The *Bulletin* in 1887 wrote of "Anglo-Colonial test matches", and also of "the so-called 'test matches' between the amateur and professional bicyclists", as if the application to cricket was familiar to Australian readers and a transfer of usage to other sport had some currency, but was not yet settled. The *Evening News,* Sydney, began its report by cable on 22 July 1890 thus: "The first of the three test matches between the

Australian Eleven and All England was commenced to-day at Lords.'' I think such usage was standard in Australian newspapers by 1890. But in London *The Times* did not, I think, use the phrase in the 1880s, though it wrote of "the real test of merit" in 1884 and had a similar phrase ("a test of the merits") in 1885. The earliest use of *test match* I have noticed in *The Times* is for 1892, and that comes from a correspondent in Melbourne, commenting on a proposal to bring out an English team at the end of that year to play "three test matches against representative Australian Elevens". The paper did not use the word in reports of the 1891—92 series in Australia, though it had the term *great match*. For Australian papers, the games in this series were "test matches" or "great test matches".[48]

P. F. Warner believed that the phrase was not used until 1894—95, and thought that it was coined then by a London evening newspaper, the *Pall Mall Gazette,* the imperially minded journal whose makers judged it worth putting more money into cables from Australia that season — up to nearly seven hundred pounds a day — than any paper had ever spent. Making the most of the difference in time which got the scores to London too late for morning papers to use, the *Pall Mall Gazette* offered readers long accounts of each day's play under headlines such as:

ENGLAND V. AUSTRALIA
FIRST TEST MATCH[49]

Warner's testimony tends to confirm my impression that the phrase entered into general usage earlier in Australian than in England. It may well be that the *Pall Mall Gazette* popularized the phrase in England that season. *Wisden's Cricketers' Almanack* first used the phrase in 1894, and its competitor *James Lillywhite's Cricketers' Annual* admitted it in 1896.

It was also in 1894 that the South Australian journalist C. P. Moody, in his *Australian Cricket and Cricketers,* reviewing the history of encounters between English and Australian teams, proposed a canon of "those which by common consent were aptly styled the test matches". Moody's list began with the match at Melbourne in 1877, omitted the Australian Eleven against MCC and Ground in 1878 as not a meeting with "the full strength of England", and proceeded through to the present with knowledge and discrimination. The canon was proclaimed in England by *Cricket,* which published Moody's "Record of Test Matches" in its last issue of 1894.[50] From now on the meeting at Melbourne on 15, 16, and

17 March 1877 was known as "the first test match", and the counting of wins, losses, and draws began with it: when Moody established the canon it contained thirty-eight matches, of which England had won twenty, Australia twelve, and six had been drawn. Some reluctance to use the term appears to have persisted in England until 1899, which is the earliest date so far cited in the *Oxford English Dictionary*. The *Annual Register* had it that year, and *The Times* had almost assimilated it: in a leading article on the 1899 season, test matches are referred to twice without quotation marks and once as "the five so-called 'test matches' ".[51] For *test* as a noun standing alone, without *match*, the *Oxford English Dictionary* cites 1908 as the earliest known usage.

It is seldom easy to plot in detail the infancy of a usage, and after so casual a study my speculation about *test match* must be tentative. I suggest two conclusions. First, it appears to have been more on Australian than English initiative that these games of cricket came to be described as test matches: I think the usage was common in Australia for as long as a decade before it was used beyond a fairly small circle in England. Secondly, like "the Ashes", the idea of a test match was nurtured and propagated by journalists. P. F. Warner wrongly but significantly thought it had originated with the *Pall Mall Gazette*. I suspect that it was admitted so late into the kind of publication noticed by the *Oxford English Dictionary* because it was judged to be a vulgar piece of journalese (itself a word used first in 1882, according to the *Oxford English Dictionary*), fit for sporting men and readers of evening newspapers and colonials, but not for writers and readers of *The Times*. Gentlemanly lovers of cricket winced at such notions as a county "championship" and a division of county teams into "first class" and "second class", both of which, like so much else in the new culture of cricket, were minted by journalists. "Cricket", as R. C. K. Ensor observes, "is a game which specially lends itself to reporting."[52] Putting my two tentative conclusions together, it may not be much of an exaggeration to say that test matches were created by Australian newspapers.

NOTES

I have had much help in the preparation of this chapter from Jan Brazier and W. L. Gammage.

1. My main source for the 1878 tour is "Argus", *The Australian Cricketers' Tour through Australia, New Zealand and Great Britain: containing a full racy account of the matches, dinners, excursions, etc. in which they have been engaged* (Sydney: Jarrett, 1878). As well as being full and racy, it is occasionally inaccurate. For

this and other tours, where figures differ I have used those given in *Wisden's Cricketers' Almanack*.

2. *Australasian*, 29 September 1877, quoted in W. F. Mandle, "Cricket and Australian Nationalism in the Nineteenth Century", *Journal of the Royal Australian Historical Society* 59, no. 4 (December 1973): 236.

3. Ibid.

4. Lord Hawke, Lord Harris, and Sir Horne Gordon, eds., *Memorial Biography of W. G. Grace* (London: Constable, 1919), p.129.

5. The match is described in *The Paddock That Grew: The Story of the Melbourne Cricket Club*, by Keith Dunstan (Melbourne: Cassell, 1962), pp.45-47, and in *The First Test Match: England v. Australia 1877*, by John Arlott and Stanley Brogden (London: Phoenix House, 1950).

6. H. S. Altham, *A History of Cricket*, 2 vols. (London: George Allen and Unwin, 1962), 1: 138-39; Lord Harris *A Few Short Runs* (London: John Murray, 1921), p.220; J. Henniker Heaton, *Australian Dictionary of Dates and Men of the Time* (Sydney: George Robertson, 1879), part 2, p.247.

7. *The Times*, 25 August 1880 (Murdoch), 28 June 1880 ("An Old Etonian"), 9 September 1880 (on Lord Harris's chivalry); Harris, *A Few Short Runs*, pp.220-21.

8. *The Times*, 30 September 1880.

9. Ibid., 5 October 1880.

10. Ibid., 29 August 1882.

11. *Cricket*, 31 August 1882.

12. *The Times*, 27 September 1882.

13. The opening of the Criterion is reported in *TheTimes*, 17 November 1873; *Punch* is quoted in "Argus", *Australian Cricketers' Tour*, p.94; the banquet is reported in *The Times*, 29 September 1882.

14. *Cricket*, 21 September 1882 (a Muscovite XI"), 7 September 1882 (on extravagance of responses), 31 August 1882 (the *in memoriam* notice).

15. *Sporting Times*, 2 September 1882.

16. John Morley, *Death, Heaven and the Victorians* (London: Studio Vista, 1971), pp.91-99; *Bulletin*, 9 December 1882, quoted in S. J. Baker, *The Australian Language* (Sydney: Currawong, 1966), p.48; R. D. Beeston, *St. Ivo and the Ashes* (Melbourne: Australian Press Agency, 1883), p.3.

17. See "'Test Matches': A Note on Usage", at the end of this chapter.

18. Alfred Shaw, *Alfred Shaw, Cricketer: His Career and Reminiscences* (London: Cassell, 1902), p.83; *Shaw and Shrewsbury's Team in Australia 1884-85* (Nottingham: Shaw and Shrewsbury, 1885), pp.25, 27.

19. Lord Hawke, *Recollections and Reminiscences* (London: Williams and Norgate, 1924), p.98; Shaw, *Reminiscences*, p.101.

20. *Australasian*, 12 November 1887; *Sydney Morning Herald*, 28 November 1891; Altham, *History of Cricket* 1: 211.

21. Shaw, *Reminiscences*, p.118; *Sydney Morning Herald*, 4 February 1892.

22. *Age*, 29 March 1892; George Giffen, *With Bat and Ball* (London: Ward Lock and Co., 1898), p.51; Dunstan, *The Paddock That Grew*, p.70.

23. K. S. Ranjitsinhji, *With Stoddart's Team in Australia 1898-98* (London: J. Bowden, 1898), p.213; *The Times*, 11 September 1899.

24. *Australian Etiquette* (Melbourne: People's Publishing Co., 1886), pp.502 3; R. E. N. Twopeny, *Town Life in Australia* (London: Elliot Stock, 1883), p.204.

25. Ibid., p.206.

26. *Australasian*, 27 November 1880; *The Times*, 29 August 1882; Oscar Asche, *His Life, by Himself* (London: Hurst and Blackett, 1929), p.18; letters of W. S. Jevons 1855-57, Mitchell Library. A. W. Martin showed me a copy of Jevons's letter.

27. F. R. Spofforth, "Australian Cricket and Cricketers: A Retrospect", *New Review* 10, no.59 (April 1894): 512.
28. *Home News*, quoted in "Argus", *Australian Cricketers' Tour*, p.23; C. F. Pardon, *The Australians in England 1884* (London: Pardon, 1884), p.512; Harris, *A Few Short Runs*, p.211.
29. Nat Gould, *On and Off the Turf in Australia* (London: George Routledge and Sons, 1895), p.195; Giffen, *With Bat and Ball*, p.1; Twopeny, *Town Life in Australia*, p.204.
30. Twopeny, *Town Life in Australia*, p.205.
31. *Argus*, 26 December 1861, quoted in Dunstan, *The Paddock That Grew*, p.21; David Adams, ed., *The Letters of Rachel Henning* (Ringwood, Vic.: Penguin, 1969), p.81; *The Times*, 19 February 1874; *Australasian*, 18 April 1874, quoted in W. F. Mandle, "Games People Played: Cricket and Football in England and Victoria in the Late Nineteenth Century", *Historical Studies* 15, no. 60 (April 1973): 526.
32. The *Australalsian's* verses are quoted in Shaw, *Reminiscences*, pp.58-59, and Melbourne *Punch*'s in Dunstan, *The Paddock That Grew*, p.48.
33. *Colonial and Indian Exhibition. Official Catalogue* (London, 1886), p.179; "Argus", *Australian Cricketers' Tour*, p.18; Gould, *On and Off the Turf*, pp.189-90.
34. *Memorial Biography of W. G. Grace*, p.103; Spofforth, "Australian Cricket and Cricketers", p.631; *Globe*, quoted in "Argus", *Australian Cricketers' Tour*, p.23.
35. Mandle, "Cricket and Australian Nationalism", pp.233-36.
36. Mandle, "Games People Played", p.526.
37. W. J. Sowden, *An Australian Native's Standpoint* (London: Macmillan, 1912), pp.40-41.
38. Hogan is quoted in Mandle, "Cricket and Australian Nationalism", p.237; for the Gaelic Athletic Association, see Mandle's study in this book; Herbert Moran, *Viewless Winds* (London: Peter Davies, 1939), p.25. But it may well be that Irish-Australians were under-represented in Australian teams. If so, why?
39. *Bulletin*, 19 March 1898, quoted in Mandle, "Cricket and Australian Nationalism", p.241.
40. "Argus", *Australian Cricketers' Tour*, pp.71-73.
41. Shaw, *Reminiscences*, p.107; Ranjitsinhji, *With Stoddart's Team*, pp.86-87; Gould, *On and Off the Turf*, p.242.
42. For one version of the story, see J. Bufton, *Tasmanians in the Transvaal War* (Launceston, n.p. 1905), p.15, quoted in "Australia's Reactions to the Boer War — A Study in Colonial Imperialism", by B. R. Penny, *Journal of British Studies* 7, no. 1 (November 1967), p.102.
43. H. S. Altham and John Arlott, *Lord's and the M. C. C.* (London: Pitkin Pictorials Ltd., 1967), p.18.
44. Quoted in *Cricket Quarterly*, Winter 1966-67, p.14.
45. *Age*, 22 July 1878; *TheTimes*, 30 September 1880; Pardon, *Australians in England*, p.175; *Cricket*, 31 August 1882; *Sporting Times*, 2 September 1882.
46. Pardon, *Australians in England*, p.177.
47. W. F. Mandle has given me the references to *Boyle and Scott's Australian Cricketers' Guide for 1883 and 1884* (Melbourne: Boyle and Scott, 1884), p.215, and to *John Lillywhite's Cricketers' Companion for 1885* (London: Lillywhite, 1885), p.6; James Lillywhite's uses are in *Shaw and Shrewsbury's Team in Australia, 1884-85*, pp.22-23.
48. *Bulletin*, 5 March 1887, 12 February 1887; *The Times*, 22 July 1884, 11 February 1885, 30 March 1892, 28 January 1892, 28 March 1892.
49. For Warner's view see "test" in *A Dictionary of Slang and Unconventional*

English, by Eric Partridge (London: Routledge and Kegan Paul, 1949); *Pall Mall Gazettre*, 14 December 1894.
50. C. P. Moody, *Australian Cricket and Cricketers 1856 — 1893-94* (Melbourne: Thomson, 1894), pp.71-72; *Cricket*, 28 December 1894.
51. *The Times*, 11 September 1899.
52. R. C. K. Ensor, *England 1870-1914* (London: Oxford University Press, 1936), p.165.

RICHARD CASHMAN

The Phenomenon of Indian Cricket

India's record in test cricket has not been impressive in terms of raw statistics: 26 wins have been achieved in 152 matches of which 62 have been lost and 64 drawn. Yet in spite of this, cricket has become more popular in India than in any other country. This fact is clear whether one examines the size of crowds, gate-money, media attention, the status of players, or the pre-eminent position of the game which is fast becoming India's national sport. This chapter will explore the nature of this popularity and suggest some possible explanations for this interest in a colonial game.

The Indian fascination for cricket has been commented upon frequently. Richie Benaud, tourist to India in 1956 and 1959, wrote that the "astonishing thing about Indian cricket" was "the spectators": "They throng to the grounds in their thousands and, over a full Test match, in their hundreds of thousands, cheerfully sitting in cramped space having bought legitimate and at times non-existent tickets after months of saving for the great day."[1] All Indian test matches are usually sold out in advance even though the grounds are only slightly smaller than their Australian equivalents. It is the good fortune of the Indian Board of Control to count on capacity crowds at each test centre on each day no matter what the strength and current form of the oppostion. Packed houses have been a feature of Indian test cricket from its inception; the first test played on Indian soil, at Bombay in 1933, drew a capacity crowd over four playing days. Consequently, an ordinary series against a moderate English Eleven, such as the 1972–73 series, with a total of approximately one million spectators in five tests, outdrew the historic Australia–West Indies clash of 1960–61, with a total of just over three quarters of a million spectators over a similar number of tests, even though this series included the world record crowd of 90,800 for one day.[2] And with the further expansion of Indian ground capacities, even larger crowds will eventuate as a matter of course.

In India a test match ticket is usually most difficult to obtain. All seats are sold well in advance. The purchase of a daily ticket is very limited; tickets are sold for the entirety of a match, often at a very high price. In the 1972–73 series against England, tickets cost as much as three hundred rupees in Delhi (which represented about two weeks' salary of a middle-level government official), two hundred rupees in Bombay and Calcutta, though only eighty rupees in Madras. Hence the comment of Neil Harvey in the 1950s that Indians constitute "probably the world's most fanatical followers" of cricket who "pay easily the highest admission prices". In spite of the prohibitive prices, the demand for tickets remains great and was a prime reason for the test "which went up in flames" in 1967. Such was the pre-test rush for tickets that the secretary of the Cricket Association of Bengal issued some fourteen to fifteen thousand tickets "entirely at his own discretion" where "it was customary for only some hundreds of tickets to be issued". Chronic overcrowding was also caused by the forgery of many tickets. Needless to say, there is a thriving black market; profiteers purchase blocks of seats in advance and make a handsome return. Several days before the Calcutta test that began on 30 December 1972, it was reported that forty persons had already been arrested for the crime. About two weeks before the fourth test of the same series some five hundred students from various colleges of Kanpur protested against the non-availability of tickets and alleged that they were being sold on the black market.[3]

Cricket enthusiasm is fuelled by a sympathetic media which treats cricket as a favourite son to the detriment of other sports, which often vanish from the sports columns when a test occurs. If national titles in minor sports, such as tennis, badminton, and table tennis, happen to coincide with a test, they are practically ignored and have to beg for public attention. Most sports have been poorly covered by the All India Radio (and recently introduced television) which did not set up a regular sporting programme or "round-up" common to other countries until 1972 and did not establish a separate sporting department. Test cricket has been the exception to this rule, and "ball-by-ball" descriptions have provided cricket with a significant fillip. In many instances cricket had monopolized more than one channel of the national radio: in north India the tests are broadcast both in Hindi and English over separate stations, while in the south there are commentaries in Tamil and English. The game is also reported extensively in the vernacular press in addition to the English-language journals.

Within India there are three contenders for media attention and for the mantle of national sport: cricket, soccer, and field hockey. Of the three, hockey has the most natural advantages, and it was the opinion of the prominent cricket official, Anthony de Mello, that "if any game can truly be described as our own . . . it is hockey". Introduced by British army officers and British army teams, the game spread rapidly in the early twentieth century to the extent that India came to dominate the Olympics from 1928 to 1964. Indian hockey was responsible for a significant refinement which brought a greater flexibility to the game: "they shortened the toe of the stick" so that the player could "turn it over for reverse play without relaxing the grip". Unlike cricket, hockey requires a minimal outlay for equipment. Soccer is also a game suited to the poor and is the most popular game played by the working classes. At the provincial level a soccer match will outdraw its Ranji Trophy equivalent. However, a vital weakness in the national promotion of soccer and hockey has been the limited number of international contests staged within India. Cricket has undoubtedly prospered for this very reason. While the Indian Eleven has not always performed well overseas, India's spectators can usually count on a close and exciting tussle on the home wickets.[4]

By the time of Indian independence, no one sport had attained pre-eminence. Professor Deodhar, pioneer cricketer and Sanskrit scholar, wrote: "There is no national game in India developed as yet in the real sense of the term."[5] This statement is still largely true. Hockey has been dominated by the Sikh community and is most popular in the Punjab and northern India, though it is also played in western and southern India. Bengalis and Goans are the most prominent soccer players; Calcutta is the headquarters of the game. Cricket is most popular in western and southern India and has its greatest following in the cities of these regions. Before 1947 it was virtually unknown at the village level. But in recent years cricket has made significant advances in the north and east, has broadened its social base, and is fast becoming India's national sport.

Before the 1970s, cricket suffered from the dominance of Bombay, which not only possessed certain historical advantages but also the added bonus of large business houses who employed a significant number of test players. The result was that Bombay dominated the Ranji Trophy after 1947 and actually annexed the trophy for fifteen years in a row from 1958–59 to 1972–73. Bombay regularly trounced its west zone opposition because in addition to its own talent it attracted some of the best players from elsewhere. Karsan Chavri, for instance, was born in Rajkot in the state of Saurashtra but migrated to Bombay to secure employment with Associated Cement Companies, an important cricket patron. Saurashtra, a weak team, could ill afford the loss. Poona (and Maharashtra) had suffered this fate in the 1940s when some key players of its champion team were lured elsewhere, for Poona was "a middle class town with education as its main activity" and "could not afford to maintain its own cricket products". Bombay's reign was finally brought to an end by the southern state, Karnataka. Possessing a salubrious climate and a vigorous administration, Karnataka established itself as a new cricket power in the 1970s and at one stage provided the bulk of the Indian Eleven. Bangalore, its capital city, was awarded a test match in 1974 for the first time. The rise of Karnataka can be explained partly by the climate, in which cricket can be played most of the year, but it is also due to the industrial development of Bangalore. Prasanna, for instance, has been employed by Radio and Electricals Manufacturing Company, and Brijesh Patel by the Mafatlals branch in Bangalore.[6]

Cricket has always been strong in southern India: Tamil Nadu (formerly the state of Madras), Hyderabad, and Karnataka have ranked second only to western India in their enthusiasm for cricket. A new development for the game is its expansion in the east and the north, traditionally weak cricket regions. The recent success of Bihar, which reached the Ranji final in 1976, underscored improvement in the east. In previous decades, Bengal, the leading team of the zone, had very little competition from Bihar, Orissa, and Assam, which placed Bengali cricketers at a decided disadvantage when they played stiffer competition outside the zone. Like Bangalore, Bihar's improvement was partly due to patronage, notably the support of the Bombay house of Tatas with their iron and steel subsidiary at Jamshedpur. Bihar's side was bolstered by the acquisition of Ramesh Saxena, previously of Delhi, and before being employed by Tatas at Jamshedpur. Cricket has also progressed in the north, which finally won the zonal competition. the Duleep Trophy, in 1973−74, though no northern team has yet won the Ranji Trophy. There has been also a greater northern component in the recent test sides, with Bedi and Madanlal from Delhi and the Amarnath brothers from the Punjab who transferred to Delhi. But while Delhi has hosted a test match from 1948, it has yet to establish a reputation as a "cricket-knowing or cricket-loving metropolis".

There are still states where cricket is weak, such as Assam, Orissa, Kerala, Kashmir, and Andhra, which suffer from limited facilities and lack the patronage of a business class. There are also important communities, such as the Sikhs, which continue to prefer other sports to cricket. India has only had six Sikh test players, and three of these have come from outside the Punjab, the home of the community. Given their enthusiasm for sports and their tall physique, they would appear to be potential fast bowlers, but of the six, four were batsmen, one was an all-rounder who bowled off spin, and one is a slow bowler. Bishen Singh Bedi's captaincy of the Indian Eleven may provide a stimulus for this community to take up cricket.[7]

It is difficult to estimate cricket's expanding social basis and to plot its spread to district towns and even villages with any precision. Since 1947 India has had a greater proportion of test players from less privileged backgrounds, players such as Chandu Borde, Nana Joshi, and Ghulam Guard, whose parents were poor and of the working class; Ramnath Parkar, brought up in a depressed section of Worli, a depressed suburb of Bombay; Eknath Solkar, whose father was on the ground staff of the Hindu Gymkhana and who has not completed his high school education; and Karsan Ghavri, who comes from a low status family. The majority of post-independence players, however, come from the middle and lower middle class; one such is Ajit Wadekar, who came up from the ranks and learned his cricket in impromptu games with a tennis ball in the lanes of Shivaji Park, "which is to Bombay what Pudsey . . . is to Yorkshire". Today there are fewer test cricketers of independent means than in the teams of the 1930s, 1940s, and 1950s, which included princes (Pataudi, Patiala, Vizianagram), captains of industry (Vijay Merchant and the Apte brothers), and Cambridge and Oxford educated professionals (C. Ramaswami, A. H. Kardar, Dr Jehangir Khan, Dr. Dilawar Hussain, and R. Divecha). Contemporary players rely more on the patronage of the government and business.[8]

In many states cricket has yet to establish firm roots outside of the large cities. The great majority of test cricketers of Bengal and Tamil Nadu, for instance, have been born in the respective capital cities of Calcutta and Madras.[9] There is evidence, however, that in some regions cricket has begun to recruit test players not only from district towns but also from villages. Maharashtra is an interesting example of this. Of the twenty-three test players born in Maharashtra, excluding Bombay, only five were born in the largest inland city, Poona, and another eight in district capitals; the remainder came from smaller towns and villages of the region.[10] No other region can yet claim such broad recruitment, but with the growing popularity of cricket, there is no reason why this pattern may not be repeated elsewhere. Maharashtra has in fact produced more test players than any other state: approximately 40 per cent of

India's cricketers have been born there. It is not surprising to read that "most members" of the 1962 team to the West Indies spoke Marathi, which created some problems for the remainder of the team, including the non-Maharashtrian captain.[11]

The broadening base of Indian cricket is paradoxical given the elitist background of the game. Cricket was a "fashionable game" in the nineteenth century played by "the few English educated citizens" of entrepôt cities such as Bombay, Calcutta, and Madras. The cost of equipment excluded all but the wealthy. Cricket paraphernalia was expensive because most of it was imported, though there were some signs of an emerging indigenous industry; advertisements include references to "country-made practice balls" which retailed for one rupee, four annas. But match quality balls, such as Ayre's International treble seam, cost more than seven rupees. Cricket's status was enhanced by princely participation, frequently as the captain of the Indian Eleven, and by munificence. Cricket could not have survived without its aristocratic patrons, the princes and the businessmen, who built ovals, recruited coaches from overseas, organized tours, employed cricketers, and provided necessary equipment.[12]

Cricket has retained its aristocratic image. It is regarded as socially prestigious to attend a test match. A first-day crowd will include the leading ministers, judges, film stars, and businessmen of the city in question. One enterprising Delhi businessman established his own 250-square-yard barricaded enclosure right in front of the pavilion at the test of 1972. It proclaimed with "four fairly large signs" of "luminous green and red" that this was the "Modi Enclosure". And just as the teams returned to the pavilion for the lunch-break, this area, almost astride of the boundary, became alive with activity:

A low table approximately 4 x 12 yards was laden with food. Behind it stood two drumfuls of drinking water. A liveried servant, impressive in his all-blue, gave the signal and the guests, including evidently the scions of the DDCA [Delhi and District Cricket Association] patron's family, left their chairs near by to be served food. . . . A former Cabinet Secretary and a former Inspector-General of Police were among the frontliners in the enclosure. There was any number of other officials, including a former Union Deputy Minister and a Rajya Sabha member.[13]

It is a frequent complaint of cricket-lovers that many of the socially privileged present have no real interest in the game and exclude the more serious students of cricket.

Cricket's appeal is not limited to the rich and powerful. There is broad support among the middle classes and poorer groups, particularly in the cities, although many will never have the opportunity to witness a test. Popular enthusiasm for the game was particularly evident in the fifth test of the 1972—73 series in Bombay, which coincided with the introduction of television to the city. Groups, sometimes consisting of more than a hundred spectators, clustered around shop-front television sets to watch the match in its entirety. It was most unlikely that the majority of this audience could follow the progress of the ball with any certainty. A television set also dominated the university library of Elphinstone College, where it was studied closely by several hundred students. Elsewhere, enterprising gentlemen hired halls and charged admission. Television had been preceded by what the *Statesman* referred to as the "transistor syndrome": "In tea shops by the wayside and in posh restaurants, in Government offices and in sedate board-rooms, in passing cars and aboard trams and buses, the monotonous drone of the wireless will obliterate all else. So overwhelming is the pre-occupation that even the Railway might consider inscribing on the walls of carriages: 'Please do not talk if it disturbs the transistors of your fellow passengers'."[14]

Test cricket fever is an occasional phenomenon which reaches epidemic proportions with the final test in Bombay city, particularly when a series is tied (as in 1974—75) or when the fate of the series still hinges on the final match (as in 1972—73). For the duration of the game all work in the city virtually stops. During the 1973 test, cabinet meetings were held "after the close of the day's play" because a majority of the state ministers were at the Brabourne Stadium "most of the time". Many heads of departments in the past have followed suit, and "such being the case, the other employees have normally taken it easy". It was estimated that at any given time "at least 75 per cent of the employees in an office were listening to the commentary". This cricket fever also occurs outside Bombay: the Tamil Nadu government decreed that 12 January 1973, the first day of the Madras test, would be a holiday for all public offices in Madras and in the Chingleput district and that the second Saturday in February would be a working day in lieu thereof.[15] It is not clear whether this action was taken out of a love of the game or whether it represented a realistic appraisal of anticipated production on 12 January 1973, or for both reasons. Cricket does not usually produce enthusiasm of such proportions in other countries. The most obvious parallels are with football: Australian Rules football in Melbourne in September, and soccer in many countries.

Popular enthusiasm for the game has produced substantial gates and returns for participants, and this has enhanced cricket's social status. The Indian test cricketer has been better paid, in recent years, than his counterpart elsewhere. In 1976–77 in the series just before the Packer "revolution" he was paid Rs 2,000 per test, which represents considerably more than the Australian 1976–77 test match allowance of $475 when comparative purchasing power and salary scales are taken into consideration. Indian cricket salaries have been augmented further by cash awards such as the Rs 35,000 in the 1972–73 series, provided by the journal *Sportsweek* together with Erasmic, a prominent business house. In the same series, additional purses were awarded by I. S. Johar, a film producer, who gave Rs 10,000 for the "Man of the Series"; Horlicks, who added another Rs 5,000 for a similar award, and the Indian Oil Corporation which donated Rs 1,000 and several prizes. Such awards for the winning team and the best players of each test are broadly comparable to the Australian Benson and Hedges awards which amounted to $20,000 in the 1974–75 series, $30,000 in 1975–76, and $39,000 in 1976–77. In addition, exceptional Indian players have always had the opportunity to reap handsome dividends through benefit matches which prior to 1975 had returned from Rs 30,000 for Nari Contractor in 1970–71 to Rs 225,000 for Shute Banerjee in 1973–74. But in February 1975 this figure was eclipsed by the Rs 500,000 presented to India's recently retired captain, Ajit Wadekar. This sum represents, in comparative terms, an equivalent purse to the record ten-year contract of $630,000 signed by Jeff Thomson in 1975. But it is not wise to push comparisons too far. Advertising provides a greater bonus for the leading Australian players than their Indian counterparts. Indian cricketers, on the other hand, should expect significant allowances from their Board of Control, which, with assured gates over several decades, has had much greater revenue than other national associations. It would be wrong to argue, or even imply, that Indian players should not agitate for a larger share of an expanding cake.[16]

However, in terms of employment, the Indian test player has been looked after by the patrons: the princes in the 1930s and 1940s, and private firms and government agencies such as the State Bank of India and the railways since that time. The Indian government, unlike the Australian and British governments, has made a substantial contribution to test cricket by the employment of cricketers. Of the recent test players, Bedi, Viswanath, and Kirmani were employed by the State Bank of India, and Chandrasekhar by the state government-controlled Syndicate Bank. Given the rewards and associated publicity, it is not surprising that cricketers in India rank as high socially, or almost as high, as film stars. Like the matinee idol, the successful batsman or bowler can count not only on a secure and comfortable future but also on a potential upward mobility and life of glamour. Two test players, Salim Durrani and Sunil Gavaskar, have appeared in films, while another, Mansur Ali Khan (formerly the Nawab of Pataudi), married a prominent actress.

One important reason for the patronage of cricket by the private and public sectors is that national victories and defeats assume large proportions in India. Following India's historic victory over England at the Oval in 1971, the plane that carried the team back to India was diverted from Bombay to New Delhi so that it could be met by Mrs Gandhi herself. Huge crowds thronged the Delhi and Bombay airports, and some 1,500,000 fans lined the route from the Bombay airport to the city hall "to show their admiration and affection". The *Overseas Hindustan Times* captured some of the spirit of the occasion:

> The entire city was dressed up for the occasion with buntings; welcome archs and what not [*sic*] as if to honour a visiting high dignitary. Indeed, for those countless fans who could not watch the historic triumph at the Oval, the return of the players seemed to be the next best thing. They mustered in strength at every vantage point and expressed their joy in a variety of ways — through colourfully brought out posters, by bursting crackers and blowing trumpets and by showering the players with rose petals and gulal. Wadekar and his gallant warriors deserved all these and even more.[17]

It was the opinion of a friend of Sunil Gavaskar that "even the Pope and Mr Kruschev" did not receive "such a tumultuous welcome in Bombay". In order to commemorate the occasion, "the cricket lovers of Indore . . . erected a huge bat of concrete" on which were inscribed all the names of the players. No doubt part of this enthusiasm reflected the forty-year wait for victory over England on her own soil, but this does not fully explain the great emphasis placed on national victories and losses on the sporting field. When the next tour to England (1974) produced a disastrous result for India (three losses), the home of the Indian captain was pelted with stones and shoes, while the same bat at Indore "was smeared with tar and defaced". Will it be cleaned and repaired, asks Sunil Gavaskar, when India next beats England?[18] The Indian hockey team suffered a worse fate after the crushing 6-1 loss to Australia in the Montreal Olympics, some of the homes of the players being razed to the ground.

The historical relationship between cricket and Indian national

identity differs from that of other colonial societies, such as
Australia. Whereas the game provided a natural vehicle for the
expression of an emerging nationalism in the antipodes, an interest
in the game had first to be created in India by the colonial government. The continuation of this element of colonial culture after 1947
attests to the thorough job done by the British. Notable among the
official patrons of the game were Bombay's cricketing governors.
Lord Harris (1890–95) was one of the founders of the Bombay
tournament when Indian teams first played European elevens.
Harris was later to become at spokesman for Indian test interests
when he was president of the MCC in 1895. Lord Willingdon,
governor of Bombay (1913–19), viceroy of India (1931–36), and
former president of the MCC, also played an important role in
India's emergence in the test arena, as did Lord Brabourne,
governor of Bombay (1934–37), who leased land to the Cricket
Club of India at only one guinea per yard for the purposes of
building a modern stadium in Bombay, which became, appropriately
Brabourne Stadium. This support was replicated by lesser officials
such as the secretary to the agent of the B. B. and C. I. (now
Western) Railway, who was chiefly responsible for the employment
of many of the leading cricketers of the day at the railway offices in
Bombay.[19] The secretary established the principle of government
patronage of cricket which was taken up in a more grand manner
after 1947.

The game was first introduced by British regiments which
frequently played against one another outside the cantonment or on
the maidan and thus created some interest in cricket, though they
did not play against Indian teams. It has been suggested by the
prominent former official Anthony de Mello that the British army
provided the principal source of inspiration for all modern Indian
sports; but in the case of cricket in Bombay, educational institutions
were also formative. Within the English-language colleges and
universities, set up from the mid nineteenth century, enthusiastic
masters and principals actively encouraged student participation in
the game and organized teams, grounds, and even tours. Such was
the interest in cricket at Elphinstone College, one of the many
colleges affiliated to Bombay University, that annual tours of three
to five weeks duration began in 1901 to such distant places as
Karachi, Calcutta, and Ceylon. The students' interest in cricket was
a natural extension of the pursuit of new forms of learning and
exploration of modern customs and values. It is not surprising that
many of India's first test players were graduates or students who
benefited from the university patronage of the game. This was

particularly true of test players from the Punjab in the 1930s Dilawar Hussein, Baqa Jilani, Jehangir Khan, Mohammed Nissar, and the Ali brothers all attended the University of the Punjab.[20]

There were a number of stated reasons for the official encouragement of cricket. The game would further the process of anglicization, the "assimilation of tastes and habits between the English and the native subjects", begun with the setting up of English-language universities in the mid nineteenth century. Indian players would develop the traits of "manliness" (on the British public school model) and teamwork, which would be character-building. They would be encouraged to adopt the more scientific and "phlegmatic" approach, characteristic of Anglo-Saxon players in the opinion of Harris, rather than the "excitable" Asiatic model. When Harris first went to India he claimed that "the amount of time wasted in calls for, and the drinking of, water by the Parsi batsmen was quite ridiculous". He noted that they later "got over their weakness".[21]

A second stated benefit of the game was that it would foster communal harmony between the various castes and communities of India who would intermingle "absorbed by the game" and learn to co-operate with one another on the cricket field.[22] It was the opinion of many officials, such as Harris, that India was a very divided society which needed some common link such as cricket could provide, to bind it together. This was a convenient and common justification for the continuity of colonial rule, since it denied the viability of an Indian nation without the mediating role of the rulers, or at least removed such a possibility into the far distant future. To Harris, cricket was an imperial gospel, since it was a better mirror of the best English values than the Established Church. There was also abundant evidence that cricket was a more acceptable imperial religion than Christianity to the indigenous elites of the country.

The need for collaboration was probably the most significant reason for cricket patronage. It was no accident that the first community to take up the game were the Parsis, a wealthy entrepreneurial group who acted as cultural brokers between the British and Indian society. Originally migrants from Persia, the Parsis formed a small community of approximately a hundred thousand, primarily located in Bombay, who had readily absorbed modern technological developments and had familiarized themselves with the culture of the rulers. They were among the pioneers of the cotton industry in Bombay, they produced some of the leading merchants and professional men of the city, and they introduced many European customs such as the use of tables and chairs. As an affluent community, they could afford to launch cricket clubs, first begun in the 1840s, and by the 1880s they had progressed sufficiently to take on and beat the Europeans of the presidency. The fixture became an annual event in 1892. The Parsis even managed to organize two extended tours of England in 1886 and 1888. Although beaten in most games (in 1886 they were only successful once against nineteen losses and eight draws), the tours provided valuable experience for Parsi cricketers.[23]

In the tradition of colonial elites, the Parsis took up the game of cricket, along with other imperial customs, partly to demonstrate their fitness for the role of collaboration. It was a matter of pride for a Parsi historian and cricketer to record how the Parsi cricketer diligently transformed himself into a modern exponent of the game by adopting pads and other appropriate equipment and by discarding his "strange and picturesque oriental costume", for he originally went to the wicket "with a white band around his forehead, giving him quite the air of the inmate of some hospital, and a still whiter apron dangling from his waist, which was encircled by the sacred thread of faith".[24] The successful adoption of the English game fitted this community for leadership in other fields.

The Parsi enthusiasm for cricket was part of a larger interest in all forms of sporting activity which was catalogued in Darukhanawala's *Parsis and Sports*. Parsis such as Dr M. E. Pavri, a player in the Parsi Eleven for twenty-eight years and a historian of their endeavours, exemplified the diversified interests of the community and the enthusiasm in the cause of sport: he was "President and Secretary of various Health and Strength Institutions of Bombay" and was "associated with almost every sport, e.g., Cricket, Skating, Scouting, Zoroastrian Physical Culture and Health League, Ambulance Association, and many others". Some of this interest may derive from the community's origins in Persia, where they played the game *Chugan Gui* (bat and ball), which has definite parallels with cricket. But it is more likely that the Parsi love for sports in general, and cricket in particular, derived from their great sympathy with European culture and customs in the late nineteenth century. Whatever the explanation, the fact remains that a tiny minority has contributed and continues to contribute significantly to test cricket: the Parsis have produced 11 test players (out of the 140 who have represented India from 1932 to date), of which the best known are Farokh Engineer, Nari Contractor, Polly Umrigar, Rusi Surti, and Rusi Modi.[25]

Although Parsis viewed cricket in the nineteenth century as a means to forward the interests of their community, their achievements in cricket helped to set in motion the first stirrings of an Indian nationalism on the sporting field. While the first Parsi victory over the Europeans in 1886 was a community triumph, watched by a large throng, including many jubilant Parsis, it was also a victory for an indigenous team which managed to defeat a European team at its own game. The success of the Parsis was also a victory for Bombay, and when the Parsis beat an English team led by G. F. Vernon, the Middlesex cricketer, in 1890, "the city went mad on the game" and "business was quite at a standstill, while the match was in progress, for two days". "The variegated oriental crowd" for what was described as "the most famous match ever played in India" included not only Parsis but "almost all the varied nationalities of the great city". Such victories assumed large proportions because most Indians accepted without question the many colonial myths, developed by the British, which suggested that European institutions and games were superior to Asiatic and that Western sportsmen were inherently superior to Eastern. "It must be admitted", wrote a prominent Parsi cricketer at the turn of the century, "that in staying power the man whose sinews are built on beef is stronger than he whose sinews are formed on curry and rice, together with the great disadvantage of an enervating climate."[26] Like many other colonial cricketers, India's first cricketers appear to have half-accepted the myth of English superiority, and even invincibility, on the sporting field. Victories in the 1880s and 1890s thus represent the first steps towards Indian self-respect on the sporting field, a process which has not been completed until the 1970s when India defeated the West Indies and England on their respective home territories. It was not uncommon to read in the 1950s and 1960s that while teams from India and Pakistan (and the West Indies) produced mercurial and lithe batsmen, who could charm crowds with oriental artistry, they often lacked phlegmatic Anglo-Saxon qualities which would enable them to act calmly in a crisis. The West Indies performance in 1960−61 and Indian victories in 1971 should have dispelled such myths.

While it was the expressed hope of Lord Harris that cricket would soften the relationships between communities, those officials who encouraged cricket helped to establish it on a communal basis in the nineteenth century. It was only natural that Parsis should follow the example of European clubs, which established the principle of restricted membership along community lines. In Bombay there was the incentive not only to beat the Europeans but also to secure victory over communal rivals. In due course the Parsee Gymkhana, founded in 1885, was followed by the Islam Gymkhana in 1892 and the Hindu Gymkhana in 1894, and the competition was extended to a triangular tournament in 1907 (Europeans, Parsis, and Hindus), a quadrangular tournament in 1912 (with the addition of the Muslims), and a pentangular competition in 1937 with the addition of the Rest, comprised of Christians, chiefly Anglo-Indians and Goans, and based on the Catholic Gymkhana.

Inevitably cricket was enhanced by communal rivalries and tensions in cosmopolitan Bombay: it was common for a Parsi crowd to taunt Hindu players, for instance, with the phrase 'Tatya, pylas ka" (literally, Uncle, did you see that?).[27] Hindu spectators retaliated by calling the Parsis "crows", a reference to the manner in which this community disposed of its dead.

With the fairly frequent occurrence of communal riots in the city from the 1890s, it is surprising that a communal tournament could exist and flourish as it did, providing the backbone of Indian cricket to 1947. Some cricketers argued that communal matches — war confined to the sporting arena — brought the communities together rather than divide them, for such matches helped to ease social tensions in the city and cemented many a friendship between players of different communities. It was even argued that on occasions a communal cricket match had helped to defuse a potential riot, though this view assumes, probably erroneously, that there is some correlation between cricket spectators and individuals caught up in communal violence. But the opponents of communal cricket — headed by Gandhi, who made his famous statement of 1941 to the Hindu Gymkhana: "I am utterly opposed to communalism in everything and much more so in sport" — eventually won out. A one-time supporter of communal cricket, Berry Sarbadhikary, changed his mind on the question when he witnessed the tensions that existed between players in the course of the 1935 and later tournaments.[28]

The abandonment of the Pentangular, the premier tournament of the century before 1947, did not harm cricket, for there was a smooth transition from communal to national cricket. While there had only been four national series and ten tests in the period from 1932 to 1947, and all were played against England, there were now frequent tours against a variety of nations, including Pakistan, which in addition to being India's foremost political rival contained a number of former Indian test players and continues to include their descendants and relatives. The popularity of test cricket was enhanced by the first victory over England at Madras in 1952, followed by series victories over Pakistan in 1952 and New Zealand in 1955 – 56.

There are a number of ingredients in the successful transition from local (Bombay) and communal cricket to the national and international sphere. It has already been suggested that the Parsis played an important role; they not only created interest in their own community but also generated enthusiasm in other communities as well. For the Hindus and Muslims of Bombay there was the double incentive to defeat both the Europeans and the Parsis, who dominated the tournament in the initial decades but who were surpassed by the Hindus and the Muslims in the 1920s.

Cricket could not have prospered in Bombay without the lavish patronage of the business community, who made certain that the game did not remain the exclusive privilege of an educated minority or of a traditional aristocracy. A generous donation of five thousand rupees by Jamshedji Nasserwanji Tata, the pioneer of the iron and steel industry, enabled the Parsee Gymkhana to become a reality in 1885. This was the beginning of a very close relationship between the house of Tata and all branches of Indian sport. Sir Dorabji Tata, son of the founder, was responsible, for instance, for Indian participation in the 1920 Olympic Games for the first time when he "paid all the expenses of the team" of four athletes and two wrestlers and "even succeeded in securing a place for India on the International Olympic Committee". Tatas have employed and continue to employ many of the leading cricketers and other sportsmen. There was similar enthusiasm among the Hindu business community of Bombay when the Hindu Gymkhana was founded in 1894 with a donation of ten thousand rupees from the Gujarati busineesman Gorhandas Parmanandas and sizeable donations from most of the leading manufacturers and merchants of the city. Business patronage has increased considerably since this time. It was the business community together with the government which took up the slack when princes were no longer in a position to employ cricketers after 1947.[29]

Such munificence was not an isolated phenomenon limited to cricket charity. The Bombay businessmen, having prospered with the growth of the cotton and allied industries in the nineteenth century, also established educational institutions and funded hospitals, reading rooms, friendly societies and a variety of welfare programmes partly to improve the quality of life of the city but often to improve the prospects of caste and community fellows in the rush to take advantage of expanding educational and employment opportunities. A successful cricket team not only provided healthy recreation and entertainment for the young, but was also tangible evidence of the community's commitment to modernity and the progress made in the realization of such goals.

In the case of the Hindu business community of Bombay, there were some additional reasons for their patronage of cricket. The majority of this group were Gujarati merchants who were influenced by Jain values, notably *ahimsa* (non-injury of life) and who abstained from meat. It is likely that cricket was an acceptable game to such men because it was non-violent, in the sense that it did not involve blood-letting and bodily contact, which could not only cause injury but also defilement. This was particularly true in the late nineteenth century, when Indian society was governed by rules that regulated human contact and ordained that indiscriminate mixing was socially dangerous. Although cricket transcended many social taboos, Untouchables (now Scheduled Castes) being admitted into the game by the turn of the century, the game benefited from the support of the orthodox-inclined merchant communities of Bombay who approved of this modern game because it was in harmony with most accepted notions of purity and pollution. This is perhaps one reason why rugby has made no progress in India, since it runs counter to traditional notions of desirable physical activity. It is perhaps an explanation why soccer is a lower-class game, since it involves some degree of bodily contact. It is significant to note that blood sports have never gained any widespread acceptance among the middle and upper castes of India, the groups that provide the core of cricket support. The exception to this general rule would be the regions heavily influenced by Islamic culture and court circles, where sports such as *shikar* (big game hunting) were popular.[30]

While Bombay initiated the premier tournament in the country before 1947 and provided substantial patronage after this time, it was the princes who established the game in many far-flung regions and helped set up a network of cricket centres throughout the country. It was also the princes who employed the majority of pre-independence test players; in fact, no less than eight of the first Indian Eleven were in the employ of India's aristocracy. The principal patrons were Patiala (who employed Lall Singh and Lala Amannath), Holkar (C. K. and C. S. Nayadu, Mustaq Ali, Sarwate), Nawanagar (A. Marsingh, Colah, Meherhomji), and later Baroda (Hazare, Kisenchand, Gul Mohammed, Shinde, Sohoni) but many other houses, such as Bhopal and Vizianagram, also contributed. Many cricketers became ranking officers in the princely armies — for example, Major (later Colonel) C. K. Nayady of Indore and Captain Vijay Hazare of Baroda — which initiated a "feudal-cum-military" axis that exercised a significant shape over the game, particularly in the 1930s. It was then considered appropriate for a "person of rank and great wealth", a prince, to lead an Indian Eleven on this modern battlefield and for the management of the team to rest in the hands of an army officer.[31] This connection with the power-holders of traditional India provided a necessary element of legitimacy for this imported game.

Perhaps the greatest contribution of the princes was to enlist the help of overseas players as coaches to improve the quality of Indian cricket. Patiala took the lead and imported many prominent English cricketers, including Hirst, Rhodes, Larwood, Leyland, and Tarrant among a number of others. Other houses, notably Cooch Behar and Nawanagar, followed suit. Even the Raja of Jath, a jaghirdar who ruled a tiny principality in western India, found it possible to import Clarrie Grimmett in 1938 to coach himself and a promising youth, Vijay Hazare. The specific task of the coaches was to improve the quality of princely elevens which were set up at Hyderabad, Patiala, Bhopal, and Cooch Behar in the late 1920s and in many other states, most notably Baroda and Holkar, in the 1930s. Princes did not restrict their interest to their state elevens; they also organized All-India tours. The Maharajkumar of Vizianagram (popularly known as Vizzy) organized a tour of India and Ceylon in 1930–31 which not only included some of the best players of the land but also two English stars, Hobbs and Sutcliffe. Vizzy not only underwrote all the expenses of the tour but encouraged his team with the promise of "extravagant prizes" and at the end of the tour every member of the team, "decked out in the resplendent Vijayanagram [sic] caps and blazers" received "a silver statuette of a batsman" while the more successful were "simply showered with trophies". Princes in fact made a habit of donating trophies for cricket: Patiala gave five hundred pounds sterling for the two-foot-high Grecian urn which became the Ranji Trophy, Nawab Moin-ud-daulah of Hyderabad provided seven hundred rupees for a gold cup for a national invitation tournament, while Vizzy, never one to be outdone by others, presented a gold trophy for a tournament at Delhi. Princely munificence greatly added to the glamour of the game, for successful players could count on many fringe benefits such as lavish entertainment at the house of Patiala, the provision of new suits, and straight cash bonuses. Finally the princes played a most significant role in paving the way for India's entrance into the test arena in 1932. Patiala was the chairman of the Board of Control, founded in 1928, which prepared the ground for India's affiliation to the Imperial Cricket Conference.[32]

The princely interest in the game derived partly from the inspiration of the legendary Ranjitsinhji (1872–1933), Jam Saheb of Nawanagar, and his nephew, Duleepsinhji (1905–59) though neither represented India and both regarded themselves as "English cricketers". In the same way in which Victor Trumper captured the imagination of Australian followers of the game, Ranji, as he was known, caused a revolution in the game through the introduction of highly original and daring strokes and by stamping his own personal genius on the game. Ranji, Duleep, and the senior Nawab of Pataudi (Iftikhar Ali) all had the distinction of scoring centuries on their first appearance for England against Australia.[33] The Nawanagar tradition was maintained by his cousin, who succeeded him on the throne and whose successful patronage of cricketers enabled the state to win the Ranji Trophy in the third year of operation, 1936–37, and to reach the final in the following year. The Jam Saheb was responsible for the apprenticeship of two more contemporary players: Inderjitsinhji, a relation of the royal house, and India's great all rounder, Vinoo Mankad, who was not a relation but who was taken under the royal wing.

There were many other reasons why cricket was considered an eminently desirable pastime by India's aristocrats. From the beginning of the eighteenth century, English cricket had been transformed from its more "humble social idiom" to become "one of the most favoured sports in fashionable society". With its "nice blend of energetic activity and dignity of behaviour", it was readily absorbed into the culture of refinement, and it attracted a number of rich and noble patrons such as Sir Horace Mann, the dukes of Cumberland and Richmond, and the Prince of Wales. Patronage was a common practice in the eighteenth century, the noble employing professional (working class) cricketers who played for the patron's team and worked as estate servants. This aristocratic transformation of the game was also made possible because cricket was "susceptible to distinctions of social class". It was the usual practice for the noble to bat and the commoner to bowl, since the latter involved a much greater degree of physical toil. This distinction persisted in English cricket well into the twentieth century particularly in the case of the fast bowler, who could count on hard labour and a relatively short career, and who was usually a professional cricketer of working-class origin. Cricket thus appealed to India's princes because it was an aristocratic game which upheld traditional notions of social hierarchy and patronage. Social rank was also reflected on the Indian cricket field, for the nobility were, with few exceptions, batsmen rather than bowlers. The superior rank of the prince was also reflected by his almost automatic choice as captain when selected in the Indian Eleven.[34]

For the ambitious prince the prize of captaincy of the Indian

Eleven provided significant rewards in terms of status and power. As captain of the 1936 team, Vizzy, a minor aristocrat from the United Provinces (now Uttar Pradesh), was able to mix with the cream of English society. Representing the team at social functions, Vizzy was "brilliantly successful"; but unfortunately he was found wanting as a playing captain, for not only was his batting below test standard but "he did not understand the placing of the team or the changing of the bowling, and never maintained any regular order in batting". Vizzy's determination to cling to the prize of leadership was one reason why the 1936 tour proved a disaster for Indian cricket both in team performance and in morale. It is interesting to note that the less glamorous sport of hockey suffered no similar princely fixation. The Indian team for much of the 1920s and 1930s possessed a "plain skipper", Dhyan Chand, who had "no problem in fulfilling social engagements". The management of cricket proved an attractive arena of endeavour for many smaller princes, for it occurred at a time when they were faced with "the prospect of being swallowed in the proposed All-India Federation". Consequently there were no less than three princely factions in 1932 (Bhopal, Patiala, and Kathiawar) vying with each other for the prize of captaincy of the new national XI.[35] When the team was announced, Patiala was captain, the prince of Limbdi was vice-captain, and Vizzy was deputy vice-captain. But before the team left for England, Patiala had to withdraw because of the pressure of state business and Vizzy resigned probably because he was ranked third in this hierarchy after Limbdi, who happened to be a fair batsman but who contributed less to the promotion of cricket than Vizzy. The ruler of Porbandar, who had no cricket qualifications to speak of, subsequently became captain, while Limbdi remained as vice-captain. At their worst the princes could be impossible. "Like spoiled children they quarrelled, sulked and were insanely jealous of one another", but they did add a certain glamour to the game. "The Maharaja of Patiala was the cynosure of all eyes as he strode to the crease, jewels flashing in the sun. The people adored him and if, plumb in front to the first ball he received, he was given not out by the umpire, who cared? He was not likely to make too many in the best company, and these he would make entertainingly."[36]

There is no doubt that this glamour, begun by the princes but maintained with the high cash stakes involved, is a significant factor in spectator interest in the game. Such glamour is important in the large urban centres of India, given the drabness of city life, the paucity of alternative entertainment, and the very limited recreational facilities available. Cricket has prospered in India partly because of the absence of competitors in the business of mass entertainment. In Bombay city, for instance, there are two potential rivals, the film and the religious festival, but both tend to complement rather than compete with cricket. In the film industry there is a predominance of romantic and escapist themes which further attest to a need to retreat from the conditions under which most people live. Theatres are, like test cricket grounds, invariably packed. Cricket represents a variant form from the film, since the game involves a very real and extended struggle, a national war, whereas the movie represents a temporary and brief flight from reality.

A more traditional form of mass entertainment in the city is the religious festival. In Bombay there is an annual ten-day festival in honour of Ganesha, the elephant-headed deity, which includes singing, dancing, feasting, religious devotions, and a mammoth final-day procession with floats, banners, and larger-than-life clay images, which absorbs the whole attention of the city in the same way that a test does. While this festival is immensely popular, and may involve a million participants on the final day, it is a traditional form of "entertainment" since it includes many spontaneous, individualistic, and non-restrictive forms of activity rather than the more disciplined modern sport which involves set teams, rules, and a finite area. Within the festival an individual or small group, usually based on a neighbourhood or a club, is free to devise his own float and to express his feelings in the procession by quiet devotion or even dionysian dancing.[37] Festivals hark back to village society and tend to reflect the parochial outlook and calendrical celebrations, whereas the modern game of cricket includes elements of combat of national proportions. The success of cricket in urban India clearly indicates that while traditional forms of recreation retain and have increased their popularity, there is also a need for some modern competitive sport which would help to alleviate tensions created between ethnic and class groups within the city. It is also likely that the restrictions and frustrations of city life together with the discipline of factory and office labour create a greater need for a sport that dramatizes conflict and permits the spectator to release some of his pent-up emotions.

The success of an imported game also underlines the absence of any traditional alternative that could be adapted to suit the needs of urban society. Whereas eighteenth-century England had some recreations that disappeared with industrial culture, such as cock-fighting and bull-baiting, it had others that were successfully transformed, such as cricket and football. India lacked any indigenous games that could make this transition. Many of the games of traditional India were too rudimentary and could not be translated into modern sophisticated sports watched by mass audiences. *Gilli danda,* still a very popular game, is played with the most primitive equipment, two sticks. Striking one stick, which rests on the ground, with the other, the batter propels the airborne stick out of the reach of fielders. *Kabaddi,* also known as *hu-tu-tu,* involves no equipment whatsoever. The game is a contest between two teams which stand facing each other, separated by a nether world, and which attempt to capture the enemy one by one through the agency of one member of the team who can operate within the buffer zone.

One ancient sport of India, wrestling, enjoys considerable popularity and often attracts large crowds, though as a body-contact sport it has less status than cricket. Wrestling also lacks a national dimension and the stimulation of nationalism, as most contests are between local sportsmen. Wrestling is most popular at the village level and in some district towns, such as Kolhapur, where sizeable crowds follow the sport. Wrestling does not yet tap, to any degree, the vast potential spectator reservoir of urban India. Western freestyle ("fake") wrestling was, and to some extent still is, an exception to this rule in that it attracted very large crowds in Bombay and other cities particularly in the 1950s and 1960s. The sport enabled one Indian, Dara Singh, to become a household name, though most of the exponents of the game, including King Kong, Flash Gordon, and Tiger Holden, were from abroad.

Although cricket is a modern sport in that it has a well-defined set of rules and is played in a finite space over a set period of time, it retains some of the rhythms of its rustic and aristocratic origins, and it is one modern game in which an epic drama is played out over a very extended period of time. It is the one modern sport that has approached the timelessness, the lack of concern with time, of traditional society.[38] Only cricket could have experimented with "timeless" games, "timeless" tests, and only such a game could extend over five or six days, to the end of allotted time, without a result. Such a game would appear to be in harmony with the traditional Indian notion of time and entertainment. Even today an Indian classical music concert may go on well into the night, unlike Western equivalents which have precise beginnings and endings, since the Indian entertainer retains some of the spontaneity, love for improvisation, and lack of concern with ending on time which were the hallmarks of a less modern society. It is therefore likely that Indian spectators enjoy cricket because they are prepared to watch the subtle and imperceptible unfolding of a drama (such as when

Bapu Nadkarni conceded only five runs in thirty-two overs) over an extended period, a drama that may have no ending.[39] The drama is centred on the unceasing and often cyclical action rather than the result.

The phenomenon of Indian cricket is part of a larger phenomenon, that of cricket itself. It began as a rustic game played in "gentle country where sheep have finely cropped the turf, and where material is readily available for wickets and bats", but was transformed in the eighteenth century into a noble game because it fitted in with aristocratic notions of physical activity and the need to maintain social distinctions on the playing field. Meanwhile, cricket continued to flourish at the village level. Cricket benefited from the aristocratic involvement in the game, for nobles codified rules, set up clubs, and constructed ovals not always out of a love of the game but to protect their sizeable stakes which were a feature of the eighteenth century game.[40] The regularization and institutionalization of the game made it possible for the importation of cricket to the cities, where it obtained a middle-class following in the nineteenth century. Thus cricket became a very cosmopolitan game, since it was appreciated in the city and country and by individuals across the social spectrum. It is perhaps this cosmopolitan character that has enabled cricket to spread to other societies and to flourish. Cricket also benefited from imperial promotion in India, since it was a game that mirrored values considered desirable for a colonial society. With its many traditional elements and with its refined and subtle notion of ritualized warfare, cricket can appeal to a society undergoing rapid modern transformation which remembers nostalgically some of its less-hurried pastoral past. It is ironic that cricket, which retains many traditional vestiges, is ideally suited to modern technology, radio, and television. It was the opinion of one prominent nationalist, C. Rajagopalachari, that "the day might come when India would give up English, but not cricket".[41]

NOTES

This paper has been enhanced by the research of Michael Murray, which was made possible through the research funds of the University of New South Wales.

1. Richie Benaud, *Willow Patterns* (London: Hodder and Stoughton, 1969), p.155.
2. Capacities vary from 73,000 (Calcutta) to 25,000 (Delhi). New Zealand tours have been an exception to this general rule. *The Cricketer* 53, no. 1 (January 1972): 6.

England v. India 1972-73		Australia v. West Indies 1960-61	
Delhi	100,000	Brisbane	45,473
Calcutta	350,000	Melbourne	198,083
Madras	160,000	Sydney	135,717
Kanpur	150,000	Adelaide	112,070
Bombay	225,000	Melbourne	274,404
TOTAL	985,000	TOTAL	765,747

Whereas there exist precise daily crowds figures for Australian test matches, the Indian figures are estimates.

3. Quoted in *Six and Out: The Legend of Australian and New Zealand Cricket*, ed. Jack Pollard, 4th ed. (Sydney: Pollard, 1973), p.348; Edward Docker, *History of Indian Cricket* (Meerut: Macmillan, 1976), p.229; Ray Robinson, *The Wildest Tests* (Delhi: Bell Books, 1974), chap. 7; *Statesman*, 30 December 1972; *Times of India*, 13 January 1973.

4. *Link*, 7 January 1973; *National Herald*, 18 November 1972; *Times of India*, 25 January 1973; Anthony de Mello, *Portrait of Indian Sports* (London: Macmillan, 1959), p.75. India won the gold medal on seven out of eight occasions in this period. John V. Grombach, *The 1976 Olympic Guide* (Chicago: Rand McNally, 1975), p.156. While a provincial soccer match will draw a capacity crowd (in Calcutta at least), it is always possible to secure tickets for the equivalent cricket contest. India has recorded seven victories, thirty-six losses, and twenty-two draws overseas, whereas at home there have been nineteen wins, twenty-six losses, and forty-two draws.

5. Professor D. B. Deodhar, *March of Indian Cricket* (Calcutta: Illustrated News, 1948), p.123.

6. In Bombay the largest private patrons are Tatas, Associated Cement Companies, and Mafatlals. Ghavri is an opening bowler who first represented India in 1974. Deodhar, *March of Indian Cricket*, p.103. Karnataka's contemporary test players include Chandrasekhar, Prasanna, Viswanath, Brijesh Patel, and Kirmani.

7. Bengal won the Ranji Trophy in 1938-39 and was runner-up on seven other occasions. *Link*, 27 February 1972. Patiala, Lall, Rai, and Milka Singh were batsmen, Kripal Singh was an all-rounder, and Bedi is an off-spinner. Lall Singh was born in Malaya, while Milka and Kripal Singh were born in Madras.

8. Ajit Wadekar, *My Cricketing Years* (Delhi: Vikas, 1973),p.5. Abbas Ali Baig, a more recent cricketer, attended Oxford University.

9. Two exceptions are N. Chowdhury (born in Jamshedpur) and P. Sen (born in Comilla, now part of Bangladesh).

10. Test cricketers born in Poona include Adhikari, Borde, Gadkari, Ranjane, and Shinde. C. K. and C. S. Nayadu, H. G. Gaekwad, Mantri, Nadkarni, Phadkar, S. R. Patil, and Umrigar were born in the district towns of Nagpur, Nasik, Kolhapur, and Sholapur. Dani, Ghorpade, Hazare, Hindlekar, Kanitkar, Kulkarni, Navle, Sohoni, Sarwate, and Rangnekar came from smaller towns and villages.

11. The birthplace of 121 out of India's 140 test players has been identified: 48 out of 121 were born in Maharashtra. Nawab of Pataudi, *Tiger's Tale* (London: Stanley Paul, 1969).

12. Deodhar, *March of Indian Cricket*, p.45; *Pioneer*, 11 and 12 November 1899.

13. *Statesman*, 21 and 22 December 1972.

14. My own observations of the fifth test, Bombay, 6-11 February 1973; *Statesman*, 20 December 1972.

15. *Times of India*, 9 February 1973; *Statesman*, 31 December 1972.

16. The figure of two thousand rupees does not include fares and board. It is not valid simply to convert rupees into Australian dollars since this does not indicate comparative purchasing power. Rather it is better to note that a middle-level government official would have earned approximately seven hundred rupees per month in 1972. *National Herald*, 6 December 1972; *Times of India*, 12 February 1973; *Cricket Quarterly* 1, no. 1 (January 1975): 42.
17. *Overseas Hindustan Times*, 25 September 1971.
18. Sunil Gavaskar, *Sunny Days: An Autobiography* (Bombay: Rupa, 1977), pp.72, 116-17.
19. W. F. Mandle, "Cricket and Australian Nationalism in the Nineteenth Century", *Journal of the Royal Australian Historical Society* 59, no. 4 (December 1973). They included P. Vithal, P. Baloo, J. S. Warden, S. R. Godambe, B. E. Kapadia, and many others.
20. Dé Mello, *Portrait of Indian Sports*, p.3; Jamshed Dinshaw Antia, *Elphinstone College Tours* (Bombay: Rupa, 1913); Deodhar, *March of Indian Cricket*, p.91.
21. Quoted in M. E. Pavri, *Parsi Cricket* (Bombay: J. B. Maryban, 1901), p.8; quoted in J. M. Framjee Patel, *Stray Thoughts on Indian Cricket* (Bombay: The Times Press, 1905), p.xv; Lord Harris, *A Few Short Runs* (London: John Murray, 1921), p.241.
22. Patel, *Stray Thoughts*, pp.xv, xvi.
23. In 1971 there were 91,266 Parsis, of whom 64,000 resided in Bombay. In 1888 the Parsis were more successful, winning eight out of thirty-one games.
24. Patel, *Stray Thoughts*, p.8.
25. H. D. Darukhanawala, *Parsis and Sports and Kindred Subjects* (Bombay: n.p. 1935); the other six are: S. M. H. Colah, J. K. Irani, R. J. D. Jamshedji, K. R. Meherhomji, P. E. Palia, and K. K. Tarapore.
26. Patel, *Stray Thoughts*, p.53.
27. Deodhar, *March of Indian Cricket*, p.48.
28. Berry Sarbadhikary, *Indian Cricket Uncovered* (Calcutta: Cricket Library, 1945), p.61; quoted in *Who's Who in Indian Cricket*, ed. M. H. Magsood (New Delhi: Z. R. Commercial Co., 1942), p.50.
29. *Platinum Jubilee Souvenir, 1885-1960, Bombay Parsee Gymkuna*, p.2; Jal D. Pardivala, "Tatas in Part and Life of Indian Athletics", unpublished paper, in author's possession, p.3; *Times of India*, 5 May 1894.
30. Sarbadhikary, *Indian Cricket Uncovered*, p.67; A. H. Sharar, *Lucknow: The Last Phase of Oriental Culture* (London: Elek, 1975), chaps. 17-20.
31. Sarbadhikary, *Indian Cricket Uncovered*, p.32.
32. Patiala also employed Robinson, Dolphin, Waddington, Kilner, Mitchell, Dennis, Hearne, Murrell from Yorkshire and Middlesex and Bromley and Scaife from Australia. Vijay Hazare, *My Story* (Bombay: Rupa, 1964), p.5; Docker, *History of Indian Cricket*, p.41; Mustaq Ali, *Cricket Delightful* (Calcutta: Rupa, 1967), pp.16-17.
33. De Mello, *Portrait of Indian Sports*, p.60. Unlike Ranji and Duleep, the senior Pataudi did represent India, captaining the side in 1946.
34. Robert W. Malcolmson, *Popular Recreations in English Society* (Cambridge: Cambridge University Press, 1973), pp.40-42; John Ford, *Cricket: A Social History, 1700-1835* (Newton Abbot, Devon: David and Charles, 1972), p.48; Dennis Brailsford, *Sport and Society: Elizabeth to Anne* (London: Routledge and Kegan Paul, 1969), p.210; Inderjitsinhji was a partial exception to this rule; he was a wicket-keeper.
35. *Indian Cricket*, September 1936, p.654, and January 1937, p.202; Docker, *History of Indian Cricket*, p.43; Deohar, *March of Indian Cricket*, p.85.
36. Docker, *History of Indian Cricket*, pp.27-28.

37. R. I. Cashman, "The Political Recruitment of God Ganapati", *Indian Economic and Social History Review* 7, no. 2 (September 1970): 347-76.
38. In traditional India, time was regarded in cyclical rather than linear terms. Such values were in tune with an agrarian society which has its regular round of feasts and festivals based on the seasons. In comparison to the regular wage labour of an industrial society, work in a rural society was spontaneous and irregular.
39. First test at Madras, 1964. Nadkarni's figures were: 32 overs, 27 maidens, 5 runs, no wickets.
40. Brailsford, *Sport and Society*, p.254.
41. Quoted in *Himmat*, 18 March 1977.

IAN TYRRELL

The Emergence of Modern
American Baseball c. 1850–80

Baseball reigned as the premier spectator sport in the United States between the 1870s and the end of the Second World War, a long period of dominance ended only by the rise of professional televised football. In many ways baseball has provided a mirror of American values. The game's fast pace, its complex set of rules and methodical organization, and its materialistic approach to the questions of professionalism and business influence in sport all seem peculiarly suited to modern American industrial society. Because baseball has mirrored so faithfully certain modern American values, it is tempting to conclude that the game has always reflected these values, that baseball has been a wholly new product of modern industrial society. Moreover, it has been common to explain baseball's emergence as a function of the game's peculiar fit with the conditions of industrial society or with the distinctive character of the American environment. Naturally the game could never have risen to prominence, let alone maintained its long hegemony without deep roots in the American social structure. Yet it is important not to assume that the rise of baseball was inevitable, that baseball was uniquely and ideally suited to the American environment in the middle and late nineteenth century.

Baseball went through three stages on the way to gaining widespread popularity. In the first stage, it was played by respectable amateurs and could hardly be distinguished from cricket. In the second stage, working-class and lower-middle-class people took over the game and made it popular in the process, but changed its character into a more dramatic sport played by semi-professionals. Finally, the third stage involved the rise of entrepreneurs — partly from the ranks of the players and partly from more respectable business groups — who put the game on a business footing and gave baseball its modern organizational structure. This social analysis broadly coincides with three key periods: first, up to the Civil War, when baseball vied with cricket for supremacy; second, the 1860s and early 1870s, when certain changes in American society provided mass support for baseball; and third, the emergence of the National League of Professional Baseball Clubs in1876.

To turn first to the comparison of cricket and baseball, it may come as some surprise that cricket was the more prominent summer game in the United States until the eve of the Civil War. Clubs were well organized in the eastern states, especially in New York, Boston, and Philadelphia, and cricket was played as far away as New Orleans. The first international matches were played not in England or Australia but on the North American continent in 1844, between the United States and Canada.[1] Moreover, the first international tour by an England team was to the United States in 1859. The invitation to the English eleven to tour the United States and Canada provides some indication of the interest cricket produced in the 1850s. Large crowds came to watch the English cricketers during the tour; over twenty-four thousand people saw the game against the United States twenty-two at Hoboken, New Jersey. Unfortunately the enthusiasm of the American crowds vastly exceeded the abilities of their cricketers. The English eleven won the game against the twenty-two by an innings. In Philadelphia, the American cricketers did resist more staunchly, for the Englishmen were obliged to bat twice to secure victory.[2] If the defeat of the American teams in 1859 evokes amusement in a contemporary audience, the slaughter did not differ markedly from the defeats inflicted on the local cricketers when English teams first toured Australia in 1861 – 62. Yet Australian cricket went on to be a major international force, while American cricket languished. In contrast, baseball quickly surpassed the English game, and by the 1870s was entrenched in the United States. There were over a thousand clubs operating by 1870, and though most of these were amateur organizations, about twenty leading clubs formed the nucleus of a professional league.[3] Already enterprising promoters had enclosed playing fields and begun to demand admission fees of spectators. Professionalism had first been practised openly in 1869 by the Cincinnati Red Stockings, but the beginnings of true professional baseball date from the formation in 1871 of a separate association, the National Association of Professional Baseball Players. Yet the association was a loose and in many ways an unsatisfactory organization. Professional clubs played only *irregular* inter-city fixtures until 1876. It was the creation of the National Baseball League in that year by a group of astute businessmen which marked the final emergence of organized baseball. No longer simply a game, baseball was now big business.

Historians have offered two general explanations for the rise of baseball and the demise of cricket. One explanation stresses the suitability of baseball to the American environment or an unchanging American national character. Cricket was too slow for Americans who wanted a game compatible with the frenetic pace of their civilization. One particularly silly example of this view is provided by Foster Rhea Dulles. Cricket, wrote Dulles, "never really took hold in America. Its leisurely pace could not be reconciled with a frontier-nourished love for speed, excitement, action. It was steadily driven to the wall" by "the far more lively game of baseball." The frontier explanation can be immediately discounted, since the game was from its inception predominantly urban; yet the relevance of the pace of American life and its relationship to the alleged speed of baseball is a question which nevertheless must be confronted in what follows. The second explanation stresses the powerful currents of nationalism present in the United States in the middle of the nineteenth century. Harold Seymour argued in his general study of baseball that Americans rejected the English game of cricket and chose baseball as their pre-eminent summer game because the latter was a home-grown product.[4]

Each of these answers reflects a failure to examine closely the character of the two sports at the time of their introduction to the American scene. Baseball may be a faster game than cricket at the present time, but there was very little to choose between the two in the 1850s, when cricket was the more widely known of the two games, and when baseball was on the rise. Baseball was in fact a much slower game in the 1850s than it has since become. Matches of four hours or more were not uncommon. As one historian of sport in New Orleans points out, "spectators came prepared to spend the day, because games were often terminated by darkness". The slow pace of early American baseball stemmed primarily from the rules of pitching, which differed substantially from the modern laws, and heavily favoured the batters. Consequently large scores prevailed, and with fifty or more runs a side common, long games were the rule rather than the exception. It was up to the batter, not the umpire, to decide what constituted a fair ball. If he wished, a batter could stand at the plate all afternoon until he received what he considered a favourable pitch. Only when he actually swung at the ball could a strike be called; in contrast, modern rules enable the umpire to call the strikes according to explicit regulations. If the pitching rules slowed down the game, so too did the scoring regulations in force in the "Massachusetts" version of baseball.

Baseball as played in New England was especially slow because the first side to get one hundred runs was declared the winner. This was not an easy task even under rules favouring the batters, and games often lasted more than one day.[5]

If baseball before the Civil War does not exactly fit its stereotype as a game suited to a hectic American environment, cricket as played in the 1850s also shatters its own stereotype as a slow game. Only international games extended beyond one or two days, and club games were usually finished in a day's or even an afternoon's play. Games tended to be short because run-scoring opportunities were low, the rudimentary character of the grounds making conditions averse to good batting. It can be argued that a fast game did have an edge in the competition between spectator sports in the United States after the Civil War — this question will be explored later — but it is difficult to explain the rising popularity of baseball in the 1850s as resulting from the pace of the game; and it would have been difficult to predict the game's later successes from its format before the Civil War. What we must discover is why baseball became a faster game, while cricket adopted a more leisurely pace. Recent developments in the cricket world, notably limited-over cricket, suggest that the sport could have been adapted to the American environment to make it a quicker game than mid-nineteenth-century baseball, should such a result have been desired.

While explanations in terms of the pace of the two games do not fit exactly, neither do explanations that emphasize the foreign origins of cricket. Such contests as Olympic competitions have been seen by some authorities as means of asserting national identities. The adoption of cricket by colonial peoples as diverse as those in Australia and in India might also be viewed in this light; cricket served as a means of asserting prestige symbolically by beating the mother country at her own game.[6] Perhaps the United States was free to reject cricket and adopt an entirely new game precisely because the American nation had thrown off its British tutelage. Certainly American historians have argued that assertive nationalism disposed Americans to reject cricket and embrace a game of local origins. In support of this view, it can be shown that some Americans hailed baseball as "the national game" as early as 1859, but these claims were essentially propagandistic exercises by promoters of the game.[7] By no means all Americans accepted baseball's patriotic pleadings, and it was not until the 1890s that the theory of baseball's uniquely American origins gained wide support. The culmination of this trend was the acceptance in 1907 by a special commission established by the baseball leagues that Abner

Doubleday of Cooperstown, New York, had invented the game in a flash of Yankee ingenuity in 1835. Before the dissemination of this myth, the claim of the English game, rounders, to be the ancestor of baseball received wide though not universal acceptance.[8] During the eighteenth and early nineteenth centuries rounders was widely played in the western counties of England. Since the probable English ancestry of baseball was well known in America, the distinctive appeal of the game against the competing claims of cricket is once again muted. Moreover, even if we accept the importance of national origins, we have still to inquire exactly what it was about the English character of cricket which impeded its growth in the United States.

To be sure, there was one important respect in which baseball and cricket differed before the Civil War. Cricket was played mainly, though not exclusively, by English immigrants, while baseball was played mainly by native-born Americans. What we need to know is why more Americans were not attracted to cricket so that it remained the game *mainly* of English immigrants. To do this we must examine the structure of cricket as played in the United States before the Civil War. Most striking are *similarities* between English and American cricket before 1860. When Englishmen brought the game to the United States, they imported the conventions, rules, and organization of cricket largely unaltered. One vital carry-over was the use of professionals by American cricket clubs to act as coaches, to take care of the grounds, and to spearhead the bowling. Almost every American club in the 1850s and 1860s had one or two English professionals. Professionalism was in fact accepted in cricket at a time when baseball remained an amateur sport. While the use of professionals improved the standard of the game, the practice did nothing to endear the game to Americans. Especially hostile to the use of professionals were those Americans who were seeking a participant sport. Native-born Americans complained that they could not possibly compete against "hired professional players" who had long experience in the game. "It came at last to be believed", reported the *New York Times* correspondent, "that no man who did not drop his H's could possibly win honors at bowling or wicket-keeping." These criticisms may seem misplaced given the rapid strides made toward professionalism in baseball between 1865 and 1876, yet the professionalism among early cricket clubs did certainly upset one group, the moralists who sought to develop healthy forms of outdoor exercise for young men. In 1858, baseball still seemed to offer the best hope for a truly amateur sport. Fifteen years later, the reverse seemed true, and the promoters of morality through sport preferred cricket. Yet the opinions of the amateurs held no weight by the 1870s, since professional baseball had already taken off as a major spectator and participant sport.[9]

Much more critical for the survival and prosperity of cricket in America were the attitudes of the English-dominated clubs towards the future organization of the game in the United States. In New York, the clubs were frequently accused of "an English exclusiveness" which had almost "squelshed the rising spirit of cricket amongst Americans in New York, and driven it into base-ball, as a means of outdoor exercise and recreation". The English-dominated clubs made no effort to introduce Americans to the game; they did not encourage the playing of the game in the schools of the city and made little attempt to publicize the game by courting the press. Especially noticeable was the absence of any sign that cricket clubs were willing to adapt the game and its rules to changing American conditions. In this sense the English origins proved to be quite important to the eventual demise of the game in America. At the very time that baseball players were speeding up their game, English cricketers did not make "the least effort . . . to Americanize the game, by ridding it of the tedious and annoying delays to it". The failure of English cricket clubs to promote the game widely in America contrasts quite sharply with the situation in India. There the colonial rulers pushed cricket because it helped to develop English values among collaborating Indian elites. Such a social purpose could not apply in the American case, where English cricketers were in practice members of an ethnic minority.[10]

Cricket proved more inflexible than baseball not simply because of its English origins, but also because the game had taken on an organized form before it reached American shores. Cricket had deveoped standardized rules by 1835, long before baseball. When Englishmen refuse to adapt the game in America, they were seeking to preserve a successful sport whose rules were already articulated.[11] In contrast, baseball's early condition was chaotic. The National Association of Baseball Players had been formed in 1857, but it was a loose organization, and the rules of the game were not fully worked out until the 1870s. In the opinion of David Reisman and Rueul Denny, the diversity of American society meant that Americans demanded highly legalistic games with explicit, standardized rules. Nothing could be left unregulated, nothing unstated, for Americans did not trust anything to be left to "fairplay".[12] Yet this explanation, when applied to the early history of baseball, does not help us to determine why baseball began to triumph over cricket, since the rules and conventions of early baseball were less clear than those of American cricket. In fact, this condition worked to the advantage of baseball, because while the game was not noticeably quicker than cricket in the 1850s, baseball's loose structure and the absence of firm traditions meant that it was able to *adapt* to changing demands for a faster game. Baseball and cricket, in a sense, moved in opposite directions. Cricket became more leisurely for reasons that will be explored below, but baseball moved toward a faster format after the Civil War. The trend was away from the longer Massachusetts game toward the shorter New York game. By changing the pitching rules after the Civil War, especially by introducing the three-strike rule, the National Association of Baseball Players speeded up the game. The difference in the rules and structure of the two sports is instructive not simply to explain the fate of these particular sports. Such factors may go part of the way to explaining the rise to prominence of a variety of sports. Historians would do well to give more attention to the institutional structure in which games took shape, and the impact of standardized rules on the adaptive capacity of particular sports.

The inflexibility of the English game — relative to baseball — provides a more convincing explanation of the game's demise in America than any other theory so far advanced. Yet such an answer is not entirely satisfactory. Cricket was indeed mainly a game for English immigrants, but nevertheless there was *some* American support for cricket, particularly in Philadelphia. The English cricketers who visited the United States in 1859 found that "the majority of the [Philadelphia team] were self-taught cricketers, being principally Americans".[13] We need to know why this small number of American-born cricketers did not seek to adapt the game to American conditions any more than immigrant cricketers did. Why did American cricketers import almost unaltered the English game? To answer this question we must first inquire into the social origins of American cricketers. The evidence for Philadelphia, cricket's stronghold in the United States, strongly supports the thesis that cricket was an upper-class game, especially from the 1860s onwards. Although cricket was first brought to Philadelphia by lower-class English artisans and factory hands in the mid 1850s, "proper Philadelphians" sought to make the game respectable and gentlemanly. Upper-class Philadelphians began to build exclusive cricket clubs so that the sons of Philadelphia's first families could play the game without associating with rough English artisans. From the 1850s onwards, such exclusive schools as the Germantown Academy and Haverford College began to dominate the game. Thereafter, the social elite of the city could be found prominent among the players and organizers of the leading cricket clubs. The sociologist Digby Baltzell found that in the game of cricket, status-conscious members of the upper class in Philadelphia discovered a suitable vehicle for the expression of their own self-image as "gentlemen at play", although why the elite chose cricket is never made entirely clear by Baltzell or anybody else.[14] The fact that it was a game played in the Public Schools of England may have impressed the social elite. One contemporary observer, Albert A. Outerbridge, attempted to account for the appeal of cricket in Philadelphia by quoting advice on discipline, playing the game, and unselfishness, drawn from *Tom Brown's Schooldays*.[15] Perhaps, as Robert Malcolmson suggested in his perceptive study of pre-industrial English recreations, "cricket was able to be absorbed more readily [than other athletic sports] into a culture of refinement and restraint, for its structure of rules allowed for a nice blend of energetic activity and dignity of behaviour". Cricket could combine better than baseball or football the "disposition to compete" with standards of gentlemanly conduct.[16] When we consider the social following that cricket began to acquire, it becomes easier to explain the general demise of cricket in the United States. The gentlemen who dominated the clubs made no effort to tailor the game to the limited leisure of the lower and middle classes. Indeed, the cricket grounds that the gentlemanly cricketers built tended to lengthen the game; better pitches and grounds improved the conditions for batting after the middle of the nineteenth century.

Against this interpretation of cricket's growing social exclusive-ness it has been argued that baseball too was originally a sport of the social elite. The American sport also began as a respectable game for young middle-class businessmen who were expected to observe "gentlemanly" standards of play and dress. Indeed, the Knickerbocker Club, the most famous and first organized ball club, tried to exclude the disreputable from participating in the game and at first limited membership to men of good breeding and social standing.[17] Yet there was an important difference between the social following of the two games, because the social respectability of early baseball has been exaggerated. Too much reliance has been placed by historians on the example of the Knickerbocker Club, and even within that club the exclusive social credentials do not appear impressive besides those of Philadelphia's cricket clubs. The New York baseballers were young middle-class businessmen; Philadelphia's cricketers came from an older, more stable, and more leisured social class. As a measure of the Knickerbockers' support, the members of its roster comprised seventeen merchants, twelve clerks, five brokers, four professional men, two insurance salesmen, a bank teller, a cigar dealer, a hatter, a cooperage owner, a stationer, a United States Marshall, and several described only as gentlemen.[18]

If baseball had some early claims to social respectability, these were lost by the 1860s. Artisan groups began to dominate the game in the late 1850s, while the same period witnessed a pronounced slide in the social status of the crowds watching baseball games. Unlike cricket, baseball always had a popular appeal among lower- and lower-middle-class native-born Americans. The artisan domination of early American baseball deserves more than the cursory notice it has so far received. Baseball teams represented in part a metamorphosis of old craft and ethnic rivalries. The game was played by such teams as the Newark Mechanics Club; the truckmen of Boston; the firemen of New Orleans; the Manhattans, a team composed of New York policemen; the Brooklyn Eckfords, a team of shipwrights; and the Mutuals, from the Mutual Hook and Ladder Company of New York.[19] Because historians have given no more than passing attention to the phenomenon of artisan participation, the precise importance of these groups is not known. The growing popularity of baseball has been interpreted simply as an example of a general sociological principle: lower classes ape the manners and sporting customs of their social betters. Thereby, social groups seek prestige through symbolic victories over their superiors. This answer wrongly assumes an exclusive character for early baseball, which lower-class groups are supposed to have challenged, but in addition, the explanation does not account for the choice of baseball rather than some other more socially desirable game (for example, polo, archery, or, more to the point, cricket). The artisan support for baseball cannot be explained simply as mimicry of social superiors. Most of the sports of the social elite did not invite mass participation because they involved considerable expense — for example, polo — or because they lacked drama or spectator appeal, as in the case of archery. Yet cricket can hardly be eliminated so easily, for the game has won wide spectator appeal in a number of different societies. Moreover, cricket did not require more expensive equipment and facilities than baseball did in the 1850s.[20]

Though the explanation for cricket's failure to compete with baseball remains uncertain, further research could profitably focus on perceptions of the two games among lower- and lower-middle-class Americans. It seems that cricket appeared too "exclusive" and "genteel", especially when socially prominent people began to patronize the game by the late 1850s.[21] In addition, the ethnic diversity of the United States may have discouraged cricket. Linking ethnic affiliations with support for particular sports is a tricky business, but German and Irish names were not found among the players of cricket, while the Irish, in particular, were prominent in the game of baseball. The Irish preference for baseball may have stemmed from their greater familiarity with the game of rounders in their homeland, and perhaps also by a negative association of cricket with the English.[22] If ethnic diversity impeded the development of a mass appeal for cricket, the social segmentation of American society also discouraged the social elite who did play cricket from seeking to popularize the game among the masses. Whereas wealthy English cricket patrons sought to encourage their worker-employees to play cricket, Philadelphia's social elite — it may be recalled — sought a game which would *separate* them from artisans and immigrant groups generally. From the 1860s onwards, wealthy Philadelphians moved out of the central city area and built sumptuous homes on the suburban Main Line; here they were geographically as well as socially and ethnically segmented. Perhaps because rank had been undermined in American society, the elite were much more self-conscious of their position and sought to develop recreations and social styles that would set them apart from the masses. In England, and in India, this was not as necessary. Social hierarchies remained distinct enough.[23] The only group comparable to the upper-class patrons who developed cricket in India and England were the businessmen-promoters of baseball. But these entrepreneurs, we shall see below, gravitated toward baseball rather than cricket because there was more money involved. Behind that preference lay the popular appeal of baseball.

What made baseball increasingly popular? One approach to this question would be to look at the reasons ordinary people gave for playing and watching the game. Unfortunately, there are few readily available accounts describing artisan participation and perceptions of baseball; nevertheless, one account of an early baseball game by Frank Pidgeon is suggestive. Pidgeon, a pitcher for the amateur Brooklyn Eckfords, revealed two possible motives when he described a game that took place with the Unions of Morrisania in 1859. "Such sport as this brightens a man up, and improves him, both in mind and body," commented Pidgeon. It may be that the desire for self-improvement underlay the urge of many artisan groups to join baseball clubs; certainly the connection between self-help clubs and baseball's early amateur organizations needs further investigation. But if such a statement emphasizes self-help, Pidgeon also stressed the sheer pleasures of physical recreation. "We had some merry times among ourselves; we would forget business and everything else on Tuesday afternoons, go out on the green fields, don our ball suits, and go at it with a rush."[24]

The demands for recreation and excitement which baseball satisfied for both spectators and players have been typically viewed as a product of industrialization and urbanization. According to the standard interpretation, these broad social changes created increased leisure time which in turn called forth new mass spectator sports. As Harold Seymour argued in his history of baseball, "industrialism created at one and the same time the need for commercialized amusement and also the increased leisure and standard of living necessary for the success of such amusements".[25]

The growth of organized baseball was undoubtedly connected with the onset of industrialization and urbanization, but the exact relationship between the sport and social change needs closer attention that it has yet been given. Industrialization created leisure time only in a limited sense. In the short term, industrialization actually appears to have reduced leisure time and repressed popular pre-industrial leisure activities. Robert Gallman's study of pre–Civil War agriculture shows considerable slackness in farm discipline, while the amount of time expended in farm labour was about one-third less than that in manufacturing enterprises.[26] Gallman's study assumes a larger significance when read alongside the work of E. P. Thompson and Herbert Gutman on the repression of pre-industrial work habits in England and America. Pre-industrial societies of the eighteenth and early nineteenth centuries were characterized by lax attitudes toward work and by a considerable mixing of play and work. In the early stages of industrialization, the amount of leisure time available for recreation actually decreased under the demands of entrepreneurs that employees work regular and long hours, and maintain sober habits.[27] Thus it is extremely difficult to sustain the simple thesis that mass sports were a functional response to increased leisure time. To be sure, industrialization made possible more regular if smaller blocks of leisure time and thus perhaps laid the basis for spectator sports. But even this modified argument runs into difficulties in the American example. In the United States, baseball promoters did not have the Saturday half-holiday to exploit, for this holiday was not widely observed in the second half of the century. Moreover, the early entrepreneurs of the game did not seek to exploit the Sunday holiday to increase their audiences. Baseball promoters were, we shall see, obsessed with respectability, and hence loath to antagonize sabbatarian opinion.[28] Baseball was frequently played during the week, and even major league games were typically played during working hours. More important than leisure time in promoting the game of baseball was the increased material standard of living which industrialization and high productivity made possible in the United States in the second half of the nineteenth century. Working hours dropped only slightly between 1860 and 1890, but real wages did rise substantially.[29] Workers may not have had more time to watch games, but they had more money to take time off to watch.

Rather than increased leisure time promoting baseball, it could be argued that industrialization and stern attitudes toward work — together with the inhibitions of many promoters against the use of Sundays for sports — created a competitive advantage for a game which involved minimal interference with working hours. By the end of the 1860s, sporting commentators increasingly recognized that baseball "comprises all the necessary elements for affording a pleasing and harmless excitement, . . . yet can be regularly practised and even played in the shape of formal matches without interfering unduly with business hours".[30] Baseball promoters like Albert Spalding began to argue that baseball had become the national game in part because "two hours is about as long as an American can wait for the close of a baseball game — or anything else, for that matter".[31] The demands for a quicker game were clearly growing, yet these criticisms were levelled initially as much against baseball as against cricket.[32] But as promoters and players began to change the rules of the American game, the charges were more and more reserved for cricket. To take just one example, during the annual match in 1876 between the American-born cricketers and the English cricketers resident in the United States, it was stated by the *New York Times* that "the Americans were deprived by business of several of their best men". Concern that sport should not interfere "unduly with business hours" was not narrowly confined. Artisans, businessmen, promoters, and players all expressed the same point.

If industrialization helped to shape baseball into a faster game by restricting leisure time and by promoting the work ethic, the process of industrialization certainly operated in other ways to promote commercialized baseball. Especially critical were changes in technology which helped to create the infrastructure of organized sports. A modern transportation system allowed the fans to reach the games and it also facilitated the inter-city competition on which commercial baseball in America has been built. Manufacturing industry made possible standardized equipment, while the telegraph and later the telephone provided a means for spreading the results of games and providing more comprehensive publicity. Urbanization, often linked with the growth of industrialization and technological change, gathered people together in greater numbers, and so helped to create the mass audiences which made professional baseball an economically viable proposition.[34]

In addition to providing the technological underpinnings of the mass spectator sports, industrialization and accompanying social changes also repressed existing pre-industrial leisure patterns. To a large extent, the rising interest in baseball and other mass spectator sports directly correlated with these broader social changes; baseball provided new recreational outlets for groups whose traditional leisure patterns were being undermined. Like eighteenth-century England, mid-nineteenth-century America had a rich recreational tradition. The pattern of leisure activities was diverse but quite unstructured. Recreation could not easily be differentiated from the complex patterns of working lives. Gambling, horse-racing, cockfighting, drinking, boxing, and competitive running, among other diversions, were all popular in pre-industrial American society, but in addition, many other activities not so obviously recreational functioned as part of a diverse pattern of popular entertainments. In rural areas, fairs, log-rollings, hunting, barn-raisings, and harvests, among other things, acted as focuses for community entertainments which often involved drinking, dancing, and popular games as central aspects.[35]

Such popular diversions were not confined to rural areas alone, but in urban areas more spectacular entertainment was provided by the antics of volunteer fire companies, while perhaps an even more important outlet for aggression was provided by the gang rivalries of ethnic and native-born artisan groups. New York, for example, had its Plug Uglies, Slaughterhouse Gang, Fly Boys, and Buckaroos in the 1850s, and gang rioting was prominent in the daily newspapers. Gangs spent their time beating up recent immigrants, controlling their "territory", and asserting their authority in the most elemental way through force. Also deserving of closer historical analysis are the violent exploits of the fire companies. Fire-fighting was, in effect, a major participant sport. Rival companies fought each other to be first on the scene, sabotaged each other's equipment, fought violent physical battles, and generally turned fire-fighting into a free-for-all. The unruly behaviour of fire-fighters stemmed in part from the free use of liquor. It was a tradition to supply the successful company with as much liquor as it desired while fighting a fire. This was one reason the companies competed so keenly, while another was the status and prestige that went with victory. Rival companies corresponded quite closely to ethnic communities in urban areas, and they had a strongly developed sense of territory. They fought rival groups to preserve their right to control their own communities.[36]

By the 1850s much of this rich if violent culture had come under attack through economic changes, and through the onslaughts of moralists determined to discipline society. Anti-gambling and anti-liquor movements originated in this period, but perhaps more effective were the activities of police and political machines. The 1850s saw the introduction of organized police forces in the major metropolitan areas, while it was at precisely the same time that urban politicians began to discipline the ethnic gangs and press them into service for political causes, which integrated the gangs into the social order. Civic authorities did not limit their actions to the repression of gang violence alone; Mike Walsh, himself a Tammany ward boss who had risen to power in the 1850s through the ethnic gangs, pointed to the repression of popular amusements of many kinds: "Ballad-singing, street-dancing, public games, all are either prohibited or discountenanced."[37]

Equally important as the activities of civic reformers were economic and technological changes. Rural amusements began to be undermined with the beginning of the shift of population from country to city in the period from 1840 to 1880, while technological change transformed some pre-industrial amusements in the 1850s and 1860s. The introduction of the steam fire-engine, for example, signalled the end of the era of volunteer fire companies and of the violence associated with them. Steam fire-engines reduced the need for large numbers of volunteers and encouraged the use of professionals who could handle the equipment. In addition, the sheer cost of the new equipment made volunteer companies unpractical; increasingly city authorities had to take over the organization of fire-fighting.[38] These changes had their impact on the evolving sport of baseball. It is interesting to note, for example, that several prominent early baseball clubs were volunteer firemen's organizations. Perhaps they were looking for alternative sources of recreation as fire-fighting became more disciplined and specialized. The prevalence of artisan groups in baseball is also suggestive. Perhaps they sought to exert prestige and to perpetuate old rivalries in new ways as police surveillance of gang warfare among artisans intensified. Instead of participating in gang violence and fire-fighting, the lower class began to watch their representatives do ritual battle on the baseball field.

If it was the eclipse of popular recreations that fed the growing support for baseball, artisans nevertheless brought to baseball many of the practices that had characterized those older recreations. Thus the infusion of artisan support imparted a decidedly plebeian tone to a game which had previously won a reputation for the "decorous conduct" of players and spectators alike. Until the late 1850s, baseball matches were apparently models of "good temper and decorum".[39] But increasingly, baseball came to be known as a sport in which, during the next fifteen years, riots were not uncommon, gambling was endemic, and drunkenness was widespread. The earliest recorded riot at a baseball game occurred in August 1860, when the Plug Uglies invaded the field at a match between the Brooklyn clubs, the Atlantics and the Excelsiors, to prevent the Atlantics from losing; gang members had gambled on the team's victory. Part of the trouble arose because as baseball grew in popularity, gamblers moved in from other sports, particularly racing and trotting. By the late 1860s, what moralists called "the devouring spirit of gambling" threatened to overrun the game.[40]

The influx of gambling was closely tied to the ethnic origins of some of the major clubs, and to their links with the corrupt world of urban political machines. Boss Willian Tweed of Tammany fame had his own club, the New York Mutuals, comprising city employees, while the Haymakers of Troy, New York, were run by John Morrisey, the ex-fight champion and machine politician. These teams served primarily to enhance the prestige of Irish ethnic groups, and to further the gambling interests of their political patrons. Under the influence of Tweed and Morrisey, several of the leading clubs combined to throw games in the 1871 season. This practice, known as *hippodroming*, quickly gave baseball a bad name among the respectable. The *New York Times* correspondent expressed the shock of respectable society when he described the changes that had occurred in baseball in the ten years since the outbreak of the Civil War:

> In the place of enjoyable amateur contests, witnessed by crowds of ladies, and governed only by those incentives of an honorable effort to win the trophy of the game, we have seen a field crowded with thousands of people who have paid an admission fee to the grounds, and the game patronized by the worst classes of the community, of both sexes, and moreover, many of the gatherings have been characterized by the presence of a regular gambling horde, while oaths and obscenity have prevailed, and fraudulent combinations of one kind or another have marked the arrangements connected with some of the prominent contests.

For ethnic groups and political machines, the criticisms of

respectable society carried no weight. Followers of the Tweeds and the Morriseys valued baseball precisely because of the opportunities for gambling which the developing sport provided.

As the example of gambling suggests, early baseball inherited a good deal of its appeal and many of its practices from pre-existing sports and recreations. Sometimes the practices and values supporters infused were specifically *pre-industrial* in character, even though baseball was shaped in many ways by the processes of industrial society. The values that seemed carry-overs from an older, pre-industrial world included, among players, resistance to regular practice, refusal to separate work and play, and refusal to consider the game not as play but as work. The difficulties managers and owners had in inculcating workmanlike attitudes to the game were clearly indicated in the many strictures against the use of alcohol by players.[42] Among both players and spectators there was still further evidence of pre-industrial values in the tendency to take unauthorized time off work to play or watch the game; and in the perpetuation of old trade and ethnic rivalries through allegiance to particular baseball clubs. The persistent influence of pre-industrial values is especially important in the American context, because of the influence of European immigration on American culture. Herbert Gutman has pointed to the survival and infusion into American life of values and practices antithetical to industrial production and American business practices. It is likely that such cultural influences as immigration helped to shape the distinctive character of American mass spectator sports. Especially through identification with ethnic heroes in baseball teams, old ethnic rivalries could be preserved and cultural identities asserted.[43]

The resilience of elements of pre-industrial cultures in America suggests that we ought to look more closely at the period in which pre-industrial sports declined and organized sports of the industrial age arose. Interpretations of the rise of baseball typically depict the game as a reflex of industrial and technological change, and given the close relationship between industrialization and the rise of modern sports, it is tempting to conclude that the appeal of these games and their social functions were wholly new. Yet it must also be remembered that pre-industrial values survived and fed the growing interest in mass sports. There has been much more con-tinuity than has been recognized between pre-industrial sports and those of industrial society.

So much for the social changes that created mass support for baseball. Without the economic viability which popularity made possible, the game of baseball could never have been successfully professionalized. Yet there remains to be considered one important aspect of baseball's early growth. The game was not simply the result of such larger changes as those imposed by industrialization. Men shaped the game of baseball within the limits imposed by larger economic forces; and among those who did, probably none had more influence than the great entrepreneurs, the businessmen who realized the potential for profits and helped to give baseball its organizational structure.

The argument that organized baseball represented a sharp break with the past has assumed the proportions of a myth or legend. Up until the 1870s, so the myth goes, baseball was threatened by gambling, drinking, and hippodroming. The game began to lose popularity as the criminals and the rabble took over. Then baseball was rescued from this fate. The "saviours" of baseball were astute businessmen led by William Hulbert, a Chicago businessman, and Albert G. Spalding, a baseball pitcher for the Chicago White Stockings and a budding sporting goods entrepreneur. Hulbert and his friends put baseball on a highly organized basis by establishing the National League in 1876, and then acted resolutely to eliminate the taint of corruption which threatened the game. The reversal of baseball's sliding popularity in the late 1870s has frequently been attributed, especially by Spalding, to the high-minded and astute actions of the businessmen of baseball. Yet the new National League never fully achieved its goal of eliminating the less respectable elements from the game. The remainder of the century saw a long war of attrition between two traditions: the entrepreneurial tradition, which sought to make baseball an attractive spectator sport for the middle classes by making the game respectable; and the tradition that gloried in the gambling, the drinking, the fighting, the fixing of games. Generally, the respectable businessmen had the better of the battle, though scandals could never be entirely eliminated.[44]

The myth of the baseball promoters must also be challenged on another ground. Though Spalding and Hulbert represented the organization of the National League as a step to clean up the game, two contesting moralities were in fact at issue. The entrepreneurial morality sought to make profits out of attendance at the game. This involved not only the owners of clubs but groups associated with the clubs such as transportation companies, companies selling refreshments and so on, and sporting goods firms, of which Spalding's quickly became the most famous and successful. The other group, led by the Tweeds and Morriseys, sought to use the game to further their gambling interests. At bottom, they did not care about the game as a spectator sport, because their own business interests were served no matter who actually attended the games. It is wrong to label one morality as superior to the other; the attempt to clean up baseball and make it more respectable harmonized very well with the business interests of the promoters of the National League. Although the businessmen who formed the National League ultimately gained the upper hand, their success probably had little to do with the organization of the game on a more respectable basis. The depressed state of baseball in the mid-1870s reflected the great depression of those years; similarly, the revival of the game's economic fortunes in the 1880s stemmed primarily from economic boom; rising standards of living provided the underpinning of the game's prosperity and of the secure position it had achieved by that time. Nonetheless, the improvement in the game's fortunes enabled the National League owners to pose as the saviours of the game; henceforth respectability and business success became closely linked in the myth of organized baseball's origins, and the League gained considerable prestige.[45]

But the triumph of the League was not entirely fortuitous, for its businessmen entrepreneurs had ample funds behind them to back professional teams. They had the support, for instance, of prominent groups of city boosters who were prepared to lose money, at least in the short term, to provide their cities and businesses with publicity. Chicago "would not see her commercial rival on the Ohio [Cincinnati] bearing off the honors of the national game, especially when there was money to be made by beating her".[46] Having a successful baseball team in a city was something prominent businessmen were eager to support with cash, and thus professional clubs could afford to woo players with good salaries. The business interests of the League clubs were safeguarded by the decision to restrict team franchises to the larger cities, and by limiting the number of franchises in each city to one. With a captive market, promoters could look forward to substantial profits in the boom years after 1880, especially if they could mould winning teams.

These baseball entrepreneurs brought more than money to the game, for they shaped baseball in the image of American business. Their model was the emerging system of industrial capitalism. Whereas the early professional clubs of the National Association of Professional Baseball Players, formed in 1871, had been led primarily by players, the new League emulated the economic system by insisting on separation of "the control of the executive management from the players and the playing of the game". This was, Spalding recognized, "the irrepressible conflict between Labor and Capital asserting itself under a new guise".[47] The League sought to exact the same kind of discipline from players as any business would from its employees. Especially important was the drive to instil into them the notion that baseball was a profession in which full attention had to be given to the game. To further this goal, managers and owners enforced regular training and invoked severe penalties against gambling and drunkenness. In general, baseball promoters introduced contractual relationships, business principles, and labour-management separation, and they attempted to enforce the paternalistic morality of respectability prominent in the larger society. The kind of baseball system that emerged reflected not simply the nation's industrial growth and its technology but its business practices and organizational forms. The popular appeal of baseball had roots in ethnic and artisan communities, yet the *organization* of the game ultimately reflected the demands and values of American big business.

Given this analysis in terms of the social groups exploiting the sport, it becomes apparent why professionalism triumphed so easily in American baseball. The idea of amateurism had little or no appeal for artisans and ethnics who simply did not have the means to resist professionalism, even if they had wished to avoid the avenues of improvement which the game presented for its most talented players. For American businessmen, amateurism was again an ir-relevancy or even an obstacle to their economic interests. The tradition of amateurism lingered only among the genteel social elites of cities like Philadelphia and Boston, where to be an amateur, and to play cricket rather than baseball, became a mark of high social status, an expression of superior social position. In Australia, pro-fessionalism was associated with moral corruption; hence it was widely resisted.[48] In the United States this same tradition existed, but there was also the tradition that linked respectability with business success and upward social mobility. Through the activities of men like Spalding, Americans could accept professionalism because it promised to clean up the sport by openly acknowledging that baseball was "a legitimate vocation" while at the same time eliminating links with the underworld and with gambling in particular. To ignore the "realities" of life seemed to Spalding to encourage the "false pretences" of semi-professionalism, that shadowy world where gambling interests threatened the corruption of sport and the "young men" of America.[49]

American mythology posits a classless society, but the dynamics of baseball's early organization suggest that its form and content were shaped by the class structure and by the values and aspirations of different social groups. Rather than tell the story of organization and administration of baseball itself, this chapter has given a good deal of attention to the general social structure and its intersection with the history of a sport in the early stages of its organization. The social history of baseball remains largely unchartered territory. To understand the appeal of the game, its social functions, and its remarkable rise and its special character, we must give more attention to the social processes which produced "America's national game".

NOTES

1. John I. Marder, *The International Series: The Story of United States v. Canada at Cricket* (London: Kaye and Ward, 1968), pp.11, 16.
2. There is an interesting account in Fred Lillywhite, *The English Cricketers' Trip to Canada and the United States* (London: Lillywhite, 1860).
3. *New York Times*, 7 April 1870.
4. F. R. Dulles, *A History of Recreation: America Learns to Play*, 2nd ed. (New York: Appleton-Century-Crofts, 1965), p.186; Harold E. Seymour, *Baseball: The Early Years* (New York: Oxford University Press, 1960), p.31.
5. Dale Somers, "The Rise of Sports in New Orleans, 1850-1900" (PhD thesis, Tulane University, 1966), p.105; *New York Times*, 13 October 1859.
6. W. F. Mandle, "Games People Played: Cricket and Football in England and Victoria in the Late Nineteenth Century", *Historical Studies* 15, no. 60 (April 1973): 526; Mandle, "Cricket and Australian Nationalism in the Nineteenth Century", *Journal of the Royal Australian Historical Society* 59, pt. 4 (December 1973): 225-46.
7. Seymour, *Baseball*, p.31.
8. Ibid., pp.8-12. There was another view, that baseball had been derived from town-ball or cat-ball, but these games also stemmed from rounders. See Robert W. Henderson, *Bat, Ball and Bishop: The Origin of Ball Games* (New York: Rockport Press, 1947), p.155 ff.
9. *New York Times*, 26 August 1858; and *New York Times*, 24 June 1869, 16 March 1873, 22 March 1875.
10. *New York Times*, 9 July 1860; *New York Times*, 13 September 1868.
11. John Allen Krout, *The Annals of American Sport* (New Haven, Conn.: Yale University Press, 1929), p.125; John Arlott, ed., *The Oxford Companion to Sports and Games* (London: Oxford University Press, 1975), pp.200, 213.
12. David Reisman and Reuel Denny, "Football in America: A Study in Culture Diffusion", in *The Sociology of Sport*, ed. Eric Dunning (London: Cass, 1971), pp.152-74.
13. Lillywhite, *English Cricketers' Trip*, p.42.
14. Digby Baltzell, *Philadelphia Gentlemen: The Making of a National Upper Class* (Glencoe, Ill.: Free Press, 1958), p.359.
15. Albert A. Outerbridge, "Cricket in America", *Lippincott's Magazine* 11: 596 (May 1873).
16. Robert W. Malcolmson, *Popular Recreations in English Society, 1700-1850* (Cambridge: Cambridge University Press, 1973), p.41.

17. Seymour, *Baseball*, p.23; David Quentin Voigt, "Cash and Glory: The Commercialization of Major League Baseball as a Sports Spectacular, 1885-1892", DSS thesis, Syracuse University, 1962), pp.51-53.
18. Seymour, *Baseball*, p.16.
19. Ibid., pp.23-24; Dulles, *History of Recreation*, p.187.
20. "Bats, Balls, and Mallets", in *New York Times*, 30 April 1871.
21. *New York Times*, 13 September 1868, 9 July 1860.
22. Voigt, "Cash and Glory", p.202. Yet another explanation has focused on the role of the Civil War. It has often been argued that the war publicized baseball on a national level, and it may be that this fortuitous event helped to secure supremacy for the game. Certainly the war did not retard the game's growing popularity, for baseball was widely played by both Union and Confederate soldiers. Yet if the war did help promote baseball over cricket, it merely accelerated the trend to baseball apparent in the years immediately before the Civil War. Baseball appears to have overtaken cricket in popularity by 1861. See Seymour, *Baseball*, pp.40-41.
23. I am indebted to Dr Richard Cashman for this comparative insight.
24. Seymour, *Baseball*, p.60.
25. Ibid., p.348.
26. See the review of *Essays in Nineteenth-Century Economic History: The Old North-West*, ed. David Klingaman and R. K. Vedder (Athens, Ohio: Ohio University Press, 1975), in *American Historical Review* 81 (June 1976): 663.
27. Herbert Gutman, "Work, Culture, and Society in Industrializing America, 1815-1919", *American Historical Review* 78 (June 1973): 531-88; E. P. Thompson, "Time, Work-Discipline, and Industrial Capitalism", *Past and Present* 38 (December 1967): 56-97.
28. Seymour, *Baseball*, pp.92, 261.
29. *Historical Statistics of the United States, Colonial Times to the Present* (Washington: US Government Printing Office, 1957), Series D 573-577.
30. *New York Times*, 24 June 1869.
31. A. G. Spalding, *America's National Game* (New York: American Sports Publishing Co., 1911), p.6.
32. Frank Pidgeon had complained in 1859 of the difficulty of getting time to practise, while employers complained when their employees watched or played games during working hours. Ibid., p.59.
33. *New York Times*, 23 December 1876, 13 September 1868; Spalding, *America's National Game*, p.59; Seymour, *Baseball*, pp.17, 55.
34. For a general survey of these changes, see John R. Betts, "Organized Sport in Industrial America" (PhD thesis, Columbia University, 1951), passim.
35. Edgar W. Martin, *The Standard of Living in 1860* (Chicago: University of Chicago Press, 1942), p.384.
36. Bruce Laurie, "Fire Companies and Gangs in Southwark: The 1840s", in *The Peoples of Philadelphia: A History of Ethnic Groups and Lower-Class Life, 1790-1940*, ed. A. F. Davis and M. H. Haller (Philadelphia: Temple University Press, 1973), pp.71-89.
37. Gutman, "Work, Culture and Society", p.572.
38. David R. Johnson, "Crime Patterns in Philadelphia, 1840-70", in Davis and Haller, *Peoples of Philadelphia*, p.103.
39. *New York Times*, 21 July, 18 August 1858.
40. Spalding, *America's National Game*, p.85; *New York Times*, 24 June 1869.
41. *New York Times*, 6 March 1871.
42. Seymour, *Baseball*, p.66.
43. Gutman, "Work, Culture and Society", passim.

44. Spalding, *America's National Game*, passim; on scandals see Krout, *The Annals*,
     p.136 for an account of the "fixed" World Series of 1919.
45. Voigt, "Cash and Glory"; Betts, "Organized Sport", pp.76-78.
46. *Lakeside Monthly* 4 (1972): 326; Voigt, "Cash and Glory", p.88.
47. Spalding, *America's National Game*, p.193.
48. Mandle, "Games People Played", pp.533-34.
49. Spalding, *America's National Game*, p.123.

BRAHAM DABSCHECK

"Defensive Manchester": a History of the Professional Footballers Association

One of the paradoxes of the growing academic interest in sport is the unwillingness of scholars to actually inquire into sport *per se*. Rather, sport is used as a vehicle through which insights into other, apparently more relevant, phenomena can be gained. There is a need to examine sports from the "inside", to inquire into the relation between sport and the participant, that which provides the spectator and academic alike with their respective vicarious existences. This chapter is concerned with examining the lot of the professional sportsmen, concentrating its attention on the problems that beset the English professional footballer, and in particular their use of a players' association in an effort to redress these problems.

The genesis of modern football has its roots in the formation of the Football Association (F. A.) in 1863. The FA established itself as a body that would govern the hitherto spontaneous development of football and promote the game. Member clubs would have to observe the "uniform" laws set down by the controlling body. The acceptance of the FA was initially slow, and it was not until after the inauguration of the FA Challenge Cup, in 1871, that clubs, *en masse,* were prepared to come under the FA's umbrella. "The Cup" quickly became a popular spectacle; and it was only a matter of time before some clubs, to enhance their chance of success, offered rewards to players to attract them to their team. The first known professional was a J. J. Lang of Scotland, who joined Sheffield Wednesday in 1876. Despite several attempts to outlaw payments to players, the FA eventually sanctioned professionalism in 1885.[1]

In 1888 the Football League (FL) was formed, being one of the many leagues which then operated under the FA's umbrella. The early years of the FL were chaotic, with individual clubs prepared to flout the rules and regulations of both the FL and FA. The complexities of this early period will not concern us here, except for two issues which pertain to the "control" of players.[2] Firstly, there was no limit on the payment of players at the time of the FL's formation, and several attempts to introduce a limit in the 1890s were unsuccessful. Eventually, in 1901, the FA sanctioned a maximum wage of four pounds a week, though the enforcement of this wage and other financial rules proved difficult in the ensuing years. In 1904 an informal understanding was reached between the FA and FL in which it was agreed that the financial affairs of FL clubs would be the responsibility of the FL. However, in 1908, the FA again attempted to assert its authority in this area; but it was forced to back down and granted a general amnesty to clubs that had conducted their financial affairs improperly, provided they would observe the FA's financial rules in the future. Secondly, there was the issue of "poaching" players. In these years the rules governing the movement of players between clubs were vague, and players moved to or were poached by clubs who showed a (financial) interest in them. To overcome this, the FL clubs agreed that each club would have the right to retain its players, and that transfer fees would be paid to the "owning" club as compensation for the loss of any player transferred. The problem, however, still remained of clubs outside the FL. The FL's response was, initially, to forbid its clubs to play matches with clubs who had poached FL players. This was vetoed by the FA — because of the effect it would have on the FA Cup — and so as to bring poaching clubs under its transfer laws, the FL formed a second division in 1892. In only four years the FL had grown from twelve to twenty-eight clubs.

Very early in the history of professional football, the principle of "controlling" the employment, or the labour market, of players became enshrined in the rules and regulations of the FA and FL. Limits were placed on the wages of players, and clubs assumed the right to retain players and to receive transfer fees for the release of a player to another club. Such wage and mobility restrictions are unique in the history of industrial employment. It is into this controlled labour market and fledging industry that an association of professional footballers was formed at the end of 1907. There is an obvious appeal in the study of any union or association of employees that seeks to advance and protect the rights and interests of members, but the progress and history of this 1907 body has an added element.[3] In addition to "normal" organizational and strategic problems, the Professional Footballers Association (PFA) has the added problem of operating in a labour market where the economic freedom of its members is highly circumscribed. Several students of sporting labour markets have argued that the formation of player associations has the potential of enabling players to increase their bargaining and economic power *vis-a-vis* the clubs.

Because the PFA is the oldest continuous association of professional team sportsmen, a study of its rich and varied history enables us to examine whether or not player associations can in fact enhance the social and economic welfare of members.[4] More generally, the PFA's seventy-year history throws light on the various constraints that impinge on the effectiveness of an association of professional team sportsmen.

The FA and FL share responsibility for the management of professional football. Depending on the issue, the PFA negotiates with either the FA or FL.[5] The once-prominent position of the FA was increasingly challenged by the FL at the turn of the century. The FA's forays into the financial affairs of FL clubs were consistently countered with the argument that these were matters best left to the FL itself. The FA's 1908 armistice marked a capitulation to the FL, and in 1910 the rules of both bodies were changed to formally acknowledge the FL's authority in the management of its own financial affairs. The only exception was the retaining wage (the minimum wage at which clubs could retain players), which remained in the FA's rule book, ostensibly, because of the belief of the FA that it would be able to safeguard the interests of players. Despite this loss of financial authority, the FA still maintained its position in the area of discipline, both field and club, and, of course, was still master of its own financial affairs. In 1929 the rules of the FA were again altered to allow members of the FL management committee full membership to the FA council. This overlapping of "directorates" helped to ensure that the two bodies worked in close co-operation.

Generally speaking, the PFA has pursued wage, transfer, and financial matters with the FL (and up until the 1960s the retaining wage with the FA). The PFA took up disciplinary issues — especially field discipline — and financial issues specific to the FA with the FA. These range from representations on behalf of non-league members, fees for England internationals, a share of the FA's television receipts — this issue lead to two threatened strikes in 1956 and 1965 — and more recently a court case over the "international" transfer of players.

Before examining the respective structures of both organizations, it is worth noting the emergence of an "amateur" association which split from the FA. The first decade of this century witnessed a transfer of power from the FA to the FL; the authority of the FA was also challenged by the "amateurs". In 1907 a group of amateur clubs split away from the FA to form the Amateur Football Association (AFA). The ostensible cause of the split was the FA's directive to county associations to allow professional clubs to play in their competitions. By 1914 peace had been restored when the AFA agreed to recognize the FA as the governing authority of football.[6]

As with most organizations, the supreme policy-making body of the FA was the annual general meeting. However, the FA council, with more than ninety honorary and representative members, was the effective policy-making body — though its size may suggest, given the FA's system of committees, that the FA secretariat, with the FL representatives, played a prominent part. The organs within the FA which were of major concern to the PFA were the secretariat and council. Negotiations were carried out with the FA president and secretary, and various vice-presidents. Generally speaking, whenever the PFA has been able to convince these representatives of the wisdom of a certain course of action, which has not necessarily been an easy matter, the FA, after the necessary round of committee meetings, has then endorsed the "agreement" entered into by its representatives.

The FL has ninety-two member clubs. The general meeting was the supreme policy-making body of the FL. However, not all clubs of the FL have entree to these meetings. Access is automatic to each of the forty-four first and second division clubs. Four representatives from the other two divisions, with less than full voting rights, were allowed to attend.[7] A three-quarters majority was necessary at these meetings to bring about changes to the rules and regulations of the FL. Between general meetings the FL was administered by the FL management committee and serviced by a "large" secretariat. The management committee has eight members plus the FL president. The PFA approached the FL secretary and the FL management committee when it wished to gain a concession. If an "agreement" was reached, the management committee made recommendations to the "clubs" at a general meeting. From the 1920s to the 1950s the PFA found it extremely difficult to negotiate agreements with the FL management committee. In the last decade the management committee has been more prepared to negotiate and reach agreements; however, they have been unable to achieve their endorsement by the clubs at general meetings.

The distinctive feature of the professional footballers' labour market was that once a player signed with a club he was bound to that club for the rest of his playing life. A player could only be employed by another club with the permission of the club he has previously signed with. Before a number of changes were brought about in and after 1961, the labour market was characterized by a maximum wage and the retain-and-transfer system.[8] These wage and mobility controls have severely limited the economic freedom of professional footballers and have been a continuing source of dissatisfaction among footballers and a rallying cry for the PFA. The rationale for such controls has been built around the notion that professional football was a "sport" rather than an "industry" and controls were necessary to ensure the maintenance of sporting equality. If any team, or a small coterie of teams, acquired the best players, uncertainty and interest in the results of various competitions would wane and professional football would loose its spectator appeal. Subsidiary arguments justifying controls have been the need to maintain team stability and the minimization of wages and costs, and a belief that clubs should be compensated for the loss of players. Recent research has challenged the view that labour market controls enhance sporting equality. Such benefits are negligible and/or illusory and hardly justify the denial of "normal" economic freedom. Moreover, there are alternative ways in which sporting equality can be achieved, consistent with labour market freedom.[9]

A maximum wage placed limits on the amount of income that a player could receive from playing football.[10] The problem with a maximum wage, especialy where the difference between the maximum and minimum was small was how to construct a (club) wage structure which would "adequately" reward the "star" members of the team. Before the abolition of the maximum wage in 1961, there were persistent rumours that some, if not many, clubs were prepared to offer under-the-counter payments to players.

Approaching the end of each season, clubs prepared two separate lists regarding players. The first was of those players the club wished to retain; the second, players placed on the transfer list. To be able to retain a player a club was only obliged to offer terms equal to the minimum retaining wage. Generally speaking, clubs tended to offer their "star" players, given the wage maxima, terms similar to those that had been in force during the previous season. With the so-called lesser players, and even some "star" players, several clubs adopted a more "niggardly" approach. If a player did not accept the terms offered by his club, or if no subsequent agreement could be reached; he was not entitled to any pay.[11] Some clubs, so as to save resources, would offer substantially reduced terms to players, and if the player refused these terms he would not receive any income during the "dispute". The alternative available to the player was to retire from football.

Transfer-listed players were not entitled to receive any wages from their "owning" club. And unfortunately for the player it was the "owning" club which determined the player's transfer fee, and, despite the right to appeal to the FL management committee for a reduction, it could be set at such a level to discourage potentially interested clubs from purchasing the player. In this situation a player could join a non-league club, but if he wished to return to league football with a new club, that club might now have to pay two transfer fees — one to his former league club, and another to the non-league club. Through such avenues clubs could escape the payment of "summer" wages. For the player this meant no income for three months. Although the player was not receiving any income from the club, not having a contract, he was nonetheless still "owned" by his club.

Players could be transferred during the season as well as at the end of the season and could ask to be placed on the transfer list, with the club setting the transfer fee. The player's signature was necessary to affect his transfer from one club to another. It may appear that a player cannot be transferred against his will, and this ability to sign one's name could be a useful bargaining ploy in the transfer market. Reality has been different. An owning club wishing to convince a recalcitrant player that he should agree to his transfer could always make it very clear to the player that if he did not sign the necessary documents he would never kick another football. The club prepared to purchase the player, in all probability, would play the player in its first team, the prospect of which may no longer be available with his current club. And by moving, the player, if he had not been the instigator of the transfer would be able to receive a share of his transfer fee; and the new club might also offer other inducements to make the move worthwhile.

The problem, in a nutshell, of the retain-and-transfer system, prior to 1961, was that all the options lay with the club. Given the inability to find alternative FL employment, players were subsequently dependent on the generosity of their clubs. While clubs have at times treated their players "fairly", on other occasions they have been quite ruthless in their dealings with players, particularly when there have been financial problems or poor team performances. Ultimately the source and focus of most player discontent in professional football has centered on this one-sided labour market.

The inaugural meeting of the PFA was held at the Imperial Hotel in Manchester on 2 December 1907. A possible reason for the emergence of the PFA at this date could lie with the more favourable environment enjoyed by trade unions following the Trade Disputes Act of 1906. Though some, if not many, players had links with "pit life", and by association with principles of trade unionism, the main reasons for the emergence of the PFA were developments within professional football. After the formation of the FL, players had tried to form a collective body for their own protection and advancement. Two earlier attempts, in 1893 and 1898, had failed because of the FA's refusal to grant recognition. If we can accept that the players had a desire to form a body such as the PFA, the strategic problem was to find the "right" time to successfully launch it. Concomitant with this, the players had to possess leadership astute enough to perceive this opportunity and to undertake the "necessary" tasks to ensure the organization's future survival and growth once it had formed.[12]

As noted above, the first decade of the twentieth century was one of struggle between the FA and FL over the question of "controlling" and supervising the finances of FL clubs; and simultaneously the amateur clubs had left the FA to form the AFA. These developments had two effects which suggest that the PFA's formation was most likely at this time. Firstly, many players were fined and/or suspended because of the FA's wide use of its powers, which had the hallmarks of an inquisition, to force clubs and players to observe the spirit and letter of their rules. Billy Meredith, the chairman of the PFA's first meeting, epitomized the problems experienced by players during this period. Meredith was one of football's most colourful and controversial figures. A player of unparalleled skill — the "Prince of Wingers", "the Master" — Meredith was at the centre of some of the financial scandals of this time. Young says that Meredith "off the field . . . like many men of genius, was a problem to the conventional . . . the prevailing factor . . . [his] inconvenient habit of demanding what he considered as his rights". At the end of the 1904—5 season, Meredith and sixteen of his colleagues were fined and suspended from playing with Manchester City again, for their participation in "illegal" financial dealings.[13] Such sentences imposed on a number of other players at other clubs created a hard core of players who felt the pressing need for a collective body for their mutual self-protection.

Secondly, the period was one in which the previously undisputed authority of the FA was being increasingly challenged. Both the professional and amateur clubs were becoming increasingly disenchanted with the FA. The more astute players correctly calculated that this was the right time to form a players' association. By adopting a restrained approach, and with the FA and FL pre-occupied with each other, it was possible that no serious opposition would be mounted against the PFA's formation. The FA, in fact, recognized the PFA almost immediately. By 1908, because of the amateur split and the continuing headaches associated with policing the finances of FL clubs, the FA wished to wash its hands of FL club finances. The FA may have calculated that the formation of the PFA would provide tactical help in resolving this problem.[14]

The need for protection against the FA and FL permeate almost all of the original objectives of the PFA, the ultimate symbol of this need being the adoption of the telegraphic address "Defensive Manchester". With only two exceptions, the objectives drawn up in the early months of 1908 have continued to guide the PFA. The first objective was "to promote and protect the interests of the members by endeavouring to come to amicable arrangements with the governing football authorities with a view to abolishing all restrictions which affect the social and financial position of players, and to safeguard their rights at all times." Other objectives were to provide members with legal advice and legal assistance; to help transfer-listed or disengaged players find employment; to provide temporary financial assistance for members and their families if and when necessary; generally to regulate relations between professional football players and their employers and to do all things necessary to help advance and promote the interests of members; and finally, "to obtain recognition by, and representation on the FA with a view to bringing before the proper authorities the grievances of its members". This representation objective was subsequently dropped at the PFA's first annual general meeting in December 1908, apparently owing to the FA's having already granted recognition and a realization that the latter half of the objective would be difficult to achieve. The only other changes to the PFA's objectives have been the inclusion of a clause granting authority to administer benevolent, accident insurance, and education funds.

Objectives were easy enough to define, but it was another thing to develop the organizational verve necessary for their pursuit and achievement. The PFA's structure was very straightforward. Any registered professional player (league or non-league), or apprentice professional, was entitled to PFA membership. Each club could elect a delegate who could be the club's representative at the annual general meeting — the PFA's supreme governing authority. An eight-member management committee was elected which was responsible for conducting the PFA's affairs between annual meetings.[15] The management committee had authority to appoint a secretary and any other full-time officials that it deemed necessary. However, other than its five secretaries (see appendix 2) only two other full-time officers have been appointed: the first, Jimmy Guthrie, as a full-time chairman from 1948 to 1957; and the second, an education officer in the person of Bob Kerry in 1970. The PFA's leaders have been recruited from within football.[16] Before their involvement in the PFA's internal affairs, these leaders had little or no experience of running a collective organization or confronting the numerous organizational and strategic problems that such leadership entails. The skills required had to be learnt "on the job". Many able and resourceful trade union leaders have gained extensive experience and "organizational" ability from moving around their own complex structures. The PFA's structure was essentially simple, and there was no recruitment procedure, other than the preparedness of a delegate to talk up at an annual general meeting, to determine whether or not a particular individual would be a capable and effective leader.[17] Of course, it was possible that the "right" persons for leadership would simply "emerge", but it was equally conceivable that they would not.

The leadership problem also had its roots from within football itself. Compared with most "normal" occupations the life of the professional team sportsmen was exceedingly short. With the unremitting pressure on maintaining form and the ever-present risk of injury (increasing with the growing number of fixtures, the introduction of a FL Cup, the various European competitions) few players spend more than ten years in the game. When a young player entered the game he was easily carried along by the game's glamour and kudos, and his thoughts were directed to establishing a regular first-team place rather than worrying about such things as the retain-and-transfer system. Club management also assured the young hopeful that as long as he realized his unlimited promise the club would always stand behind him. With the passing of the years the glamour of the game frequently began to wear off. They then would start to think more seriously about their profession and perceive the possible role that the PFA could play in advancing the cause of players. Such players might be prepared to become a club delegate and/or members of the management committee. But by this time the player would have only a few years of his career left. It might also take the player a certain amount of time before he became sensitive to the dominant issues of the moment. An adept and hard-working group of leaders might emerge. But this group might be quickly and easily diminished with several retirements from the game. And players at the end of their career, who would undoubtedly be concerned about their next occupation on retirement, might not be able to concentrate their full attention on a particular thorny issue which was then confronting the PFA. As we will see below, effective and able leadership has been a problem that has periodically haunted and handicapped the PFA.[18]

The PFA was formed because the players of 1907 believed that collective action was necessary if improvements to their economic and social position were to be achieved. By forming an organization and by pooling and centralizing resources, players, both individually and collectively, would be more able to act as a countervailing force to the FA and FL and would also be able to provide "mutual insurance" benefits for members. This latter activity has traditionally taken up much of the time and resources of the PFA.

We will concentrate on one aspect of the PFA's programme, the accident insurance scheme, because of its illustration of the various twists and turns of the PFA in its efforts to provide benefits for members. In 1909 the PFA successfully pursued a number of court cases which found that professional footballers were "workmen" within the meaning of the Workmen's Compensation Act of 1906. The implication of these decisions, and the following unsuccessful appeals by the FL, was that injured players were entitled to receive an income while injured; necessary medical expenses should be paid by the employer; and in the case of an injury that forced a player to retire, the player was entitled to a lump-sum payment as compensation. The PFA's solicitors represented and conducted the negotiations of the various players so affected with the Football Insurance Federation, a body formed by the FL to meet the club's responsibilities following the 1906 Act and the attendant court cases.

The area of accident insurance was relatively trouble free for the PFA until the mid-1930s, when a High Court judge, Mr Justice Roche, used a level of income to determine whether or not a person receiving wages could be regarded as a workmen as implied by the Workmen's Compensation Act and other similar acts. After a test case, it was eventually decided that a player receiving more than £350 income in the twelve months before receiving an injury was not a "workman". The PFA responded to this by approaching the FL to see whether or not the clubs were prepared to cover the £350 plus players, even though they were not covered by the Workmen's Compensation Act. After a deal of procrastination, the FL eventually acceded to this request. At the end of the Second World War, representations by secretary Jimmy Fay were successful in extracting *ex gratia* payments from the FL for players who had suffered permanent injury during the war-time "competitions", but because of the war were not covered by the Workmen's Compensation Act.[19]

Although the FL continued to make *ex gratia* payments after the war, the PFA was unhappy with the amounts offered, and in 1946 decided to take out their own block insurance scheme which would provide permanently injured players with a £500 cover. Unfortunately, the premium required to maintain this cover quickly increased, in 1947 the insurance premium was £2,750 and in excess of £6,000 in 1951; this latter figure constituted more than 50 per cent of the PFA's income for that year. The insurance premium was a continuing headache in these years; a headache which was removed in two parts by unexpected developments.

In the middle of the 1950s the FA Cup and other matches controlled by the FA were shown on television. The PFA had unsuccessfully tried to negotiate fees for players with the FA, and in March of 1956 threatened a ban of members playing in televised games if the FA continued their stance of non-negotiation. The threat was successful, and after a series of meetings the FA agreed to pay a share of their television receipts to finance a joint accident insurance scheme.[20] Over the next decade the FA's television fees financed more than half the premium needed for the maintenance of the accident insurance scheme.

The next major change occurred in the 1964–65 season when the FL tried to discontinue the provident fund (unilaterally) and put pressure on the FA to discontinue the joint accident insurance scheme. After a threatened ban on televised games, and resulting negotiations, the FL took over the PFA's joint accident insurance scheme, providing a £750 cover, and maintained the provident fund at a lower rate; and the FA agreed to make donations of further television moneys to the funds of the PFA.[21]

The 1909 dispute between the PFA and FA has been almost totally misreported in the literature. Previous authorities have all presented the dispute as being caused by the PFA's affiliation with the General Federation of Trade Unions (GFTU), a body created by the Trades Union Congress of 1899.[22] Rather, GFTU affiliation resulted from a dispute whose origins were firmly rooted in the internal machinations of professional football.

The immediate cause of the dispute was the PFA's intention to initiate legal action over arrears of wages and the Workmen's Compensation Act on behalf of members. Such action was in contradiction to the FA's rule 48, which did not allow those coming under its "authority" to pursue legal action without the prior consent of the FA council. The FA adopted a very hard line in this dispute, and pursued a policy designed to crush the PFA. The reasons for such an intransigent stance require an explanation, especially given the FA's earlier recognition of the PFA. The FA were opposed to the PFA's taking "disputes" to the courts because they feared a further erosion of their position and authority within the football world. Almost half a century earlier, the FA had established itself as football's governing authority. If the PFA were to have disputes settled in the law courts, the courts rather than the FA would become the governing authority of football. In this context, the split with the amateurs and the FA's inability to enforce financial discipline on FL clubs should be remembered. We can probably interpret the FA's response to the PFA's action as "the last straw" — the FA had to stand up and fight and reassert its former past role. The issue at stake was equally crucial for the PFA. Legal representation was one of the PFA's objectives, and if it was to be denied the right to pursue such cases it would be for ever reduced to a mutual benefit society. The dispute represents a fundamental struggle between two organizations — one seeking to find its feet and the other clutching for past glory and status. The eventual PFA victory marked an end to the previous prominent role of the FA in English football; the once proud father was to be reduced to younger brother status.

Secretary H. C. Broomfield expressed the PFA's reaction to the FA's opposition to the proposed legal action in a letter in February 1909 which said: "The Management Committee are not convinced that they are expected to regard seriously the opinion that a football player forfeits a common legal right on entering into a professional engagement with a football club." The FA regarded this letter as "bombastic", and the FA council, on 8 March, withdrew their recognition of the PFA and significantly, at this stage, decided to include in the standard player's contract a clause whereby signing players had to agree to abide by the FA's rules. The PFA were not worried by this turn of events, and Broomfield advised members to sign contracts for the next season, as according to legal advice the "extra" clause was ineffective anyway. This retort further irritated the FA, and the FA council, on 23 April, altered their rules to include players against whom games could be prohibited. On 3 May the FA council resolved: "Such of the officers and members of the Committee of the [PFA] who do not before the 17 of May give an undertaking that they will in future act in accordance with the rules of the FA will be suspended from taking part in football or football management." The FA went on to say that the PFA's leadership had not consulted its members and "suggested that a special general meeting be called without delay for the purpose of registering their opinion upon the policy of the Committee".[23]

The PFA management committee met for three and a half hours, on 7 May, to determine their position *vis-a-vis* the FA council's resolution, but did not announce their "position" until more than a week later. The reason for the delay was tactical; other parties had to be contacted, and undertakings received, before the PFA could announce its "official" position. The problem was that the FA had launched its attack at the end of the season, and as a *Sporting Chronicle* reporter noted, the PFA realized that the summer is a time in which it is impossible for them to act. The plan was to ride out the summer, wait for the start of the next season, and counter-attack in the form of a threatened strike. The PFA's "official" response to the FA's resolution was for members of the management committee to resign their positions on the committee, except for H. L. Mainman (the chairman) and Broomfield, who would carry on to the annual meeting in August and "give the whole of the members an opportunity of deciding whether they would support the PFA or not". In the meantime the PFA would seek affiliation with the GFTU, try to arrange matches with the AFA to raise income to help members if a strike was necessary, and explain their present strategy to members. It is important to stress that the PFA only sought affiliation with the GFTU after the FA council's resolution of 3 May.[24]

The FA remained apprehensive about the developing situation. They initiated inquiries into why a number of leading players had not yet signed their contracts. At their annual meeting in June, the FA suspended Mainman and Broomfield *sine die* for not giving the undertaking demanded in their 3 May resolution, and even went further when the FA council decided: "Members . . . having also failed to avail themselves of the opportunity of putting the PFA upon a proper basis, so that it could be carried on according to the rules of the FA must cease membership . . . before July 1, or their registration with the FA shall be cancelled."[25]

On 21 June the PFA held a meeting of Lancashire and Yorkshire players in Manchester who pledged their support for the PFA. This was to be the first of a series of meetings, held up and down the country, where Broomfield was to report to members and seek their continuing support in the struggle with the FA. Broomfield was a capable and resourceful leader who entered successfully into the propaganda warfare that was now raging. He saw the dispute as hinging on "whether the professional player is to be a man or a puppet in the hands of the FA". He had a number of retorts to the FA's new ultimatum. Firstly, members did not have to pay subscriptions in the off-season; they need only become financial in

September. Secondly, many players with dependants had advised him that they had given the FA the undertaking it wanted to secure summer wages, and once the season started they would resume their membership. Thirdly, Broomfield speculated about the legal position of players who had signed contracts with their clubs, but had been barred from playing by the FA; he predicted further court cases which would not only bypass but also question the role of the FA.[26]

Developments in the dispute occurred on five fronts. Firstly, clubs attempted to sign players and secure the necessary undertakings required by the FA. The players of the Manchester United Club, the reigning league champions, were most conspicuous in their public refusal to do so, the key figure being the captain, Charlie Roberts. Players of other clubs similarly supported the PFA; but the extent of this support is difficult to gauge given the continual claims and counter claims in this period. Secondly, tentative arrangements were made between the PFA and AFA to arrange a fund-raising match. Matches against the universities were suggested, but the most likely opponent was the Corinthians for the Dewar Shield, a charity match organized by the Sheriff of London to be played in September. With the eventual settlement of the dispute on 1 September no game was played. Thirdly, the GFTU and the FA entered into negotiations. Two meetings occurred on 4 and 18 August, and at a subsequent meeting on 26 August, which also included the PFA, the dispute was almost resolved but stalemated over the issue of pay arrears — thirty-eight pounds — for disqualified players. It was later revealed that the FA representatives had divided four to three over this issue. Concurrent with these negotiations, the GFTU was drumming up moral support for the PFA from trade unions and trade councils throughout England. Fourthly, in August, the courts announced their favourable decision with regard to the PFA's representations on behalf of members coming under the Workmen's Compensation Act. These decisions would have further confirmed and strengthened the PFA's stance. Fifthly, as the possibility of a strike seemed more likely, various FL clubs began to criticize the FA's handling of the dispute, especially their recalcitrant and uncompromising attitude.[27]

By now the dispute had aroused the interest of members of parliament. Arthur Henderson, the Labour Party chairman, suggested that the dispute should be resolved through voluntary, binding arbitration. The FA refused this request because it was "now too late to consider arbitration when the PFA were willing to accept it". The FA had one last ploy. They would invite representatives of the players, non-PFA members, to a meeting in Birmingham on 31 August for an exchange of views. The FA council also resolved: "to assist the players, if they so desire, to the formation of another organization to promote their interests, and that the FA will assist in such formation by advice, or financially, as may be desired by the players".[28]

Immediately before this meeting, Colin Veitch, the Newcastle United captain, who had been involved in the 26 August negotiations, approached the FA president, (later Sir) Charles Clegg, and secured his agreement to allow PFA members into the meeting.[29] At the meeting, players endorsed their support of the PFA and the FA agreed to a truce on suspended players to allow clubs to pay wage arrears and to consider immediately other requests of the PFA. In addition, the FA agreed to the PFA's right to represent members before the courts, while the PFA, for their part, agreed to first present a "dispute" to the FA to give them a reasonable time to resolve it. The only stumbling block to a satisfactory settlement was the PFA's affiliation with the GFTU. The FL who were now about to take over "responsibility" for the financial affairs of FL clubs, wanted the PFA to disaffiliate from the GFTU: J. J. Bentley, the FL president, objected to the GFTU's strike clause. Though he admitted they had "done much good in preventing strikes" and were "a useful industrial institution" what would happen "if within half an hour of a kick-off the players determined on a strike, and that with 30,000 or 40,000 people on the ground? That would mean a riot. Such a thing as a strike, however remote, was not sport." Both the PFA and W.A. Appleton, the GFTU secretary, pointed out that the right to strike was not a condition of GFTU membership but was guaranteed by the 1906 Trade Disputes Act. Appleton added, however: "Whether the PFA retains its affiliation or not is a matter of small moment to the Federation, but while it does so it is assured of advice and assistance."[30] The PFA were prepared to ballot members to determine whether or not GFTU affiliation should be continued. The ballot was in the negative, 172 to 470, and at their second annual meeting in November, after expressing thanks to the GFTU, the PFA announced its decision to disaffiliate.

After this victory, the PFA was to experience, for the first time, the leadership problems referred to above. Both Mainman and Broomfield resigned their positions and were replaced by E. H. Lintott and A. J. Owen. Within a year Lintott resigned from the management committee and Veitch was elected to the position of chairman. Thus within a few years the PFA lost the expertise gained from the successful conclusion of the 1909 dispute. For the FA the dispute settled once and for all that the various leagues could be responsible for the "governorship" of their own financial affairs. The PFA now proceeded to bargain with representatives of the FL and the Southern League (SL) in an effort to win concessions. The PFA argued for freedom of contract, but if this could not be achieved an increase in the maximum wage from four pounds to six pounds in ten-shilling yearly increases, and the introduction of a win-draw bonus. The response of the leagues was to offer a "take-it or leave-it package" in which the maximum wage would be increased to five pounds with two ten-shilling instalments to be paid after two years, a bonus for successful championship and cup teams, and the PFA's agreement that the clubs would have "the power, subject to appeal, to get rid of incompetents, malingerers, and non-triers on giving fourteen days notice". Despite objections to this last condition, the PFA representatives ultimately agreed to this package. In 1911 the PFA unsuccessfully made representations to the FL for increases to the remuneration of players. According to the *Athletic News,* the FL refused to sanction these requests because "the financial regulations . . . passed last spring, had not yet had a fair trial . . . and . . . the clubs . . . were really not in a position to undertake any further financial responsibilities".[31]

To hark back to 1910, the FL and SL entered into a transfer agreement where both leagues agreed to the payment of transfer fees for players moving from one league to the other. The minutes of PFA management committee meetings reflected a desire to test the legal validity of these laws. A possible test case presented itself when a Mr Kingaby initiated legal proceedings against the Aston Villa club. Kingaby had played for Aston Villa in 1906, but had not been able to establish himself as a regular member of the team and had joined a SL club in 1907. After the 1910 transfer deal, Aston Villa demanded a £350 transfer fee, later reduced to £300 on appeal, for his services. An approach was made to Kingaby's solicitors and it was agreed that the PFA would represent Kingaby in a test case of the transfer system. However, during 1911, for reasons which are not clear, the PFA and Kingaby fell out. Firstly, Kingaby either lost interest in the case or decided to proceed without the PFA. Consequently, at the 1911 annual general meeting the PFA decided to drop the Kingaby case. Secondly, it was later reported that Kingaby's solicitors were to initiate legal proceedings over a supposed libel contained in the PFA newsletter.[32] Either because of this threatened libel or because of a desire to test the transfer system's legality come what may, the action was continued with.

Unfortunately, the presiding judge, Mr Justice Lawrence, only concerned himself with whether or not Aston Villa had observed the FL's rules, rather than the "broader" question of whether or not these rules were "legal". Hence he found against Kingaby and the PFA. The PFA could not meet the resulting costs and were fortunate, in a sense, when the FL agreed to absorb them until the PFA were more financial. In a 1913 issue of their newsletter, secretary H. J. Newbould wished "to publicly thank the. . . League for the fair and generous way in which they have met the [PFA] with regard to the costs of the transfer system test case. Of course, the action was taken in friendly spirit and in the interests of all, but at the same time, the League had it in their power to be either generous victors or harsh victors, and they choose the former attitude."[33]

However, the FL's "generosity" implied dependence and vulnerability and had previously helped to bring about Owen's resignation as secretary. After the Kingaby case the PFA attempted to organize a game to raise money to help pay the FL the money owed. Such a match required the permission of both the FL and FA. The FA, however, failed to grant the necessary permission, ostensibly because the PFA had previously transferred money from its benevolent funds to the general account. In addition, the FA had a few old scores to settle. After a series of unsuccessful approaches to the FA for a reversal of this decision, Owen published a bitter letter in which he strongly attacked the FA for their high-handed attitude. The FA and FL would not agree to sanction the game until the PFA's management committee not only disassociated themselves from Owen's letter but also publicly rebuked him. The management committee agreed to this, and, in the circumstances, Owen decided to tender his resignation.[34] This financial dependence on the FL hampered the PFA up until the First World War. It was not removed until 1919.

In 1915, competitive football and the payment of wages were suspended by the FA because of the war. With the signing of the armistice in November 1918, football recommenced. The FL management committee on 29 November introduced a one-pound-a-week training allowance. Following this decision, a number of prominent London players called a meeting for 14 December, where it was decided to form a players' union and "to protest against the niggardliness of this amount". The leading figures of this "new" body were Harold Hardinge and Frank Bradshaw of the Arsenal club. Unlike the 1907 body, these players received organizational support from a number of London trade union leaders. This new body quickly became a registered trade union and proceeded to draw up a list of demands and organize meetings of players in other parts of the country. While the FL did not welcome the formation of a players' body so quickly after the war, it did ask each of the clubs to bring its captain and another player to an "open and free" conference to be held in Bermingham on 13 January 1919 in the spirit of comradeship which pervaded the early months after the armistice. In the immediate hour before the conference, Charlie Roberts persuaded Hardinge that this new players' body should join forces with PFA. The most important result of the conference was that the FL agreed to increase the training allowance to two pounds from the start of February to the end of April; and for the first and only time in its history the FL "taxed" the rich clubs so as to enable such payments to be made to the players of poorer clubs.[35]

Within the next few months the PFA negotiated a fairly substantial wage increase from the FL; for the thirty-nine weeks of the playing season only, the FL agreed to a maximum wage of ten pounds a week and a minimum of six pounds a week. And again, in the following year the PFA secured an all-year maximum wage of nine pounds a week, a minimum of five pounds a week, with one-pound increments determined by a yearly seniority system, and the introduction of two pounds a win and one pound a draw bonus money. It is not clear, however, if these wage increases resulted from the bargaining skills of the PFA leaders *per se* or if they were more a result of the general price inflation experienced after the war and a realization by the FL management committee that they had little choice but to pay such wages and in the circumstances it was best to appear to be reasonable and generous. This "calculative" interpretation of the FL management committee is consistent with the events of 1922, where they successfully forced a 20 percent wage cut on professional footballers.

In 1920 and 1921 the FL decided to form a third division south and north respectively. At the end of the 1921—22 season, several third division (mainly northern) clubs found that the small crowds they were attracting did not enable them to meet their financial obligations to players. It is conceivable that some of these clubs might have threatened to leave the FL unless something was done to alleviate their financial distress. In the light of the problems of these clubs, and given the generally depressed level of economic activity and the atmosphere of wage cuts which pervaded these times, the FL management committee summoned representatives of the PFA to a meeting in April and informed them of their decision to lower the maximum wage to eight pounds a week in the playing season and six pounds a week in the close season. Even though there had been rumours of this action beforehand, the PFA representatives were completely taken by surprise. They had not developed any specific plan with which to answer the FL. In the subsequent extraordinary and general meetings that followed, the PFA leadership exhibited indecision and uncertainty about how to respond to the FL, though there were suggestions for strike action from some delegates.[36] The PFA was again going through a leadership hiatus. Charlie Roberts, the chairman after the war, had earlier retired to manage the Oldham Athletic Club; the present chairman, Jimmy Lawrence, resigned within a year, and secretary Newbould was incapable or not prepared to initiate a campaign similar to that of Broomfield's in 1909. Resolutions expressing dissatisfaction with the FL were passed, and legal action was initiated to ensure that players who had signed "new" contracts before the introduction of the FL's changes received their wages. But the lack of more decisive action was to cost the PFA dearly, for players could no longer see the widsom of belonging to an organization that had responded so meekly to the FL.[47] Membership crumbled to a mere few hundred, and for the rest of the 1920s the PFA was really only an organization in name, helping the odd member with mutual insurance benefits. It had to wait for a new secretary and a new generation of footballers before the threads were taken up again.

With the death of Newbould in 1929, Jimmy Fay, who had been the PFA's non-playing chairman from 1922, was elected to the position of secretary. He had to confront the daunting task of rebuilding the PFA. In 1940 Fay stated that "his main object during the past twelve years [had been] to build up funds of the [PFA] to enable it to function through any crisis that may arise".[38] Fay had become a member of the management committee in 1912 and had witnessed how the PFA's financial dependence on the FL, after the Kingaby case, had stultified the PFA. His years as chairman in the 1920s must have been most harrowing and frustrating. Fay's approach was to increase the PFA's membership and to build up assets before attempting to seek any major concessions from the FL. After his election, Fay initiated a series of successful visits to clubs in an effort to increase membership. By 1931 membership had increased to more than a thousand, and it had almost reached two thousand by the start of the Second World War. In these early years Fay stressed the mutual insurance benefits available to members, and in particular the benefits to be gained under the Workmen's Compensation Act in the event of injury. The hundreds of pounds won for members in these cases, which were of obvious benefit to players, only involved the PFA in the minimal legal expenses that were necessary to bring about their successful completion.

By the mid 1930s, with the internal renaissance well on the way, the PFA began to move slowly towards taking on the FL. At first the contacts were basically defensive. Reference has already been made to the successful approach to the FL to cover £350-plus players after Mr Justice Roche's decisions regarding the Workmen's Compensation Act. And in 1934 PFA opposition led the FL to drop a proposal that would have freed clubs from paying wages to players who had suffered long-term injuries.

In 1937 the PFA moved on to the offensive. At the 1937 annual general meeting a motion was passed to request the FL to receive a deputation to obtain "better terms and more equity for the players". The FL turned down this request, but the PFA were not so easily fobbed off.[39] An extraordinary meeting of delegates was called, and it was again decided to approach the FL for a joint meeting. This time the FL agreed to come to the conference table, but despite a courteous exchange, the FL showed little response to the PFA's submissions. The 1938 annual general meeting came to the conclusion that friendly chats might not be enough to achieve concessions, and for the first time in many years a motion was passed threatening "drastic action". Players also began to pressure the leadership for action. Early in 1939 Brentford players sent a letter to the management committee claiming "that they were dissatisfied with the present conditions and were of the opinion that they were not getting the value of their . . . membership". This resulted in two extraordinary meetings which drew up a list of demands for further talks with the FL.[40] The FL readily agreed to a joint meeting, and the ritual of listening to the players' demands followed by inactivity was again repeated. Sammy Crooks, the PFA chairman, stated at the 1939 annual general meeting: "We do not appear to get much further than meeting the League and arguing the different questions which arise each year." "Drastic action" was again threatened; but the start of the war put an end to whatever the PFA had in store for the FL.

Most importantly, the PFA decided to maintain an office during the war (unlike during the First World War). Fay in fact ran the PFA from his home in Southport.[41] This decision and the intermittent meetings that occurred during these years, with Crooks, Fay, and a handful of other players in attendance, kept alive the momentum built up in the years preceding the war. The *desire* to confront the FL and secure improvements for members was maintained. Immediately after the war the FL were no doubt surprised by the fervour and commitment of the PFA. But as the PFA were to learn, *desire* in itself was not enough to secure concessions from the FL; an extra ingredient was still required.

The twelve years after the war were a frustrating and troublesome period for the PFA. They were beset by related external and internal problems. Firstly, even though the PFA were to find it relatively easy to bring the FL (and FA) to the conference table, this in itself did not guarantee the winning of concessions. Joseph Shister, in "The Logic of Union Growth", has pointed to the importance of organizations' (unions') having leadership able to adapt to new situations and challenges — and in particular acquiring the ability to "successfully" conduct a bargaining relationship with the employing unit. In this period the PFA did not enjoy leadership capable of dealing with the FL at the negotiating table. Moreover, as the management committee members were only too painfully aware, both the FL and FA made decisions without bothering to consult, let alone negotiate with, the PFA.[42] Secondly, the period was one of internal controversy and discord, the major issue being the paid chairman and chief spokesman, Jimmy Guthrie.

In both 1945 and 1946, threatened strikes were necessary to force wage and other concessions from the FL. Another strike threat, following the FL's refusal to negotiate, led the Ministry of Labour to impose arbitration under the war emergency controls which were still in force. Though the PFA were to regard the National Arbitration Tribunal's decision as a victory, it was to lead the PFA, and especially Guthrie, to habitually depend on and turn to "external" bodies whenever the going became too rough with the FL. In turn this reliance on external supports became a substitute for bargaining and made success at the bargaining table even more unlikely. During this period four external aids were relied on. Firstly, there were sympathetic members of parliament prepared to espouse the cause of the PFA. Secondly, there was the Ministry of Labour and its various appendages. After the 1947 National Arbitration Tribunal decision, the PFA increasingly relied on the Ministry of Labour. It was the ministry that helped establish the Joint Standing Committee in 1949 — even though this had been recommended by the National Arbitration Tribunal in 1947 and joint meetings were occurring anyway; and it was the ministry that established the 1951 committee of investigation into football. And again in 1953 the PFA turned to the Industrial Disputes Tribunal when negotiations with the FL became difficult. Thirdly, the PFA joined the Trades Union Congress in 1955; Guthrie reasoned: "In view of the attitude of the FA and FL . . . this would add strength to our case and would be of great assistance to . . . our committee in . . . future negotiations."[42] And fourthly, Guthrie made various statements to the press about his various schemes and policies. Sports writers were always more receptive than the FL.

The problem for Guthrie was that these tactics backfired. For example, despite the concessions gained through the committee of investigation the exercise turned out to be a public relations disaster when the committee endorsed the FL's rationale for the maximum wage and the retain-and-transfer system.[44] Also, at joint meetings, the FL would point to Guthrie's various newspaper statements and use this as a delaying tactic at the bargaining table. Throughout these years Guthrie was criticized persistently by other members of the management committee for his press comments, which, it was argued, frustrated attempts to win concessions from the FL.

The major criticism of Guthrie was his failure to work with the management committee. He would pronounce, by way of the press, on matters of policy without consulting other members of the management committee; but more importantly he developed the habit of going his own way after an issue had already been discussed and decided upon in committee.[45] The problem was dramatically illustrated by the following exchange between Guthrie and committee member Oscar Hold at a meeting on 9 August 1953 concerning Guthrie's placement of the accident insurance premium without consulting the management committee:

> Hold: "You are an employee . . . a paid official, you must do as you are told by the committee."
> Guthrie: "I will dictate the policy while I am the Chairman."
> Hold: "You will not dictate to me or the committee."
> After further lengthy consideration and criticism the Chairman was ordered by the committee not to give statements to the press or make any decisions on behalf of the committee unless he was instructed to do so by the committee.

The minutes of these years were riddled with numerous criticisms and resolutions regarding Guthrie's behaviour, and undoubtedly this period of internal feuding was the darkest in the PFA's history. These disputes spilt over to annual general meetings, and several delegates expressed discontent about how the affairs of the PFA were conducted. These continual internal disputes served to weaken the PFA and to distract attention from more serious matters. Eventually, at the 1957 annual general meeting, Guthrie failed to win re-election as chairman.

It fell to secretary Cliff Lloyd to heal these internal wounds and to set about the task of winning concessions from the FL. Luck also changed for the PFA when the FL (and FA) provided a rallying cry when, near the end of the 1956–57 season, five Sunderland players and later two officials were suspended *sine die* for their involvement in "illegal" pay. These suspensions raised anew the question of the maximum wage and the possibility that other players could be similarly suspended for a practice which in various degrees was fairly widespread. These suspensions and the consequent court case the PFA was mounting dominated developments within football for the next few years. The FL increased wages for the start of the 1958–59 season (see appendix 1), but did not consider abolition of the maximum wage and changes to the retain-and-transfer system. Joint meetings occurred infrequently and yielded little. Jimmy Hill, the PFA chairman, described the attitude of the FL representatives after one such meeting: "It seemed that these members were prepared to listen to anything we had to say, any argument we could put forward, knowing we could only go on for so long, and at the end of three hours we would have spoken ourselves out. All . . . arguments were so obviously falling on stony ground."[47]

As it became more apparent that negotiations would not yield results the PFA notified the Ministry of Labour of the dispute that existed between themselves and the FL. The ministry tried to bring the sides closer together, but all to no avail, and a strike notice was issued to take effect from 21 January 1961. This threat forced the FL to the negotiating table, and they agreed to the abolition of the maximum wage, increases to the minimum and a number of procedural changes to the retain-and-transfer system. In particular, a player in dispute with his club while negotiating a new contract was to receive the minimum wage appropriate to his division.[48]

In 1958 the PFA again sought a case to test the legal validity of the retain-and-transfer system. The opportunity presented itself when Newcastle United player George Eastham unsuccessfully attempted to join another club. Although eventually released to Arsenal, Eastham and the PFA continued to pursue the matter. In this they were successful when Mr Justice Wilberforce found "that the combined retention and transfer system" was "an unjustifiable restraint of trade".[49] The resulting negotiations established a number of significant modifications to the retain-and-transfer system. New contracts contained an option clause which could be employed at the club's discretion. If the club was not prepared to offer a player the same terms as in his past contract, the player was to receive a free transfer. If there should be a dispute between a player and a club over terms, the dispute would be settled by an independent tribunal,[50] and during the course of the dispute the player would receive the same terms included in his past contract.

In 1966 the FL made representations to the secretary of state for education and science "about the deteriorating financial position of the game and the need for money for its improvement and administration". The secretary agreed to set up a committee to undertake an inquiry, and a report (The Chester Report) was presented in March 1968. This resort to the government was a public relations disaster for the FL. Amongst a number of unpalatable recommendations for the FL, the Chester Report was significantly opposed to football's contract system, particularly options for renewal resting solely with the club, and recommended "that every contract between club and player should be for a definite period at the end of which either party should be free to renew it".[51] Like it or not, if the FL were to receive financial help they would first have to negotiate changes to the employment contract with the PFA. An agreement was reached between the PFA and the FL management committee at the end of 1969; but the latter were unable to persuade the clubs to accept it.

Following the rejection of this package by the FL clubs, the PFA reported the problems associated with negotiating agreements with the FL to the various responsible government departments. This led the government in 1973 to request the Commission on Industrial Relations "to examine and report on the question of industrial relations between professional footballers and their employers . . . and the promotion of any improvement in these industrial relations that appears to be necessary or desirable". In its report of August 1974 the commission stated: "To continue with the retain-and-transfer system . . . could ultimately lead to chaos. The system is open to legal challenge at any time and, if it were to be declared to be an unreasonable restraint of trade, clubs would immediately face a very uncertain situation from which it might take some time to recover." The commission also endorsed the Chester Report and added: "There is room for negotiations and agreement in this matter . . . at the very least there is room for experiment, and we would regard discussions on this question as a matter of priority."[52]

Following this report, the PFA and FL spent over two and a half years negotiating the player's right to join another club, on the expiration of his contract, subject to compensation determined by a formula based on the player's age and the division of the FL club to which the player was joining.[53] However, the FL management committee again were unable to secure the necessary three-quarters majority of member clubs at an annual general meeting on 17 June

1977. A leading advocate of the "no" vote was Jimmy Hill, the former PFA chairman, who became general manager of the Coventry City Football Club.

Throughout its history, the PFA has had to confront a variety of internal and external problems. The major internal problem has been acquiring leaders with the necessary bureaucratic and other skills required for successful leadership. At crucial points the PFA's inability to find a leader able to respond to the immediate task at hand has resulted in a number of major defeats. Externally the PFA has had the constant problem of securing concessions from the FL and FA. The various FL and FA representatives have been "funny people to deal with", and the FL have been unprepared to grant concessions unless forced to by legal or threatened strike action.[54]

This study has demonstrated, firstly, how difficult it has been for professional footballers to win back their economic freedom once it had been appropriated by the clubs and the FL. Even the proposed new agreement, which establishes the right of players to join new clubs, incorporates the principle of compensation. Secondly, the study has indicated the importance of and the problems associated with leading an association of professional sportsmen in this quest for economic freedom. Although the PFA may become embroiled in organizing and conducting a strike campaign, and there will be new substantive issues to take up with the FL and the FA, the eventual retirement of their current secretary should be used as the occasion to rethink and reorganize their structure and to employ more full-time officers in the continuing attempt to advance and protect the interests of members. And thirdly and fundamentally, it has highlighted the numerous and persistent problems associated with being a professional team sportsman.

APPENDIX 1
Maximum and Minimum Wages in Professional Football 1901-61

Year Introduced	Maximum per week	Minimum per week
1901	£4	£4
1910	£5, two ten-shilling increases each to be paid after two years extra service. Maximum payable in 1914	£4
1915	Wages abolished (by FA) during war	
1918	£1 training allowance	
1919 February	£2 training allowance	
1919 September	£10 for 39 weeks	£4

Year Introduced	Maximum	Minimum
1920	£9 all season	£4
1922	£8 playing, £6 close season	£4
1939	£1 10s	
1943	£2	
1944	£4	
1945	£9	
1946	£10 playing, £7 10s close season	
1947	£12 playing, £10 close season	£7 and £5
1951	£14 playing, £10 close season	£7 and £5
1954	£15 playing, £12 close season	£7 10s and £5 10s
1957	£17 playing, £14 close season	£8 10s and £6 10s
1958	£20 playing, £17 close season	£8 all season
1961	Maximum abolished	*per annum*
		Div. 1 £780
		Div. 2 £726
		Div. 3 £676
		Div. 4 £624

Source: PFA Records

APPENDIX 2
PFA Office Bearers 1907-77

Chairman		Secretary	
H. L. Mainman	1907-10	H. C. Broomfield	1907-10
E. H. Lintott	1910-11	A. J. Owen	1910-13
C. Veitch	1911-19	H. J. Newbould	1913-29
C. Roberts	1919-21	J. A. Fay	1929-53
J. Lawrence	1921-22	C. Lloyd	1953-
J. A. Fay	1922-29		
H. Matthews	1929-30		
A. Wood	1930-31		
D. M. Robbie	1931-36		
A. F. Barrett	1936-37		
S. D. Crooks	1937-46		
J. C. Guthrie	1946-57		
J. W. T. Hill	1957-61		
T. S. Cummings	1961-63		
M. C. Musgrove	1963-66		
N. Cantwell	1966-67		
J. W. T. Neill	1967-70		
A. D. Dougan	1970-		

Source: PFA Records

NOTES

Thanks are expressed to the officers and staff of the PFA, Mr Cliff Lloyd, Mr Bob Kerry, Miss Hardman, and Miss Hilton, for their help in providing documents and information regarding the PFA. Similar thanks are expressed to Mr Neil Donald of the Advisory Conciliation and Arbitration Service.

1. Geoffrey Green, *The History of the Football Association* (London: Naldrett Press, 1953), chaps. 1, 2, and 4. For details of the earlier history of football, see P. M. Young, *A History of British Football* (London: Stanley Paul, 1968), chaps. 1-7, and James Walvin, *The People's Game: The Social History of British Football* (London: Arrow, 1975), chaps. 1-3; Maurice Golesworthy, *The Encyclopaedia of Association Football*, 12th ed. (London: Robert Hale, 1976), p.166.

2. Green, *History of the Football Association*, chaps. 5, 6 and 9; C. E. Sutcliffe, J. A. Brierly, and F. Howarth, *The Story of the Football League* (Lancashire: Football League, 1938), pp.6-15 and 113-17.

3. Similar types of controls operate in a variety of other professional team sports. See R. G. Noll, ed., *Government and the Sports Business* (Washington: Brookings Institute, 1974); Braham Dabscheck, "Sporting Equality: Labour Market v. Product Market Control", *The Journal of Industrial Relations* 17 (1975); P. J. Sloane, "Restriction of Competition in Team Sports", *Bulletin of Economic Research* 28 (1976). For a discussion of whether or not the PFA can be regarded as a trade union, see S. W. Gamble, "A Study of Unionization: The P. F. A. in the English Football League" (MSc project, Department of Industrial Relations, London School of Economics, 1973).

4. The organization formed at the end of 1907 was called the Association Football Players' Union. There have been two subsequent name changes — the first in 1919 to the Association Football Players' and Trainers' Union; and the second in 1958 to the PFA. To avoid confusion we will use the current name throughout the paper. See E. G. Krasnow and H. M. Levy, "Unionization and Professional Sports", *Georgetown Law Journal* 51 (1963); Noll, *Government and the Sports Business*; Braham Dabscheck, "Industrial Relations and Professional Team Sports in Australia", *The Journal of Industrial Relations* 18 (1976). There were two earlier unsuccessful attempts to form a players' body in 1893 and 1898. Sutcliffe, Brierly, and Howarth, *Story of the Football League*, pp.6-15 and 113-17; Green, *History of the Football Association*, pp.389-401; Golesworthy, *Enclyclopaedia of Association Football*, p.165. The 1960s have witnessed a world-wide mushrooming of player associations. Noll, *Government and the Sports Business*; Dabscheck, "Industrial Relations and Professional Team Sports in Australia", and *Professional Football*, Commission on Industrial Relations Report 87 (London, 1974), appendix 7.

5. Tripartite — i.e., PFA, FL, and FA — negotiations occurred after the formation of the Joint Standing Committee from 1949 to 1956. Since 1956 the PFA has negotiated with each organization separately. Tripartite, and wider, talks occur over broad issues pertaining to the general welfare of football.

6. In 1934 the AFA altered its name to the Amateur Football Alliance.

7. In 1920 a third division south was formed, followed by the formation of a third division north in 1921.

8. The retain-and-transfer system is still in existence; the 1960s have witnessed the introduction of reforms to reduce the discretionary power of clubs.

9. These issues have been discussed elsewhere. Braham Dabscheck, "Economics, Power and Sportsmen", *Politics* 11 (1976), for an up-to-date bibliography; Sloane, "Restriction of Competition in Team Sports", has moved from being a defender of labour market controls to a cautious and qualified opponent.

10. See appendix 1 for a wage sheet for the period 1901-61. Other legitimate sources of "football" income have been win/draw bonuses, bonuses for successful Cup and League championship teams, signing-on fees, transfer fee shares, benefits for long-service players, a provident fund and television appearance (match) money.
11. A player could appeal to the FL management committee about the unreasonableness of this wage offer.
12. Derek Dougan and P. M. Young, *On the Spot: Football as a Profession* (Newton Abbot, Devon: David and Charles, 1975), pp.47-48, suggest this as a possible reason, together with the ill-feeling of players towards (increasing) transfer fees and the limits on their wages. For an account of general developments within industrial relations at the turn of the century, see Henry Pelling, *A History of British Trade Unionism*, 3rd ed. (Harmondsworth, Mddx.: Penguin, 1976), pp.123-30. After its formation, the PFA quickly attracted members. At the end of its first year it claimed thirteen hundred members from seventy League and non-League clubs. See Minutes of Annual General Meeting (hereafter MAGM), in December 1908 and *The Athletic News and Cyclists Journal* (Manchester), 21 December 1908. The "founding fathers" do not appear to have had any outside help from other trade unions at the time of the PFA's formation.
13. P. M. Young, *Manchester United* (London: Heinemann, 1960), pp.48-51, 76-84. On his deathbed Meredith asked a visitor to reach under his bed and drag out a carton full of medals, international caps, and assorted trophies. He then reminded the visitor that players cannot live on caps and trophies alone. This event has an interesting sequel. In an interview for the PFA's newspaper, in 1948, Meredith strongly hinted that his hundred-pound fine was paid by FA secretary (later Sir) Frederick Wall. The relevant section from the article is: "So, although the receipt was made out to Bill Meredith, the fine was paid by — now guess!" The only other name mentioned in the interview was Wall's. *Soccer*, official journal of the Football Players' Union, vol. 1, no. 5 (April 1948).
14. *Athletic News*, 23 March 1908. As well as finding it difficult to administer their financial rules, the FA also found it difficult to divest themselves of responsibility. Many FL and Southern League clubs found the FA's rules convenient to hide behind.
15. Up until 1919 the management committee had twelve members, and at various times, to ensure its "representativeness" there have been area and/or divisional qualifications on membership.
16. Bob Kerry is an obvious exception; secretaries A. J. Owen and H. J. Newbould had previously been respectively an auditor and in football management.
17. This ignores the question of the qualifications of those who do the selecting. This leadership problem within trade unions is discussed more fully in Joseph Shister, "The Logic of Union Growth", *The Journal of Political Economy* 61 (1953): 429-32.
18. For these and other reasons, Krasnow and Levy ("Unionization and Professional Sports" and *Professional Football*) have suggested the amalgamation of player associations with larger trade unions. The Scottish Professional Footballers Association amalgamated with the General and Municipal Workers Union in 1975. The organizer is a former professional player who became a branch secretary within the GMWU when he entered the "industrial" workforce. American baseball's Major League Baseball Players' Association appointed a "professional" union organizer as its general secretary in 1966.
19. Sutcliffe, Brierly, and Howarth, *Story of the Football League*, p.126-30; MAGM,

21 August 1933, 20 August 1934, 26 August 1935, 24 August 1936, 19 August 1946.

20. Minutes of Management Committee Meeting (hereafter MMCM), 4 March 1956. The PFA had other demands regarding both the FA and FL, including the payment of fees for players playing in floodlit matches. Players received a five-pound television appearance fee; the maximum wage being fourteen pounds. MAGM, 18 January 1957, and Minutes of Joint Meeting between PFA and FA, 13 March and 4 June 1956.

21. The provident fund had been established in 1949. MAGM, 3 November 1964 and 29 November 1965, Minutes of the National Negotiating Committee (PFA and FL), 10 September and 27 November 1964, 5 April 1965, and Minutes of Joint Meeting between PFA and FA, 29 April 1965.

22. Sutcliffe, Brierly, and Howarth, *Story of the Football League*, pp.15, 118; Green, *History of the Football Association*, pp.411-14; Young, *Manchester United*, pp.67-68; Young, *History of British Football*, pp.220-21; Dougan and Young, *On the Spot*, pp.54-55; Walvin, *People's Game*, p.85; and Golesworthy, *Encyclopaedia of Association Football*, p.165. The GFTU was a weak and "conservative"body. For an examination of its role in British industrial relation, see B. C. Roberts, *The Trade Union Congress 1868-1921* (London: Allen and Unwin, 1958), pp.162-79; E. H. Phelps Brown, *The Growth of British Industrial Relations* (London: Macmillan, 1959), pp.257-63; H. A. Clegg and A. F. Thompson, *A History of British Trade Unions Since 1889*, vol. 1: 1889-1910 (London: Oxford University Press, 1964), pp.355-77.

23. *Athletic News*, 22 February, 8, 15, 29 March, 10 May 1909; *The Sporting Chronicle* (Manchester), 8 and 24 April 1909. A joint meeting occurred between PFA and FA representatives on 28 April. The FA's minutes of the meeting are reproduced in *Athletic News*, 30 August 1909. It is clear that both sides were unable, or were not prepared, to resolve their differences.

24. *Athletic News*, 17 May 1909; *Sporting Chronicle*, 8 and 17 May 1909; there had been communications between the PFA and the GFTU following the FA's withdrawal of recognition on 8 March. The GFTU had advised the PFA "to postpone any action" with regard to the England-Scotland international. *Athletic News*, 5 April 1909. At a meeting on 17 April the management committee resolved "that the question of joining the Trades Federation be deferred until the Annual Meeting in August". GFTU affiliation only became an issue after the dispute had been settled — in effect a loser's medal — and was opposed by the FL in the immediate period before the FL took over the government of the financial affairs of its clubs.

25. *Athletic News*, 24 May, 14 June 1909.

26. Ibid., 28 June 1909; *Sporting Chronicle*, 28, 29 and 30 June, 10 and 13 July 1909.

27. For details of these developments, see *Athletic News* and *Sporting Chronicle*, July and August 1909.

28. *Sporting Chronicle*, 31 August 1909.

29. On the Saturday before this meeting, two hundred players again endorsed their support for the PFA at a meeting in Manchester which was chaired by J. T. Jones of the Municipal Employees' Association. For details, see the *Manchester Guardian*, 30 August 1909.

30. *Sporting Chronicle*, 1 September, 11, 15, and 24 October 1909; *Athletic News*, 6 and 13 September 1909; MMCM, 7 October 1909.

31. For details of the "package" and the negotiations, see *Athletic News*, 28 February, 7, 14, 21, and 28 March 1910, 17 and 24 April 1911.

32. MMCM, 22 August and 12 September 1910, 6 November 1911. There is no surviving copy of the "offending" newsletter.

33. For details of the decision, see *Manchester Guardian*, 27 and 28 March 1912; *The Times*, 28 March 1912; Sutcliffe, Brierly, and Howarth, *Story of the Football League*, p.120; Green, *History of the Football Association*, pp.419-20; *Football Players' Magazine*, official journal of Association Football Players' Union, vol. 3, no. 10 (September 1913).
34. *Sporting Chronicle*, 18 October 1912, for a copy of the letter. For details of this dispute, see *Sporting Chronicle*, 4, 10, and 24 September, 13, 18, 23, and 29 October, 8 and 16 November, 17 December 1912, and 14 January and 11 February 1913; and MMCM, 28 October, 2 December 1912, 20 January and 10 February 1913.
35. For details of the 1918 body, see *The Times*, 13 and 30 November, 16, 18, and 30 December 1918. Hardinge agreed to dispense with the organizational and other help received from the London trade union leaders. The FL of course were opposed to trade union involvement. It is conceivable, in the light of subsequent developments, that the PFA may have erred in severing this relationship. *Athletic News*, 13 and 20 January 1919.
36. *Sporting Chronicle*, 13 April 1922; *Athletic News*, 9 January, 10 and 17 April 1922; Minutes of Extraordinary Delegates Meeting (hereafter MEDM), 23 April and 7 May 1922, and MAGM, 20 August 1922.
37. There is evidence that several of the more affluent clubs were prepared to have the maximum wage increased to ten pounds and could not see the need for wage reductions at all. The FL management committee was probably able to sway the clubs by pointing to the problems of the poorer clubs, and by arguing that if the clubs could stay solid now, they could deal a crushing blow to the PFA and reduce its further interference in football "management"
38. MAGM, 26 August 1940.
39. Notwithstanding this, it is possible to interpret the FL's introduction of the Jubilee Fund in 1938 — a fund designed to give financial help to players — as a response to the PFA's renewed pressure. For details of the fund, see *Sporting Chronicle* and *Athletic News* (Manchester), 9 January 1938.
40. Minutes of Joint Meeting between PFA and FL, 21 April 1938; MMCM, 23 February 1939, and MEDM, 27 February and 13 March 1939.
41. The headquarters were moved back to Manchester in 1953 when Cliff Lloyd became secretary.
42. Shister, "Logic of Union Growth", pp.429-32. Examples of this include the FA's refusal to negotiate television fees, the Wembley Indoor Tournament in 1949, the 1953 Coronation Tournament, the FL's take-it-or-leave-it stand on the provident fund in 1949, the wage increases of 1951, and the reduction in the provident fund in 1956.
43. National Arbitration Tribunal, Award No. 942, 11 April 1947; Ministry of Labour and National Service, Conciliation Act, 1896, *Association Football: Report of a Committee of Investigation into a Difference Regarding the Terms and Conditions of Association Football Players* (March 1952); Industrial Disputes Tribunal, Award No. 399 (July 1953); MAGM, 1 November 1953.
44. Committee of Investigation, p.13.
45. This by itself is not necessarily a criticism. In the hurly-burly of industrial life, "leaders" cannot always consult other members of their organization before they make statements.
46. MAGM, 30 November 1953, 1 November 1954, and 14 November 1955, 18 January 1957; Jimmy Hill, *Striking for Soccer* (London: Peter Daniels, 1961), pp.13-14. For Guthrie's account of this period, see Jimmy Guthrie and Dave Caldwell, *Soccer Rebel: The Evolution of the Professional Footballer* (London: Pentagon, 1976).

47. Hill, *Striking for Soccer*, pp.14-15.
48. Ibid., pp.19-90 for a useful account of the dispute; and MAGM, 27 March 1961. The FL reneged on allowing a player who does not accept the club's offer to be placed on the transfer list at their general meeting. The Sunderland players' suspensions were subsequently removed in an out-of-court settlement.
49. Judgement by Mr Justice Wilberforce, Eastham v. Newcastle United and others (mimeo), 1963, p.24.
50. Consisting of a representative of the FL, PFA, and an independent chairman.
51. *Report of the Committee on Football* (chairman D. N. Chester), Department of Education and Science (London, 1968), p.81.
52. The PFA decided to seek registration under the 1971 Industrial Relations Bill, a decision that was to cost their membership of the TUC. For details of the bill, see Pelling, *British Trade Unionism*, pp.276-81: *Professional Football*, pp.iii, 76, and 78.
53. The negotiations have been based on a Dutch model. See *Professional Football*, pp.109 and 110. Joint administration of the education fund has also been on the agenda of these discussions.
54. A comment of Charlie Roberts in 1921. MEDM, 2 February 1921.

IAN TURNER

The Emergence of "Aussie Rules"

The origin of Australian football is poised between the folk football of pre-industrial times and football as organized into a regular competition by the colonial middle class. It counts its beginning from 1858 — from a game played in Melbourne between boys of the Scotch College and the Church of England Grammar School, and from the formation of the Melbourne Football Club. But, in one form or another, football is a very old game. Nearly two thousand years ago a Chinese poet, Li Yu, wrote: "A round ball and a square goal/Suggest the shape of the yin and the yang." The people of Florence played a kind of football in medieval times. In one of the more blood-thirsty Elizabethan dramas, a character expressed the hope that he might play at football — using his rival's head for a ball.

The early football was a game that people played rather than watched. It was a game with few rules, a folk game played on high holidays and involving the whole community. Other than a reference to "football" as one of the Christmas games played at the Duke of York Hotel in Prahran (Melbourne) in 1858, I have found no evidence that the folk game was played in the Australian colonies; but this must have been Australia's first football.

I have seen the game played in England — at Ashbourne, a small town in Derbyshire, where it is played each year on Shrove Tuesday and Ash Wednesday. There were few rules. The object was to strike the specially decorated ball against one or other goal — respectively a millstone and a barn-door — each of which was about a mile and a half from the centre of the town. The streets, the backyards, the river, and the surrounding fields were the playing arena. Anyone could take part, and most of Ashbourne's able-bodied citizens did. After eight hours play on each of the two days, the game ended in a characteristic English football result — drawn game, one all.

The Australian climate and the prosperity of the Australian colonies (particularly Victoria after gold) provided favourable conditions for the rapid growth of leisure activities. As William Westgarth wrote in *The Colony of Victoria* in 1864:

Victoria, notwithstanding a full share of the modern ardour for commerce and enterprise, bids fairly to exemplify the common association of bright skies and a warm climate with plentiful recreation and holiday-making. The colony reproduces the sports and games and festivities of the old country, but seems to be already far ahead of the maternal example in the proportions of her recreation.

Leisure time was more generally available in Victoria than at Home. The stonemasons and other skilled artisans had, beginning in 1856, won the eight-hour working day — "Eight Hours Labour, Eight Hours Recreation, Eight Hours Rest". One of the reasons they gave for claiming this "boon" was the heavy physical burden of work in the enervating Melbourne climate; recreation did not seem so heavy a burden as did work. Another was that a reduction in the hours of labour would "tend to improve our social amd moral condition"; there were some who deplored that the new leisure hours were spent in recreation rather than in intellectual pursuits — but others argued that the recreation itself represented a moral and social advance.

The artisans' forty-eight-hour working week was for the time still spread over six working days, and Sunday was still a "day of rest". But the young gentlemen who spent their working hours in banks and offices and counting-houses already enjoyed the "Saturday half-holiday", and workers in "shops and manufactories" were claiming this boon as their right, too. It would, said *Bell's Life in Victoria and Sporting Chronicle*,[2] be good for the physical and moral health of Victoria if they were able to enjoy it. "To possess the leisure to enjoy out-of-door pastimes denotes that the bulk of those who do so (and all classes come within this category in Victoria) are in easy circumstances, and can surrender half a day and an occasional evening once a week to this sort of recreation without injury to themselves or to their families."[3] To *Bell's* it seemed that this was a more equal society than most. The working men of Melbourne, sitting down with their families to their Christmas dinner, did not share the "festive board" with the ghost of poverty. "Here — and the fact cannot be too frequently thrust down the throats of the stump orators and the grievance mongers — there is no oppressed class. Although wealth is not equally diffused, there is no community in the world of which it may be said that its inhabitants have neither inherited poverty nor riches with so much truth as of Australia."[4]

It was true that this was a society in flux — that the class divisions of the initial pastoral settlement had been obscured by the flood of gold-inspired immigration and the sudden growth of Melbourne;

that the element of luck involved in the search for gold, and the opportunities for speculation in trade and in land, made this a more mobile society than perhaps any other; that a firm and clearly recognizable class structure was yet to emerge. But it was already there in embryonic form. Those who spoke of Victoria as a classless society were representative of the articulate, affluent, urban middle class; working men and small farmers knew, without having to be told, that class divisions persisted in Victoria and worked to their disadvantage. The spokesmen of the middle class placed a high value on "classlessness" — presumably because, if they could persuade the less privileged colonist that this was truly a classless society, that very belief would reinforce middle-class privilege.[5] And they believed that colonial recreation contributed greatly to this ideal, that one of the major benefits flowing from the growth of sport was "the fusion of classes it will promote, and . . . the absence of those lines of demarcation which it will help to efface".[6] But the emerging class divisions were almost as apparent in leisure as they were in work.

The colonists brought with them the sports and pastimes of the mother land. It was part of their desire for cultural continuity, of the need to recreate familiar patterns, to make "a new Britannia in another world". But some of them travelled cabin, and some steerage. The immigrants imported not only the popular recreations of the English villages and towns but the games of the public schools and the sports of the gentry.

The pubs of Melbourne and the goldfields offered their patrons, at Christmas, New Year, and Easter, the traditional "Old English Sports" — among them foot-racing; jumping in sacks; the various English styles of wrestling; wheelbarrow racing blindfold; dipping in the tubs of flour and water for money; boys eating rolls and treacle; climbing the greasy pole; the pig with the greasy tail; and "grinning through horse collars, after the manner of their ancestors".[7]

These were the rough amusements of the common folk. The more genteel of Melbourne's "young men and maidens" celebrated the end of the year with "picnic and water-parties, with races and regattas, quiet flirtations in shady gardens, and al-fresco fiddlings and feastings." (But all classes had this in common: "The religious character of the season is almost lost, and it has gradually assumed the nature of a new Carnival."[8] The colonists found it easy to adapt recreation to the new environment; religion did not acclimatize so readily.)

The organized games and sports were at first the exclusive property of the middle class. Pre-eminent among them was cricket:

the Melbourne Cricket Club was founded in 1838, and by the mid-1860s some twenty clubs were competing in inter-club matches in Melbourne. In 1856, the first inter-colonial cricket match between New South Wales and Victoria aroused a "wholesome spirit of rivalry between the young men of the adjacent colonies". On New Year's Day 1862, two Melbourne restaurateurs promoted, in return for the takings at the gate and a monopoly of the catering, the first match between English and Australian cricketers. The visit of the Englishmen, said *Bell's,* "will do more than anything which has occurred for many years to break down the Imperial assumption of colonial inferiority, and give the lie to the detractors who have ventured to assert that democratic institutions had already made us a nation of blatant money-grubbers, and mendacious boasters".[9] The colonial cricketers were "gentlemen", the Englishmen were "players", but the two teams fraternized quite happily — a comment, perhaps, on the more open colonial society. And, among the thirty thousand or more who paid to watch the game (to the great profit of the promoters), there must have been many working men and women. But the game in Melbourne belonged to the middle class. As did "pedestrianism" (running and hurdling) and the "velocipede" (at seven to ten pounds, the bicycle was hardly the working man's mount), and above all horse-racing. It might have been that, as *Bell's* said, this was the sport that "most effectually dissipates care, promotes enjoyment, breaks down class barriers, and fuses a great assemblage of people, drawn from all parts of the country and representing all sections of the community, into a homogeneous whole";[10] but it was the wealthy who owned and raced horses.

It was the young gentlemen of the Melbourne Cricket Club who gave birth to Australian football. On 10 July 1858 *Bell's* carried a letter from a well-known cricketer, Thomas Wentworth Wills:

Sir, — Now that cricket has been put aside for some few months to come, and cricketers have assumed somewhat of the chrysalis nature (for a time only 'tis true), but at length will again burst forth in all their varied hues, rather than allow this state of torpor to creep over them, and stifle their now supple limbs, why can they not, I say form a foot-ball club, and form a committee of three or more to draw up a code of laws[25]. If a club of this sort were got up, it would be of a vast benefit to any cricket-ground to be trampled upon, and would make the turf quite firm and durable; besides which, it would keep those who are inclined to become stout from having their joints enclosed in useless super-abundant flesh. If it is not possible to form a foot-ball club, why should not these young men who have adopted this new-born country, for their mother land, why I say, do they not form themselves into a rifle club, so at any-rate they may be some day called upon to aid their adopted land against a tyrant's band, that may some day "pop" upon us when we least expect a foe at our very doors. Surely our young cricketers are not afraid of the crack of the rifle, when they face so courageously the leather sphere, and it would disgrace no one to learn in time how to defend his country and his hearth. A firm heart, a steady hand, a quick eye, are all that are requisite, and with practice, all these may be attained. Trusting that some one will take up the matter, and form either of the above clubs, or at any rate, some athletic games. I remain, yours truly, **T. W. WILLS.**

This was the founding document of a new national game, and it was appropriate that Wills should have written it.

Edward Wills, the grandfather of Thomas, had been transported to New South Wales for highway robbery; he later did well in sealing and shipping. After Edward's death, his widow married George Howe, a convict and the first editor of the *Sydney Gazette*. Tom's father, Horatio, had overlanded his livestock and his family (Tom was then one) to the Port Phillip district in 1836. One of Tom's aunts had married Dr Redfern, transported for sympathizing with the naval mutineers of Spithead and Nore. Another aunt had married Major Henry Colden Antill, an aide-de-camp to Governor Lachlan Macquarie. Tom was named for his uncle, Thomas Reiby, ex-convict, land-owner, and a director of the Bank of New South Wales, and for the great Australian patriot, William Charles Wentworth, whose father, D'Arcy, had narrowly escaped transportation, having been allowed instead to "leave his country for his country's good".

Tom Wills's colonial ancestry was impeccable, but his football did not spring from colonial soil. For his father, Horatio, having escaped the convict stain, sent young Tom home to England — to Dr Arnold's Rugby — for his education. There, as well as cricket, he played the game which the young gentlemen of Rugby had played since 1823, the year in which the legendary hero, William Webb Ellis, "first took the ball into his arms and ran with it", thus creating a new dimension of "football".[11]

Wills first came to colonial prominence in the cricket season of the summer of 1857–58. He had brought back with him from England a "modern style" of bowling, round-arm, which enabled him to project the ball much more rapidly than could the bowlers who used the customary under-arm style. He also introduced a new element of danger into the game; a New South Wales batsman had to be carried off the ground after being hit by one of Wills's deliveries. Punters who had invested their money on New South Wales were prominent among those who protested that Wills's bowling was unsporting and unlawful; Wills replied that the interests of gamblers should "in no way . . . be allowed to have any weight with the players, or with the friendly games".[12]

Wills was a foundation member of the Melbourne Football Club and one of a committee of five, appointed in May 1859, to draft the first rules of Australian football. But his contribution to football was overshadowed by that of his cousin and brother-in-law, Henry Colden Antill Harrison.

Harrison was born at Picton, New South Wales, in 1836. His mother was at the time visiting her relative, Major Antill, for whom she named her son. Harrison's father had been a sea captain but had taken up a sheep run in southern New South Wales. In 1837 he followed Horatio Wills in overlanding his stock and family to the Port Phillip district. The Harrisons were not successful on the land; they moved to Melbourne, where Henry was enrolled in the Church of England Grammar School. He took employment in the Customs Department and later in the Titles Office, where he eventually became registrar-general. But his main interest was in "almost every kind of sport".[13]

Henry Harrison played cricket alongside Tom Wills. He became Victoria's champion "pedestrian". In a football career which stretched from 1858 to 1872, he captained at various times the Richmond, Geelong, and Melbourne Football Clubs. He drafted the 1866 code of rules, which established the principles of the Australian game. In 1877, he was appointed the inaugural vice-president of the Victorian Football Association, and in his old age he was made a life member of the Australian National Football League and honoured with the title "father of Australian football".[14]

It was, however, Tom Wills who supervised the occasion that Australian football records as its foundation — the match between the boys of Scotch College and the Church of England Grammar School, played on 7 August 1858 in the Richmond Paddock, a stretch of land surrounding the ground set aside close to Melbourne for the use of the Melbourne Cricket Club. The reports of this match were scrappy. The *Argus* noted that it was an "excellent game". The match was undecided, each side having scored one goal during the course of the afternoon's play. A week later — one of the school teams having failed to turn up for the deciding goal — the *Argus* reported "an impromptu game . . . among several members of the Melbourne Cricket Club and others who happened to be present" at Richmond Park. And, later in September, twenty-six players of Melbourne met a like number from South Yarra, watched by a curious and amused group of spectators. "The game was most keenly contested for nearly three hours, and terminated about half-past five o'clock by the Melbourne men kicking through the goal of their opponents in capital style."[15]

From the brief descriptions of these games, it seems that football, as first played by public schoolboys and middle-class young men of the cricket clubs, was a contest between roughly equal numbers of players, on a defined ground with goals at either end, victory going to the team which either scored the first goal ("won the first game"), or scored the best two of three goals (the "match"). This was close to folk football, though the rules may have been rather more extensive and clearly defined.

To the *Argus,* it seemed that football was "coming into fashion in Melbourne":

> "As it is a most manly and amusing game we hope that it may continue to grow in favour until it becomes as popular as Cricket. To lookers-on a well-contested football match is as interesting a sight as can be conceived, the chances, changes, and ludicrous *contretemps,* are so frequent and the whole affair so animated and inspiriting. Let those who fancy there is little in the game, read the account of the one of the Rugby matches which is detailed in that most readable work, "Tom Brown's Schooldays", and they will speedily alter their opinion.[16]

The game Tom Wills had played placed great stress on "manliness", which seemed to mean a cavalier disregard for physical danger. Most of Rugby took part, and the two teams sought, by strength and weight of numbers, to carry the ball across their opponent's goal-line. The physical clashes were fierce. Players involved in a "scrummage" were permitted to "hack" (kick) their opponents in shin or ankle (although they were forbidden to wear iron plates on their boots). And a player could trip or "maul" (tackle) a player who was running with the ball (although the rules held that throttling or strangling an opponent in a "maul" was "totally opposed to all principles of the game"). Tradition demanded that the players show their "mettle": "Meet them like Englishmen . . . and charge them home."[17]

But, when Tom Wills came to draft some rules for Melbourne football, he did not adopt the Rugby model. As he explained later: "Boys have plenty of time to nurse their wounded shins, and now and then their broken limbs, for it sometimes comes to that, but men, however their courage might prompt them, cannot afford to become victims in such a cause, especially as there is little skill required in a scrummage, but rather any amount of brute force."[18]

The 1859 football season began modestly: football was outspaced in *Bell's* by other sports — hunting, boxing, even ratting. The first games were scratch matches played between the members of the Melbourne club. There was no certainty as to the rules (particularly whether it was legitimate to handle the ball), but "the greatest good humour prevailed", and one match was so exciting that it moved the reporter to verse in praise of one of the scratch captains, Hammersley, who —

> Swift as an eagle on the wing
> Holds fast the ball, then with a sudden spring
> He leaps high in air and kicks the volume round.
> The ball emits a hollow moaning sound.
> Obedient to this hero's skilful care,
> The foot-ball rushes whistling through the air
> Then — as a bomb, by blazing powder thrown
> High in mid-air, when rapid it has flown
> Describes a curving parabola there —
> So turns the ball its bending course and fair.
> It falls, and far beyond the "true-blues" base.
> With many a bound it stops its headlong race.[19]

Fanciful reportage of this kind assumed an educated middle-class audience; it did not survive the development of football as a mass spectator sport.

Over the next few years, new clubs were reported from the rapidly growing suburbs of Melbourne — South Yarra, St Kilda, Emerald Hill (now South Melbourne), Richmond, Collingwood, Royal Park, Essendon, all at that time places of residence of the middle class. The Grammar School, the Scotch College, the newly established university, the Melbourne warehousemen, and the customs officers all fielded teams. Outside the city, clubs were formed in Geelong and Bendigo and Ballarat. Sometimes matches were played among the members of the club — between teams picked by two of the leading players, or "Civilians vs. Volunteers", or "Australians [i.e., native born] vs the World". But soon the emphasis shifted to matches between club and club.

One club might challenge another, but there was no guarantee that the match would take place. Players sometimes failed to appear; the match was abandoned, or a scratch match played. There was no fixed number of players; teams varied from fifteen to twenty-five, and they were not always evenly matched. The players wore jumpers or shirts, usually white, and long, close-fitting trousers. Sometimes they wore distinctive club-colours — sashes or caps — but it was not always possible to distinguish which side was which, or even how many players were on the field. Goal-posts were set up at either end of the playing-field, and the boundaries were marked with flags, but the going was often rough:

> Backwards and forwards, on this side and on that, now out of bounds — and this, unfortunately, was too frequently the case — amongst the crowd, and again in the ditch by the fence; now into old Dennis's cabbage-garden, and again kicked into branches of those horrible gums; now kept in exciting closeness to the Melbourne goal, and then with a fine spurt taken to the suburban headquarters, wavered the much-abused ball; and for two hours and a half the closest observer could not tell which side had any the best of it.[20]

The ball was a bladder encased in leather, but each club was responsible for supplying its own balls and there was no uniform size or shape; generally the ball was round, but sometimes an oval ball was used (the first was noted in 1860), and there was argument about what kind of ball bounced and carried through the air most truly.

As in England at this time, the growth of inter-club competition required the acceptance of a common code of rules. The Melbourne Football Club had drawn up its rules of 1859; gradually and with many modifications, these were accepted by other clubs. The offer of trophies for inter-club competition by the Caledonian Society in 1862 and by the Melbourne Athletics Club in 1865 — helped to stabilize both the clubs and the rules.

Melbourne football drew on English public school precedents for its rules; the amalgam which emerged was closest to the game played in Harrow, but it was unique to Australia. There was no fixed calendar of matches; clubs were free to challenge one another and to arrange between themselves the time, place, and duration of play and the size of the teams. The early games were commonly played between twenty-five men of each club; later, twenty a side became the established rule. Each goal constituted a "game"; a "match" constituted the best two of three "games". Play commonly began early in the afternoon and ended when the "match" was completed, or at dusk. But sometimes play began in the morning and broke for lunch; the consumption of "beef and bottled beer" could alter the post-lunch fortunes. If the match was not decided on the first day, play could be resumed at a later date.

The object of the play was to kick the ball through the opponents' goal — between two uprights, which stood seven or eight yards apart, there being no cross-bar as in rugby or soccer. The ball had to pass clear through the posts; on one occasion, it was recorded that "just as the ball was passing through the posts, it struck a small boy on the head, and then glanced off, touching one of the goal posts" — the goal was not allowed.[21] Goals were often disputed. In the early days there were no umpires. The opposing captains resolved any arguments; sometimes the excited spectators intervened and disrupted the play. Later, umpires were appointed — one by each side — to watch the goals.

The main argument over the rules was about how the ball should be moved towards the goal. The rugby code allowed catching and carrying the ball; Eton and other English public schools disallowed any hand-play. It was there that Australian football developed its most distinctive features. A player could pick up and carry the ball (at first only if it came to him on the first bounce, but this limitation was soon abandoned). He could not throw it (the rugby "pass") but had to kick it. An opponent could try to dispossess him by charging but not by tripping, and "hacking" was forbidden. If a player caught the ball on the full from the boot of another player, he could call "mark" and take a "free kick". (Commonly, place-kicks were used in kicking off at the beginning of a match, or after the change of ends which followed when a goal was scored. Punts or drop-kicks were used in the course of field-play.) The duties of the umpires were extended to determine when a free kick should be awarded, whether for a mark or a breach of the rules. And — most unusual of all — there was no offside rule; a player was permitted to kick the ball forward for a team-mate to mark and take a free kick: "When the kick is made, the ball generally takes an upward course, thereby causing that most enlivening scene, a charge on both sides to get first catch or kick at the falling ball."[22] The high mark was already part of the Australian game.

The rules caused a new distribution of players which became characteristic of Australian football. Where the offside rule was played, all the players were required to be behind the ball — or, if they were ahead of the ball, to refrain from play until they had become onside; consequently, the play consisted of a series of forward charges into a solid wall of defence. In the Australian game, which allowed both for the forward charge and for forward passing from man to man, the team placement added to the back and side players and the central phalanx a new category, the "goal sneaks", who hung around the enemy goal hoping to mark a forward kick and win a free kick for a goal. The playing field began to look more like two opposing networks of players than two lines of battle;

I think the ground should be free to all, so that the captain of each side could dispose of his forces in any position he likes; and when this is done, and the ball is carried on from one end of the ground to the other, by a succession of good, well-directed kicks, to the hands of those the ball was intended for, and so effectually brought close up to the goal, it has a very pretty effect, and is the result of some skill.[23]

Thus did Tom Wills define the Australian style of play.

Football was already well established as a winter sport, involving ten or more clubs, when in 1863 *Bell's* began to look more closely at the ideology of the game. The debate began with a reprint of an article from the English sporting weekly, *The Field,* urging the claims of football against those who held that it was a "rough, dirty, and even dangerous" game, "a mere wrestling and shinning match, more fit for coalheavers and bargees, than for our gallant volunteers and gentlemen at large". On the contrary, the article said, it was potentially a game of skill rather than force. It had the advantage over cricket that it involved less expenditure of money and time; the equipment was not expensive, the ground needed no special preparation, and a match might be played in sixty or ninety minutes — "as much time as this might easily be spared occasionally in these steam money-making days". It involved more people, more actively; and it was more attractive to spectators — "they understand it better than cricket; it is more exciting".[24]

Over three months in 1864, *Bell's* reprinted a series of articles by John D. Cartwright — the most detailed exposition of football that had yet appeared. Cartwright was quite clear about the significance of the game. For boys of the British upper and upper middle classes, the inhabitants of the British public schools, book-learning was far from everything. "The education of the playground, and the lessons learned from schoolfellows and college friends" was "of the highest practical value" in preparing them "to command a division, lead a cavalry charge, bear the brunt of battle, the hardships of the field, or accept the responsibilities devolving upon the men to whose hands is entrusted the government of the nation". The "manly sports" were "lessons in the art of power" which it was their "main business to learn". Unhappily, football was not playing its part. What was naturally a simple game had been made unduly complex by the differing traditions that had grown up in various public schools. What was needed was a set of "universal and simple rules" which could make football a national game. "We live in the days of the competitive system, and there is no system like it." Football should be made into a national competitive sport, in which the men of the public schools could meet on common ground with one another and with their brethren, the common folk of the villages and towns, to the benefit of both individuals and the nation. Cartwright pointed to the rules recently adopted at Cambridge and by the newly formed English Football [i.e., soccer] Association, as harbingers of a hopeful future.[25]

Living in a more open society, the colonial devotees of football were not so confident of their class position as was *The Field*, even though their game was firmly embedded in the middle class. Tom Wills noted that, "by a very curious coincidence" (he was reluctant to suggest any direct influence), the recent English rules to which Cartwright had referred were very like those which had been agreed upon by the Melbourne clubs some five years ago. The Victorian code was "as simple, rational, concise, and at the same time comprehensive, as the veriest glutton for mauling and scrimmaging can desire."[26] The virtues of the game consisted in the enjoyment it provided for players and for spectators, and in the physical well-being it induced (which might make some contribution to defence). The argument for the game was not developed in terms of the qualities needed to maintain the strengths of a hereditary ruling class.

The Melbourne rules were consolidated in the code of 1886, drafted by Henry Harrison, which established all the main features of the Australian game: no offside rule; position play, kicking forward, and the "mark"; running with the ball provided it was bounced every five or six yards; the charge or bump, but no tripping or hacking. The game owed something to its English origins;[27] but the local players had introduced some major new elements and, taken as a whole, the game was unlike any football that was played at Home. And already there were colonial patriots to argue that it was a superior game to any played elsewhere in the world.

Football had established itself as the predominant winter sport, but it was developing in ways that were not yet understood by its most ardent advocates. The competition between clubs, by now firmly based on the municipalities of Melbourne, was beginning to overrun the pleasure of the individual players; scratch matches, open to all club members, were displaced by the contests between the "first twenties". The regulation of the hours of work and leisure in modern, industrial, urban society put a premium on a game like football, which could be reasonably confined within a Saturday afternoon; and, as more people came to be bound by the clock and the calender, the demand grew for entertainment to fill the regulated leisure.

The first games of football attracted as spectators only the immediate friends and families of the players, but within three or four years crowds of several hundred and up to two thousand were reported at the matches of the day. Many observers commented on the large numbers of the "tender sex" who turned out to watch their men at play. But, more importantly for the future of the game, as workers began to enjoy more of the leisure which had earlier been the privilege of the middle class, the social composition of the spectators began to change, and the crowds continued to swell. Almost imperceptibly, football was ceasing to be a game men played for their own pleasure; instead, it was becoming one that was designed to enhance the prestige of the club, its players and officials, and the community of which it was part, and one that provided the spectators with an emotional outlet, a focus of group loyalty, and — so some would say — a diversion from the more serious social problems that confronted them.

NOTES

The material for this chapter is drawn from the opening chapters of a forthcoming book on the social history of football in Melbourne.

1. That is, Australian Rules football — as distinguished from rugby, soccer, gridiron, and Gaelic football — which began in Melbourne and now predominates in Victoria, South Australia, Western Australia, and Tasmania.
2. Melbourne's first sporting paper, published weekly from 3 January 1857, and modelled on the London *Bell's Life*.
3. *Bell's Life in Victoria and Sporting Chronicle* (hereafter *Bell's*), 30 September 1865.
4. Ibid., 28 December 1861.
5. This grossly oversimplifies the class structure of colonial society. I am using "middle class" to describe a number of groups whose interests were far from identical but who had a common interest in promoting the myth of classlessness — that is, pastoralists, land-owners, traders, employers, professionals,and salaried employees of government and private enterprise. Apart from them were tenant farmers, selectors, artisans, and labourers.
6. *Bell's*, 30 September 1865.
7. These traditional amusements are described in Joseph Strutt, *Sports and Pastimes of the People of England* (London: J. White, 1801).
8. *Bell's*, 28 December 1861.
9. Ibid.
10. *Bell's*, 30 September 1865.
11. An inscription on a tablet in the Close, Rugby. See W. J. Morgan and G. Nicholson, *Report on Rugby* (London: Heinemann, 1959), p.32.
12. *Bell's*, 23 January, 1858.
13. H. C. A. Harrison, *The Story of an Athlete* (Melbourne: A. McCubbin, n.d. [1923]), passim.
14. Ibid., p.100.
15. *Argus*, 9 August, 10 August, 30 August, 27 September 1858.

16. Ibid., 16 August 1858.
17. *Tom Brown's Schooldays, by an Old Boy* [Thomas Hughes] (London: Macmillan, 1857), chap. 4.
18. Harrison, *Story of an Athlete*, p.89; see also "Free Kick" in *Bell's*, 21 May 1864.
19. *Bell's*, 4 June 1859.
20. Ibid, 28 July 1865.
21. Ibid., 9 June 1860.
22. "Free Kick", *Bell's*, 14 May 1864.
23. Ibid., 21 May 1864. I am persuaded, from internal evidence, that "Free Kick" is T. W. Wills, though I have not been able to establish the point.
24. *Bell's*, 9 May 1863.
25. Ibid., 9 April to 2 July 1864.
26. "Free Kick", *Bell's*, 14 May 1864.
27. But, despite popular belief, nothing to Ireland. The similarities between Gaelic and Australian football seem to be coincidental.

M. N. PEARSON

Heads in the Sand: the 1956 Springbok Tour to New Zealand in Perspective

The 1956 tour of the South African rugby union team, the Springboks, to New Zealand was a particularly important one. South Africa was firmly established as the dominant force in world rugby, having won all four tests at home in 1949 against the All Blacks. Many New Zealanders attributed this disaster to biased refereeing, dirty play, and the difficulties of travel in South Africa. The 1956 tests were grudge matches which had to be won. The All Blacks eventually won three of the four tests in 1956, and claimed supremacy in world rugby.

It was a magnificent sports triumph, yet something was left out of the accounts of the tour. The Springbok team came from racially segregated South Africa, a country deliberately implementing policies at variance with the ideals of the rest of the world, and especially of New Zealand, which perceived itself as a paradise of racial harmony in a divided world. Yet this was ignored: New Zealanders were able to keep sport and politics divorced and discrete. In this time of innocence, rugby-playing Springboks were just good sports, foes to be defeated on the field. Left aside completely was any discussion of their position as official representatives of a country with ideals and policies in direct conflict with those of New Zealand, and with the emerging force of Afro-Asian nationalism.

The main object of this chapter is to reflect on this curious silence in 1956. However, to put this in perspective, a brief survey of the later controversies about sporting contact with South Africa is needed.[1]

An All Black team, if it is selected on merit, normally includes several Maoris; in fact they are usually over-represented. They make up about 10 per cent of the total population but typically have three or four players in an All Black fifteen. This may reflect Maori occupational patterns, or an "inherent" ability, but more likely it is simply a case of Maoris preferring rugby to other sports. In the total sporting population rugby is dominant, but among Maoris it is over-whelmingly the preference. Relatively few play rugby league (which is surprising, as rugby league's players and image are urban and working class), let alone hockey or soccer. The number of Maoris who have become prominent in summer sports like cricket or tennis is infinitesimal. This reflects preference, not lack of ability. Maoris like rugby, do well at it, and have made large contributions to All Black successes.

On the other hand, sport and society in South Africa had been segregated long before the Nationalist Party under Malan gained power in 1948. Until forced to do otherwise, the South African authorities had classified Maoris as non-whites, and so ineligible to visit South Africa with All Black teams. No Maoris toured in 1928 or 1949: the All Blacks of these years were, ironically, all white. Nevertheless, at a state farewell to the 1949 team, Keith Holyoake could say that "the team were ambassadors and emissaries of New Zealand. The honour and prestige of the whole of New Zealand were in the team's hands."[2] Nor did anyone in 1949 point out that the Springboks had won four tests not against the best players in New Zealand but only against the best *pakeha* (New Zealander of European origins) players. Another All Black team was due to tour South Africa in 1960, but this time there was strong opposition to the exclusion of Maoris. Politicians lay low, as did the Rugby Union. Proponents of the tour said that they were certainly not racists, but that they were not prepared to expose Maoris to the "intolerable indignity" that South Africa's "way of life" would inflict on them.

The majority of New Zealanders simply thought that to cancel such an important tour was to carry principle too far. Once the tour, without Maoris, was definitely on, editorials counselled the protesters to be "good losers" and "get behind" the team. In short, *pakeha* New Zealand had it both ways. Everyone was proud of the protest (or at least of that part of it which was "moderate" and "dignified") for did this not again demonstrate how dearly white New Zealand cared for its Maoris? But *pakeha* New Zealand also had its tour. Critics claimed that the issue was whether rugby or Maoris were most important, and the result showed that rugby was. Yet a year later, in 1961, New Zealand in the United Nations expressed warm support for the "gallant men and women who are resisting apartheid in South Africa". Unfortunately, New Zealand was too far away to aid them directly, but her voice would always "be strong for those who seek to establish multi-racial co-operation in that country".[3]

In 1965 the Springboks toured New Zealand and were warmly

welcomed. Nevertheless, there were some protests against sporting ties with South Africa, and these increased before the scheduled departure of the All Blacks to South Africa in 1967. This time the protests succeeded: the tour was postponed, and when it took place in 1970 four Maoris were in the team.

The issue of Maoris having been won, the protesters now tried to stop all sporting contacts with South Africa. In this aim they received powerful support in international bodies from Afro-Asian, and especially Black African, countries, and from the Kirk Labour government, which finally stopped the scheduled 1973 Springbok tour of New Zealand. The issue is still very much alive, partly because of the unfortunate timing of tours of South Africa: in 1960 the tour was just after Sharpeville, in 1976 just after Soweto. In the latter year the All Blacks, with Maoris, toured South Africa. Protest was vociferous, both nationally and overseas. Many Black African nations boycotted the Montreal Olympic Games in protest. But the prime minister, Robert Muldoon, said that New Zealand would play sport with anyone, "even Australia". Whether this defiance of world opinion can continue is doubtful. New Zealand is now almost completely isolated on the issue, as is shown by Malcolm Fraser's strong condemnation of racism in sport, both at the June 1977 Commonwealth Conference and earlier. Muldoon was subject to great pressure at this conference, but it is not yet clear whether he has altered his basic stance on the issue.

In 1956 there was no questioning and no opposition. The Springbok tour was a great sporting event which dominated New Zealand life for three months. During the tour normal business proceeded with difficulty, if at all. The Waikato Diocesan Synod had the misfortune to be meeting at the same time as the Springboks were playing their second game in New Zealand. The bishop told the assembled churchmen that they could get the score at afternoon tea time. "Twice during the afternoon, however, the session was interrupted and the bishop gave progress reports on the match." A meeting of the then governing New Zealand National Party conference was even worse timed, for it conflicted with the third test. Despite opposition from women delegates, who wanted to get on with business, the meeting was adjourned so that the members could listen in to most of the second half. The motion to adjourn put it: "There are matters of national moment taking place at present. I move that the conference adjourn." Three days later parliament was poorly attended, as most members were present at Athletic Park to watch another Springbok game or were at least in the corridors listening to the radio commentary.[4]

Schoolboys were particularly enthusiastic. During the tour the Springboks visited many schools. "The effect of such kindliness upon the boys and girls of the country was prodigious. No one who did not see children milling around Springboks can have any conception of how intensely their minds were filled by the tour; and probably only parents could tell how many Springboks are enshrined in children's hearts as Public Favourites, Heroes, Gods."[5]

At one large public boys' high school a prefect was allowed to interrupt the sacrosanct evening preparation period to announce the names of two trial teams for the All Black selection. The disciplinarian headmaster spent hours of school assembly time on the Springboks. His son, a medical student, saw one of their early games. His father read out in full his detailed comments on players, and tactics, to the school assembly. When the team visited the town, two live Springboks were triumphantly produced before a special school assembly. One crazed sports fanatic unprecedentedly broke the rigid lines of uniformed boys to secure autographs from the two players; a normally authoritarian headmaster beamed indulgently. After winning the last test the All Blacks received three rousing cheers *in absentia* from the assembled school.

Not only schoolboys were enthusiastic. An extraordinary number of New Zealanders saw the Springboks play. In 1956 New Zealand's population was just over 2,000,000. During the three months the Springboks were in the country nearly 666,000 people saw their twenty-three games, and paid £239,000 for the pleasure.[6]

During the tour the Springboks seemed to be omnipresent. They received a civic welcome at the Auckland Town Hall, a welcome from the "Maori People" and a national welcome at a government reception in Parliament Buildings. Here the acting prime minister, Keith Holyoake, extended the "warmest possible welcome" and noted that "the two countries had not met often enough, but they would not have known each other nearly so well as they now did without Rugby football."[7] The manager, Dr Danie Craven, spoke in public frequently, sometimes on rugby topics, other times in sermons (he was an ordained minister), and once in opposition to drink and Sunday sport.

The press coverage, at least if New Zealand's largest-circulation daily paper is typical, was quite overwhelming.[8] New Zealand's best-known cartoonist, Minhinnick, practically forgot politics for the duration of the tour. During these three months, twenty-five cartoons out of a total of about fifty-five were about the Springboks or used them or rugby to comment on non-sporting topics.

Commentary on the tour in fact started early in the year. Summer coaching for New Zealand players, and trials in South Africa, were covered in full. The names and full playing information of 120 South African players who participated in these trials were listed in detail. The final Springbok selection was the main local news story of the day, and a third leader also commented. Later the interminable series of trials to choose the All Blacks was similarly covered in full. The arrival of the Springboks in Sydney in May was narrated in enormous detail, and their first training run at Coogee Oval rated a three-column report.

Reports on games, and team selections for the tests, were often rated as the main local news of the day. Editorial and letters columns featured the Springboks frequently. Reams of paper were used for feature stories about the team as tourists, as players, and as heart-throbs. As an example of this trivia, in August the Springboks arrived in Wanganui to a warm and joyous welcome. The "Sprinkboks turned their procession in vintage cars and fire engines from the railway station to their hotel into a riotous comedy, in which a star turn was played by J. A. J. Pickard. With a water pistol he kept squirting the crowd." The last week of the tour, which included the fourth test, was given saturation coverage, including a first and second leader on the same day. Numerous valedictory letters were published, along the lines of "splendid athletes . . . an inspiration to our youth . . . forged another link in the chain of Commonwealth unity and friendship". At the airport the president of the New Zealand Rugby Football Union said, "All New Zealand joins with us in saying farewell to the greatest team to visit New Zealand. It has been a wonderful tour and we must thank the South Africans and the South African Rugby Union for it." A message from the prime minister, who in fact had been overseas for much of the tour, noted that "Saturday afternoons would be dull now" and stressed "the pleasure that the tour had given to hundreds of thousands of people in this country".[9]

This fanatical interest in a sports tour is unexceptional, even if a trifle excessive. What is interesting is not what is said but what is left unsaid. This was, after all, an all-white team from a black-majority country which refused to allow Maoris to visit. Yet in 1956 the issue was not confronted at all. It is true that the whole controversy would be more clearly defined when it was a case of Maoris being excluded from All Black teams touring South Africa; indeed, the 1956 Springboks played against Maoris in virtually every game, and also played a match against a New Zealand Maori team. Yet the issue should have been put. Race relations in New Zealand even in the 1950s were far from ideal, and South Africa in 1956 was a country far along the road to apartheid. New Zealand preferred to keep politics out of sport and welcome her rugby visitors. T. P. McLean's book on the tour has no mention of the problem. His chapter on the controversies of the tour deals exclusively with rugby: refereeing, standards, rough play, strange selections. All these are regrettable as they interfere with pure sportsmanship and "the highest principles of sporting friendship".[10]

The protests since 1959 are well known in New Zealand and Australia. They point to an awareness that politics and sport are, and must be, inextricably linked. The interesting question, however, is why it took so long for this link to be seen. Why were the Springboks greeted in 1956 in a purely sporting, apolitical, way? These questions need to be asked for two reasons. First, New Zealand has always prided itself on being the most successful country in the world in race relations. The indigenous Maori population is treated equally with the majority *pakehas*. There is no discrimination. Ultimately, indeed, there are no Maoris or *pakehas:* there are just New Zealanders. If this self-perception means anything at all, it should mean that New Zealanders are uniquely sensitive to racism and strenuously opposed to it, for racism should be seen as an affront to a cornerstone of the New Zealand ideal. In particular, it is legitimate to expect New Zealanders to be deeply concerned about, and opposed to, apartheid. But in reality it seems that even today a majority of New Zealanders are hypocritically prepared to play sport with white South Africa. Since 1959 the issue has at least been raised. In 1956 it was not, and this silence obviously needs to be explained.

The second point to be made is that sport and politics were, in other areas, obviously mixed in together long before 1956, and were seen to be linked. This is perhaps best shown in the vicissitudes of the Olympic Games, under Avery Brundage the archetypal expression of the separation of sport and politics. In reality the Games have been politicized for most of their modern existence. The 1908 London Games severely strained relations between American and British athletes and their supporters. The Berlin Games in 1936 were notoriously political, designed by Hitler and Goebbels to celebrate "Aryaness". Politics played a role in the 1948 London Games also, for they were meant to demonstrate the resilience of Britain soon after the Second World War. Japan and Germany were excluded.

The 1952 Helsinki Games were the most politicized to that date, partly because the USSR competed for the first time since the 1917 Revolution. The USSR could have competed in 1948, but preferred to wait until 1952 and, by means of intensive preparations, make a successful debut. Rivalry between American and Russian athletes was intense, and success was openly seen in Cold War terms. Nor was this the only area where politics were important in 1952. East Germany applied and was rejected. West Germany applied and was accepted. China also was accepted, whereupon Taiwan withdrew. China then failed to compete anyway.

The point had been made clearly even before the Berlin Games. The *New York Times* opposed American participation in these Games. When the Nazis "deliberately and arrogantly offend our common humanity," the paper argued, "sport does not 'transcend all political and racial considerations.' " This principle was, or should have been, universal. Whether in Olympic Games or in rugby tours, politics could not and should not be kept out of sport. It is thus an important and valid historical question to ask how, in New Zealand of all places, could politics and sport be kept separate as late as 1956.

There seem to be three elements which help to explain why in 1956 New Zealand sports fans, and indeed apparently most of the country, could ignore the wider implications of sporting contacts with South Africa. First, rugby occupied so central a role in New Zealand society, and in New Zealanders' stereotypes of themselves, that any opposition to such an important tour would be ignored if possible. The tour was sacrosanct, as was rugby. Second, New Zealanders were less likely to get upset by a team from South Africa because of the racism latent at this time in New Zealand. Third, in 1956 New Zealanders did not appreciate the strength of Black African nationalism, the significance of the end of colonialism in Africa and Asia, and the effect this would have on sporting contact with South Africa. The press played an important role here, for it did little to educate its readers in these matters.

Taking the role of rugby in New Zealand society first, the extreme interest in the 1956 tour of New Zealand was only an exaggerated case of the country's century-old obsession with rugby. It is not only a spectator sport. Literally thousands of New Zealanders *play* rugby on Saturday. It was estimatd in 1956 that at least fifty thousand New Zealanders played every winter Saturday. In 1970–71 there were 3,250 club and secondary school teams in New Zealand.[11] Taking account of reserves and fluctuating team selections, it is probably about right to count twenty per team, which means that about sixty-five thousand New Zealand males were active in the game at that time. Given that hockey, rugby league, soccer, and other minor sports are also played, these figures show an unusual willingness to participate. The total New Zealand male population between the ages of ten and thirty-four, roughly the rugby-playing age, was 585,652 in 1971: over 11 per cent of the possible total therefore actually played in organized rugby competition.[12]

Descriptions of rugby in New Zealand become, in this matter-of-fact land, almost poetical. As an official history put it: "The story in the following pages is the story of Rugby Union Football in New Zealand; the story of a great pastime and of its rise from a humble beginning to occupy pride of place as New Zealand's national game; the story of men of prowess on the green-sward; of sportsmen; of New Zealand's young manhood at its best." A quasi-official history of the game enlisted academic help: "A New Zealand professor of history gave his opinion that if the chief event in Auckland in 1956 was the defeat of the Springboks, the next was the exhibition of the sculpture and drawing of Henry Moore. Few would challenge his order of reference; the Aucklander sees more beauty in the towering posts of Eden Park than in sculpture with holes in it." Indeed, rugby is not just a good game, it is the best game: "Some talk of great moments of cricket, of soccer, of runners, of tennis, but for every one of these you can choose a hundred from Rugby." Given this position in New Zealand, the rewards for the successful participant are great: "For generations rugby in New Zealand has been a sport of idols and idolators. An All Black might not be a king, but within his circle, large or small according to his ability and reputation, he could very often live like one."[13]

In fact, anyone who is good at rugby is automatically a good citizen. "The rugby type of New Zealand is a fine type, even though maligned by some people who could not pick up a ball even before the air is added." The chief justice recently gave a light sentence to a rugby player convicted of rape because he was only nineteen and was a "good sportsman". His Honour observed: "it is very rarely indeed that we see one who does well at Rugby before the court. You are letting down the game as well as yourself."[14]

Rugby reinforces (or creates) various parts of New Zealanders' self-perceptions. It is too important to be interfered with by politics or morality (indeed, it is above politics), because it is so central to New Zealand's ethos that criticism of rugby is criticism of New Zealand. A complete analysis of rugby's role in New Zealand society would involve writing a sociology of New Zealand. The following are simply a few preliminary observations which touch on some aspects of New Zealand society.

The role of international sporting success in fostering or creating national pride is something of a cliche in the literature. Victory serves to reinforce ideas of national worth, and indeed to legitimize the very existence of a small, dependent, culturally undifferentiated country in the South Pacific. Defeat on the other hand is a national disgrace. As Bob Scott noted, "the 1949 tour of South Africa [when New Zealand lost all four tests] was a terrible shock to New Zealand, the worst we have ever had." Great players are legitimate national heroes. The years in which Colin Meads dominated the All Black scrum were also years of unprecedented success for the team as a whole. "It is not easy to convey what Meads has meant to New Zealanders. They have ridden on his back to glory in the field which means most to them."[15]

Rugby has other international implications. The fiery combat of sport has often been claimed to reveal true character and to open up friendships between men, even on an international level. Terry McLean quotes approvingly the following: "I have failed to find anything in the whole field of human pastimes — unless it be war — that can bring men closer together than sport. . . . Sport can open up a door, as it were, between men." The great wing Ron Jarden stresses that any unpleasantness is left on the field. "I regard nearly all the players whom I have marked myself on these [test] occasions as men of the highest character and would always welcome them, as I have done, into my home."[16]

The New Zealander tends to think of himself as more handy and practical than most people. He may repair his own car, build his own house, construct a boat in his backyard, or at least be able to do repairs and renovations to his own home. The emphasis is on physical aptitude. A university professor standing for parliament played down his considerable academic achievements and instead stressed that he had once been a good boxer, and that on weekends he roughed it in his "bach" like any other typical Kiwi. The other side of this coin is a distrust of the artistic or intellectual, which was clearly revealed in the year of the 1956 Springbok tour by an exhibition of Henry Moore's sculpture in Auckland. The mayor opined that the pieces "desecrated" the Art Gallery, for they were a "nauseating sight" and "repulsive". "One man, similarly dissatisfied, ran out of the gallery in a rage . . . and said 'That man ought to be shot.' " A female viewer said "Some evil influence in the world is trying to demoralize us." Yet another man the next day seemed to put his finger on the exact problem with modern sculpture: it was, he said "tripe. . . . Lot of nonsense. I know — I'm a tradesman."[17] People do not really have holes in their bodies and tiny heads; who better to point this out than a man who works with his hands?

Rugby serves to reinforce the myths of this practical, pioneer society. University teams, and also the French, are often seen as being too brainy and incurably flighty. What is needed for a good All Black pack is plenty of farmers: the myth is overwhelmingly of huge hairy farmers with big feet crashing into rucks. The ubiquitous Winston McCarthy noted of the forwards in the 1963—64 team that they were very tough. "They were all outside workers, most of them farmers." The facts are otherwise. Of the ten forwards McCarthy lists in this context, six were farmers and four had non-manual white-collar jobs. Of all the sixteen forwards in the team, seven were farmers, one other was a manual worker, and eight had white-collar jobs.[18] We lack complete information on All Black occupations, but in four All Black teams (those of 1960, 1963-64, 1972-73, and 1974), with a total of 120 players, farmers accounted for 23.4 per cent of the total, other manual for 11.6 per cent, and white-collar for 65 per cent. In the total New Zealand male working population in 1966, 15.3 per cent can be classified as farmers, 49.2 per cent as other manual, and only 35.5 per cent as white-collar. These discrepancies need more evaluation: they tend to discount the myth outlined above. In part they reflect the social and occupational mobility which rugby prowess can provide. Large companies have been increasingly happy to employ All Blacks in sales, public relations, and executive jobs. It may also be noted that the Springboks are even more non-manual than the All Blacks. Of a total of sixty-four players in their 1956 and 1965 teams, only seven were farmers, two others did manual work, and fifty-five were white-collar, including ten students.[19]

It seems that while top rugby players achieve some mobility, the material rewards for sports success in New Zealand are much less than in other countries. This fits several parts of the New Zealand ethos. New Zealand society is usually considered to be egalitarian, with class divisions either non-existent or at least of little importance. The dominance of rugby fits perfectly here: "everyone" plays rugby, and "anyone" can, regardless of size, occupation, or wealth. As a great coach noted, "They must make allowance, in most other sports, for differences in ages and weights and experience and physical attributes. But there are few allowances in Rugby. At each and every level, there is one constant, inescapable demand: Manliness."[20] The sport in New Zealand is almost completely declassed; an upper-middle-class English game was taken over and democratized. The stockbroker plays with the fisherman, the doctor with the farmer, the graduate with the boy who left school at fifteen, the Maori with the *pakeha*.

This is related to rugby's proud status as an amateur game. Professional sport attracts to it American and Australian style hoopla and crassness: cheer-leaders, advertising on uniforms, gambling. How much better is a pure amateur game that all can play, where the local sports star is a farmer like you just down the road, not a man who sells used cars on television. New Zealanders are so competent, so versatile, that they can hold down regular jobs and still beat the world.

Rugby also builds character and discourages unnecessary softness or a desire for frills and luxuries. These ideals of course fit well the New Zealand traits of making do and of egalitarianism: what is all right for us *should* be all right for anyone else:

> The Minister in charge of Tourism and Publicity, Mr. Eyre, said yesterday that glib comment on the need for luxury hotels for tourists was often heard in New Zealand, but his own view was that most tourists were satisfied with accommodation which met the requirements of the average New Zealander. . . . Super-luxury accommodation, he said, was hard to provide, and it was doubtful whether it was needed. Most of New Zealand's tourists would come from Australia and he was sure that they would be satisfied with accommodations which satisfied New Zealanders.[21]

New Zealand rugby reinforces these plain hard ideals. It is, as a semi-official history notes, "based on physical strength rather than subtlety of mind, it is a game of bodily contact". A famous player and administrator warned that "there is no place in Rugby for the squealer. Play the game; take the hard knocks; give them; and afterwards shut up and forget them." As Bob Scott put it, "Rugby in terms of manliness, sportsmanship, and fair play has so much to offer a virile nation".[22]

The stress on participation, on playing the game almost regardless of aptitude or desire, relates to New Zealand's give it a go ideal. As McLean notes, and I can confirm, in the good old days "a medical certificate was the only escape from rugby in Secondary school". Players, even successful ones, who played any winter sport other than rugby had to justify themselves to their peers. Those who played individual sports, such as athletics, were seen as competing only for their own selfish glory, while the member of the first fifteen was considered to be playing altruistically for the school. This attitude leads to the organization of even seven- and eight-year-olds into regular competitive teams: this activity fits them for life's battles. A photograph in a rugby history sums it up perfectly: a real lineout on a full-size field of little boys with bewildered expressions, knobbly knees, and spindly arms, all in real uniforms and short hair. Savage-looking parents patrol the sideline.[23] One can find other New Zealand character traits reflected in rugby. The All Blacks have notoriously played safe rugby, with grinding, efficient forwards, and backs who usually kick rather than open up play. Many critics have noted a similar concern for safety and conformity in New Zealand life as a whole: paralysingly boring suburbs, opposition to heterodoxy, bigotry, authoritarian schools, and a claustrophobic stress on external compliance. Yet a reverse interpretation of the role of rugby in New Zealand life can also be attempted. There have been many studies of the role of sports, for both participants and spectators, as a safety valve for modern man trapped in assembly-line jobs, smothered by conformity, and afflicted by urban anomie. Antisocial behaviour is allowed, or even encouraged, in this isolated, neutral area of activity. Spectators used to queue up all night before big games, and heavy drinking was the norm at these times. The drinking, accompanied by destruction of property, throwing of empty beer bottles, and generally loutish behaviour, continued during the game itself. After the game, beer parties went on into the night. This sort of saturnalia is tacitly condoned: it is no accident that the rugby-playing rapist was let off lightly.

Some biographies and autobiographies of All Blacks stress the role of the coach as a father figure, especially for younger players from rural areas. This dependency is sometimes attributed to the role of the overweening and omnipresent Welfare State in New Zealand, which allegedly discourages initiative and enterprise. This need for security, to be dominated by someone, was best expressed by the great forward Peter Jones, a sparsely educated rustic who, because he came from the backblocks, was called "Kumara" by his team-mates. Jones notes that in 1953 his local selector came to Wellington especially to see him play in an important trial. "And that helped a lot, having him there especially, giving me someone to play for." Later Jones met the famous general, Lord Freyberg. His comments are especially revealing: "Now *he* would have been a man to play for. That's what I always needed — someone to play my heart out for."[24]

At least until recently New Zealand has seen itself as a frontier, male-dominated society. This dominance has created some curious phenomena in relations between the sexes. On one hand the editor of the high-brow *Listener* presented a very traditional view when he wrote that "women unable to have children are unfulfilled, unless they find fulfilment vicariously, as in the care of the young". This advice seems to be taken to heart. New Zealand has an extra-ordinarily high rate of illegitimate births, though this is probably more a result of naivete than of unusual promiscuity. Deviation from the heterosexual norm is discouraged. As an extreme example, in 1964 six youths aged between fifteen and seventeen went to a Christchurch park to pick up and assault any homosexual they might find. They went too far and killed their victim, but were acquitted by a jury, apparently because the victim was homosexual.[25]

Rugby seems to reflect some of these attitudes. The publicity for Colin Meads's biography states: "This book is fascinating reading whether one is a devotee or not — and will be enjoyed by most males of all ages — and by a significant number of women too." Bob Scott, in his biography, notes of his children that "Bruce will be the player and Wendy, like her mother,will be the enthusiastic onlooker." Ron Jarden put the role of rugby into a wider perspective by saying: "I feel that a lot of housewives should be grateful to me in that I have provided their husbands over the years with the opportunity of releasing a great deal of frustration which might otherwise have been expended on the domestic battle front." Other aspects of New Zealand's sexuality also appear. There is an interesting ambivalence in Terry McLean's description of Barry John, the star of the 1971 Lions tour of New Zealand. His team-mates joked about "the adoration of multitudes of New Zealanders, by no means all of them young and, despite his distinctively handsome looks, perhaps more of them male than female".[26]

It is something of a cliche that sports administrators and players tend to be conservative socially and politically. Many critics have stressed these aspects of New Zealand society in general. Conservative conformist sportsmen can be national heroes in a conservative conformist country. Thus Colin Meads is devoted to the Royal Family, along with rugby and farming. Almost no players question the authoritarian role of the New Zealand Rugby Football Union. The mayor of Tauranga suggested that vandals could be stopped by forming vigilante groups of rugby players and suchlike who have "vim and vigour. . . . Some of the troublemakers could end up with broken necks." The great halfback Chris Laidlaw, now an iconoclast, notes rugby is "an establishment activity. Distressingly so. It is normally played and administered by conservative elements in society. . . . [Players are] thundering bores with short hair and a suspicion of 'lefties', particularly those who break up their matches for some cause as obscure as a protest against apartheid. Today's players are by and large tomorrow's Tories. Society seems to have passed them by."[27]

A most interesting case, demonstrative of authoritarianism, and implicitly of sexuality, concerned the 1956 Springbok team. They had a practice of "borselling", the Afrikaans verb *borsel* meaning "to brush". An offender was lifted to chest height and beaten on the backside by the bare hands of his team-mates. In extreme cases the offender was borselled naked. Early in the tour borselling was very frequent, and even a local New Zealand rugby official attached to the team once suffered this fate. "It was, in one sense, a form of initiation and in another of punishment." Later in the tour the practice was ended. McLean notes sagely that "everyone had grown thoroughly tired of what was, though sometimes useful, basically a rather childish amusement for grown men".[28]

The myth that New Zealanders cherish most is that their country is a shining example of racial tolerance in the world, that Maori and *pakeha* are one, living peacefully together. Indeed, rugby is claimed to have played an important role in creating this happy racial situation. "Maoris as tribal warriors, as modern soldiers, as successful farmers, and as mighty players of religious rugby, command respect." McLean comments on rugby's "ancient, traditional and immensely valuable role as a catalyst between the white and non-white communities."[29]

Until recently most New Zealanders, at least *pakehas,* believed in the specific role of rugby and generally that their islands were a speck of tolerance in a bigoted world. Recent studies paint a very different picture, one of a far from ideal climate of race relations which is deteriorating. It is true that during the last decade or so the situation has worsened, thanks to an influx of Pacific islanders, rapid urbanization among Maoris, and a failure of governments or white society in general to take cognizance of the problem. Nevertheless, the situation has never been as good as most New Zealanders thought, at least in the North Island where most Maoris live. In the 1950s a distinguished Maori was refused service in a private hotel bar, and a hairdresser cut only *pakeha* hair. Such incidents were condemned, and *pakeha* New Zealand relapsed into righteous complacency. More significantly, a major study of New Zealand published in 1958 by an acute, if acerbic and sometimes wrong-headed, American, David P. Ausubel, claimed that while race relations were good, they were not perfect. With remarkable prescience, Ausubel said: "For as long as New Zealanders persist in deluding themselves that all is well in the sphere of race relations, the only realistic prospect for the future is the emergence of a brown proletariat segregated in the urban slums and living in a state of chronic tension with their white neighbours."[30]

As a sensitized outsider, Ausubel could see more clearly than most New Zealanders. Yet it must be stressed that white attitudes and stereotypes in the 1950s revealed at worst very deep-seated contempt and hostility towards Maoris and at best a bland patronizing attitude. This point needs to be demonstrated at a little length, for along with the just-discussed centrality of rugby to the New Zealand ethos, it helps to explain why New Zealand was able to divorce so completely sport and politics in 1956: had it not been for this at least incipient racism, the Springboks and the New Zealand Rugby Football Union could not have escaped so lightly.

Some New Zealanders are simply unconsciously patronizing. Terry McLean said that he "believed that New Zealand as a predominantly white nation was deeply indebted to the Maori people. Without Maoris, there would be no tourist industry. Without Maoris, there would have been in post – Second World War times, no New Zealand Army serving abroad." Bob Scott wrote of the "age-old politeness of the Maori". Ron Jarden broke his leg "on Ben Couch's head. The Maori five-eighth was not affected by the incident." The famous commentator Winston McCarthy in typically jocular fashion pointed out that "trying to identify a Maori among a pack of others [on the football field] when you are seeing them for the first or second time is like trying to pick out a particular sheep in a flock. They all look the same."[31]

The press had, before the 1956 Springbok-Maori game, played up the likelihood of an entertaining time at Eden Park, with mass hakas from Maoris in the crowd. These did not eventuate because, as McLean said, "someone had forgotten that the Maori, when out-numbered by the *pakeha,* is inordinately shy and becomes confident and capable of performing only by the most careful and subtle coaxing". The same author says, concerning the Maori scrum in 1921, that "these were the days when all Maoris seemed to have heads like cannon-balls".[32]

None of this demonstrates overt racism; it will be noted that some of the stereotypes are favourable. Nevertheless, they are insensitive stereotypes which, no matter now kindly or unconscious or well-intentioned, do in sum tend to lump Maoris together as different and subtly inferior. From this it is only a short step to more overt statements and actions. In 1956 a man hit a Maori on the head with a piece of wood, and said "he would hit any Maori who came inside his gate. He had a bias against all Maoris." He was fined five pounds. In the same year a magistrate in Whakatane said about Maoris that

"their main purpose in living seems to be to swill beer and get into trouble." . . . Mr Freeman said the sooner the authorities realised the true position the better. With the existing unrestricted sale of liquor to them, the Maoris could not resist buying it. It took white men all their time to resist it, and there were enough of them who got drunk.
Maori drinking was assuming serious proportions and something should be done about it, said the magistrate.
He was well aware that what he was saying would probably be advertised by the press. He hoped it was.[33]

This report was published without comment by the *Herald,* and no letters on the subject were received, or at least none were published. Perhaps in the case of the *Herald* it is not surprising, given that in 1949 it could publish an editorial headed "Maori Votes bought by Labour" which concerned the results of the 1949 election (which Labour's opponents, the National Party, had won anyway):

In all their four electorates, the Maoris of New Zealand yesterday gave majorities to a party which had used the taxpayers' money quite shamelessly to buy their votes. The whole affair represents one of the least edifying episodes in New Zealand politics. Doubtless the Maoris themselves have voted according to their rights. It is in the authentic Polynesian tradition to live as easily as possible with the least exertion in labour. In a hundred years the Maori character has not changed sufficiently to eradicate a natural improvidence. And to trade votes for easy living must seem to the majority of Maoris a perfectly normal and sensible transaction.[34]

New Zealanders in 1956, and earlier and later, could read, write, and speak such things quite unconsciously, still firmly convinced that New Zealand was a paradise of racial harmony. Harder questions, such as the rival merits of assimilation or integration, were simply not put, let alone discussed. The issue became a matter for general debate only in the late 1950s, and even then only spasmodically.

The third element that helps to explain why the 1956 Springboks received bouquets rather than brickbats, deference and delirium rather than denunciation, was New Zealand's ability to ignore trends in South Africa and in the world at large. In this the press appears to have played an important role, for it took care not to link sport and politics. The *New Zealand Herald* failed to address the problem of sport and politics until late in the year, when three editorials during the Melbourne Olympic Games gloomily concluded that sport did have political implications. The USSR was mostly to blame for this unhappy situation. This issue seemed to have been forced onto the attention of the *Herald:* certainly it had chosen not to draw the obvious parallel during the Springbok tour. Yet a responsible paper should have seen the Springbok tour as raising important issues for New Zealand to consider which were closer to home than the Olympics. Instead there was silence on the political and moral issue. But the Springboks received massive coverage both on sports and news pages, and for the duration of the tour they even replaced the Royal Family in photographic coverage, an almost unprecedented feat. (If British royalty and the Springboks were inactive, other royalty were pressed into service: the Dutch family especially, while Princess Grace of Monaco rendered yeoman service for the *Herald* in 1956.) The "Pom cringe" was very much in evidence. British political news was covered in great detail. Churchill's *History of the English Speaking People* was serialized. Googie Withers and Earl Mountbatten visited New Zealand and received ridiculously adulatory coverage. The letters column was small, its content and tone relentlessly trivial. Subjects covered at length in 1956 in the column included outsize peaches; teaching Latin in schools; noisy lawnmowers; the propriety of erecting a cross over the grave of Opo, the Friendly Dolphin; modern art; wine in restaurants; Anzac Day observance; Sunday entertainment. It could be argued that these are the subjects on which the *Herald* received letters, but one visitor doubted this, and claimed the New Zealand press distorted dissenting comment and deliberately selected letters hostile to dissent.[35]

Perhaps the most intriguing news story to appear in the *Herald* in 1956 lifted the veil for a moment. It reported a speech by the assistant manager of the Springbok team near the end of their tour. Typically it attracted no editorial or letter comment, for it got rather close to the nub of a problem which New Zealand and the *Herald* had so far been able to ignore. Mr de Villiers noted that while most New Zealanders are friendly, some disliked South Africa, and this was "not healthy".

> "Why must you dislike us as South Africans?" he asked. "You people should not think you are so safe. With the present situation over the Suez Canal you may find that all your dairy products may have to be shipped through Cape Town, knowing that it has to go through a port peopled by a race that you do not like or may hate."
> The Springboks, Mr de Villiers concluded, had come to New Zealand not only to play Rugby but also to promote mutual understanding.[36]

At this time the *Herald* chose not to comment or tell its readers what to think about South Africa. Yet the year was a most significant one for the development of apartheid in South Africa, for it saw the successful conclusion of the Nationalist Party's efforts virtually to disenfranchise coloured voters. The need was to get them off the common (i.e. white) voting rolls; after considerable constitutional difficulties the Senate was gerrymandered and the coloured voters could then be put on a separate roll from which they elect four white MPs. The significance of these measures was that they showed how committed Prime Minister Strydom and his party were to apartheid and how they were prepared to go to any lengths to achieve it. The measures, and opposition to them, were covered in a series of small reports in the *Herald* in the early months of 1956 in a neutral factual way. Protests by British MPs and South African coloureds and journalists were reported, and a hostile editorial from the *Manchester Guardian* was reprinted. The *Herald* did not comment editorially on these important events itself, though it did on racial tensions in America. One hostile letter was published, but this focused on constitutional rather than racial issues.

The *Herald* also published without comment short reports on other developments in South African apartheid. These included criticism in the United Nations, student demonstrations in South Africa against segregation in universities, government attempts to move a whole tribe of seventy-five hundred blacks from their home area, the introduction of segregation among nurses, and a report that blood for transfusions was to be racially segregated. European blood was to be kept in bottles with white labels, and native blood in bottles with black labels.

It was not until December that the *Herald* used its editorial columns to comment on South Africa. In that month 140 black leaders were arrested in dawn police raids. The *Herald's* first leader denounced rather severely both the raids and apartheid in general. While welcome, this stand was curiously late. In the development of apartheid, the raids were less important than the earlier constitutional manipulation, which the *Herald* ignored. Perhaps the editors thought it would be inhospitable to comment while the Springboks were in New Zealand.

Apart from this one late editorial, there appeared virtually no hostile comentary. All that could be found in the *Herald* was a very favourable review of the anti-apartheid book *Naught for Your Comfort,* a hostile review of a pro-apartheid book, and a tiny report that the leader of the opposition, Walter Nash, had denounced apartheid as a "most terrible indictment of the whole of the people in the area". These cheeps of indigenous protest were overwhelmed by other comments. A New Zealand woman visitor to South Africa said it was unsafe to go out alone after dark in South African cities. The "natives were still firm believers in their witch doctors and this influence, until eradicated, would always be a stumbling block to their progress". A South African visitor, in New Zealand to renew wartime friendships, told the Hamilton Rotary Club that "very many of his country's vast black majority were still primitive people, running around without clothes and living on queer diets. 'A chap who wanders around with no clothes and never takes a bath is not the person you want to sit in your lounge,' he said." A story headed "Government Helps Coloured People in Africa" quoted a South African businessman as saying some sort of segregation was "necessary" and that government policy was "absolutely sincere". Race relations would improve "if handled firmly". The government the previous year had spent thirty million pounds on native services, and Europeans provided 75 per cent of this sum.[37]

More generally, the *Herald* chose to quote rather fully some comments by a visiting member of the BBC talks department who ostensibly was promoting stronger Commonwealth ties. He did not comment directly on South Africa, but "he also noticed that the initiative in colour prejudice seemed to be passing from the white people to the coloured. The Bandoeng conference was supposed to have been a political alignment of anti-colonial against colonial interests, but on looking closer it was a matter of coloured nations versus white." A leader in the *Herald* commented in a remarkably insensitive way on race relation in Africa. It noted that if all Europeans in Africa had been like Livingstone and Charles Gordon then there would be fewer problems today, but it was also necessary to remember that Gordon was killed by Africans. Some Africans were worse than the Boers. Britain was the only colonial power leading Africa to self-government, yet she had been met by Mau Mau terrorism. The need was for courtesy and good will on both sides.[38]

The point is not that the *Herald,* or New Zealand, was racist, but neither were they favourable to black nationalism. The news was reported, but the *Herald* made no effort to point out its significance for the Commonwealth or race relations generally, and New Zealanders apparently chose not to correlate Springboks and apartheid. This was still a time when it seemed best (and seemed possible) to ignore nasty reality.

Thus 1956 was still a time of innocence for New Zealand. Most of Africa was still a colony of one European power or another; black nationalists were treated with amused contempt, or were ignored. The possibility of their influencing New Zealand sport was quite inconceivable. The Afro-Asian bloc in the United Nations was in the future; its progenitor, the Bandung Conference, took place only in 1955. Its significance was not realized in New Zealand. At home, race relations were ignored or were waved around as an example for the rest of the world. For those who cared to see, New Zealand was becoming offside with the rest of the world, but at this time, blinded by complacency, ill-informed by the media, and doubtless influenced by her own incipient racism, New Zealand was able to slumber on. This torpor, this anachronistic ability and desire to keep morality and politics out of sport, was disturbed only in the 1960s and shattered only in the 1970s.

NOTES

1. The subject has been admirably covered in the works of Richard Thompson: "Rugby and Race Relations: A New Zealand Controversy", *Journal of the Polynesian Society* 69, no. 3 (September 1960): 285-87; *Retreat from Apartheid: New Zealand's Sporting Contacts with South Africa* (Wellington: Oxford University Press, 1975); *Race and Sport* (London: Oxford University Press, 1964).
2. Quoted in Thompson, *Race and Sport*, p.6.
3. Ibid., pp.62-63.
4. *New Zealand Herald*, 14 June, 20 and 23 August 1956.
5. T. P. McLean, *The Battle for the Rugby Crown* (Wellington: Reed, 1956), p.24.
6. R. J. Urbahn and D. B. Clark, *The Fourth Springbok Tour of New Zealand* (Wellington: Hicks, Smith, 1965), p.198.
7. *Herald*, 22 June 1956.
8. The *New Zealand Herald* had a circulation of over 176,000 in 1955, about fifty per cent greater than its nearest rival (*Herald*, 27 March 1956); R. H. T. Thompson, "Maori Affairs and the New Zealand Press", *Journal of the Polynesian Society* 62, no. 4 (December 1953): 368-69. This is part of a series of articles on the press in this journal, vols. 62-64, 1953-55, by Richard Thompson.
9. *Herald*, 7 August, 4 and 6 September, 1956.
10. McLean, *Battle for the Rugby Crown*, pp.103-9.
11. *Herald*, 21 June 1956; Terry McLean, *Lions Rampant* (Wellington: Reed, 1971), p.87.
12. *New Zealand Official Yearbook* (Wellington, 1976), p.83.
13. A. C. Swan, *History of New Zealand Rugby Football*, 2 vols. (Wellington: NZRFU, 1948-58), 1: ix: G. C. Slatter, *On the Ball: Centennial Book of New Zealand Rugby* (Christchurch: Whitcombe and Tombs, 1970), p.73; F. R. Allen and T. D. McLean, *Fred Allen in Rugby* (Auckland: Cassell, 1970), p.224; Terry McLean, *All Blacks Come Back* (Wellington, Reed, 1975), p.14.
14. Harry Morton, *Which Way New Zealand?* (Dunedin: John McIndoe, 1975), p.236; Gordon McLauchlan, *The Passionless People: New Zealanders in the 1970s* (Auckland: Cassell, 1976), p.136.
15. R. W. H. Scott and T. P. McLean, *The Bob Scott Story* (Wellington: Reed, 1956), p.64; A. R. Veysey, *Colin Meads, All Black* (Auckland: Collins, 1975), p.13.

16. McLean, *All Blacks Come Back*, p.15; R. A. Jaden, *Rugby on Attack* (Christchurch: Whitcombe and Tombs, 1961), p.xiii.
17. *Herald*, 19 September 1956; 20 September 1956.
18. W. J. McCarthy, *Haka: The All Blacks Story* (London: Pelham, 1968), p.291; *Herald*, 23 September 1963. A three-way division of New Zealand occupations is obviously rather gross and indiscriminate. Essentially I have counted "dirty hands" jobs other than farming as "other manual", and all "clean hands" jobs, whether outdoor or indoor, as "white-collar". Thus a farm appraiser like Wilson Whinerary is counted as white-collar, for desk work and walking around a farm are clearly not manual occupations.
19. T. P. McLean, *Beaten by the Boks* (Wellington: Reed, 1960), pp.9-11; *Herald*, 23 September 1963; Terry McLean, *They Missed the Bus: Kirkpatrick's All Blacks of 1972-73* (Wellington: Reed, 1973), pp.310-11; McLean, *All Blacks Come Back*, p.157; *New Zealand Official Yearbook* (Wellington, 1970), pp.928-30; McLean, *Battle for the Rugby Crown*, pp.231-32; Urbahn and Clark, *Fourth Springbok Tour*, p.179.
20. Allen and McLean, *Fred Allen on Rugby*, p.226.
21. *Herald*, 3 May 1956. Curiously, six days later Eyre announced a publicity campaign in the United States to attract American tourists to New Zealand: *Herald*, 9 May 1956.
22. Slatter, *On the Ball*, p.357; N. A. McKenzie, *On with the Game* (Wellington: Reed,1961), p.164; Scott and McLean, *Bob Scott Story*, p.ix.
23. McLean, *Lions Rampant*, p.86; Slatter, *On the Ball*, facing p.42.
24. P. F. H. Jones, *It's Me, Tiger: The Peter Jones Story as Told to N. Harris* (Wellington: Reed, 1965), pp.30, 33. A kumara is an indigenous sweet-potato.
25. M. H. Holcroft, *Graceless Islanders: A Selection of Editorials from the New Zealand Listener* (Christchurch: Caxton, 1970), pp.145, 45-47.
26. Veysey, *Colin Meads*, p.1; Scott and McLean, *Bob Scott Story*, p.x; Jarden, *Rugby on Attack*, p.43; McLean, *Lions Rampant*, p.32.
27. McLauchlan, *Passionless People*, p.136; Chris Laidlaw, *Mud in Your Eye* (Wellington: Reed, 1973), p.6.
28. McLean, *Battle for the Rugby Crown*, pp.19-20.
29. Colin M. Tatz, *Four Kinds of Dominion* (Armidale: University of New England Press, 1972), p.19; McLean, *All BLacks Come Back*, p.108, and see also p.15.
30. David P. Ausubel, *The Fern and the Tiki. An American View of New Zealand: National Character, Social Attitudes and Race Relations* (Sydney: Angus and Robertson, 1960), p.155.
31. McLean, *Lions Rampant*, pp.108-9; Scott and McLean, *Bob Scott Story*, p.30; Jarden, *Rugby on Attack*, p.11; McCarthy, *Haka*, p.257.
32. McLean, *Battle for the Rugby Crown*, p.212; T. P. McLean, *Great Days in New Zealand Rugby* (Wellington: Reed, 1959), p.31.
33. *Herald*, 23 May, 26 September 1956.
34. Quoted in "Maori Affairs", by R. H. T. Thompson, *Journalpson, Journal of Polynesian Society* 63, no. 1 (March 1954): 4.
35. Ausubel, *Fern and the Tiki*, pp.125-26.
36. *Herald*, 31 August 1956.
37. *Herald*, 21 February, 26 April, 10 and 29 May, 12 and 24 July 1956.
38. *Herald*, 19 May, 13 August 1956.

CHRIS CUNNEEN

The Rugby War: the Early History of Rugby League in New South Wales, 1907–15

In 1907 rugby union was booming in Sydney. The "handling game" of football had arrived in New South Wales about 1870 and was organized four years later with the formation of the Southern Rugby Union, later called the New South Wales Rugby Football Union. This body adopted the rules of the parent Rugby Football Union in England, including the strict enforcement of amateurism among players. Interstate matches against Queensland began in 1882, and in that year also a New South Wales team first visited New Zealand. Two years later a New Zealand team visited New South Wales followed in 1888 by a team from Britain. Matches of full international status commenced in 1899.

The growth of the city of Sydney by 1907 had made mass spectator sport possible. Tramway and railway routes had spread since about 1880, and suburban growth had gathered pace after the depression of the nineties. Between 1871 and 1901 the city's population had more than trebled. Certainly some of the dwindling open space was fenced, for by 1901 four of the grounds used by the Rugby Union were enclosed and an entrance fee was charged.[1]

Before 1900 the local rugby union matches in Sydney had been between clubs. Some, like Randwick (a strong team), were linked to a suburb, but there were no residential qualifications and many, such as University, Wallaroos (both strong clubs), and Pirates were not linked with specific localities. After some years of dissatisfaction with this system, which tended to result in strong players being attracted to a few powerful clubs, district competition was introduced in 1900, and in the next seven years the sport grew in popularity, stimulated by the novel element of local district loyalties. Numbers were placed on jerseys of players in first grade matches in 1904. Control of the Sydney district competition was in the hands of the Metropolitan Rugby Union, and its annual reports revealed the code's growing prosperity. Australian rules and association football (soccer) were also played in Sydney at this time, but rugby union was the popular winter sport in New South Wales. The heights to which its popularity had risen can be measured by the attendance on 30 June 1906 of sixteen thousand spectators at an ordinary club match between Eastern Suburbs and Glebe. The following year nearly fifty-two thousand people, one tenth of the population of Sydney, crowded into the Cricket Ground to see the first test between Australia and the New Zealand All Blacks; this was the largest attendance then seen at a sporting match in Sydney.[2]

The pattern of the growth of football in Britain had been for football clubs to own their own grounds. This had not been the case in New South Wales. But in 1905 the New South Wales Rugby Union, forced to pay a large proportion of each Saturday's takings to the trustees of various playing fields, began looking around for a ground of their own. In 1907 they decided to purchase, for fifteen thousand pounds, Epping racecourse at Forest Lodge, near Glebe.[3] This decision, which revealed how prosperous the organization had become, was causing a deal of controversy when, in July 1907, Sydney newspapers reported that a team of professional rugby union footballers from New Zealand was planning to tour Britain, to play against the professional teams of rugby footballers known as the Northern Union.

The first professional football in England had been soccer in the 1870s, bred in the northern industrial cities, particularly in Lancashire. In the 1890s the coal and steel cities of western Pennsylvania had produced professional football in the United States of America. At about the same time in England, disputes over non-payment of amateur rugby union footballers for broken time was causing tempers to flare in the northern cities, but the southern clubs blocked all attempts to introduce payments to players for lost working time. In 1895 the rugby code split, and the Northern Rugby Football Union (later known as the English Rugby Football League) was formed, in which players received six shillings to cover the loss of their Saturday's wages.[4]

By the mid-1890s in Britain, therefore, there were two rugby organizations, one amateur, one professional, both playing the same code. But, spurred on by the ardour of revolution and by the need to lure paying customers away from the rival amateur code and through their own turnstiles, the League, the professional organization, began to alter the rules of rugby to produce a more entertaining game. Important changes were the abolition of lineouts, changed points for goals, new play-the-ball rules, abolition of "charges" at free kicks (which encouraged the emergence of star goal kickers), and awarding scrums when the ball was carried into touch. In 1906 the teams were reduced from fifteen to thirteen men.

The new code became strong in the north of England, in parts of Lancashire and Yorkshire ousting association football as the local working-class sport, but failed to develop significantly elsewhere in Britain.

In 1905–6 the first New Zealand All Black rugby union team toured Britain. On this tour some amateur New Zealand footballers first came into contact with the professional organization, starved of the prestige and drawing power of international games since 1893. The germ of professionalism returned with those players to New Zealand. George Smith, one of the team, and Albert Henry Baskerville, a Wellington civil servant, also a rugby union footballer, began to organize a professional team to visit England and play against the English rugby league players. The news that this team was to visit Britain was the spark that ignited the tinder in the rugby union code in Sydney.

There was considerable discontent in rugby union circles in Sydney. The major problem stemmed from unrest among the players. Despite the large amounts of money which the purchase of the Epping ground produced for the rugby union administration, the stars, who drew the crowds and created the profits, were out of pocket. A particular grievance was that footballers injured during the game lost working time and consequently wages and had to pay their own medical fees. But the players were not the only disgruntled element. Some spectators urged changes in the rules to improve the game. There was criticism of the slavish adherence of the local body to the parent English Rugby Union. Moreover, aspirants for administrative positions were chafing under a conservative rugby establishment which was overloaded with conservative politicians and old stalwarts. For example, J. J. Calvert was president of the New South Wales Rugby Union from its foundation in 1874 until his death in 1915.[5]

There were other agents for change. The *Bulletin* on 25 July 1907, reporting the plans for Baskerville's professional team of New Zealanders to visit Britain commented: "The idea of professional football proves very alluring to a number of people in Sydney and some N. S. W. capitalists are considering the question of organizing three or four professional teams to play in and around the big Australian cities." The most important of these "capitalists" was James Joseph Giltinan.

Born in Sydney in 1866, son of a coach-builder, Giltinan is recorded on electoral rolls as "draughtsman", but other sources describe him as a commercial traveller, salesman, or manufacturers' agent. He was prominent in the cricket world and had officiated as an umpire in representative matches. Presumably, it was through his association with cricket that he had met Victor Trumper. Trumper was born in Sydney in November 1877. A cricketer of legendary skill, he was also a man of considerable charm and status. His association with the early organization of rugby league in Sydney was an important factor in its public appeal, though his ownership of a sports depot in Market Street, Sydney, and later a larger shop in George Street, was to lead to accusations that he was reaping private advantage from the new code.

The rugby league tradition has it that in meetings at Trumper's shop in Market Street Giltinan and Trumper conceived the notion of forming in Sydney an association of professional footballers. Others said to have been present at these gatherings were Harry Hoyle, a real estate agent, formerly a politician, and Peter Moir and Alec Burdon, prominent amateur rugby union players. Burdon had suffered an injury, variously described as to his arm or shoulder bone, which was said to have occurred either on a tour of northern New South Wales or in a representative match against Queensland. "He paid his own medical expenses and received no compensation for time lost at work."[6]

Henry Clement Hoyle, the fifth member of the group, provides the first of a series of links between the new football code and the Australian Labor Party. Born in Sydney in 1852, Hoyle was an employee of the New South Wales railways dismissed in 1890 for activity in strike agitation. On the strength of the public notice he received as a result, he won the seat of Redfern in the Legislative Assembly in 1891. He did not join the Labor Party and lost the seat in the next election. However, he later joined the party and won the seat of Surry Hills in 1910, eventually rising to cabinet rank. On 8 August 1907, at Bateman's Crystal Hotel, George Street, Hoyle chaired a meeting of fifty, comprising several leading players and officials, the first primary evidence of the birth of rugby league.

By this time Giltinan had already invited the New Zealand professional players, who came to be known as the "All Golds", to play three matches in Sydney *en route* to England. The meeting of 8 August resolved to form a body called the New South Wales Rugby Football League and elected Hoyle as president, Giltinan secretary, and Trumper treasurer. A committee comprising captains of three first-grade clubs was chosen to select the players to meet the New Zealanders. Four days later Hoyle chaired a second meeting at the same hotel, at which Giltinan revealed that he had written to the English Rugby League proposing that an Australian team tour Britain in 1908.[7]

Three matches were played in Sydney between New South Wales

players, whose blue jerseys bore a kangaroo emblem, and the New Zealand professional team. Played according to rugby union rules, the games were a financial success and secured valuable publicity for Giltinan's scheme. Unfortunately, an attempt by John Wren to arrange a game in Melbourne had to be cancelled because of the tightness of the All Golds' schedule. All the New South Wales players who had played, the "pioneers", were promptly expelled from the Rugby Union. These twenty-two and the other players who had attended the meetings at Bateman's Hotel were the basis for Giltinan's plan to establish in Sydney a full district competition the following season. In the meantime, interest in the new code was kept alive by newspaper reports of the progress of the New Zealand professional team in Britain. One particular reason for the attention the All Golds received in the Australian sporting press was that it included one Australian, Herbert Henry ("Dally") Messenger.

Messenger was born in Balmain in 1883. The son of a boat-builder, he later became apprenticed to his father and worked at the family boatshed at Double Bay. After playing rugby union at school, he entered Eastern Suburbs second-grade side in 1905, and by 1907 it was evident that the young three-quarter was one of the greatest rugby players Australia had produced. A tricky, unorthodox runner with the ball and a phenomenal place-kicker, he had quickly become the star of the rugby union in Sydney. His capture by Giltinan was a major factor in their success. He had performed well in the matches in Sydney against the New Zealanders, who then invited him to join their team for the tour of Britain. There he was the outstanding player in a successful series of games against the English Rugby League and, £350 richer for the tour, he returned in April 1908 in time for the opening of the first season of club rugby league in Sydney.

During the Australian summer of 1908 Giltinan, Trumper, and Hoyle had organized meetings which set up nine district clubs. The first to be formed, on 8 January, seems to have been Newtown.[8] Other clubs that took part in the first year of competition were Glebe, South Sydney, Balmain, Eastern Suburbs, North Sydney, Western Suburbs, Cumberland, and Newcastle.[9] An attempt to form a St George club failed, despite a meeting at Rockdale, probably partly because a St George club had only recently been admitted (1906) into the Metropolitan Rugby Union district competition.[10] However, the failure to establish a rugby league club there in what was in 1908 a relatively middle-class suburb, does point to the working-class nature of the League. The strong clubs were South Sydney, Newtown, Balmain, and Eastern Suburbs. Easts included a fair proportion of the inner-city districts, such as Woolloomoolo, and a down-at-heel boat-building village around Double Bay, unaffected by the cocoon of wealth forming around it.

Glebe, since 1900 a stronghold under the Rugby Union administration (it had won the premiership in 1900, 1901, 1906, and 1907) at first provided only a few of its top players to the League. One area whose adherence to the new code was to be particularly strong was South Sydney. It had won the district rugby union premiership in 1905, but by 1911 was only able to field a first-grade union team by withdrawing from second and third grade competition. Its record in the rugby league competition is, on the other hand, unrivalled.

The class composition of the early Rugby League, underlined by its strength in those areas of inner Sydney where the Labor Party had become firmly established, such as Surry Hills and Balmain, is also discernible in the occupations of the players who joined it. Of the twenty-two "pioneers" disqualified for playing against the All Golds there were four labourers, two painters, two carpenters, one storeman, one waterside worker, one boat builder, one "athlete" (later a fireman), one cleaner, one compositor, one clerk, one dealer (in fish), one boilermaker, one journalist, one draper, one tailor, and two unknown.

The first season of rugby league club football, in 1908, won by South Sydney, was moderately successful. More union players changed to league, and two touring teams from New Zealand, one composed entirely of Maoris, helped to stimulate public interest. The weather was good for the big games, and so, in its risky first season, the Rugby League survived by popular support and the capital of its early promoters.

The headquarters of the new code was undoubtedly Sydney, but rugby union had also been popular in Brisbane, and the upheaval in New South Wales also extended to Queensland. In 1908 a body called the Queensland Amateur Rugby League was established in Brisbane and a team visited Sydney to begin a long series of defeats at the hands of the New South Wales rugby league footballers. One of the founding players in Brisbane was J. A. Fihelly, later to be a minister in Queensland Labor governments.

Fihelly, with Messenger, Burdon, and thirty-two other players, at the end of the 1908 Australian season left for the much-heralded first Australian tour of Britain, managed by Giltinan. The team adopted a Kangaroo hat badge and became, in rugby league terms, the "first Kangaroos". Unfortunately, despite the great financial success of the New Zealand tour the previous year, Giltinan's was a failure. They were dogged by terrible English weather and depressed economic conditions in the north of England. The expected crowds failed to materialize, partly, it was suggested, because the games were played on association football grounds such as Fulham's "Craven Cottage". Their failure was made more bitter by the success of the first Australian rugby union team to tour England and Wales, which occurred simultaneously. At first nicknamed "the Rabbits" by some papers, the union team, captained by Dr H. M. Moran, had met to vote on another, more dignified title and chose "Wallabies". Members of this team won for Australia in 1908, at London, gold medals for rugby football in the Olympic Games.

After the disastrous Kangaroo tour, Giltinan and his team returned, broke, to Australia to find the local Rugby League organization in complete disorder. In his absence a coup had been effected, and Giltinan, Hoyle, and Trumper were voted off the committee for having, apparently, established a "secret fund". Giltinan was forced to carry the expenses of the Kangaroo tour himself and was in consequence bankrupted.[12] The finances of the infant body were in complete disarray and the original founders of the League discredited. In contrast the Rugby Union's organization was solid, their finances strong despite a loss incurred by the Wallaby tour, and their returning team triumphant. Union officials must have felt that they had defeated their upstart rivals. But seven Sydney clubs and Newcastle continued in the 1909 metropolitan district competition.[13] Again matches were played against Queensland and a New Zealand Maori team. Then, at the end of the season the League effected a spectacular coup through the intervention of James Joynton Smith.

Smith's background is hazy, but in the 1880s he had arrived in Sydney from New Zealand and set about making money in the hotel business and in pony racing.[14] It had been Smith who had sold Epping racecourse to the New South Wales Rugby Union in 1907. In August 1909 he was persuaded to finance a series of exhibition matches between the Wallabies and the Kangaroos and devote part of the proceeds to South Sydney Hospital. Members of the Wallaby team were first offered £50 each to defect. By the time the deal was closed, thirteen were to receive £100 each, one, rumoured to be E. F. Mandible, £150, and another, probably Vivian Farnsworth, who had not actually been in the Wallaby team, £50. The *Bulletin* exclaimed: "Few of the footballers earn more than £2 per week; so they were guaranteed practically a year's salary each for a series of three matches. It is reducing football to private enterprise."[15]

The Wallaby v. Kangaroo deal was not without its difficulties for the League. A. Knox, a vice-president of the League and one of those behind the ousting of the early entrepreneurs, resigned in protest, threatening legal action, and the controversy led also to the resignation of E. W. O'Sullivan, MLA who had succeeded Hoyle as president. The scheduling of the Sydney district competition final as a curtain-raiser for the fourth of the Wallaby v. Kangaroo matches caused one of the teams, Balmain, to refuse to play in protest at the loss of gate receipts.[16] Their opponents, South Sydney, thereby won the premiership by forfeit. But these were minor disadvantages of what was in general a decisive success, which secured for the league season of 1910 a new crop of crack players. The New South Wales Rugby Union suddenly realized that they would have to fight the new code for the attention of the Sydney public. The League restructured the Sydney district competition by bringing in a new club, Annandale (with J. J. Giltinan on its committee), in place of Newcastle, which thenceforth conducted its own suburban competition. Better grounds were secured for the League, such as the new Metters Ground, in Newtown, provided by Metters stove company, and North Sydney Oval, which the trustees enclosed with a high fence to ensure profitable gate takings. The League had arranged for an English team to tour Australia during 1910. In retaliation, the Rugby Union announced, as rival attractions, tours of a New Zealand, a Maori, and an American universities team. The *Bulletin* commentd: "The Rugby war is to the knife, and will only end when one crowd is pushed out of existence."[17]

As early as 28 May the trend was emerging. Between fifteen and sixteen thousand turned out to watch a local league club match (Souths v. Newtown) at the Agricultural Ground, compared with twelve thousand at the interstate union game (New South Wales v. Queensland) played on the Sydney Cricket Ground on the same day. A week later forty thousand saw New South Wales play the English rugby league team while the rival code could manage only nine thousand at the New South Wales v. Maoris clash. Later in the month nearly thirty thousand preferred the rugby league nostalgia match, Kangaroos v. England, the proceeds of which after the touring team had taken their percentage were paid to the Kangaroos, who had received only five shillings in 1909 for their matches against the Wallabies. On the same day only fifteen thousand were drawn to the union carnival at the Cricket Ground where two internationals were played — Maoris v. Yankees and All Blacks v. Australia.[18]

Successes such as these caused more footballers to desert rugby union. The league clubs were "becoming choked . . . [with] more players than they [could] provide games for".[19] At the end of the season it was clear that the League had won the rugby war. To some extent the reason was that clashes between England and Australia in any sport would of course attract the crowds, and in the future, regular contests against England were to be a feature of the rugby league programme. Partly, the crowds found that league was a far more entertaining game for the spectator, with movements clear and possession of the ball changing less haphazardly, as well as being less likely to cause serious injury to the player. Partly the league games were more entertaining because they had succeeded in obtaining the star players of the union code. In gratitude, the League turned on a special benefit match for Messenger, which earned him £280, "a pleasant little souvenir for a season of glory". The New South Wales Rugby League, its finances buoyant, was able to boast that it paid two pounds a week to injured first-, second-, and third-grade players.[20]

The Metropolitan Rugby Union, on the other hand, was in "a straitened position". It had not recouped the expenses of the 1909 season and the Wallaby tour. The losses due to the visits of the Maoris, New Zealand and, especially the American universities team were heavy. In March 1911 the Metropolitan Rugby Union announced that it could not provide clubs with the costs of insurance, trainers, or jerseys. Unable to meet the annual payment due to the Sydney Sports Ground, the Union was forced to relinquish that arena to the League; next year the Sydney Cricket Ground Trust was also to decline to renew its agreement with the Union. All these factors contributed to further erosion of support for the amateur game, and by May 1912 the Union had been forced to "get rid of" Epping racecourse.[21]

During the steady deterioration in strength of its rival, the position of the new code continued to improve. The 1911 season was Messenger's most successful in Sydney district football, and he was largely responsible for the victory of his club, Eastern Suburbs. In the Australian summer of 1911-12 a tour of Britain by the "second Kangaroos" captained by one of the former Wallaby team, Chris McKivat, was a remarkable success. Though, like its predecessor, the team suffered a financial loss, it convincingly defeated the English team in the test series on their home grounds, a feat not achieved again for another fifty years. By the start of the 1913 season the League had secured the Sydney Cricket Ground for its matches and was solidly entrenched in Sydney.

A fair proportion of the credit for the successful consolidation of the League after Giltinan's departure belonged to Edward Rennix Larkin. A former policeman and representative union player, Larkin had been appointed full-time secretary to the League in June 1909. For the next five years he was tireless in the cause of the new code

— travelling the state and addressing meetings — cajoling union players into the League. He was assisted by a new committee which seemed less associated with the entrepreneurial adventures of the early days of the code. True, Joynton Smith was the president, but he seems to have been, after his early coup, largely a figurehead. More closely involved in the organization were Fred Flowers (a Labor MLC) and C. H. Ford, who were vice-presidents, and H. R. Miller, treasurer. Larkin had attended St Joseph's College, Hunters Hill, run by the Marist Brothers, and a significant achievement of the committee was the establishment, in 1913, of rugby league as the football game in Sydney's Marist Brothers schools, with the New South Wales Rugby League providing the referees.[22]

In December 1913 Larkin surprised everyone by winning the Legislative Assembly seat of Willoughby for the Labor Party — its first victory on the north side of the harbour. It was a striking continuation of the link between the league code and the Labor Party evidenced by Hoyle's career and Flowers's connections. Larkin's political career was tragically short-lived. He enlisted in August 1914 and was killed at Gallipoli on 25 April 1915.

The effect of the First World War upon the rugby league code was to strengthen it. In contrast to the Rugby League in England, which virtually ceased to exist during the war, and the Rugby Union in New South Wales, which suspended all competition, the Rugby League in Sydney continued to function throughout the war. This reflected its solid working-class composition and the attitudes of that class towards the war. Messenger had retired, but a new crop of crack players, such as the young South Sydney star Harold Horder, continued to draw league supporters to the Sydney Cricket Ground. And, in the absence of any rival code, union followers went too. It was not to be until the late twenties that rugby union began to recover from the effects of the rugby war and the world war.

Rugby League was, in its early stages, essentially a city game in both New South Wales and Queensland. Attempts to form country leagues were not successful, so that Newcastle's area for the first season extended as far north as Tamworth. It was not until 1915 that the League began to consider "a comprehensive scheme for the administration of the game in the country districts".[23]

It is not clear how much players were paid or how "professional" they were. Amateur sporting bodies in Sydney had been persuaded by the Rugby Union authorities to rule that anyone who played rugby league, whether he was paid or not, was a professional. This attempt to stifle the new code was obviously absurd. On the other hand, in the first few years of league, its promoters denied that any player was a professional and claimed that, like Australian cricketers, its footballers received only reimbursement for loss of salary or time while playing the game. But individual players certainly received considerable sums, as the payments to the Wallaby team and to Messenger revealed. The *Bulletin* claimed that the Wallabies' professional opponents in those famous matches in 1909 received only five shillings each, but they too received more the following year.[24] Perhaps the best evidence of how much a good Sydney league footballer received in the early years is provided by J. D. ("Dinny") Campbell, a fine Eastern Suburbs player, who was engaged by an English club. He stated: "In the big matches in New South Wales . . . [I received] a most satisfactory return and on the average in my last season in Sydney would work out to £4 each match." The men who were first-grade footballers in these early years of rugby league were largely of the working class, and to them four pounds a match, as Campbell remarked, was "a most satisfactory return", and probably justifies the label "professional".[25]

In the same interview, no doubt partly to explain the financial rewards received by Australian players, Campbell drew attention to the fact that in the Sydney and Brisbane Rugby League first-grade players had "a powerful representation in the official circles and club circles".[26] This was true; playing footballers held important positions in the administrative organization of the code, reflecting the manner in which the Rugby League was founded in New South Wales. Whereas in England a group of clubs and officials declared unilateral independence, in Australia individual players were lured to the code by entrepreneurs. The players themselves were virtually the founders of new clubs and were strongly represented on management committees. This did cause some problems with the English Rugby League, in particular over the transfer of Australian players to English clubs. The practice of the English body was that the bonus transfer fee was paid to a player's club. The New South Wales Rugby League took the view that its players had the right to make any contract they please with any body not absolutely under its own jurisdiction.[27] Consequently, many Australian players such as Campbell received large sums to play with English clubs.

In some accounts of the emergence of rugby league, the decision to continue competition during the First World War is seen as being the decisive factor in its victory over union for the patronage of the Sydney public.[28] I believe that the rugby war had been won in the seasons 1910–12. By 1915 the new code had consolidated its position to such an extent that the Rugby League was considering itself as more than merely a body to administer football matches. In February 1915 the *Referee* reported: "The Rugby League is not idle during the summer months. It has taken over the United Services Club and means to bring together men who are in sympathy with its aims and to foster the social side all the year round."[29] So was born the first leagues club in New South Wales.

The emergence and growth of rugby league was a reflection of the structures of working-class organization in Sydney. It was no coincidence that many of its leading figures had close links with the Labor Party, nor that the new code should have early established itself in Catholic schools. Its solid grounding in the working class was, indeed, the basis of the new code's strength. A Sydney rugby league supporter was able through the game to give expression to his community and district loyalty in inter-club games, and to his wider loyalties in the matches against Queensland, New Zealand, and, particularly, England. To working men it was no infringement of any particular moral code for the representatives on these occasions to be paid.

For other elements in society, however, payment to sportsmen had disturbing connotations. In 1896, commenting on the hold rugby union had obtained in New South Wales and Queensland, the *Sydney Mail* had been driven to see football as either "a means of physical and moral discipline" or, if freed from proper control, as degenerating into a source of evil.

> There is nothing more all-pervading and more exacting than the discipline of the football field . . . upon it the player is taught to curb his passions, to stand without flinching hard knocks which must come to all sooner or later, to exert his physical powers to the best possible advantage, to practise a ready chivalry, to be vigorous without being rough, and to obtain a control of temper and of impulse which cannot fail to be of value in after life . . . Where . . . rules are not observed, however, both physical and moral harm must come.[30]

The holders of such exalted views of the value of sport were unable to reconcile the amateur ideal with payment for the participants. "The moment a money interest enters a game", warned the *Sydney Morning Herald,*

> it begins to fall a prey to a host of evils . . . professionalism . . . destroys the instinct of legitimate sportsmanship very quickly for the player, and it teaches the onlooker as quickly to mistake the "play" for a contest of gladiators — hired at that. The best thing about our English sports, apart from their intrinsic healthfulness, is that they maintain for us in after life the traditions of the great public school, and extend those traditions into every grade of society.[31]

The split in the ranks of rugby football reflected the inappropriateness of such sentiments in the Sydney of 1907.

Looking back in 1939, H. M. Moran, former captain of that victorious first Wallaby rugby union team of 1908, discussed the effect of the defection of rugby league from the parent body:

> When professionalism was established . . . the game became cleaner because we lost some of the rougher element, but it was not all gain for us. In 1904 Amateur Rugby was still a game for all the classes — just as it is to-day in Wales. There were no social distinctions, nor any systematic professionalism . . . We all stood on a level of equality . . . Those who later became professionals . . . created a social discrimination in Australian rugby.

For Moran, the division of rugby on a class basis meant that "University players were shut out from friendships with men in the ranks called lower and their education suffered by it . . . they now were sentenced to be weaker in humanity".[32] The First World War, as Michael McKernan shows, dramatized the distinction between the amateur and the professional, the middle-class and the working-class view of sport. But in Sydney this division had emerged in 1907 when the players formed the Rugby League and the working men went along to watch them. The success of rugby league in New South Wales during its early years, 1907–15, is an indication not only that it was a more entertaining and spectacular game than its rival codes, but that it stemmed from a secure base in the Sydney community.

NOTES

I am grateful to Sir William McKell, Bede Nairn, Barry Andrews, Don Wilkey, and other colleagues for comments on earlier versions of this paper.

1. Peter Spearritt, "An Urban History of Sydney 1920-1950" (Ph.D. thesis, Australian National University, 1976), chap. 1; J. W. McCarty, "Australian Capital Cities in the Nineteenth Century", *Australian Economic History Review* 10, no. 2 (September 1970): 131.
2. *Daily Telegraph,* 21 May 1900; *Sydney Mail,* 4 May 1904; *Bulletin,* 5 July 1906; *Town and Country Journal,* 17 July 1907.
3. *Sydney Mail,* 10 July 1907; *Bulletin,* 8 August 1907.
4. James Walvin, *The People's Game: The Social History of British Football* (London: Arrow, 1975); Paul Gardner, *Nice Guys Finish Last: Sport and American Life* (London: Allen Lane, 1974); Keith Macklin, *History of Rugby League Football* (London: Stanley Paul, 1974), pp.15-21.
5. *Referee,* 24 March 1918.

6. Jack Pollard, *Ampol's Australian Sporting Records* (Sydney, 1969), p.395.
7. *Sydney Morning Herald*, 10 and 13 August 1907.
8. Pollard, *Ampol's Australian Sporting Records*, p.405.
9. *Sydney Mail*, 20 May 1908.
10. *Arrow*, 7 March 1908.
11. *Town and Country Journal*, 4 November 1908.
12. *Bulletin*, 9 September 1909; *Referee*, 4 February 1914.
13. Cumberland had merged with Western Suburbs after the first season.
14. Sir Joynton Smith, *My Life Story* (Sydney: Cornstalk, 1927).
15. *Bulletin*, 9 September 1909; for further details of payments, ibid., 23 September 1909.
16. *Arrow*, 25 September 1909.
17. *Bulletin*, 28 April 1910.
18. *Bulletin*, 2 and 9 June 1910; *Arrow*, 2 July 1910; *Bulletin*, 30 June 1910.
19. *Bulletin*, 7 July 1910.
20. *Arrow*, 20 June 1908, and Sydney *Sportsman*, 9 September 1908 (for entertaining safer game); *Bulletin*, 13 October 1910 (for Messenger); *Arrow*, 3 September 1910.
21. *Referee*, 25 January 1911; *Arrow*, 11 March 1911; *Referee*, 15 February 1911; *Sportsman*, 8 May 1912.
22. *Referee*, 7 May 1913.
23. *Sydney Morning Herald*, 16 June 1915.
24. *Bulletin*, 17 March 1910.
25. *Referee*, 19 May 1915.
26. Ibid.
27. *Referee*, 18 June 1913.
28. For example, Pollard, *Ampol's Australian Sporting Records*, p.378.
29. *Referee*, 3 February 1915; see also 5 May 1915.
30. *Sydney Mail*, 8 August 1896.
31. *Sydney Morning Herald*, 6 August 1907.
32. H. M. Moran, *Viewless Winds* (London: Peter Davies, 1939), pp.36-37.

The Sport of Kings and Commoners: the Commercialization of British Horse-Racing in the Nineteenth Century

During the nineteenth century, horse-racing changed considerably in character, in structure, and in organization. At the beginning of the century, racing was basically a national sport carried on at local level. Generally, meetings were annual, one-day affairs intimately associated with local holidays; along with the racing there would be sideshows, itinerant entertainers, and other amusements. The degree of commercialization within racing was low: spectators did not pay for their pleasure, most jockeys were little more than liveried servants, and even the best thoroughbred stallions could not obtain a stud fee of more than fifty guineas. By the end of the century, racing drew its spectators from far and wide, the carnival atmosphere had been dampened down, and the sport had become much more commercial. Racing companies had enclosed courses and were charging spectators entry fees; even ordinary jockeys, if these extraordinary individuals can ever be so termed, were earning a thousand pounds a year; and a fashionable stallion, able to command six hundred guineas a service, could be yielding his owner in excess of twenty thousand pounds per annum.[1] Other changes followed in the wake of commercialization: sprints, handicaps, and two-year-old racing began to dominate race cards previously full of long-distance, weight-for-age events; licensed professional officials working throughout the racing season generally replaced the amateur starter or handicapper who officiated at one or perhaps two meetings a year; and a racing press developed to throw open the stable doors to the working-class punter. These changes, and the factors producing them, are not merely of significance to racing: they can throw light on nineteenth-century living standards, on the general development of mass leisure industries, and on the performance of the Victorian entrepreneur.

Horse-racing in 1800 was much the same as it had been for the past fifty years or more. Most meetings were one-day, annual holiday events to which the local community came to enjoy the fun of the fair; travelling shows, gaming booths, beer tents, cockfights, boxing and wrestling matches, open-air dancing, and, for a privileged few, balls and dinner parties, all contributed to a full day's entertainment along with the racing. This social function aspect of racing was one reason why many meetings held races not just for thoroughbred racehorses but also for half-bred horses, hunters, or even ponies. The local race meeting was a high point of the community's sporting and social calendars. Starved of organized public entertainment, the local populace came determined to enjoy *their* meeting, and if it was possible to participate at more than spectator level then people wished to do so; hence farmers raced, and frequently rode, their half-breeds and others their thoroughbred hunters and racing stock.[2] A further reason for the variety of equine competition was that as long as horses had to be walked to meetings they tended to race only locally, which restricted the number of thoroughbred entrants at any particular gathering. Heats were another device to obtain a full day's racing from a limited supply of horses. The winner of an event was the first horse to win two heats; this could often require four or more races.

Unless they wished to view from the grandstand (not that there always was one), spectators at these meetings did not have to pay to see the horses run.[3] Possibly the race committee, usually local notables or their nominees, were deterred from charging entrance money by paternalistic feelings of responsibility towards the community: something along the lines that racing was an integral part of a local holiday and the basic ingredient of that day should be provided free. However, there were also practical problems associated with the introduction of gate money. Entry fees to the grandstand could be collected, as access was relatively easily restricted: two or three burly gatemen could see to that. For the racecourse as a whole, however, restricted entry was not so easily attained. Enclosure would have been necessary and this was not possible where racing took place on common ground. Elsewhere it was legal but expensive, and it was far from certain that the returns would justify the outlay. If they were not to be grossly uneconomic, enclosed meetings would have to be held more regularly than were the existing annual social gatherings so as to cover the increased overhead costs, but there was no guarantee that sufficient spectators could be persuaded to come to race meetings more regularly, particularly if they would have to pay for their viewing.

Clearly there was plenty of time available for recreation.[4] Conditioned by the climate and the ecclesiastical calendar, agricultural work, the dominant economic activity well into the nineteenth century, was unevenly spread over the year. In addition, independent farmers, task-work labourers, craftsmen, and domestic industry workers had some choice in their working routine. Although with the Industrial Revolution there came an insistence by industrial capitalism that time was now spent, not passed, it was only in large-scale, machine-powered industries that working hours were almost totally inflexible, and relatively few members of the occupied population were factory employees. Whether potential racegoers had the money as well as the time is not so certain. Professor Flinn's survey of price and wage data concluded that "from such figures as we have . . . it would be a brave historian who would assert that real wages were generally advancing" before 1788–92 and suggested that "there are relatively few indications of significant changes in levels of real wages either way before 1810/14".[5] Even if both time and money were available, there was still the transport problem, for the poor state of inland communication limited the spectator catchment area of any course. When all is said and done, it was far easier for the race committee to continue along traditional lines than to attempt to create an enclosed meeting.

Although racing at the beginning of the nineteenth century retained much of its traditional character, there had been changes, and these intensified as the century progressed. Younger horses were being raced, long-distance heats were gradually being abandoned, races for heavyweight amateur jockeys were becoming increasingly difficult to find, and sweepstake races with several entrants were being substituted for matches between two or possibly three horses.[6] Perhaps there was simply a growing awareness that younger horses could produce races just as exciting as any by mature animals; possibly long-distance heats died out because they became farcical with the first two miles of a four mile heat being taken at little more than walking pace;[7] and it is possible that the rise of the sweepstake race reflected a desire to prove that one's horse was a true champion, capable of taking on all comers and not merely a few selected challengers. But all these changes can also be explained in terms of a growing commercial attitude towards racing on the part of some owners: sweepstakes meant that owners risked less for the chance of winning more; employing specialist, professional jockeys increased the chances of winning; and racing younger horses meant that investment in bloodstock could yield a return much earlier than before. Once younger horses ran, shorter races and lightweight jockeys followed almost inevitably; owners did not have to be in racing for the money to appreciate the foolishness of risking the breakdown of valuable horseflesh.

The problem is to account for this changed attitude on the part of owners. It can be tentatively suggested that the changing norms and values of a rural society in transition came to be reflected in all the activities of that society. Britain had undergone an agricultural revolution in the process of which economic behaviour had become increasingly conditioned by the profit motive. It is not beyond the bounds of credulity to suggest that some owners took this attitude into their leisure pursuits; others then adopted their practices, if not their motivations, in order to compete effectively with them in racing. Whatever the reason for its development, there is evidence for the growing importance of economic attitudes in racing: in the 1830s both Ascot and Newmarket, despite their social and racing prestige, found difficulty in attracting sufficient runners because of their inadequate level of prize-money; and in 1842 the York race committee established a public subscription for the purpose of making additions to the prize fund as such added money had "materially contributed to the prosperity of racing at other places".[8]

Although racing had changed, the degree of change should not be exaggerated. Even by 1840 many race meetings remained one-day, annual holiday affairs; social functions rather than economic events.[9] Two factors were restricting development: the limited amount of prize-money and the problems of transport. Most prize-money came from the owners themselves in the form of stakes and forfeits. In addition there would be subscriptions from local hoteliers, victuallers, brewers, and others who stood to benefit financially from the meeting, rents from the proprietors of the beer tents and gaming booths, financial patronage from the local gentry and from the borough or county member of parliament, entry fees from those using the public grandstand, and rentals from the owners of private stands. Prize-money had risen, from £115,000 in 1807 to £143,000 in 1839, but until the spectator was made to pay at the gate, a potential major source of funds was not being tapped. However, the solitary attempt to charge entrance money — at the Bayswater Hippodrome — ended in financial disaster, as insufficient racegoers were willing to pay a shilling to view what was available elsewhere without charge.[10]

The other limiting factor was transport. Although a few meetings, notably Ascot, Epsom, and Goodwood in the south and Doncaster in the north, had attained more than local social significance, they, like all other meetings,[11] drew the vast majority of their supporters from the immediate surrounding population; before the coming of the railways, only wealthy racegoers could afford to travel far. Transport, of course, was of importance to more than spectators. Any owner wishing to race any distance from his horse's training quarters had to set his animal walking well before the race: from Goodwood to Epsom or Ascot took four days, to Newmarket a week, and to Doncaster almost a fortnight.[12] Yet, despite the difficulties, by the late 1830s the desire of owners to race further afield had led to the emergence of half a dozen racing circuits, within which the better horses travelled to take on each other and also local challengers. However, except for large stakes and prestige events, racehorses rarely left their chosen circuits. For both spectators and horses, racing still remained very much a national sport pursued at local or regional level.

The first major breakthrough in transport came in the 1830s with the development of vanning. Credit for pioneering this is usually given to Lord George Bentinck. When he could not get the odds he wanted on his horse, Elis, for the 1836 St Leger, Bentinck made no apparent effort to send the animal to Doncaster; Elis was still in his Goodwood training quarters only days before the race and the betting fraternity naturally assumed that he would not run. The odds widened till they reached a level that satisfied Bentinck, whereupon he placed his bets and dispatched the horse northwards in a van drawn by four horses; the victorious Elis left far more to his rear at Doncaster. Despite the publicity, Bentinck was not the first to van a racehorse. Twenty years previously Mr Territt's Sovereign had arrived at Newmarket having come from Worcester in a padded bullock van; Territt was a grazier and often sent his quality fat bullocks to auction on horse-drawn floats.[13] The time-lag between Territt and Bentinck is not easy to explain. It probably had something to do with expense; a pair of post-horses could cost upwards of two shillings a mile, and Elis's trip reputedly set Lord George back about a hundred pounds. Such outlays could not be warranted by the level of prize-money, especially when horses could be walked anyway. All that vanning saved was time, and this was money really only to gamblers: it must be conjectured that Bentinck was the first among them to appreciate the possibilities. Owners had little to gain. Perhaps vanning would have allowed horses to race more frequently, but the racing circuits that had evolved enabled horses to undertake walking tours, competing at meetings arranged to fit in with their travels. Although vanning allowed them to race outside their chosen circuits, it was expensive, especially in relation to the prize-money that could be won. Nevertheless, the publicity given to Bentinck's venture did stimulate a move into vanning. In 1838 the *Sporting Magazine* reported: "The system of transporting horses by van is being felt everywhere, and Scotland particularly reaps the advantage in common with every far-off district."[14]

The era of vanning was short-lived. Within four years of Elis travelling to Doncaster by van, the clerk of the course at Newcastle was anticipating the arrival of southern horses sent north by rail. The railways could offer all that vanning could, and more. They were much cheaper and so worth using even if the level of prize-money had remained unaltered, but in fact the railway companies helped raise the level of prize-money from £143,000 in 1839 to £315,000 in 1874. They did this indirectly by bringing more spectators and directly by sponsoring races. This increased prize-money, attracted larger fields, which in turn further raised the volume of prize-money from entry fees and stake money. Railways were also much faster than vans: horses did not need to leave their training quarters till the day before the race or even on the morning of the race day itself, which cut down the risk of a horse being "got at", something always easier outside the security of the stable. Once the railway network had extended into the provinces there was no real alternative for most owners and trainers. Horses could easily race outside the traditional circuits without undue cost or waste of time; in fact the railways produced a shift in the circuits so that eventually, instead of half a dozen regional ones, there emerged a nation-wide circuit of major meetings and a fluctuating set of lesser events, extremely local in character and seldom having a permanent date in the racing calendar.[15]

Spectators as well as horses gained from the speed of the railway. The provision of special race trains encouraged followers of the turf to attend race meetings other than the ones in their immediate vicinity. All courses close to a station found their spectator catchment area both widened and deepened by the speed and convenience of railway travel. Racing did not need these extra spectators; although the atmosphere a crowd created heightened its own enjoyment, this did not positively benefit racing. Nevertheless, although the new attenders, like the old, did not pay entrance money, they contributed indirectly to the prize fund since their spending encouraged the booth proprietors to pay increased rentals. Most race committees thus welcomed them.[16]

By now more people could afford to go racing. It is generally acknowledged that real wages rose after the 1840s. Even Professor Hobsbawm, no optimist in his interpretation of the effects of the Industrial Revolution, admits that although "there may or may not have been deterioration between the middle 1790s and the middle 1840s . . . thereafter, there was undoubted improvement". There was certainly improvement in the 1860s; perhaps an increase of 10 per cent in average real wages compared with the previous decade.

But did the mass of the population have the time to go to the races? One leading social historian has argued that by the 1830s or 1840s the industrial worker had so absorbed the values of industrial capitalism that he accepted long and unremitting hours of labour.[17] Nevertheless, in other sectors of the economy there remained ample opportunity for daytime midweek leisure activity. Agriculture, with its irregular work patterns, was still the largest single employer in 1850; outwork survived in several manufacturing industries; the docks and ports had an army of casual labour; and large numbers of self-employed craftsmen maintained control over their working hours. Even in the factories there is evidence that at times workers simply took time off to attend their local race meeting.[18]

Rising incomes, sufficient leisure time, and improved transport facilities encouraged the emergence of new meetings: in the 1850s there were sixty-two new events, and in the 1860s there were ninety-nine. There was also a distinct trend towards holding both longer meetings and more than one meeting a year. A few of the new meetings were revivals of languished social gatherings, but most were commercial speculations, designed to extract money from the racegoer by way of the stands, booths, or facilities of the town.[19] At the rougher meetings there were sometimes brute-force attempts to collect entrance money, but there were still no enclosed, gate-money meetings: no entrepreneur was yet convinced that there was a market large enough to warrant the initial expenditure. The rate of failure among the newly founded meetings could not have been encouraging. Of the sixty-two begun in the 1850s, only twenty-nine lasted for at least five years and only sixteen for ten; and of the ninety-nine founded in the 1860s, fifty lasted for at least five years but only twenty-four for ten.

In 1875, however, Sandown Park opened its turnstiles as an enclosed course, entry to which required a fee from *all* racegoers. It was an instant commercial and racing success. Others followed where Sandown had showed the way, and within two to three decades racing was taking place at enclosed courses all over Britain.[20]

The success of the enclosed meeting was a function of its ability to attract paying spectators. Here two groups attained new significance: women and the working class. Before the advent of the enclosed meeting, relatively few women went to race meetings. Of course the upper-class women went to Ascot, where there was the royal enclosure and the lawn to accommodate them; Epsom and, especially, Goodwood, run under the aegis of the Duke of Richmond, also were part of the social season. Elsewhere, however, even at Newmarket, ladies were rarely seen except for a few in carriages or in private or stewards' stands. Respectability inhibited them from making use of the free areas or even the public grandstands. This social precept was acknowledged by the enclosed courses when they attempted to attract female spectators. From its inception Sandown encouraged their attendance by the formation of a racing club whose membership was carefully vetted to ensure an aura of respectability. Although club membership was a male prerogative, members who subscribed at the higher rate obtained two ladies' badges, and other subscribers could take in two ladies on the payment of a small fee. Similar clubs were formed at all enclosed courses to provide pleasurable racing for the wealthier supporters of the turf and their womenfolk: the races, luncheon, the musical accompaniment, even just strolling around the lawns and flower beds could all be enjoyed in comfort. For many, racing would merely be a backdrop for other activities. By the turn of the century several thousand women could be expected to attend the most important meetings.[21]

The other major new source of revenue was the working class, more of whom became both able and willing to pay to see racing. There are, of course, difficulties in generalizing about *the* working class; at any time the skilled artisan could probably afford a wider range of recreational activity than the labourer or the factory hand. Most economic historians, however, would accept that, for the bulk of the working class, real incomes rose between the 1850s and the end of the century. Admittedly before the 1880s most of the rise was attributable to money wages moving ahead of prices and was thus probably restricted to those groups with the strongest bargaining power, but from then on falling prices brought greater prosperity to the working class on a broad front. Overall, between 1850 and 1900 average real wages rose some 70 per cent. Initially, spending was possibly expanded along conventional consumption lines, but certainly by the 1880s new spending patterns were emerging; entrepreneurs had responded to the new market stimulus and had developed goods and services suited to a "mass consumer" society, among them commercialized leisure. It may be that the Sandown Park executive was not attempting to tap the working-class market in any depth since their minimum admission charge before 1914 was never less than half a crown which contrasts unfavourably with the sixpence generally charged to see a top-class football match.[22] Most other enclosed courses, however, took a shilling as the basic entry fee; this was still expensive relative to soccer but within the pocket of sufficient working men to satisfy the course management. It must be stressed that it is not being argued that every worker could afford to go to race meetings; clearly the contemporary social surveys repudiate such a notion. However, it should also be pointed out that a basic deficiency of many budgetary studies which show how much was left for recreational purposes after necessary expenditure is their reluctance to admit that *all* spending is optional. Human beings are perverse creatures, often finding greater satisfaction in activities other than those meeting basic physiological needs. How many spectators at race meetings nutritionally could not afford to be there is a matter for conjecture. Nevertheless, it seems reasonable to correlate the rise of the enclosed race meeting with the increase in working-class spending power.

Of course, that the working man had more money in his pocket for recreational expenditure did not mean that he would necessarily spend it at the races. Not only had racing to compete against other leisure activities, but even among racegoers the enclosed course did not have a captive market; the railways had seen to that. Although the Jockey Club organized the racing calendar so as to prevent serious fixture clashes, courses were still in competition with one another for spectators, as the average racegoer had limited funds and leisure time at his disposal. If he was to be persuaded to pay for his pleasure rather than frequent a meeting which did not charge gate-money, then he had to be offered something different for his money; in other words, the product of the gate-money meeting had to be differentiated from that of the unenclosed course.

One way was to offer Saturday afternoon racing. This was partly forced upon the new, enclosed courses because many existing meetings, to whom the Jockey Club gave priority, would not have a Saturday, traditionally a day for taking horses home from a meeting, but no doubt as the Saturday half day became more common there was a positive advantage in choosing to race on a Saturday. It was also made easy for the racegoer to attend; almost all the new courses had a railway station within a short walking distance, often with a covered walkway from the platform to the stands. The racing at the enclosed meetings was usually of a high standard, featuring top-quality horses and jockeys. Spectators could always be attracted by great performers, who in turn were attracted by the high level of prize-money offered by the gate-money meetings, itself partially a product of the numbers attending. Primarily, however, the race promoters attracted their audience by offering the type of racing that the crowd wished to see: two-year-old races, sprints, and handicaps, all of which had a sufficient degree of uncertainty about the result to make for exciting racing.[23]

Giving the spectators the type of racing they preferred also served another purpose. Before courses were enclosed, crowd disorder at race meetings was virtually taken for granted.[24] Although the beer and gaming tents contributed to the crowd problem — no doubt alcohol and gambling losses provoked many a fracas — the race fund needed the rents from the booths. At most meetings the clerk of the course would simply employ a few pugilists to protect the horses and other racing property, and a gentleman or two to keep undesirables out of the stands. At the society events, police would also be in attendance to control the rough element with a strong hand. Generally, however, as long as the masses, in their anger or exuberance, damaged only themselves and did not offend anyone who mattered, those in charge were content. Anyway to keep the crowd firmly in order would have required a force of policemen, and most race committees could not afford this. Others saw no need to, for at many meetings there was little property that could be damaged.

With enclosure, things changed. There was too much property at risk if the crowd got out of hand, so the course executives took steps to improve crowd behaviour. One way in which they reduced the crowd's propensity to riot was by employing licensed, specialist officials so that the public had less reason to suspect malpractice by handicappers, starters, or judges. Segregation was also seen as a way of reducing trouble. It was done by differential pricing for the different enclosures, by vetting the membership of the racing clubs, and by absolute exclusion.[25] Traditionally, segregation had merely been a matter of keeping the riff-raff out of the stands; now the lower elements of the racing world were not even to be allowed on the course. Thus pickpockets, thimblemen, coiners and forgers, thugs, welshers, and prostitutes would be much less likely to provoke trouble. Licit ancillary activities were also cut down. Gaming and drinking became stringently controlled: booth rents were less important now that spectators were paying at the gate, so the enclosed course executives restricted such facilities both in volume and character. It was not merely beer and betting that were controlled. Itinerant entertainers, tipsters, and traders all found themselves less welcome than before: indeed the whole holiday atmosphere of racing was dampened down. However, in order to encourage the racegoing public to accept the change, racing itself was changed and spectators were offered sprints and handicaps rather than the traditional weight-for-age, staying events.[26]

Not all enclosed meetings were successful. Portsmouth Park, Hedon Park (Hull), and Four Oaks Park (Birmingham), where a hundred thousand pounds was lost, were conspicuous failures, partly because of an inability to obtain suitable dates. Nevertheless, the majority of the new, enclosed meetings were financial and racing successes; so much so that many older, established fixtures were forced to follow suit and adopt the style of the modern racing company by rebuilding stands for the general public, creating club enclosures for more select racegoers, and charging a shilling for admittance to the outside portion of the course.[27] Even where they did not enclose to the extent of Sandown and its imitators, they offered less free space than before. Primarily this was done not to make money but to preserve the quality of their racing. They could only hope to attract the best horses by increasing their prize-money to a level commensurate with that offered by the enclosed meetings, but this could only be done if the funds were available. Admittedly, owners were still basically racing for their own money — even in 1905, entry fees from owners provided two-thirds of all prize-money — but prizes had to be underwritten, for there was always the possibility that insufficient entries would be forthcoming to guarantee the promised reward.[28] Contributions could be solicited from local hotel-keepers, shopkeepers, and railway companies; and there was always half the surplus from "selling races".[29] The best way to make sure of having sufficient funds, however, was to charge at the gate, and this involved some form of enclosure. Without this it would be difficult to compete against the gate-money meeting. The choice was simple: either you erected fences or you went to the wall. Most unenclosed meetings either disappeared or struggled along with racing of an inferior quality. The situation was no doubt aggravated by a Jockey Club ruling of 1877 which demanded that race committees provide a minimum of three hundred sovereigns added money for each day of racing.

One can only speculate about the demise of the "social" race meeting, so dominant in the eighteenth century. Many simply lost their traditional local character and patronage as the railways brought participants and spectators from far afield. Possibly, at least for the rural population, the point-to-point replaced the flat meeting as the local social sporting event of the year.[30] Certainly for the urban workers new forms of paternalistic leisure emerged under the aegis of muscular Christianity and productivity-conscious employers in the form of works football and cricket teams, brass bands, and sponsored outings.

That prestige and a good name for racing was insufficient to preserve an open meeting intact is clear from the experience of Newmarket. Here, despite the testing variety of courses and an acknowledged racing reputation, the Jockey Club found that the level and quality of entrants was such as to leave it "no alternative but to march with the times, to build stands, to make enclosures, to substitute the white rails of modern civilisation for the old-fashioned ropes and stakes of our forefathers". Pedestrians and horsemen were still allowed free entry to most of the Heath, but heavy tolls were exacted from carriage owners everywhere and from all who used the stands and other spectator facilities.[31]

A few open meetings, however, did far more than merely survive: at Ascot, Epsom, Goodwood, Doncaster, and York, racing flourished. The charisma of traditional prestige events may have offered some protection; but if this was true, why had the prize-money for the Derby, the blue riband of the turf, to be raised to a level comparable to the best prizes at the enclosed meetings? Their real protection lay with their position in the social calendar: members and would-be members of high society felt a social obligation to put in an appearance at these meetings. Certificates of social seaworthiness, however, did not come cheaply — a private box at Ascot could cost over twelve guineas. The payments of the elite produced ample funds for prize-money — in 1900, Ascot gave over thirty-seven thousand pounds to its twenty-eight races — and it was this which was the major attraction for owners. Yet even these major open courses still found "it necessary from time to time to alter their programmes and keep step in the quick march of the day, lest they too should be fair to take their place in the rear of the companies".[32]

The admission money of paying spectators enabled a greater volume of prize-money to be offered: in 1874 £315,000 was won; by 1905 the total was £495,000. The greater rewards encouraged more horse ownership, and the number of horses in training rose from 2,534 in 1869, the highest pre-enclosure total, to 3,957 by 1902. Estimates suggest that in the period 1877 to 1891 investment in racing bloodstock rose from £1.7 million to more than £3 million and jumped to between £7 million and £8 million by 1913. Here there was another influence at work besides that of the gate-money meeting. The late nineteenth century witnessed a move into race-horse ownership by successful men from industry and commerce.[33] These men were probably seeking social rather than economic returns from their investment in horseflesh. Nevertheless, their spending had economic consequences for racing. Successful in business, they were determined to be equally to the fore in racing. They wanted success and they wanted it quickly: unwilling to wait till they had bred a good horse, they frequented the sale-ring.

Competitive bidding pushed up the price of horses, thus reinforcing the trend begun by the enclosed course and by increased prize-money.

As owners sought to buy success, the pressure on the bloodstock industry sent stud fees soaring. In 1869 only the leading stallion in the country could command a service charge of a hundred guineas, but by 1909 twenty-four stallions obtained such a fee and the leading stallion was making six hundred guineas a mare, whether or not she became pregnant. The technological spin-off from thoroughbred breeding also changed. Apologists for racing had always defended their sport on the grounds of public utility, namely the improvement of British bloodstock. Certainly the improvement of the thorough-bred led to improvements in the quality of other breeds, particularly light horses, but was racing necessary to attain this? Of course it was, said the supporters of the turf, for how else could the relative merits of thoroughbreds be assessed adequately. Looks would be an illusory method, as they did not demonstrate the possession of soundness, speed, and stamina: the racecourse test alone did this.[35] In a way, the argument that racing improved the breed was fallacious, for racing performance in itself is not hereditary. Genetic inheritence merely set the limits; how near those limits were approached depended on many factors, not least the abilities of trainer and jockey. A more important flaw in the argument was that the type of racehorse produced was dictated not by the needs of the country, or the light horse industry, but by the level of prize-money offered for different types of racing, and increasingly as the nineteenth century progressed this money was going to two-year-old and spring racing, not the kind of events that would encourage breeding for stamina and strength. The development of the enclosed course and the ensuing competition for both spectators and horses further increased the prize-money available to two-year-olds. By the late 1880s all the principal meetings had valuable events for such horses, and at most meetings there was more money for sprints and two-year-old racing than for stamina-testing distance races. The response of owners and breeders was predictable: as a proportion of all horses racing, two-year-olds increased from about 20 per cent in 1849 to 40 per cent and over in the last decades of the century.[36] Such a concentration was not good for the general bloodstock industry; immature horses were susceptible to breakdown, and sprints hid stamina deficiencies. How could horses running only five or six furlongs carrying a mere seven stones or so contribute to the improvement, or even the soundness, of hunters, hacks, or, of more importance, army remounts? Clearly at the end of the nineteenth century little deliberate linkage can be seen between racehorse breeding and general bloodstock improvement.

Naturally owners had always wanted to win, but increased prize-money and rising stud fees for those horses which had been successful on the track now placed an even greater premium on winning. Other things being equal, and often when they were not, it was the skill of the jockey that determined the result of the race. There was thus a high and increasing demand for the services of top-class jockeys, and since the supply of such talent was extremely limited, the normal working of supply and demand ensured high rewards for the gifted. Although the basic riding fee was three guineas with an extra two guineas for winning, presents and retainers to the top-rank riders produced "an annual total before which 2,000 guineas in bare riding fees shrinks into insignificance". It is possible to trace instances of valuable presents throughout the nineteenth century, but generally in the first two-thirds of the century they were either for classic victories or were isolated examples of an individual's generosity or eccentricity. After that, however, large presents became the norm for any big race. Retainers rose strikingly in the latter decades of the century. Frank Butler, Sam Rogers, and Jem Robinson, all leading jockeys in the 1830s and 1840s, respectively received retainers of a hundred pounds, fifty pounds, and twenty-five pounds. These can be contrasted with George Fordham's perennial thousand pounds in the 1880s, Fred Archer's thirty-six hundred pounds in 1881, Tod Sloan's five thousand pounds in 1899, the fifteen thousand pounds given to Tom Cannon for a three-year retainer in the 1880s, and the eight thousand pounds obtained by Danny Maher in 1910.[37] Admittedly, even before racing came under the influence of the enclosed course, one or two jockeys had made five thousand pounds in a season, but in the last two decades of the nineteenth century at least ten jockeys a year were making such an amount. By this time any competent jockey, capable of winning a handful of races, could be earning a thousand pounds a year, and, it was enviously claimed, "even the commonest jockey-boy in this company of mannikins [could] usually earn more than the average scholar or professional man".[38]

By the close of the nineteenth century, racing had changed significantly from its eighteenth-century form. The prime reason for this was growing commercialization within the sport, a development stimulated by rising living standards, improved transport, and entrepreneurial talent. Above all, the enclosed, gate-money meeting stands out as an agent of change: indeed, it forced transformation upon the turf, for if race committees did not innovate to meet its challenge they frequently disappeared. Although commercial enterprise had always been associated with race meetings, the enclosed-course executives took it beyond the refreshment tents and gaming booths. By differentiating their product from that of the traditional style of meeting they persuaded the racegoer to pay to see racing. Previously, most race committees had put the owner before the spectator, but with enclosure it became impossible to serve the owners' interests without also considering those of the crowd. In offering the crowd what they wanted to see, race committees were tempting spectators to pay for their pleasure, and this money, by underwriting the increased level of prize-money, had further consequences for racing as seen in the increased ownership, rising stud fees, and high rewards for jockeys. Clearly, by the end of the nineteenth century, racing was as much a part of the economic as the social scene: it was an industry as well as a sport.

NOTES

The author gratefully acknowledges financial help in the preparation of this paper from the Carnegie Trust for the Universities of Scotland and from the research funds of Edinburgh University, and the Flinders University of South Australia.

1. In these inflationary days it is difficult to put these figures in perspective, but in terms of 1970 spending power a thousand pounds of late Victorian money would equal somewhere between six thousand and eight thousand pounds.
2. This is brought out in the surveys of racing in the *Victoria County Histories*. It is becoming clear that in the eighteenth century there was a wide range of recreational activity pursued by the lower ranks of society, but to a great extent this was self-made entertainment. What *organized* entertainment there was tended to be irregular and frequently on a one-off basis. See Robert W. Malcolmson, *Popular Recreations in English Society, 1700-1850* (Cambridge: Cambridge University Press, 1973); J. H. Plumb, *The Commercialisation of Leisure in Eighteenth Century England* (Reading: Department of History, University of Reading, 1974) argues that leisure was becoming increasingly commercialized and supports his case by listing an array of activities which involved consumer expenditure, but he does not show that such activities were regularly organized or that they were available to the mass of the population.
3. Plumb, *Commercialisation of Leisure*, p.10, argues that eighteenth-century racing had a paying public, but he does not cite any supporting evidence. Possible he has become confused between spending to see the races and spending at the races. Most spectators wanted more than a view of the horses, a fact well appreciated by the lessees of the gambling booths, beer tents, and food stalls.
4 See E. P. Thompson, "Time, Work-Discipline, and Industrial Capitalism", *Past and Present* 38 (December 1967), and Malcolmson, *Popular Recreations*.
5. M. W. Flinn, "Trends in Real Wages, 1750-1850", *Economic History Review* 27 (1974): 395-411. T. R. Gourvish's challenge to Flinn has not really changed the position. "Flinn and Real Wage Trends in Britain, 1750-1850": A Comment",

Economic History Review 29 (1976): 136-42. The very fact that there has been controversy over the course of real wages lends support to Professor Flinn's claims of only modest gains: one can argue about the existence of fairies at the bottom of the garden, but the presence of giants can hardly be a subject for debate.

6. At the beginning of the eighteenth century, few horses raced before the age of five. Races for two-year-olds and three-year-olds developed from the mid-century, but though the latter soon became generally acceptable, as symbolized in the foundation of the Derby, Oaks, and St Leger in the 1770s and 1780s, the former received no such stamp of approval till 1827 when the Criterion Stakes was begun at Newmarket. In 1797, eight per cent of horses that raced were two-year-olds; in 1832 the proportion had risen to sixteen per cent (figures calculated from the *Racing Calendar*). Unfortunately for the eighteenth century, our evidence is impressionistic rather than quantified, but certainly there was a sharp drop in the importance of matches in the nineteenth century. One estimate suggests that in 1807 matches made up twenty-six per cent of all races but had declined to seven per cent by 1843. H. J. Rous, *On the Laws and Practice of Horse Racing* (London: A. H. Bailey, 1850), p.x.

7. C. J. Apperley, "The Turf", *Quarterly Review* 49 (1883):388.

8. C. J. Cawthorne and R. S. Herod, *Royal Ascot* (London: Longmans, 1900), p.58; *New Sporting Magazine* of 1833 cited in Richard Onslow, *The Heath and the Turf* (London: Barker, 1972), p.41; entry in Minute Book of York Race Committee, quoted in *Notes for York Race Committee*, p.5. York Racecourse records.

9. In 1823 the *Racing Calendar* listed 95 racecourses, of which 87 had only one meeting a year. In 1840 the proportion was 120 out of 137. (There may be an illusion of an increasing volume of racing because of the incomplete coverage of the Racing Calendar in those years.) In 1848, by which time the *Calendar*'s coverage was more comprehensive, sixty-one meetings were one-day events, fifty-six lasted at least a day longer, but only thirteen courses hosted more than one meeting a year.

10. *Select Committee on Gaming* 1844 VI, q. 1267-70, 1301; Rous, *Laws and Practice*, p.x; J. C. Whyte, *History of the British Turf* (London, n.p., 1840), pp.xiv, 189, 2747-77; James Rice, *The History of the British Turf* (Lonon, n.p., 1879), pp.202-5.

11. Newmarket was the solitary exception to this. Here racing was almost exclusively for the upper-class owner and spectator. In contrast to Epsom where, on Derby Day, a crowd of over a hundred thousand could be expected, attendances at Newmarket rarely exceeded five hundred "and they [were] mostly of the higher classes, the majority on horseback, with perhaps a few close carriages and barouches for invalids and ladies". Here racing existed "in perfection" with no crowds or booths to obscure the view and "none of those discordant sounds which make a perfect Babel of other racecourses". Whyte, *History of the British Turf*, p.209. At Newmarket, racing was the only thing of importance; a third of all registered racehorses were trained there, all to participate in the seven annual meetings, each of which lasted several days. Royal patronage, Jockey Club authority, and ideal, if testing, ground for racing and training had all contributed to raising Newmarket to a pre-eminent position as the headquarters of British racing.

12. Earl of Suffolk and Berkshire, and Arthur Coventry, *Racing and Steeplechasing* (London: Longmans, Green, 1886), p.211.

13. John Kent, *The Racing Life of Lord George Cavendish Bentinck M. P.* (London: Blackwood and Sons, 1892), pp.60-70. Suffolk, *Racing and Steeplechasing*,

pp.44-45, says that Bentinck borrowed a van that Lord Chesterfield used for show cattle, but modern writers, such as Roger Mortimer, *The Jockey Club* (London, Cassell, 1958), pp.59, 66, and Roger Longriff, *The History of Horse Racing* (London: Macmillan, 1972), p.120, suggest that he had it specially constructed; The Druid, *Scott and Sebright* (London: Warne, 1895), p.67.

14. Suffolk, *Racing and Steeplechasing*, p.212; Robert Rodrigo, *The Racing Game* (London: Phoenix Sport Books, 1960), p.25; quoted in *The Racecourses of Scotland*, by J. Fairfax-Blakeborough (London: Reid-Hamilton, 1955), p.25.

15. James Radford to John Bowes, 4 July 1840. *Racing and Personal Correspondence of John Bowes* D/St. Box 162 Durham County Record Office; Whyte, *History of the British Turf*, p.189; *Racing Calendar*, TheDruid, *Post and Paddock* (London: Warne, 1895), ed., p.5, dates this point of no return in the mid-1850s; Charles Richardson, *The English Turf* (London: Methuen, 1901), p.156.

16. Again the one great exception was at Newmarket: here racing was for the privileged few, and more especially it was for those on horseback. The pleasure-seeking, holiday racegoer was not wanted. Indeed, when the Great Eastern Railway began to run excursions to Newmarket, the stewards there countered the invasion by taking full advantage of the Heath's many courses and staging the finish of consecutive races literally miles apart so that only the mounted gentry could effectively view the racing. Edward Moorhouse, "Then and Now — Racing", *Badminton Magazine* 36 (1913): 480.

17. Flinn, "Trends in Real Wages", p.396. E. J. Hobsbawm, *Industry and Empire* (London: Weidenfeld and Nicolson, 1968), p.74; Based on B. R. Mitchell and P. Dane, *Abstract of British Historical Statistics* (Cambridge: Cambridge University Press, 1962), p.543; Thompson, "Time, Work-Discipline", pp.90-91.

18. M. B. Smith, "The Growth and Development of Popular Entertainment and Pastimes in the Lancashire Cotton Towns 1830-70" (M. Litt. thesis, University of Lancaster, 1970), pp.136-46.

19 By 1870 thirty-two courses held more than one meeting a year, and the number of meetings lasting more than one day had risen to eighty two. The worst of these commercial speculations was a group of London meetings organized by local publicans and bookmakers simply as a means to sell beer and take bets with no interest in the sport as such. As they attracted the dregs of the metropolis, fraud, violent robbery, and mob rule became accepted features of the meetings. Eventually parliamentary legislation was used to put them down. See Wray Vamplew, *The Turf* (London: Allen Lane, 1976), pp.36, 99

20. This development is discussed more fully in Vamplew, *The Turf*, chap. 3.

21. Richardson, *English Turf*, p.176. As elsewhere in Victorian society, ladies found their role in racing severely restricted. They could not become members of Tattersalls; they were not allowed to act as officials or trainers, and the thought of female jockeys would have produced apoplexy in Jockey Club circles. For most of the nineteenth century, female owners generally took male pseudonyms. For a general view of the situation, see Caroline Ramsden, *Ladies in Racing* (London: Stanley Paul, 1973). Racing clubs were not new, but the previous ones at Epsom, Stockbridge, and Lewes were much smaller and did not admit ladies. Charles Richardson, *Racing at Home and Abroad*, vol. 1 (London: London and Counties Press Association, 1923), p.262.

22. Calculations based on Mitchell and Deane, *Abstract of British Historical Statistics*, pp.343-44, suggest that an index of average real wages rose from 99.8 in 1850-59 to 171.0 in 1890-99; A. E. Dingle, "Drink and Working-Class Living Standards in Britain, 1870-1914", *Economic History Review* 25 (1972): 615-16, 618; Hobsbawm, *Industry and Empire*, p.138. This response on the part of

entrepreneurs lends support to the current re-evaluation of the performance of British entrepreneurs in the late Victorian economy, which suggests that they have been overly condemned as failures. See, e.g., D. N. McCloskey and Lars Sandberg, "From Damnation to Redemption: Judgements on the late Victorian Entrepreneur", *Explorations in Economic History* 9 (1971): 89-108; P. L. Payne, *British Entrepreneurship in the Nineteenth Century* (London: Macmillan, 1974). An associated development was the emergence of the popular racing press. Sporting journals before this time catered for a high-class clientele, horse-racing being covered along with other pastimes of the leisured classes. In 1840 there were four such monthlies, the *Old Sporting Magazine, the New Sporting Magazine*, the *Sporting Review*, and the *Sportsman*. As the latter cost 1s 6d and the others 2s 6d, they were all beyond the pocket of the working man (Whyte, *History of the British Turf,* p.xiii). Two weekly sporting magazines, *Bell's Life* and the *Sunday Times*, were cheaper, but they aimed above the heads of even the literate lower-class punter. Provincial newspapers would break out into a rash of turf articles at the time of their local meeting, but racing columns were not a regular feature. Really there was no racing press as such until the substantial rise in working-class spending power. By the late 1870s there were one daily, one bi-weekly, and six weekly papers wholly devoted to sporting, particularly racing, matters; by the early 1890s three dailies and a dozen weeklies were devoted exclusively to racing; and at the turn of the century twenty-five sporting papers were published in London alone (Rice, *History of the British Turf,* pp.xi-xii; L. H. Curzon, *A Mirror of the Turf* [London: Chapman and Hall, 1892], p.v.; *Select Committee on Betting,* 1902, V, q. 3842). In addition, there were innumerable tipsters' circulars masquerading as newspapers and racing sheets emerging at intervals on race days from 10 a.m. onwards (*Select Committee on Betting* 1902, V, q. 1600); Richardson, *The English Turf,* p.175.

23. The attraction of the top performer is difficult to substantiate historically, but certainly it was the common belief of racecourse executives interviewed by the author. From personal experience, the author would be adamant that in 1972 the appearance of the horse Brigadier Gerard swelled the crowd at both York and Newmarket. Most studies of spectator sports claim that the uncertainty of the result is more conducive to attendance than a predictable game. See, e.g., Henry G. Demmert, *The Economics of Professional Team Sports* (Lexington, Mass.: D. C. Heath, 1973); R. G. Noll, "Attendance and Price Setting" in *Government and the Sports Business,* ed. R. G. Noll (Washington: Brookings, 1974).

24. The question of crowd behaviour is dealt with more fully in Vamplew, *The Turf,* chap. 8.

25. Ibid., chap. 7. This policy of differential pricing became firmly entrenched: the Ilchester Committee, which examined racing in the 1940s, believed that "to make admission to the Grandstand too cheap would be to flood it with the more noisy and undesirable elements who now confine themselves to the cheaper stands". *Report of the Racing Re-organisation Committee* (London, 1943), para. 44.

26. It should be stressed that it was not betting on the horses that was attacked by the executives but the operation of roulette, E/O tables, and card games, all of which were highly susceptible to sharp practices. How well their successors believed that they had succeeded in dampening down the whole holiday atmosphere of racing is illustrated in the Benson Committee's report on *The Racing Industry* (London, 1968), para. 203: "The Racecourse Association said that, in the main, the public attends for the purpose of seeing racing and betting. Bands, side shows, and other attractions tend to irritate the ardent

racegoer, as he is in the main fully occupied in the intervals between races. However, in the cheaper enclosures at certain courses, and particularly wherever a holiday atmosphere prevails, other attractions may be acceptable, although it is doubtful whether they would bring out increased attendance by the paying public."

27. Richardson, *English Turf,* p.197; John Rickman, *Homes of Sport: Racing* (London: Peter Garnett, 1952), p.30; Sandown Park had originated as a partnership but became a limited company in 1885. Almost all other enclosed meetings adopted company status.

28. Several contemporary commentators pointed out that it was the level of prize-money that primarily interested owners. E. g., Hawley Smart, "The Present State of the Turf", *Fortnightly Review* 38 (1885): 542, "A few [owners] may race here and there for whim, or a liking to run horses in their own neighbourhood, the majority of them go where the stakes are highest"; and even before the enclosure movement reached its height, Lord Cadogan was convinced that owners of horses were "no longer satisfied with the prizes offered for competition at old-fashioned meetings". "The State of the Turf", *Fortnightly Review* 37 (1885): 109; Lord Hamilton of Dalzell, "The Financial Aspects of Racing", *Badminton Magazine* 23 (1906): 252.

29. Selling races were a device to obtain money for the prize fund while at the same time giving owners a chance to get rid of relatively poor horses. Entry conditions stated that the winner would be sold for a certain sum, usually a hundred pounds. The difference between the actual auction price and the nominated selling price was divided equally between the race fund and the owner of the second horse; Richardson, *English Turf,* pp.149-55.

30. Some support for this view can be found in R. F. Mersey Thompson, "Ethics of Horse-Racing", *National Review* 33 (1899): 608.

31. Suffolk, *Racing and Steeplechasing,* pp.74-75, 95.

32. Several commentators noted that the big-stake races staged by the gate-money meetings undermined the Derby's reputation. Vigilant, "Recollections of Epsom and the Derby", *English Illustrated Magazine* (1891-92): 656; L.H. Curzon, *The Blue Riband of the Turf* (London: Chatto and Windus, 1890), p.19; Smart, "Present State of the Turf", p.534; Cawthorne and Herod, *Royal Ascot,* pp.123, 191-93; Richardson, *English Turf,* p.74; Suffolk, *Racing and Steeplechasing,* pp.74-75.

33. Calculations based on data in the *Racing Calendar,* L. H. Curzon, "The Horse as an Instrument of Gambling", *Contemporary Review* 30 (1877): 378; Curzon, *Mirror of the Turf,* p.61; *Bloodstock Breeders Review* 5 (1917): 189. The motivations and rewards of ownership are further discussed in Vamplew, *The Turf,* chap. 11.

34. Calculated from data in the *Racing Calendar* and *Bloodstock Breeders Review.*

35. On this, see W. S. Dixon, *The Influence of Racing and the Thoroughbred Horse on Light Horse Breeding* (London: Hurt and Blackett, 1924); A. E. T. Watson, "The Turf", *Badminton Magazine* 4 (1897): 732; Lord Durham, "Turf Reform", *New Review* 2 (1890): 278.

36. Calculated from data in *Racing Calendar.*

37. T. A. Cook, *A History of the English Turf* (London: Virtue, 1905), pp.521, 544; John Welcome, *Fred Archer: His Life and Times* (London: Faber, 1967), p.88; Richardson, *English Turf,* p.276; S. G. Galtrey, *Memoirs of a Racing Journalist* (London: Hutchinson, 1934), p.184.

38. Calculated on the far from extreme assumptions of a retainer of around a thousand pounds and presents of five per cent of the prize-money won. Curzon, *Mirror of the Turf,* p.346; John Runciman, "The Ethics of the Turf", *Contemporary Review* 55 (1889): 613.

JIM FITZPATRICK

The Spectrum of Australian Bicycle Racing: 1890–1900

The first safety bicycle was imported into Australia within one year of its development in England in 1885.[1] The pneumatic tyre, invented in 1888, arrived a year later. By 1890 Australia was faced with a *fait accompli:* the pneumatic-tyred safety bicycle, a reliable, technologically advanced form of personal transportation that required little further development or modification for Australian conditions; a device that captured the imagination of the populace and the energy of inventors and mechanics; and the fastest form of locomotion on the continent, barring a train on rails.[2] As the decade progressed, a cycling craze developed in Australia as it had in Europe, North America, and certain other locales, although the depression of the early 1890s and the antipodean lag appear to have inhibited it initially. The previous cycling boom of the 1880s, occasioned by the "ordinary" bicycles, had partially subsided. The danger of the machines, their weight, unsuitability to a variety of surfaces (partly as a result of the hard tyres), slowness, and cost meant that they would not become the mount of the masses. Although machines, riders, and clubs were still to be found, the few cycle journals had folded and the general state of cycling affairs was not robust.

The safety bicycle changed all that. That lightweight, deceptively delicate-looking mechanism, embodying several ingenious technological innovations (the roller bearing chain, tangential-spoked wheel, tubular frame, and pneumatic tyre) permitted a unique man-machine interaction. Mounted atop, a man could achieve a sustained speed not possible with any other form of animate power. But it represented an interaction in which that speed depended ultimately upon the rider himself: the machine was the mechanical multiplier, the man was the multiplicand. It simultaneously provided a challenge and a way to meet and measure that challenge — and in the process furnished an almost synergistic self-exhilaration. In addition, as a result of its lightness, strength, and reliability, it could be used in extremely difficult conditions. It could be ridden over rough roads and tracks, or none at all. Its lightness allowed it to be readily pushed or carried by the alternatively pedestrian power source. It was, in essence, a machine with a human engine, with all the physical possibilities and limitations that entailed.[3]

Australia soon found itself in the mainstream of the bicycle boom. The machines were being imported from North America and Europe along with the cycle journals, social attitudes, and accompanying debates. By mid-decade, among other things, "cyclistes" were not uncommon on the streets; churches still argued, albeit less adamantly than previously, about the morality of Sunday cycling; doctors debated the physical effects; the military pondered the potential of the machine; rumours filtered out of the Western Australian goldfields regarding marvellous bush cycling feats; numerous cycle journals were about to spring forth; bicycle dealers were gaining reputations formerly attributed to horse traders; and dogs chased everyone. By 1897 about 130 different models of bicycles were available, either imported *in toto* or assembled from imported components by local "manufacturers".[4]

The sheer speed of the bicycle amazed many, and it was demonstrated in various ways, including competition against horses. In Colac, Victoria, a cyclist conceded a horse a quarter-mile in a two-mile race and won by two hundred yards, while a relay ride from Albany to Perth in 1899 had as a side objective the besting of the coaching record. In Queensland an eighty-mile race held at Winton matched a rider with two horses against a cyclist. The horseman could use his horses in any way he wished and was given a one-hour start as incentive. The cyclist passed him after sixty miles. In addition, occasional runner/cyclist matches were held. However, a "race" between two distinct forms of locomotion is nonsensical in that they have quite distinctive performance curves. Ultimately it is a case of trying to determine a theoretical "break-down" distance over which the two can be matched. This fact makes such contests inherently unsatisfactory. Given the relatively few reports of such events, they appear to have been neither popular nor common. Although the speed of cyclists gradually crept upward, many local newspapers were hesitant to credit "mile-a-minute" Murphy's ride in the United States of over sixty miles an hour when first reported. Even given wind assistance, it was almost too much to believe initially.[5]

The greatest interest in bicycle sports arose from track races. In the early days of both safety and ordinary bicycles these were frequently held in conjunction with other activities such as athletic events or agricultural shows. However, as they increased in popularity they gradually evolved into relatively exclusive events. Large numbers of entrants often necessitated numerous heats for each of the various distances, and a scheduled programme of six to ten races could occupy much of the day. In smaller communities the lack of entrants or the poor quality of racing led to organizers occasionally suggesting foot-races or other events to provide variety and generate more interest and larger gates. In at least one instance horse and camel races were added to the agenda.

Cycle tracks were found in innumerable locations, ranging from the major city centres to cleared areas in the bush. Australian cycle racing was helped immensely by the existence of cricket and football ovals which were of an excellent size and shape, plentiful, and consequently easily adapted for racing. As the financial benefit accruing to the grounds' governing bodies was often considerable, they were willing to co-operate. However, it appears that their co-operation occasionally verged on extortion, at least in some eyes. The Western Australian Cricket Association ostensibly earned 80 per cent of its revenue for the period 1895-99 from cycle racing, charging up to one-third of the profits from cycle meetings, while retaining booth rights. In 1897 cycle officials argued that the WACA was using cyclists to help make up lost revenues incurred by a visiting "professional" cricket team and other activitires. Given that apparently almost as many persons were turning out for cycle *training* sessions at the ground in 1897 as turned out to see the inter-colonial cricket match, there may have been some truth in the allegation. Even a WACA member agreed that the charges were high, but complained only because in its greed the association had "brought cricket to the low level which professionalism had brought cycling". The sentiments were echoed in Coolgardie, where the Coolgardie Recreation Association reportedly "netted a profit of £800 on their two [Westral Wheel] meetings, and [had] not spent same on the track, but for the benefit of footballers, cricketers, and any other class of sport bar cycling". The committee bowed to pressure and asphalted the track.[6]

The quality of tracks varied enormously and was not necessarily equated with rental charges or ancillary facilities provided. The surfaces ranged from claypans, packed dirt, and gravel to asphalt and concrete. At the WACA ground the surface was packed with a calcareous material containing shells. After heavy rains partially dissolved and degraded the surface, the exposed shell edges played havoc with the thin racing cycle tyres. In Northam, Western Australia, "double-gees" (the spiny fruits of the weed *Emes*

Australis) rendered the track virtually useless at one time, and in Albany some of the club's races "had to be abandoned on account of the incoming tide and sea weed".[7] The local ovals, being a venue for other groups as well, posed problems for cyclists while training. Children and dogs wandered the tracks, and complaints were issued against cricket balls, footballs, and footballers finding their way onto the track, resulting in some serious falls. The circling cyclists undoubtedly provided excellent and tempting targets for the other "sportsmen", and the enmities are not heavily masked in some of the writings of the era. Night lighting was provided in some locales. While it was lauded and drew a large crowd initially, promising a revival of racing interest in some communities, occasional writers noted that it was questionable whether the sport could sustain the possible increase in the number of events that might result. A relative decline in interest in cycle racing was already in evidence by the time many lighted facilities were being established in the late 1890s. They only provided a brief respite from the decreasing patronage and enthusiasm.

The issue of Sunday riding, which had long been debated by various facets of society, appears to have been substantially settled sometime after mid-decade. The original criticism of the bicycle *per se* had radically declined, partly because respectable people rode it, church parades were popular, and ministers used bicycles to get from Willoughby to the West Australian goldfields. However, as a precaution, possible against latent wrath, Sunday cycling does not appear to have been common. Yet, all was not quiet on the western front. In Perth the Reverend G. E. Rowe criticized the use of the WACA ground for training on Sundays and was offended at the vile language encountered there. One cycle journal, reporting the sermon, supported his views on language but was surprisingly silent on whether or not the track should be closed. However, the silence is perhaps understandable when it is realized that the Reverend Mr Rowe was an officer of the Perth Cycling Club, to which many prominent cyclists and personages belonged; the disagreement obviously required considerable diplomacy. A few days later a local newspaper pointed out that Rowe had been perhaps a bit harsh in singling out cyclists, while ignoring "tennis players (who used the same ground), rowers, and golf players". In Rowe's defence it was made clear that far from being an unfeeling man, "no one wished pure sport more success than he did . . . but no one more strongly deprecated vice in sport than he did . . . he would set his face against Sabbath desecration by sportsmen of every kind." On the other hand, the paper continued, "young men had a perfect right to develop their muscles, and to train for that object. Sport had the sanction of Christ, for he had recommended the training of the soul, the mind, and the body, and what God had joined together, let no man put asunder." Even the Reverend Mr Rowe must have been swayed, for the potential sundering of cyclists' bodies was arrested by allowing training on Sundays, but only before half-past nine in the morning; at least the cycling organizations could not be accused of condoning cycling during the hours of service.[8]

On the goldfields, however, apparently the interpretation of God's sentiments was more variable. Not only did men train on Sundays, but occasional road races and other activities were held. One Sunday road race in fact was carried out in Cue only two weeks before a visit to the area by Mr Rowe. In addition, less than three months later it was rumoured that one of his fellow ministers, the Reverend H. Poole, of Menzies, a well-known cyclist and "a scorcher at that", had challenged the Reverend Mr Jenkins of Perth to a mile match. This should not be taken as a complete religious licence for the goldfields, however, since on several occasions the Coolgardie police took it upon themselves to stop Sunday cycle races scheduled in their jurisdication.[9]

On the track the cyclists constituted a colourful group. "Half the charm of cycle racing to the general public is the beauty of the scene when, a dozen or more riders in divers colours sweep along together," the *W. A. Cyclist* commented. Assigned racing colours were eventually abandoned. A bit too colourful for some, it appeared. The costumes became progressively briefer and complaints were laid about the disgraceful clothing: "skin tight singlet, a pair of trunks displaying the leg to the hip, and so tight as to expose the whole form". All of this was considered an affront to the crowds, composed as they were of a significant number of women, particularly at the larger, more socially notable meetings. The substitution of trunks for knickers was looked upon as virtually indecent by some, and riders were occasionally fined. If the costumes were a danger for morals, the hats they wore were considered a danger to other riders, and the racers were chastised about casting them off during an event.[10]

Flying hats would appear to have been the least of rider's worries. The occasionally poor track conditions, the lack of safety facilities, and the furious riding resulted in exciting racing and some spectacular and dangerous crashes. The Austral Wheel of 1898 had upwards of two score heats, and at the ANA Wheel Race in Melbourne in 1899 there were 1,134 entrants for seven events. To reach the finals, riders were forced to win several heats, an arduous task, and in the attempts there were many falls. The hazards of the race are summed up in an anonymous poem, "To the 1897 Austral":

> After the Austral's over,
> After the track is clear —
> Straighten my nose and shoulders,
> Help them to find my ear.[11]

The riding was hard and often rough because there was frequently much at stake. Prize-money could be extremely high, and some Australian races ranked with the most lucrative individual races held in North America or Europe. The Westral, ANA, and Austral Wheel races eventually paid between £200 and £300 each to the winner. In addition, some firms paid separate awards or gave gifts to winners mounted on their machines. The winner of the 1898 Austral Wheel stood to pick up an extra £100 if he happened to be mounted on a Swift bicycle, for example. The seven-race card at the ANA races of 1899 paid a total of over £800 to place-getters, while Victorian professional races during the 1897-98 season distributed a reported £6,348 in prize-money.[12] Given the going wages of the day, there was indeed a lot of incentives and rewards for the physically endowed and fortunate rider. The big money was not always restricted to the major centres either. Races in the West Australian goldfields consistently offered prizes equalling or exceeding anything available to Perth race winners. The road races held on the goldfields also paid much larger prizes than any in the metropolis. However, these prizes, typically £10 to £20, were not large in comparison with the track rewards. In addition, individual contests occasionally pitted two riders against each other in match races. Although these were not generally given patronage by any cycling body and were for relatively small amounts, they could become expensive affairs; two goldfields riders of note rode for £100 at Day Dawn, a £60 track being laid for the event.[13] All in all, cycle racing was a good candidate for being the most lucrative sporting activity an individual could attempt throughout the 1890s.

The riders were not the only ones to profit from the races. The Melbourne Bicycle Club cleared fifteen hundred pounds from the 1898 Austral Wheel Race, for example, and the financial benefits accruing to the grounds' governing bodies have already been mentioned.[14] But the biggest winners or losers of the races were the bicycle manufacturers and dealers, at least in some views. As the philosophy was bluntly put, record setting and race winning meant sales. In tyre sales the Dunlop company had a near monopoly.

Virtually all long-distance riders in Australia and the vast majority of all cycle race place-getters were shod with Dunlops. Yet the company did not appear to rest on its laurels and worked hard to preserve its envied position. It was the single greatest promoter of cycle activities in Australia. Some cycle firms, battling one another for any possible advantage in sales, became enmeshed in the problem of subsidizing riders and teams. Some firms questioned the wisdom of this, as many dealers and the public realized that the differences between most machines were often negligible, if there were indeed any at all. What differences did exist in performance probably resulted from the various riders' capacities, and in any case racing-bicycle characteristics did not necessarily carry over into the other lines of cycles, such as the touring bicycles. Ultimately the amount of corruption attaching to the sport generally, the dubious returns with respect to the total outlay required for a rider or team, and the general decline in cycle sales towards the end of the decade led many firms to opt out of the arrangements.

With so much money to be made for so many groups, it is not surprising to find that there was considerable circulation of riders. North American, European, and other international riders toured the country, and Australians occasionally went abroad to try their luck. Within the country, national and local champions made the rounds of the major centres, competing against one another. Some problems arose as a result of this movement, not the least of which was the matter of riders changing their names. Those not yet particularly prominent, but still of high calibre, could find it profitable on occasion to assume a different name and register as an inexperienced rider, perhaps even lose a couple of races, so as to obtain a relatively small handicap for a lucrative race. And, while most communities enjoyed the prospect and experience of witnessing the best riders, not all locales welcomed them with open arms. Queenslanders complained that their annual cycling carnival was harmed by an influx of champions. "Bananaland has been the happy hunting ground of the professional racing man during the winter months," the W. A. Cyclist said of the years 1897 and 1898.[15] The resultant economic extractions apparently only stimulated the growth of the parochial seeds of the colony.

Cycle racing provided an alternative outlet for gambling, and the money that consequently changed hands resulted in prize-money paling into insignificance in comparison. There were some opposed to any form of financial rewards being involved in cycle racing, of course, whether they were prizes, trophies, or wagers on the outcome. Many, however, seemed to accept, if resignedly, the dictum that "betting is the life and soul of any sport", cycling included. Despite the speed and excitement of cycle races, many felt that "unless one had his 'little bit' on the man of his choice one cannot raise three ha'porth of enthusiasm over such a race" Technically it was illegal to bet at most cycling venues, but the society, police, and officials generally overlooked it. It was so blatant, in fact, that the complaints about the bookies were not that they should be removed from the venue itself but from in front of the grandstand, where they blocked the view of the finishes. On the control of gambling, one writer pointed out:

> The method adopted in Melbourne is to carefully notify by advertisement that care will be taken to suppress betting — otherwise some of the bookies might miss the fixture and go to the racecourse — and then to mark out special places for the ringmen to stand, by sticking up notices that betting is strictly prohibited. If the weather is hot and these notices are in shady places, they invariably provide a favorite rendezvous for the books, the bobbie, and the "battlers"; the books laying the odds, the "battlers" punting, and the bobbies looking on, which has the admirable effect of minimising welching and preventing clamour.[16]

Unfortunately, even for those willing to accept gambling at cycle races, it became obvious that the racing was not a model of purity. The cycle agents themselves were sometimes involved in officiating at events, and this led to complaints that they might be less than objective about disqualifying or charging riders, depending upon whether or not they were riding the agents' machines. Far more ominous, however, were the continued complaints about the blatantly "stiff", "dead", "cronk", and "crook" riding that was occurring. While some suggested that cycling officials should take more notice of such matters, others pointed out that the officials themselves were often to be found doing business with the bookies. The temptations, opportunities, and rewards accruing from race-rigging were too great to be ignored, and it is probably unrealistic to expect that they would have been. "Major" Taylor, one of the world's greatest cyclists, sometimes found it difficult to win in Australia, even though he proceeded to set most colonial, state, and national time records whenever he rode. He quite bluntly questioned what chance any honest rider could have against the rampant team riding that was common in the country. A New Zealander noted: "A stranger has no show against the numerous cliques on the track, and stands a good chance of being punched if he rides well." The reaction of many was expressed in the bitter assessment that cycling had "degenerated to the level of a money-making game almost on an equality with pony racing and pedestrianism", while one went so far as to suggest that even "pony racing was angelic to this".[17]

There were various suggestions about how to regulate matters: cycling bodies should provide greater supervision, police should enforce the no-gambling edicts, bookmakers should be licensed and their books and activities inspected closely, and so forth. In Western Australia in mid-1898 there was a move afoot by the League of Wheelmen to introduce legislation permitting the establishment of totalisators on the cycle course. The proponents assumed that such an action would contribute to restricting the opportunities for corruption, which was undermining the races at the time. The counter argument was based essentially upon the assumption that to legalize gambling — in effect, to recognize its existence — would be detrimental to the sport, since many riders, particularly those who "rode for the love of the sport and for the honour and glory", would withdraw from the league. The move was defeated and it was decided instead to request the police to enforce the laws on the books. In Coolgardie it was suggested that all riders should be put in one room, where the heats would be drawn, and subsequently the riders would be individually escorted to their marks without having the opportunity to talk to friends, managers, or bookies, as they were accustomed to do. However, the potential inefficacy of that kind of proposal was pointed out in the question: "Do they never notice, what others see, signs and motions of attendants of the competitors when the latter are getting on their marks? Does it never strike the officials that these attendants are conveying the latest 'information' to those outside the railings?"[18]

Ultimately the cycling fraternity and the public never came to grips with the problem of race fixing. Prophecies concerning the imminent demise of cycle racing were eventually fulfilled. The Austral Wheel Race of 1901, which involved large sums of money and dubious riding, caused subsequent public criticism, and during the next couple of years the mass popularity of cycle racing declined markedly. "It came to be realised that there was too much of unanimity of spirit amongst the riders; for the participants, at least, the placing had not the charm of the unexpected. Public support then ceased abruptly."[19]

However, gambling by itself did not end the heyday of professional cycle racing in Australia. The introduction of motorcycles and automobiles captured the imagination, and their greater speed usurped some of the bicycle's claim to glory. In addition, as wealthy and influential people turned to the new devices, the prestige of the bicycle diminished, and it gradually became commonplace. The gambling aspect only added a perhaps premature *coup de grace* to a probable inevitability. Although a certain minority remained loyal to the bicycle and bicycle races, by the turn of the century it had lost much of its mass appeal.

During the latter half of the 1890s, however, cycle racing was extremely popular. "Every town of any importance has its racecourse," the *Coolgardie Miner* noted, "and now each centre of population is deemed incomplete without its asphalted cycling track." Most communities attempted to rectify the matter as soon as possible. In some areas, such as the West Australian goldfields, the inability to provide regular horse-races meant that cycling achieved a tremendous degree of popularity. About eight thousand persons turned out for the Westral Wheel Race alone, for example. However, the largest crowds by far were assembled in Melbourne at the annual Austral Wheel and ANA Wheel races in December and January respectively. The entrants, heats, and other preliminary details were telegraphed throughout Australia. The races, though not attracing interstate visits on the same scale as the Melbourne Cup were nonetheless great social events. Crowds of thirty thousand attended the heats and finals. In 1898 the ANA attracted a reported total of fifty thousand, and in 1899 sixty-five thousand.[20]

Women were also associated with the cycling scene. The crowds that turned up at the socially important functions like the Austral Wheel and ANA Wheel Races and the like were composed of a significant proportion of females. Their interest in and knowledge of cycle racing was often keen, and they occasionally demonstrated a considerable familiarity with the terminology and action. However, men (and women, generally) did not accept females as an on-track component of the racing scene, whatever the extent of their involvement off the track. That women did ride bicycles was a fact that not all segments of society could yet live with easily; to ask that women also be accepted on the track, with its physical danger, language, gambling, and eventual low moral repute, was almost too much to expect, given the social climate of the time. Almost . . . but not quite. It appears that women's races in Australia were proposed following their success and popularity in London and Paris. The *Austral Wheel,* perhaps the best of the Australian cycling journals and a staunch advocate of women's cycling, registered a strong protest at this suggestion, adding its voice to those of many cycle clubs, leagues, and other associations:

> That women's races will be held is unfortunately unavoidable, because there is a class of unmanly men which will derive pleasure from seeing

girls with perspiring faces and heaving breasts "riding all out" for some paltry prize, or for a daily wage, as they lately did in London; and will look on with satisfaction while they are lifted half fainting from their machines, or are carried hurt and bleeding to the casualty room after a fall. And there are others who will get up such races for the sake of the gate money and the advertisement. We hope, however, that the better class of cyclists will discountenance the thing, and will *let it be publicly known* that they do so.

The *Austral Wheel* was accurate in its prediction that such races were unavoidable. While they never caught on, spectators did see the occasional one. And again, as predicted, a lady "as if to guarantee the fact that she had done her best, after the post had been passed, fainted". However, the matches were deemed poor racing fare, and while the curiosity value alone may have supported a few such stagings, the dubious financial benefits and the social attitudes of the time made them less than attractive as a feature of cycle racing cards.[21]

Perhaps the most publicized event in the country involving a racing cycliste was the tour of Mademoiselle Serpolette, "the champion lady cyclist of the world", sponsored by the Gladiator cycling firm. The young French girl, "hardly out of her 'teens, good-looking, with pleasant expression and jet-black hair, charming in manner, and vivacious", had been a virtual terror-on-the-track in Europe for over three years. Her mid-1898 six-month tour of Australia, undertaken to promote the firm's machines, included exhibitions behind pace at tracks and during the interval of football matches, touring, coaching at riding schools, demonstrating her motorized tricycle, and racing. One writer, commenting on her racing, said that she was certainly "capable of shifting her machine to a lively tune"; but he continued, "with all due respects to Mademoiselle, we think the game unladylike. The morbid curiosity attracted by these exhibitions is one not likely to influence the pastime for its good." Mlle Serpolette was available to meet any woman on even terms. One columnist's reaction was that it was "extremely improbable therefore, that she would be seen in competition". Australia had no one to match her. While Mlle Serpolette's appearances and reputation received considerable press coverage, she was apparently relegated to giving demonstration rides at meets around the country, riding her motorized tricycle, and other innocuous activities.[22]

The one off-track possibility that was readily open to Australian women was the establishment of long-distance cycling records. The rides between the major cities were initially undertaken as touring efforts. However, by definition the first lady held the "record" for the distance, and it is not surprising that subsequent cyclists gradually lowered the times. By no stretch of the imagination could it be said that women flocked to the challenge, or opportunity, as the case may be. While these rides were not noticeably criticized as being inappropriate for women, they were not given great publicity. They received a few lines or paragraphs, rarely more. Hence, while this opportunity for competitive riding existed for women, it was relatively unpractical, unattractive, and, if the resultant publicity is any guide, not greatly encouraged. Australian cycle racing in the 1890s was definitely a male-participant sport. Road races never achieved the popularity of track races, partly because they were ridden in relative isolation and the progress could only be monitored by occasional telegraphic reports. The difficulty of covering the races was substantially attributable to the fact that the bicycles were the fastest things around. In the 1897 Beverley – Perth race, for example, the starter and contingent who flagged off the contestants arrived back in Perth two hours after the riders, despite their taking the train over a route some fifteen miles shorter. Another complaint about road racing was that the winner was often the man who negotiated the distance without a mishap. This made it as much an element of luck as of skill or endurance. In this context the road riders, like many touring organizations of the period, emphasized the poor state of the roads. The early Perth bicycle road races could not be held around the metropolitan area. The Beverley – Perth Race was originally meant to be started at Bunbury, but was changed because the Bunbury road was effectively impassable after rain.[23]

Narrow, rough roads through the countryside with carts, cattle, sheep, and other obstacles led one paper to suggest that in preparation for road races clubs should organize a "class for instruction in ambulance work" and make the "best arrangements possible for medical attendance and payment of services of a doctor". They were needed. Riders were killed. In the 1898 Victorian Road Championships the League of Wheelmen's medical officer stated that it was "asking men to attempt suicide in an unusual manner" to race under the conditions that prevailed. Within three-quarters of a mile nineteen of the seventy-six starters crashed on the narrow road. Frequently less than half the starters even finished a race. The road conditions were not the only obstacles: tacks and other items were occasionally put on a road deliberately, and the police in Victoria declared road races illegal at one stage. While one could ask why men raced under such circumstances, the very element of difficulty undoubtedly made it an attraction to many competitors. The road race was perhaps the ultimate extension of W. P. Forlonge's observation that "the *soupcon* of danger and risk attaching to the riding of a bicycle tends to give a flavour of excitement to the exercise".[24]

But the road races and various relay rides had an aspect that appealed to many: the demonstration of the machine's practical utility. In discussing road races one writer made the point: "We have in cycling a pastime which has possibilities possessed by no other form of pleasure, a sport from whose adherents the nation can in times of need draw men capable of covering any distance within a reasonable time"; if necessary he may "supplant both railroad and telegraph".[25] The application of racing cyclists to message delivery on the West Australian goldfields had more than proved the validity of the point. This led to efforts on the part of occasional government officials, cycle companies, and Dunlop to encourage relay rides to demonstrate the bicycle's potential value to the military. There appears to have been a sincere conviction on the part of many that the bicycle had a definite role to play in some future, if nebulous, defence of Australia. However, the financial benefits if the government adopted large numbers of bicycles — and required tyres — was undoubtedly not overlooked. These relay rides culminated in the 1909 and 1912 Dunlop Military Dispatch Rides, endorsed by the Department of Defence, between Adelaide and Sydney, via Melbourne. The 1,149-mile distance was covered by sixty-four relays of cyclists in 69½ hours both in 1909 and in 1912. Though beaten by a car and motorcycle in 1912, the military judged the bicycle to be the most reliable means of dispatch delivery on the continent, even at that late date.[26] In contrast, an earlier relay ride in Western Australia in 1899 from Albany to Perth was not the success the promoters had anticipated. The railway refused free transport for riders to isolated legs of the route (so much for supplanting trains!) and consequently some riders had to ride long, hard stretches of road. The projected fifteen-hour journey took twenty-five hours. Worse, the dispatch was lost by one of the riders in a collision with a kangaroo.[27]

Besides organized road races, numerous riders undertook individual long-distance record rides, most commonly between the major cities. The Adelaide–Melbourne run attracted considerable attention and effort because not only did it entail sheer speed and endurance, but it also required the rider to pick one of several alternative routes in the South Australian section: he had to balance the varying lengths against the road conditions prevailing at the moment. The inter-city rides were not always best achieved on the local roads, either. One rider gave up the Broken Hill–Adelaide attempt in 1897 because the roads were too rough. However, the following year another cyclist covered the distance in thirty-three hours by abandoning the road at Cockburn (near the South Australian border) and heading across country at night to Burra.

In the matters discussed up to this point, Australia's cycling scene was not unlike that in North America, Europe, and other countries, such as New Zealand and South Africa. Track racing was popular; amateurism versus professionalism was debated; road races were held; social issues and implications were argued; crowds, money, fame, and corruption flowed around many a rider; and the society was swept along in the current of general cycling sports, including such things as cycle polo and quadrilles. There were differences, of course. Handicap racing was developed here more than in most other countries. Also, those essentially inhumane six-day bicycle races, so popular elsewhere, never caught on here. Possibly this was because there were no adequate enclosed stadiums. However, Australia held a relatively unique position in the cycling world in one respect: overland cycling. As the years passed, enough experience had been gained in rural areas to demonstrate conclusively the reliability and practicality of the bicycle and the Dunlop tyres for bush use. In November 1896, Arthur Richardson became the first to cycle across the Nullarbor. He pedalled from Coolgardie to Adelaide in thirty-one days. Within two years at least a score of known cyclists made the crossing. By late 1898 one rider had cut the time to a blistering nineteen days, an average of one hundred and ten miles per day through the bush, sand, and dirt that comprised the roads, tracks, and natural surfaces of the route. In early 1897 the first Adelaide–Darwin ride was made in the deliberately slow time of seventy-four days (the solo cyclist spent a week touring some two hundred miles in the Alice Springs area, for example). Immediately a team of noted Victorian racing cyclists were sent to lower the "record". They met near disaster, had to be rescued by telegraph line patrols, and managed to better the time by only a few days. Clearly, for overland rides it was necessary to start with experienced bushmen and then add bicycles — not to start with cyclists and hope they would develop into experienced bushmen on the way. The following year a telegrapher with four years' experience in the Northern Territory mounted his machine in Darwin and proceeded to pedal through to Adelaide in twenty-nine days, capping it off with a last-day effort of 185 miles. This ride, as well as all others in the 1890s, was on a fixed-wheel machine.[28] Most of the long-distance rides were undertaken by one or two men against time. However, occasionally there were man-against-man matches. The most notable was the 1898 race between J. Denning and Frank White from Perth to Brisbane. They passed and repassed each other through Adelaide, Melbourne, and Sydney. The contest ended abruptly with a severe fall and the hospitalization of Denning at Armidale, New South Wales. White continued on up the coast to Rockhampton, taking only sixty-two days for the journey, and then turned around and pedalled back to Perth.

By 1899 there was only one important untried long-distance ride left: around Australia. That year White left Melbourne with two others to ride around the continent in a counter-clockwise direction. Several weeks earlier, Arthur Richardson had left Perth alone with the same goal in mind but in a clockwise direction. The first two efforts thus became a virtual race. It was less exciting in some respects than the earlier White/Denning match, for the distance was much greater and reports from the Top End were often weeks in reaching the public. Ultimately Richardson won the race and added the honour of the first and fastest circum-cyclist to his previous Nullarbor laurel. White, who admittedly rode in 1898 for the fame, must have regretted his failure to continue on around the continent at the end of his race with Denning.[29]

Australian overland cyclists were in a unique situation. The continent was relatively flat, could be ridden year-round, and possessed no notable linguistic, political, economic, or social barriers to such efforts. It simultaneously provided a challenge combining long distances, scarcity of water, loneliness, flies, heat, and danger from hostile Aborigines: a fact greatly exaggerated by the press but nonetheless real, as the White party was twice attacked in the North-West. The rides were not easy, as the machines had to be alternately ridden, pushed, carried, and floated across streams. At least three parties nearly perished (Richardson personally helped relieve the distressed White party in the Northern Territory). Some overlanders refused to undertake subsequent rides for which they were invited, stating flatly that once was enough. The riders' motives varied, but nearly all were encouraged by the cycle and tyre companies' assistance in providing equipment and administrative aid. Whatever the reasons, the result was a period during which the overlanders became momentary heroes and made Australia the long-distance cycling centre of the world. And yet, for some strange reason their adventures were also forgotten fastest in the minds of most Australians; the few subsequent writings on Australian cycling races and exploits have ignored them almost completely. Perhaps the very remarkableness of the rides placed them outside the commonly conceived realm of bicycle "sports".

The Australians' fascination with the bicycle was manifested in a variety of ways during the 1890s. The same machine could be used for rural work, urban commuting, track and road racing, church parades, courting, military purposes, and as a mark of social status. The bicycle was perhaps the first of the mass technology sports items. Yet, because of the very fact that the machine could serve many functions and was exclusive to none, it raised many questions about the very nature of the concept of "sport" itself. The bicycle, in particular, both derived from and demonstrated the inextricably intertwined nature of the society's economic, social, technological, and sporting activities. For the historian seeking fresh perspectives on the Australian society of the 1890s, the role and impact of the bicycle, sporting or otherwise, is illuminating.

NOTES

1. A Melbourne Safety Bicycle Club was formed in early 1886; *Punch*, 29 April 1886. *Safety* refers to bicycles as now commonly ridden, with two equal-size wheels and chain drive to the rear one. *ordinary* refers to the penny-farthing machine.
2. An 1898 interview with a long-established figure in the Australian cycle business indicates that safeties were commercially available in 1889, and that pneumatic tyres were not commercially fitted until the following year ("Mr E. W. Rudd", *Austral Wheel*, May 1898).
3. A good survey of bicycle technology is presented in C. F. Caunter, *The History and Development of Cycles* (London: HMSO, 1955).
4. This figure is quadruple that cited by Keith Dunstan, *Sports* (Melbourne: Cassell, 1973), p.247. Mine is a cumulative tally drawn from every source yet surveyed.
5. *W. A. Cyclist*, 6 October 1899; *Austral Wheel*, October 1899; *W. A. Cyclist*, 21 July 1899.
6. For the WACA and cycling, see *West Australian Wheelman* (hereafter *WAW*), 26 March, 16 April 1897, 2 June 1899; for Coolgardie, see *W. A. Sportsman*, 20 July 1901.
7. *Morning Herald* (Perth), 24 June 1897; *WAW*, 28 October, 2 December 1898.
8. *WAW*, 14 May 1897; *Morning Herald*, 20 and 24 May 1897.
9. *Mt. Magnet Miner* and *Lennonville Leader*, 26 September 1896; *WAW*, 24 December 1896; *Kalgoorlie and Boulder Standard*, 27 December 1897.
10. *W. A. Cyclist*, 12 May 1899.
11. *WAW*, 31 December 1897.
12. Ibid., 24 June 1898.
13. Ibid., 5 March 1897.
14. *Austral Wheel*, December 1898.
15. *W. A. Cyclist*, 5 May 1899.
16. *WAW*, 23 July, 29 October 1897; *W. A. Cyclist*, 26 May 1899.
17. *Morning Herald*, 16 July 1898; *Western Mail*, 1 July 1898; *Austral Wheel*, February 1899.

18. *W. A. Cyclist,* 26 May 1898, citing a goldfields newspaper; for the reply, see *Austral Wheel,* February 1899.
19. Gordon Inglis, *Sport and Pastime in Australia* (London: 1912), p.261.
20. *Coolgardie Miner,* 23 February 1895; *Austral Wheel,* February 1898 and February 1899.
21. *Austral Wheel,* May 1896, *WAW,* 5 February 1897.
22. *Western Mail,* 29 April 1898; *New South Wales Cycling Gazette,* 18 June 1898; *WAW,* 17 June 1898; *N. S. W. Cycling Gazette,* 2 July 1898.
23. *WAW,* 23 July, 30 July 1897.
24. *Morning Herald,* 9 August 1897; *West Australian Sporting Judge* and *Wheelman,* 27 August 1898; *Western Mail,* 9 September 1898; *WAW,* 30 June 1899; W. P. Forlonge, "Cycling: Comparison with Other National Athletic Sports", *Austral Wheel,* September 1896.
25. *WAW,* 1 October 1897.
26. See Australian Archives (Brighton) Defence records, MP 84/1, file nos. 1947/1/57 and 1947/1/58.
27. *Morning Herald,* 23 October 1899; *W. A. Cyclist,* 4 November 1899.
28. For Adelaide-Darwin, *Adelaide Advertiser,* 20 May 1897; for Darwin-Adelaide, ibid., 20 September 1897.
29. *Morning Herald,* 5 February 1900.

RICHARD BROOME

The Australian Reaction to Jack Johnson, Black Pugilist, 1907–9

The historian seeks to identify patterns of continuity and change in the past — to mould coherent meaning out of the chaos of past human events. This generalizing task often endangers the historian's ability to examine particular events closely, although this is a necessity if he is to discover what actually happened in the past. A necessity, because through the examination of the particular, the historian comes closest to the pulse of the people he is seeking to understand. The single event is of great interest to the historian, because as well as its long-term significance, it can have a large contemporary impact, especially if it is of a kind to encapsulate important social themes and is able to dramatize these to the community as a whole. This chapter examines once such event of great contemporary power as well as long-term importance — a prize-fight, which took place at the Sydney Stadium on Boxing Day 1908. It formed a new stage in modern boxing and was a landmark in relations between black and white in Australia. In this fight, before a waiting world, the American Negro Jack Johnson triumphed over the white title-holder, Tommy Burns, to become the first black man to win the prestigious title of heavyweight champion of the world.

Boxing contests are always potentially dramatic events which can produce great ambivalence in their audiences, because they encompass elements of struggle, violence, and courage. They have a compelling primitiveness about them. The fact that this particular fight was between a black and a white man threatened to further electrify the proceedings. Here I will focus solely upon the racial overtones and reactions to the fight, although the ripples it caused activated other social responses in Australian society. Above all else, this gloved contest demonstrated to many Australians the private and social significance they attributed to the notion of race, and it was an important historical incident in the moulding of these racial assumptions.

Pugilism in colonial Australia moved slowly from being a sport that was not tolerated by the respectable to one that achieved some acceptance by 1890. However, "decent people" did not object so much to amateur and recreational boxing, which allegedly developed manliness, as to fights to the finish for a cash prize. Despite this objection, and consequent attempts to outlaw them, prize-fights flourished at secret venues unknown to the "traps". William Hazlitt in 1826 had noted the English passion for boxing, and many Australian colonists in their rough-and-tumble convict surroundings seemed to relish the sport even more. After the loser of one particular bout in 1831 was carried off half-dead after thirty-three rounds, the spectators were so excited that they staged three impromptu contests for the fun of it. Despite their illegality, prize-fights remained popular largely because of the blood, drama, and gambling that surrounded them. Big contests were staged on the goldfields, where masculinity was the prevailing ethos. Part of Ned Kelly's charisma a generation later was due to his twenty-round bare-knuckle victory over "Wild" Wright in 1874 when only nineteen. Prize-fighting was prominent enough to be singled out by Dr L. D. Bevan in his sermon in 1892 attacking the sporting craze. He declared that, judging by the press, "there was not the slightest doubt that your pugilist was a much more important member of society that any monarch".[1]

The years around 1890 saw a change in the fortunes of prize-fighting as opposed to amateur boxing, which by now had become standard fare in most schools. This was largely due to the codification and civilizing process which most popular sports experienced in the late nineteenth century. After visits by the British champion James (Jem) Mace in 1877 and the Marquis of Queensberry in 1888, the colonial prize-fighters began to adopt the new scientific and cleaner Queensberry rules. Larry Foley, who was instructed by Mace, established a boxing saloon in Sydney, and this remained free of police harrassment. Gloves, clean fighting, and strict rules were decisive in bringing a measure of respectability to colonial boxing. The police attended prize-fights, but only intervened if one man was taking too much physical punishment. Now that the sport was out in the open, it burgeoned, encouraged by the activities of trainers, managers, and promoters. The bulk of their activity was centred on Foley's gymnasium at the back of his White Horse Hotel in George Street. Foley's attracted not only the boxing fraternity but a wide spectrum of the Sydney sporting world. That inimitable sportsman, Nat Gould, had his own chair at ringside.[2] It was here that Larry Foley trained or influenced a line of fighters who became prominent in world pugilistic circles, notably Peter Jackson, Peter Slavin, Albert Griffiths, and Bob Fitzsimmons. By 1900,

Australia was an important whistle stop on the itinerary of overseas pugilists, and there was never a shortage of local boxers to accommodate them. Bouts were staged at the Gaiety Theatre, Sydney, and the Cyclorama in Melbourne, and the regular crowds of up to three thousand might have been larger with bigger venues. By 1906, John Wren controlled boxing in Melbourne, but his efforts were soon eclipsed by those of the Sydney promoter, Hugh D. McIntosh.

It was McIntosh who put Australian boxing on the map in 1908. He was born in Sydney in 1876. His adventurous spirit, which may have stemmed from his Scottish father, a veteran of the Indian Mutiny, began to show when young Hugh left home at the age of seven to make his fortune. He worked in the Broken Hill mines and as a rural labourer and then as a chorus boy, until he finally made his fortune in the 1890s as a middle man in the greatest of all Australian trades — selling pies in parks and at sporting fixtures. From here he gravitated to sports promotion.[3] However, his early successes in cycling were outclassed by his invitation to the world heavyweight boxing champion, Tommy Burns, to defend his title in Australia against Bill Squires, the Australian champion. The Canadian, now resident in America, readily accepted, because as he had beaten Squires overseas twice before, it seemed like easy money.

Burns arrived in Perth in August 1908, and was feted all the way to Sydney by men of all classes, notably civic leaders. He was cheered through the streets of Perth while touring with the mayor in a four-in-hand, mobbed outside St Francis Xavier's Cathedral, Adelaide, and toasted by John Wren, the sporting fraternity, and the state Labor leader, G. M. Prendergast, while in Melbourne. Cheers erupted as he passed through every station between Melbourne and Sydney, especially at Albury, where he changed trains around the chilly hour of six as Australians had done for half a century. At Central Station in Sydney, this adulation continued as eight thousand people greeted him, and later many of these choked the roadway outside the Crystal Hotel in George Street, where he was welcomed by Alderman English and the MLAs E. W. O'Sullivan and Colonel Ryrie. At all these receptions the speakers were at pains to eulogize boxing, as they preferred to call the sport others pejoratively termed prize-fighting. They claimed it developed manliness, and in the clearest terms Colonel Ryrie stated that "boxing was an important element in the bringing up of Australians. It was necessary that they should have a sturdy young Australia to protect their hearths and homes, and who would be put in the forefront of the battle — not those milksops who cry out against it."[4]

The Canadian bathed in the adulation of the Australian sporting public. However, one thing marred the glory enjoyed by the world champion — the spectre of Jack Johnson on the horizon, the acknowledged "coloured champion of the world". Australians were well aware of the unsuccessful efforts of overseas promoters to match Burns and Johnson, and the fight talk that surrounded these efforts. Rumour alleged that Burns was dodging Johnson, though many others felt it was right that the Canadian should draw the "colour line", as all the previous white champions had done, and refuse to fight Johnson and other black pugilists. However, it appeared that Burns was more interested in money than race pride, because he declared that he would fight Johnson, but only for a sizeable six thousand pounds win or lose. Burns was questioned on all this at each of his receptions. When in Melbourne he bluntly posed the question in racial terms : "There are a lot of newspaper stories that I don't want to fight Johnson. I do want to fight him, but I want to give the white boys a chance first." In Sydney the following day Burns added: "Another thing, I don't think he is game."[5] The Australian sporting public were awaiting a Burns-Squires encounter, and being tempted by a much larger drama — the struggle between black and white. Little did they dream at this stage that they would have ringside seats.

While the sporting fraternity were thrilled by these developments, the Protestant clergy, the wowsers, and the moral improvers in general were shocked by what they saw as a barbaric excrescence on the nation. These upholders of civilization opposed prize-fights as part of the whole syndrome of barbarism which they claimed revolved around drinking, gambling, coarse behaviour, and physical activity, to the detriment of religion and mental culture. Letters of protest were sent to the premier of New South Wales, C. G. Wade, demanding an end to prize-fights. These zealous moral reformers might reasonably have expected some success from their protests, because only recently they had made real gains for the cause of sobriety and respectability with the aid of the conservative Carruthers and Wade ministries. As recently as 1907, the temperance forces had won a significant victory over the evils of drink, because a majority of electors in the local option vote had favoured a reduction in the number of hotel licences.[6]

The Reverend W. H. Ash fired a salvo for the civilizers in a letter to the *Sydney Morning Herald* in early August 1908. He claimed that the coming Burns-Squires fight would attract "the worst men in Sydney, with their worst side uppermost", and added that if parents had any sense, they would "suppress the brutish element in their children, and develop the higher side of their natures. The man who does otherwise is, in my opinion, false to civilization and to Christianity." Several correspondents alleged that, on the contrary, boxing developed character and the higher side of human nature. H. F. McHugh, a school headmaster, declared that "to test a man's grit, honour, courtesy, and generosity, put the gloves on with him. No other exercise so quickly shows moral failings, no other sport so quickly mends a defective character." Rev. T. Roseby introduced more rationality to the clergy's case by pointing out that most Christians did not object to amateur boxing or sport generally, which developed manliness. However, he added that they did oppose prize-fights, which were carried out merely for money and which encouraged brutality and, consequently, the bloodlust of the spectators. Modern sport, he argued, was making Australia a nation of barrackers rather than participants.[7]

All the Protestant Churches and the New South Wales Evangelical Council made formal protests to the premier, but to no avail. Wade merely promised that the police would be present as usual to ensure gloves were used and that none of the boxers became too distressed. He also agreed to prevent prize-fights from being held on government property.[8] Therefore, while the civilizers might reduce the evils of drinking and gambling, they made little impression on the sporting instinct.

Gripped by the notion that only big ideas produce big money — a view that was to make him a millionaire — Hugh McIntosh rented a market garden at Rushcutter's Bay. He informed the unsuspecting owner of this "out of town" paddock, that he wanted "to put on a two-man show to make a few bob out of the sailors" from the visiting American Fleet, and by this ruse secured a long lease at a trifling rental.[9] On the site he erected — at a cost of two thousand pounds — a wooden open-air stadium to seat sixteen thousand in which to stage the Burns-Squires fight. However, such daring proved conservative, when on the day of the fight an enormous concourse of forty thousand men flocked to the stadium (for only males were permitted entry), to see their native son battle for the title of heavyweight champion of the world. The spectacle was swelled by numbers of American sailors of the Great White Fleet which was then in Sydney on its official visit. Only fifteen thousand could squeeze inside, but the other twenty-five thousand remained outside to share the excitement, and three of these, atop telegraph poles, actually had a distant view of the fight. The crowd's expectations were not met, because Squires was outclassed and after making a courageous showing, was knocked out by Burns in the thirteenth round. Yet, the crowd showed their sportsmanship by warm applause for Burns, who after all was a real "white man". Colonel Ryrie commented that the crowd was so orderly that it "may have been assembled to listen to a high-class pianoforte recital, instead of a boxing contest".[10] A week later, nineteen thousand Melbourne men packed into the South Melbourne Stadium (built for McIntosh in an amazing twelve days along the lines of the Sydney Stadium), to see Bill Lang, the Victorian champion, challenge Burns for the title. The huge crowd cheered Lang throughout the fight, especially after he had knocked Burns off his feet in the second round, but Lang was hopelessly outmatched by the American in-fighting skills of his opponent. He was knocked out by Burns in the sixth round.[11]

A lot of money could be made in prize-fighting, but you had to be somebody. For these two fights, Burns received £4,000, about five times the annual salary of an Australian professional man. Squires received £1,000 for the punishment he took from Burns, and Lang received £600. Yet, handling fees and expenses were large; Lang, for instance, only netted £200 after these were deducted. Still, this was a large sum compared with the £217 10s he had earned from his previous eight fights. But it was really the promoters who won the prize, because from these two fights McIntosh grossed about £20,000 and netted at least half this sum after expenses. This sum was swelled by the receipts from screenings of the fight films; one showing at the Sydney Stadium required trams at 1½-minute intervals to transport the huge crowd.[12] Film had introduced new possibilities for sport. The excitement and horror of a boxing match could be seen again and again, by perhaps all the family. With his bank balance handsomely swollen, McIntosh promptly offered Burns £6,000 to fight Johnson "the coloured champion" win or lose, and he snapped up the offer. Money had burst through the "colour line" in boxing — the fight was on!

Jack Johnson arrived in quick time in late October, eager to fight Burns at long last. He later claimed it was the first fight in which he ever felt vindictive towards his opponent. Johnson badly wanted the title, but he also wanted revenge for being publicly called "yellow". Johnson was in an aggressive mood when interviewed in Perth and exclaimed: "No man living knows more about boxing than I do." He added: "How does Burns want it? Does he want it fast and willing? I'm his man in that case. Does he want it flat footed? Goodness, if he does, why I'm his man again. Anything to suit; but fast or slow, I'm going to win."[13] The first round of the verbal fighting which preceded the contest scheduled for twenty-sixth of

December was over. The sporting public were titillated and the clergy were aghast at the larrikin street-talk of Johnson.

The Australian public were bemused by this style, which came straight from the black areas of Galveston, Texas. Johnson was by profession a pugilist, who had won his first fight at the age of fifteen — a scuffle with the local top pug. He developed his magnificent 185-centimetre frame lifting cotton bales on the Galveston wharf. However, there was more to Johnson than physical prowess. He apparently sang well and played the double bass at every chance. He was a great talker, quite a wit, and an extrovert of the first order — altogether a man of considerable intelligence for those who cared to see it. Johnson was also political in that he was a leading member of his local (black) Methodist church, and also involved in municipal politics in Galveston, at a time when black civil rights were coming under renewed attack in the South.[14]

The sporting community had been tantalized before by this flamboyant black boxer, because Johnson had been in Australia eighteen months earlier, seeking a bout with the Australian champion Bill Squires. As Squires was soon to tour America, his manager John Wren threw difficulties in the way of an encounter in case Squires suffered a reputation-damaging defeat. The see-sawing negotiations, which teased the public, finally broke down with both sides accusing the other of evasion. Thus the acknowledged "coloured champion of the world" had to be content with knocking out fellow black man Peter Felix in 2½ minutes at the Gaiety Theatre. Johnson had his manager offset their expenses by screening to large audiences the film of the recent Burns-O'Brien title bout. A week later fifteen thousand rain-soaked men at Richmond Racecourse jeered "the coon" (Johnson), as he stepped into the ring attired in a gaudy boxing robe to meet the Victorian champion, Bill Lang. Some commented that it looked like a woman's dressing-gown, but this derision was soon silenced as Johnson took command of the fight. Within a few hits he remarked to his seconds, "Dis is a joke", and after carrying Lang for six rounds, he cut loose and floored him twice in the seventh, four times in the eighth, and once and for all in the ninth round.[15] He gained further notoriety, and a five-pound fine, when he pulled his white manager's nose after being called "a black bastard" in a dispute over money. Stories circulated about his relationship with theatre ladies, and it was rumoured that he had married while in Sydney. More fights were scheduled, including a novelty event against two middle-weights at the one time, but he mysteriously left Australia before these eventuated. He turned up in America praising

Australia and a certain Miss Lola Troy, who was reportedly a wealthy Sydney lady as "white as her gold was yellow".[16] Thereafter, boxing enthusiasts closely followed Johnson's career and the speculation about a match with Burns for the title.

Johnson's style was far different from the other black fighter well known to Australians — Peter Jackson. Jackson was a West Indian who fought as an Australian and who in 1901 chose Queensland as his resting place when he was dying from rapid consumption. He was a world heavyweight contender in the 1890s, but the white champions drew the "colour line" against him. Most ring commentators who tended to look down on "niggers" believed Jackson was a gentleman. He was immensely popular with the Australian boxing public, who erected a monument in his honour over his grave, because, as the *Brisbane Courier* described it, he was "modest".[17] The white could tolerate, even show affection for, a black man if he knew his place, but if he was an upstart like Johnson . . .

From the moment Johnson arrived in Australia, the sporting public became absorbed with the magic of the contest. Tommy Burns retired to a training camp befitting a world champion at the Hydro Majestic Hotel at Medlow Bath. He could afford such luxury; besides, he only had one handler, which Johnson (who had an entourage) thought niggardly and unbecoming a champion.[18] Burns ran miles on mountain tracks and displayed the dedicated attitude of a title-holder. Johnson, who for years had been forced to fight only other black boxers for small purses, installed himself in the more lowly, yet accessible, Sir Joseph Banks Hotel in Botany. But what style he had! For one shilling the fans could watch Johnson spar, shadow box, and hit the bag and speed ball. They came in large numbers to be entertained by his smiles, speeches jokes, and selections of the double bass. Burns later moved to Sydney and held two public training sessions a week, after the fans had complained that he was too isolated from them. Besides these sessions and the pre-fight rumours that circulated, the Sydney supporters were thrilled by exhibition bouts. At the Stadium, seven thousand watched Burns spar with Snowy Baker, the Australian amateur middleweight champion, who had missed an Olympic gold medal by a whisker. A big crowd attended an exhibition between Johnson and the Australian great, Larry Foley, at the Manly Skating Rink, which was concluded with a few selections by Johnson's small orchestra formed from his handlers.

One surprising element was that while it was custom that women were not permitted to attend prize-fights, they were admitted to these training sessions. The tradition was based on the belief that women were to be protected from the brutal sights and sounds of physical combat, and doubtless from the spectacle of near-naked male bodies in physical embrace. However, the *Bulletin* claimed that McIntosh was deluged by letters from women asking to be allowed to view the training sessions as they would not be allowed to see the fight itself. McIntosh obliged by allowing them to view Burns on Wednesday and Saturday afternoons, free of charge with tea and pastries thrown in. "The McIntosh has a tender feeling towards the fight-loving female," the *Bulletin* explained. "She is going to make the cinematograph pictures profitable after the war is over." Johnson similarly welcomed the ladies, but they had to pay a shilling to see his splendour. They came in considerable numbers to sum up his virility, for this was an age when bare chests were hard to come by in public.[19]

Though the colour of the boxers' skin provided the greatest drama, it was the more generalized venom they felt for each other that was most prominent early in the public verbal fighting. Each capital from Perth to Sydney held receptions for the boxers, and at these and in the press generally, each denounced his opponent. Johnson declared: "No one has yet found the yellow streak Mr. Burns speaks of. That is a thing any man in the world would take offence at. When he steps into the ring we shall see where the yellow streak is." Burns snarled: "He wanted me, and he'll get me. Talk's cheap, and my answer will be given to all that on the day of the fight."[20] This confrontation was not a promotional exercise, though it had that effect. Thirteen thousand man packed the Stadium two weeks before the fight, just to see the fighers' sparring partners box, largely because Burns and Johnson were the seconds in this bout. The venom between these two had been vented for too long to be contrived, and referees, commentators, and the boxing fraternity alike believed it to be genuine.

The pugilists' hatred for each other spread in this tense atmosphere. Johnson became concerned that he would not get fair treatment from the Australian public. One reporter, commenting on the strength of the hatred for Johnson, stated: "Citizens who have never prayed before are supplicating Providence to give the white man a strong right arm with which to belt the coon into oblivion."[21] Johnson demanded two judges. He also had good reason to suspect that McIntosh might be prejudiced against him, because the promoter had originally negotiated with the American ex-champion

Jim Jeffries to act as referee. Yet Jeffries had refused to fight Johnson or any other black men while he was champion! Antipathy between Johnson and McIntosh developed. There were several public arguments, and they almost came to blows when Johnson greeted McIntosh with "How do, Mr. McIntosh? How did you drag yourself away from Tahmy?" Norman Lindsay claimed that McIntosh kept a lead pipe rolled up in music in his office in McIntosh's words, "for that big black bastard if he ever comes any funny business with me." The camouflage was appropriately the score of "Sing Me to Sleep, Mother".[22]

The developing bitterness was so intense that one columnist alleged that McIntosh was concerned lest in this "wowser-ridden community" such bad blood might cause the authorities to stop the fight. Certainly the civilizers tried to achieve this. The Protestant clergy groaned at the adulation given to the fighters, which confirmed their worst fears of the inordinate love of sport among Australians. Their distaste for Catholic morality was also strengthened when Cardinal Moran was photographed on the cathedral steps with Tommy Burns. In early October, a deputation of Protestant clergy visited Wade and demanded that he stop the fight. While he concurred in their distinction between prize-fighting and "legitimate" boxing, he argued that if glove contests were banned, amateur boxing which did so much for the manliness of Australian youth would also have to be eliminated. Wade merely promised the usual presence of the police to ensure severe injury did not occur.[23] The Protestants remained unsatisfied. The Congregationalists recorded their disgust at the brutality and barbarity of prize-fighting, while the Sydney Anglican Synod shuddered because this coming spectacle with "its inherent brutality and dangerous nature", could not fail "to corrupt the moral tone of the community".[24] However, these and other protests were to no avail. Although the Protestants had achieved many moral reforms with the help of Wade, he was not going to challenge the sporting instinct by stopping this fight without evidence of wider support than the clergy could at present muster for such action.

The general fight fervour was encouraged further by the images of the coming struggle projected by the press. Burns was depicted as a clean-cut spartan with massive head, arms, legs and torso, which were all accentuated by his remarkably small stature (of 170 centimetres) for a heavyweight champion. His boxing brain and courage were the attributes most journalists stressed. "I do not think Johnson is his equal in the all important matter of brains", was a typical comment.[25] This was probably due less to empirical evidence than to the prevailing ideas about the lower intelligence of the black races. On the other hand, racist ideas current in boxing and other circles suggested that black men could withstand more pain, at least on the head, because they were less civilized and sensitive than white men. Some even suggested physiological and medical evidence for this.[26] Johnson, who was 185 centimetres tall (and some even alleged 195 centimetres), was said to have massive natural strength, but it was claimed that he trained on women and champagne, when he bothered to train at all. However, a few journalists did suggest that this was a ruse fabricated by Johnson's own camp to keep the odds long. The fight was portrayed as a contest between the brains and dedication of Burns and the brute strength and flashness of Johnson. The image was of Beauty and the Beast. It was as much racial prejudice as knowledge that caused ex-champions J. J. Corbett and Jim Jeffries, most of the journalists, and the sporting public to predict (and hope for) a Burns victory.

The racial theme had been there all along seething below the surface. In early November the *Bulletin* had sneered: "The coloured man is accompanied by his wife, a white woman, somewhat addicted to jewellery." However, several weeks before the fight the racial issue burst through unabashed. The *Australian Star* published a cartoon on its front page depicting the fight in progress, watched by representatives of the white and coloured races, with the caption: "A Waiting World. Race War Cloud!" Underneath was a letter from a correspondent who claimed that "this battle may in the future be looked back upon as the first great battle of an inevitable race war . . . there is more in this fight to be considered than the mere title of pugilistic champion of the world."[27] The Norman Lindsay poster that McIntosh distributed widely to publicize the fight must have imprinted this idea on many people's minds. There, on the billboards and telegraph poles around the city, was the powerful Lindsay image of a towering black facing a courageous, smaller white. This must have evoked the deepest feelings Australians held about the symbols of blackness and whiteness and evoked the emotiveness of a big man versus a small man and the populous coloured races versus the numerically smaller white race.

It must be stressed that while this fight was not the first encounter between a black and a white man in Australia's history, it was unique. From early colonial times onwards, visiting or resident Negroes and a few Aboriginal boxers had fought whites. However, these matches were in a totally different class from the Burns-Johnson fight. Johnson was seen as a flash black who appeared not to know his place. Furthermore, he dared to challenge a white for the prestigious title of top dog in the boxing world. Similarly it must be remembered that in the late nineteenth century, most Australians were deeply influenced by the prevailing ideas about race and human development. The most popular notion was that there was a hierarchy of races based upon their material development, which placed the Anglo-Saxon race at the top and the dark-skinned peoples at the bottom, nearest the primates. Social Darwinist thought heightened this belief in unequal and competing racial types which were all involved in the struggle for existence.[28] These ideas existed against the background of Aboriginal-European conflict; the long struggle to establish immigration restriction legislation to keep Australia white; and the increasing fear after 1900 of an invasion of the wide open Australian spaces by the Asian "hordes". It was in 1908 that this race struggle pressure forced the *Bulletin* to abandon its parochial banner of "Australia for Australians" and proclaim, "Australia for the white man".

Therefore, the struggle between the white and black races with which many Australians had become obsessed was here dramatized before their very eyes, portrayed as a battle between good and evil, civilization against animalism, the brainy Spartan against the brutish braggard. The racial assumptions of this community committed to whiteness were being laid on the line in this symbolic struggle. It was reported that on the eve of the fight, most people, even women, talked of little else. Three trainloads of spectators had just arrived from Melbourne, while a party was making its way from the West Australian goldfields. Although the tickets ranged in price from ten shillings to ten pounds (the minimum wage then being forty-two shillings a week), still they sold, and McIntosh had men working feverishly to enlarge the Stadium to hold twenty thousand people.

Overnight rain cleared on the morning of the fight, which was scheduled to start at 11 a.m. to enable the filming of the great contest. At 6 a.m., five thousand men were at the gates of the Stadium and well before 11 a.m. it was packed by twenty thousand spectators who paid a world record £26,000 gate money. Outside the Stadium, a huge concourse of thirty thousand people who had been unable to squeeze inside were kept orderly by two hundred police, as they milled around hoping to hear news of the events inside. Six hundred miles away, over five thousand Melburnians crowded outside the *Argus* office to listen to progress reports, and throughout the country, crowds gathered at post offices to hear fight developments. The contest attracted males from all classes — and a few women. A special concession was accorded to Mrs Jack London, who was allowed to sit at ringside beside her famous novelist husband while he reported the fight for the Melbourne *Argus.* It was alleged that another half-dozen women had sneaked in disguised as men. Johnson received only polite applause as he sprung into the ring dressed in a greyish robe. He grinned, bowed, pirouetted and threw kisses to the crowd. Some of the spectators cat-called and yelled "coon" and "nigger" — but Johnson only grinned wider. As the *Bulletin* explained, the crowd had not come to see the fight "so much as to witness a black aspirant for the championship of the world beaten to his knees and counted out".[29] Burns emerged amid deafening cheers which lasted for over five minutes. Nervously, as if he was the challenger rather than the champion, he took off his old blue suit and placed it in his battered suitcase. It was Johnson who showed the style of a champion as he bounded across the ring grinning, and shook the tenuous hand of a startled Burns. The betting favoured Burns, but this was misdirected race optimism, and it is significant that overseas boxing circles overwhelmingly supported Johnson. Johnson favoured himself, and as the fight was about to begin, he leant over the ropes and in an audible voice asked his handler had he got "that bet on". The bell sounded, and McIntosh, who had been appointed referee to break the impasse over who would control the match, brought the two men together.

The first round was as sensational as the whole fight. No sooner had it begun than Burns was floored by a heavy uppercut for the count of eight. He rose shaken and even the champagne applied to his face by his seconds failed to revive him fully. Johnson showed his contempt for the pressmen at ringside by ejecting a mouthful of water over them. Burns only made a showing in the third round, to the cheers of "Good Boy Tommy, Good Boy Tommy!" For the most part, Johnson dictated the fight both physically and mentally. He even dominated the in-fighting, which was Burns's forte. By the sixth round, Burns's face was swelling and his lips were puffed, his right eye was swollen and his white torso reddened. Johnson remained unscathed, belying the pre-fight jokes that his eyes would be "blackened". The fight slowed after the sixth round, because Johnson, grinning all the while, decided to amuse himself further. He stiffened his abdominal muscles and allowed Burns to hit them at will. He waved and smiled to the crowd, and even dropped his guard and taunted Burns. The champion's futile close work was greeted with: "I thought you were an in-fighter", and when Burns evaded Johnson, the latter quipped: "Say, little Tahmy, you're not fighting. Can't you? I'll have to show you how." As Burns took more punishment, Johnson patted him on the head and sneered at his virility: "Poor little boy, Jewel won't know you when she gets you back from this fight." His seconds shouted to Johnson to stop talking to the crowd and watch Burns, and Johnson merely jeered:

"I see him, oh yes, though he is so small." All this taunting of the smaller and outclassed white drove the crowd to a fury. Some yelled: "Flash nigger" and "That's flashness", referring derogatorily to Johnson's showy manner, but he only grinned, waved, and posed to them over Burns's shoulder. Their rage increased. Few actually heard Johnson's taunts at the time, but they gauged their import and read a full and deliberate account of them the next day. Burns had also engaged in this verbal fighting, but his unimaginative remarks of "You cur", "You big dog" and so on, were not highlighted at all. Johnson clearly intended to punish and humiliate Burns as well as defeat him, and he openly admitted this after the fight. It was little wonder that this calculating and controlled performer had the nickname back in Galveston of "the Iceberg". By the eleventh round he ceased talking and proceeded to reduce Burns to a pulp. By the thirteenth round a series of blows to Burns's battered face and body had the champion immobilized and swaying like a reed in the wind. As the fourteenth round opened, the cries of "that's enough" from the crowd had become insistent, and after Burns sank to his knees under a flurry of blows, Superintendent Mitchell intervened and stopped the fight. Johnson was announced the winner. A few cheered, but almost to a man the Stadium fell quiet and was emptied in a record twelve minutes as twenty thousand men slunk onto the waiting trams. Outside the Stadium, pictures of Burns had plunged to a penny, while Johnson's were sixpence but no one was buying. The whole country was stunned into silence. Even in the distant Solomons, anxious planters hid the newspaper reports from the "natives". Still, some sportsmen at Caulfield that afternoon took the hint and backed black horses for allegedly handsome wins.[30]

Not only did twenty thousand Australians actually witness the humiliation of the white, but the remainder could read about it in the voluminous press reports. The images the journalists evoked in these reports were particularly significant for the racial ideas they contained. Jack London stated frankly that while his sympathies lay with the white, Burns was not only defeated, but massacred. Most of the morning dailies were unemotional, yet in their quiet way they conjured up the image of a towering black, a bronze statue, a mass of archetypal darkness, playing with the smaller and helpless white, as a man would with a boy. The *Daily Telegraph* suggested it was a battle between civilized man and a barbarian, and printed this caption under a cartoon depicting Burns's defeat:

> And yet for all we know and feel,
> For Christ and Shakespeare, knowledge, love,
> We watch a white man bleeding reel,
> We cheer a black with bloodied glove.

Several newspapers likened the fight to a struggle between man and a beast. *Fairplay*, the Liquor Trades' weekly, remarked that it "seemed a reminiscence of a huge primordial ape . . . carrying off a pre-Adamite man, worrying his victim in deathly playfulness". The *Bulletin* fostered this image in its cartoons and likened the shaven-headed Johnson to a reptile. Characteristically, the *Truth* managed to go one lower when it remarked: "The coon towered over the Canadian like a Brahma Pootra over a bantam . . . Mistah Jahnsing you is It — and sorry we are to say it." However, the crudest and most racist account was written by the bombastic Randolph Bedford. It was so strong that it earned some very angry letters objecting to its bigoted and unfair remarks. Bedford alleged that if the fight had been held in America, Johnson would have been shot for his flash talk, and his executioner acquitted. "Even at the Stadium", he said "there was all the hatred of twenty thousand whites for all the negroes in the world." He depicted the fight in archetypal terms, drawing on the several ingrained value meanings that white and black had for the Caucasian mind: "Yet the white beauty faced the black unloveliness, forcing the fight, bearing the punishment as if it were none . . . weight and reach were telling against intrepidity, intelligence and lightness . . . His courage still shone in his eyes; his face was disfigured and swollen and bloodied. He was still beautiful by contrast — beautiful but to be beaten; clean sunlight fighting darkness and losing." But for the English slave trade, Bedford added, "Johnson might still be up a tree in Africa." Another of the *Bulletin* school, Henry Lawson, was infuriated by the triumph of black over white.

> It was not Burns that was beaten — for a nigger has smacked your face.
> Take heed — I am tired of writing — but O my people take heed,
> For the time may be near for the mating of the Black and the White to breed.

Lawson was moved like many others by the sexual fears and fascinations behind the contact of black and white.[31]

Why had fifty thousand Sydney men attempted to actually see the fight, and why had countless others held their breath around Australia waiting for the result? The simple answer is that the strength of the sporting instinct in Australia was compounded by the racist desire to see the black man beaten by the white favourite. However, many thousands of people flocked to see the fight film afterwards, despite the knowledge that the black man had won. Large crowds saw the film at the Sydney Stadium, and the Melbourne *Age* reported that for four or five days hundreds were refused admission at the matinee and evening performances, despite the venue being the Melbourne Town Hall and the fact that the cost of the seats ranged from a shilling to five shillings. One Melbourne reviewer wrote that even though they were without sound, the pictures "worked the audience up to a pitch of excitement which finally found vent in prolonged cheers or deafening boo-booing as Burns or Johnson scored in the final rounds".[32] The fight caught up the disparate themes of the struggle between good and evil, the fascination with physical prowess and violence, the expression of sexuality in a sexually suppressed society, and the racial and racist notions of a committed white nation, and dramatized them to the whole community. This was the complex fascination! The fight displayed to Australians the values they held, or at least the social themes they saw as significant. Above all else, it reflected the ambivalence born of fear, hate, sexual myths, and admiration that many Australians felt towards the black races. Norman Lindsay for one was in this predicament. He thought that Johnson was the most magnificent physical specimen he had seen, and yet he was black. His artistic portrayal of Johnson reflected this ambivalence, because it portrayed Johnson as magnificent evil. Similarly, the titillated public flocked to the fight films, at the Sydney Tivoli or Melbourne Opera House, to cheer and boo Johnson in some confusion. The Melbourne larrikins were less ambivalent. One tampered with Johnson's car, while others muddied and mutilated Johnson's posters and scrawled "The Bank Cow", "The Big Black Skite", or worse over his image. Burns's likeness was adorned with "Good Old White Man" and other eulogies.[33]

Johnson himself had much to do with this ambivalence, for both in the fight and afterwards he presented a different image than had existed before the fight and confused the conception of "niggers" that many Australians held. He bragged that he could beat Burns in any sport or musical activity. Then he stated that he had invented improvements for the flying machine. Even more astonishing, he revealed a working knowledge of archeological concepts and, turning the knife a little more, added: "Your central Australian natives must have been men of genius to have turned out such artistic and ideal weapons." Always in control of the situation, Johnson declared that he had never expected to find sympathy among Australians because of his colour and race. "As I am a descendant of Ham," he said, "I must bear your reproaches because I beat a white man." With a final twist of the knife he added that he was unperturbed by all this, as he could always find solace in his favourite books — *Paradise Lost, Pilgrims Progress*, and *Titus Andronicus*.[34]

Johnson not only evoked a racial reaction in many Australians, but also contributed to the development of the English language. Oral evidence has revealed that "long johns" were now dubbed by some "Jack Johnsons", while many free-spoken Australians who grasped for a simile of darkness exclaimed: "Its as black as Jack Johnson's arse!" One of C. J. Dennis's verses in *The Songs of a Sentimental Bloke* (1915) entitled "The Stoush o' Day", evoked the image of a black and white prize-fight to describe the cycle of night deposing day deposing night. In *Goodbye to All That,* Robert Graves records that the Allies on Flanders' fields called certain deadly German shells "Jack Johnsons", because of the menacing black smoke they emitted. Most poignant of all in describing the emotion many whites felt for this flash black who married white women was the term *Johnson* to describe a prostitute's bully — if he was black.[35]

In the two weeks after the fight a public reaction swelled up, some of it directed at Johnson and the black races, and some of it directed inwards. The latter was the controversy between the moral reformists and the sporting fraternity over whether prize-fights should be staged. The *Sydney Morning Herald* lead the case for prohibiting such contests, when it claimed that the recent fight was a "nakedly brutal scuffle", not sport, and added in moralistic and middle-class terms that prize-fights "stimulated the brute not only in those who actually witness them . . . but upon that unfortunately all too numerous class at the bottom of society, to whom the mere 'bruiser' is ever the supreme type of hero".[36] Even the more sporting-minded press disliked the new American trends in prize-fighting of in-fighting, slanging-matches, and the large money prizes. There was a general resentment against the growing professionalism in sport which endangered manliness and thus national life. The moralistic line of the civilizers reached its most hysterical in some of the clergy. The Reverend H. Worrall of Bendigo denounced the fight as a "carnival of savagery". All those memorable pulpit phrases were used to show that these exhibitions encouraged blood-lust and the worship of Mammon. The *Sydney Morning Herald* sponsored an amazing debate in its columns, publishing 101 letters on the fight in the eight issues after the contest. The editor of the *Daily Telegraph* was less liberal with his newsprint; he published only thirty-six of "a very large number of letters", because the views were so repetitive. The whole debate was about the relation between prize-fighting and national strength. In brief, the clergy, women, and "the decent people" (as Rev. W. H. Ash called them), argued that prize-fights were brutal, coarse, and barbaric events which threatened the community's morals. Their opponents argued that

the moral improvers had no right to curb the freedom of those who
wished to enjoy such contests. They attacked the clergy for leading
the country to "namby-pambyism" and debilitating the nation's
defence potential. The moral improvers replied that watching prize-
fights had little to do with knowing how to handle a horse or a gun
for national defence. Yet, one man who attended the fight believed
he had learnt "a few wrinkles" which would hold him in good stead
if the "Japs" came.[37]

The moral debate had circled back to the more central racial
theme. Many of the correspondents did not use the word *if,* but
when, because they believed that a race war was inevitable. Many
Australians were convinced of this before the fight, but never
before had the race struggle been so dramatically impressed on their
experience. One Australian saw his country as "a rich plum, ripe for
the plucking of the land-hungry foreigner" and thus, because of this
inevitable "struggle for existence, the fighting instinct had to be
perpetuated in the Anglo-Saxon race". Some even took comfort
from Burns's defeat, because though much smaller, he showed the
pluck and courage needed "to maintain white Australia, and avert
the yellow peril".[38] Others damned Burns for humiliating the white
race for money. Jim Jeffries echoed this sentiment from America.
However, most were certain that a suitably sized white man would
soon defeat Johnson. There were a few correspondents who
defended Johnson against the racial insults he had been subjected to
and the unsporting and unmanly booing of his victory.

The fight and the controversy that surrounded it alarmed the
government. The chief secretary, William Wood, though reportedly
a boxing enthusiast himself, stated that if another such bout was
organized, it would be prevented and the principals prosecuted. He
claimed that the Burns-Johnson encounter, which he witnessed
himself, had "savoured more of the brutal and repulsive than of the
scientific", and it was "highly undesirable that Sydney should
correspond to the Pacific Slope of America as the settling ground for
every phase of pugilistic undertaking'.[39] McIntosh replied that he
had merely wanted to achieve a coup for his native city of Sydney by
staging this fight, and also guard against the "namby-pambyism"
and degeneration of his race. He did not mention the fact that he
made twenty-seven thousand pounds clear on the fight itself and
netted eighty thousand from the Australian and overseas film rights.
McIntosh added: "The Stadium will never be let again for such a
fight as that recently decided."[40] Had the civilizers won? Premier
Wade, out of the state at the time of the fight, agreed that it seemed
"unsavoury and debasing". On his return he proposed regulations

to prevent in-fighting and to make six-ounce gloves standard — two ounces more than those used in the recent fight.[41] Unfortunately for the civilizers, the legislation was never introduced, and prize-fights, admittedly of a less spectacular nature, became common fare again. The conjuncton of a title fight and a racial struggle had provided sufficient drama to give the moral improvers more social leverage than they usually enjoyed. But it was short-lived, and as always in Australia, the sporting instinct won through.

Burns left the country on 2 January 1909, claiming that it was now his ambition, if given a chance, "to win the championship back again for the white race". But no one took him seriously. The public began to lose interest in Burns, not because he had lost but because of his mercenary nature, the excuses he made, and the claim that if the fight had not been stopped he might have won.[42]

Jack Johnson, who some believe to be the greatest heavyweight of all time, was hooted and booed in a so-called sporting country because he was black, because he was a "flash nigger", and because he had beaten a white man. His presence in Australia and his fight with Burns had interpreted to Australians the notions and values they held about race in the most dramatic form they had ever been presented. The fight was thus a significant historical incident in the development of Australian racial thinking. On the other hand, the Australian experience also further shaped Johnson. He won the title here and was able to survive a tense racial situation. Johnson now became a black hero in America and a symbol in the struggle for Negro emancipation.[43] In his future career he continued to infuriate whites because of his fascination for white women — he married four — and his extravagance and style, which set the pattern for future boxing champions. Finally, the whites got even. They eventually found a 198-centimetre cowboy, Jess Willard, who in 1915 beat Johnson in twenty-six rounds, when Johnson was thirty-eight years old and weakened by living the good life in Europe. In 1920 the Americans also gaoled him for a year, under the prostitution provisions of the Mann Act, for transporting his wife-to-be across state lines. But all this is to leap too far ahead.

On the eve of his departure from Australia in mid-February 1909, Jack Johnson paused in Brisbane to visit the grave of Peter Jackson, who had died in poverty eight years earlier. Jackson, unlike Johnson, had never broken the "colour line". For a few silent moments, on this Toowong hillside, the perennial smile slipped from Jack Johnson's face.

NOTES

My thanks go to Inga Clendinnen and Rhys Isaac of La Trobe University, and to my wife Margaret Donnan, who all pushed me beyond what I had first seen in this subject.

1. William Hazlitt, "Notes from a Journey through France and Italy 1826", in *The Boxing Companion*, ed. Denzil Batchelor (London: Eyre and Spottiswoode, 1964), p.25; *Australian*, 7 January 1831 (courtesy of John Hirst); Colin Cave, ed., *Ned Kelly: Man and Myth* (Sydney: Cassell, 1968), p.155; Keith Dunstan, *Sports* (Melbourne: Cassell, 1973), p.192.
2. Frank Gerald, *A Millionaire in Memories* (London: George Routledge, 1936), pp.201-10.
3. *Triad*, 2 February 1925.
4. *Sydney Morning Herald* (hereafter *SMH*), 5-12 August 1908; for Colonel Ryrie's speech, 7 August 1908.
5. *SMH*, 11 August 1908; *Australian Star*, 11 August 1908.
6. *SMH*, 12 August 1908; Richard Broome, "Protestantism in New South Wales Society 1900-1914" (PhD thesis, University of Sydney, 1975), chap. 6.
7. *SMH*, 8-15 August 1908.
8. *Australian Christian World*, 21 August 1908; New South Wales Congregational Union Papers, Mitchell Library, uncatalogued, box 12, secretary's minute book, 11 August 1908; *SMH*, 12 August 1908.
9. John Hetherington, *Australians: Nine Profiles* (Melbourne: Cheshire, 1960), p.49.
10. *SMH*, 25 August 1908; *Australian Star*, 25 August 1908.
11. *SMH*, 4 September 1908.
12. *Australian Star*, 27 August, 3 September 1908; for Lang's previous earnings, see court case reported in *Bulletin*, 14 November 1908; for McIntosh's earnings, see *Australian Star*, 26 August 1908.
13. *Lone Hand*, 1 December 1908; *Australian Star*, 22 October 1908; *SMH*, 23 October 1908.
14. *Lone Hand*, 1 December 1908.
15. For the fight against Felix, see *Australian Star*, 20 February 1908; for Lang, see *Illustrated Sporting and Dramatic News* (hereafter *Illustrated Sporting*), 19 March 1907.
16. *Australian Star*, 19 March 1907; *Illustrated Sporting* 4 April, 4 July 1907.
17. *Brisbane Courier*, 29 December 1908.
18. *Lone Hand*, 1 December 1908.
19. *Bulletin*, 3 December 1908; *Bulletin*, 12 November 1908. The enthusiasm for a glimpse of Johnson reflected white folklore which related blackness to virility and lustfulness; see Sol Encel, "The Nature of Race Prejudice in Australia", in *Racism: The Australian Experience*, ed. F. S. Stevens, vol. 1 (Sydney: Australian and New Zealand Book Company, 1971), p.33.
20. *SMH*, 30 October, 24 October 1908.
21. *Illustrated Sporting*, 15 November 1908.
22. Ibid., 3 December 1908; Norman Lindsay, *My Mask* (Sydney: Angus and Robertson, 1970), p.211.
23. *Illustrated Sporting*, 15 November 1908; *Australian Christian World*, 11 September, 13 November 1908; *SMH*, 3 October 1908.
24. *N.S.W. Congregational Union Year Book*, 1909, p.129; *Votes and Proceedings of 14th Sydney (Anglican) Synod*, November 1908, p.62.
25. *Australian Star*, 20 November 1908.

26. Eugene Corri, *Fifty Years in the Ring* (London: Hutchinson, 1933), pp.101, 221-23; J. G. B. Lynch, *Prominent Pugilists of Today* (London: 1914), p.137; *Age*, 24 October 1908.
27. *Bulletin*, 5 November 1908; *Australian Star*, 5 December 1908.
28. M. C. Hartwig, "Aborigines and Racism: An Historical Perspective", in Stevens, *Racism* 2: 9-24; Henry Reynolds, "Racial Thought in Early Colonial Australia', *Australian Journal of Politics and History* 10 (1974): 45-53.
29. *SMH*, 28 December 1908; *Bulletin*, 31 December 1908.
30. For reports of the fight, see especially *Australian Star*, 26 December 1908; *SMH*, *Daily Telegraph*, *Age*, and *Argus* for 28 December 1908; *Bulletin*, 31 December 1908, *Sporting Judge*, 2 January 1909, and *Illustrated Sporting*, 31 December 1908; for the reaction in the Solomon Islands see Jack McLaren, *My Odyssey* (London: Jonathan Cape, 1925), pp.238-39.
31. *Argus*, 28 December 1908; *SMH*, 28 December 1908; *Daily Telegraph*, 28 December 1908; *Fairplay*, 7 January 1908; *Bulletin*, 31 December 1908; *Truth*, 27 December 1908; Randolph Bedford's account is in the Melbourne *Herald*, 26 December 1908; for the replies see *Herald*, 28, 29, and 31 December 1908. Henry Lawson's poem is quoted by Humphrey McQueen in *A New Brittania* (Ringwood, Vic.: Penguin, 1971), pp.111-12.
32. *Age*, 6 January 1909; *Argus*, 4 January 1909.
33. John Hetherington, *Norman Lindsay: Embattled Olympian* (Melbourne: Oxford University Press, 1973), pp.74-75; *Bulletin*, 14 January 1909.
34. *SMH*, 31 December 1908 and 4 January 1909.
35. Eric Partridge, *A Dictionary of the Underworld British and American* (London: Routledge and Kegan Paul, 1968), p.369.
36. *SMH*, 28 December 1908.
37. *SMH*, 28 December 1908. *Daily Telegraph*, 5 January 1909; *SMH*, 30 December 1908 and 2 January 1909.
38. Oscar Young, *SMH*, 30 December 1908; Sylvester Browne, *SMH*, 5 January 1909.
39. *SMH*, 31 December 1908.
40. *Illustrated Sporting*, 25 March 1909; Hetherington, *Australians*, p.51; *Australian Star*, 31 December 1908.
41. *SMH*, 5 January 1909.
42. *Australian Star*, 1 and 2 January 1909.
43. Nat Fleischer, *Fifty Years at Ringside* (New York: Fleet, 1958), pp.280-81 and pp.75-76.

Select Bibliography

Altham, H.S., and Swanton, E.W. *A History of Cricket.* 2 vols. London: George Allen and Unwin, 1938.

Arlott, John, ed. *The Oxford Companion to Sports and Games.* London: Oxford University Press, 1975.

Aronson, S.H. "The Sociology of the Bicycle". *Social Forces* 30 (1952).

Ball, Donald W., and Loy, John W., eds. *Sport and Social Order: Contributions to the Sociology of Sport.* Reading, Mass.: Addison-Wesley, 1975.

Bennett, Scott. *The Clarence Comet: The Career of Henry Searle 1866-89.* Sydney: Sydney University Press, 1973.

Betts, John Rickards. "Organized Sport in Industrial America". Ph.D. thesis, Columbia University, 1951.

Bowe, Rowland. *Cricket.* London: Eyre and Spottiswoode, 1970.

Boyle, Robert H. *Sport: Mirror of American Life.* Boston: Little, Brown, 1963.

Brailsford, Dennis. *Sport and Society: Elizabeth to Anne.* London: Routledge and Kegan Paul, 1969.

Butt, Dorcas Susan. *Psychology of Sport.* New York: Van Nostrand Reinhold, 1976.

Caillois, Roger, *Man, Play and Games.* New York: Free Press, 1961.

Canes, Michael S. "The Economics of Professional Sports". Ph.D. thesis, University of California at Los Angeles, 1970.

Caunter, C.F. *The History and Development of Cycles.* London: HMSO, 1955.

Clawson, Marion, and Knetsch, Jack L. *Economics of Outdoor Recreation.* Baltimore: Johns Hopkins University Press, 1966.

Dabscheck, Braham. "Economics, Power and Sportsmen". *Politics* 11 (1976).

——— "Industrial Relations and Professional Team Sports in Australia". *Journal of Industrial Relations* 18 (1976).

——— "Sporting Equality: Labour Market vs Product Market Control". *Journal of Industrial Relations* 17 (1975).

——— "The Wage Determination Process for Sportsmen". *Economic Record* 51 (1975).

Daws, A.G. "Origins of Australian Rules Football". BA Hons. thesis, University of Melbourne, 1954.

de Mello, Anthony. *Portrait of Indian Sports.* London: Macmillan, 1959.

Demmert, Henry G. *The Economics of Professional Team Sports.* Lexington, Mass.: D.C. Heath, 1973.

Department of Tourism and Recreation. *Leisure — A New Perspective.* Canberra: Australian Government Publishing Service, 1975.

——— *Sport: A Reference Paper.* Canberra, 1962.

Docker, Edward. *History of Indian Cricket.* Meerut: Macmillan, 1976.

Dougan, Derek, and Young, P.M. *On the Spot: Football as a Profession.* Newton Abbot, Devon: Stanley Paul, 1975.

Dunn, J. *Australian Rules Football: An Illustrated History.* Melbourne: Cassell, 1974.

Dunning, Eric, ed. *The Sociology of Sport.* London: Frank Cass, 1971.

Dunstan, Keith. *Sports.* Melbourne: Cassell, 1973.

—— *The Paddock That Grew: The Story of the Melbourne Cricket Club.* Melbourne: Cassell, 1962.

Durso, Joseph, *The All American Dollar: The Big Business of Sports.* Boston: Houghton Mifflin, 1971.

Edwards, Harry. *The Sociology of Sport.* Homewood, Ill.: Dorsey Press, 1973.

—— *The Revolt of the Black Athlete.* New York: Free Press, 1969.

Flint, Rachel, Heyhoe, and Rheinberg, Netta. *Fair Play: The Story of Women's Cricket.* Sydney: Angus and Robertson, 1976.

Ford, J. *Cricket: A Social History.* Newton Abbot, Devon: David and Charles, 1972.

—— *Prize Fighting.* Newton Abbot, Devon: Stanley Paul, 1971.

Ganefo, I. "Sport and Politics in Djakarta". *Asian Survey* 5 (1965).

Gardner, Paul. *Nice Guys Finish Last: Sport and American Life.* London: Allen Lane, 1974.

Geertz, C. "Deep Play: Notes on the Balinese Cockfight". In *Interpretation of Cultures,* edited by C. Geertz, chap. 15. London: Hutchinson, 1975.

Gould, Nat. *The Magic of Sport, Mainly Autobiographical.* London: John Long, 1909.

Green, Geoffrey, *The History of the Football Association.* London: Naldrett Press, 1953.

Grimsley, Will. *Tennis: Its History, People and Events.* Englewood Cliffs, NJ: Prentice-Hall, 1971.

Gruneau, Richard S., and Albinson, John A., eds. *Canadian Sports: Sociological Perspectives.* New York: Addison-Wesley, 1976.

Harris, H.A. *Sport in Britain: Its Origins and Development.* London: Stanley Paul, 1975.

—— *Sport in Greece and Rome.* Ithaca: Cornell University Press, 1972.

Hart, M. Marie, ed. *Sport in the Socio-Cultural Process.* Iowa: William C. Brown, 1974.

Hoch, Paul, *Rip Off the Big Game: The Exploitation of Sports by the Power Elite.* New York: Peter Smith, 1972.

Howarth, F. *The Story of the Football League.* Lancashire: Football League, 1938.

Huizinga, Johan. *Homo Ludens: A Study of the Play Element in Culture.* Boston, 1950.

Inglis, Gordon. *Sport and Pastime in Australia.* London: 1912.

Itzkowitz, D.C. "Peculiar Privilege: A Social History of English Foxhunting 1753-1885". Ph.D. thesis, University of Columbia, 1973.

Jaques, T.D., and Pavia, G.R., eds. *Sport in Australia: Selected Readings in Physical Activity.* Sydney: McGraw-Hill, 1976.

Jobling, Ian F. "Sport in Nineteenth Century Canada: The Effects of Technological Changes on Its Development". Ph.D. thesis, University of Alberta, 1970.

Kenyon, G.S., ed. *Sociology of Sport.* Chicago: Athletic Institute, 1969.

Lasch, Christopher. "The Corruption of Sports". *New York Review* (28 April 1977).

Longrigg, Roger. *The History of Horse Racing.* London: Macmillan, 1972.

Loy, J.W., and Kenyon, G.S., eds. *Sport, Culture and Society.* New York: Macmillan, 1969.

McGonagle, S. *The Bicycle in Life, Love, War and Literature.* London: Pelham Books, 1968.

McIntosh, P.C. *Sport in Society.* London: C.A Watts, 1968.

Macklin, Keith. *The History of Rugby League Football.* London: Stanley Paul, 1974.

Malcolmson, Robert, W. *Popular Recreations in English Society 1700-1850.* Cambridge: Cambridge University Press, 1973.

Mandle, W.F. "Cricket and Australian Nationalism in the Nineteenth Century". *Journal of the Royal Australian Historical Society* 59, pt.4 (December 1973).

—— "Games People Played: Cricket and Football in England and Victoria in the

Late Nineteenth Century". *Historical Studies* 15, no. 60 (April 1973).
—— *Winners Can Laugh: Sport and Society.* Ringwood, Vic.: Penguin, 1974.
Mason, Nicholas. *Football! The Story of All the World's Football Games.* London: Temple Smith, 1976.
Menke, Frank G. *The Encyclopedia of Sport.* 4th ed. New York: Barnes, 1969.
Miller, George. "A Study of the Economics of Professional Spectator Sports". Ph.D. thesis, Claremont Graduate School, 1965.
Miller, R. "Gambling and the British Working Class 1870-1914". MA thesis, University of Edinburgh, 1974.
Mullens, C.C. *History of Australian Rules Football.* Carlton, 1968.
Mulvaney, D. *Cricket Walkabout: The Australian Aboriginal Cricketers on Tour, 1867-68.* Melbourne: Melbourne University Press, 1967.
Natan, A., ed. *Sport and Society.* London: 1958.
Noll, R.G., ed. *Government and the Sports Business.* Washington: Brookings, 1974.
Oakley, Barry. *A Salute to the Great McCarthy.* Ringwood, Vic.: Penguin, 1970.
Padwick, E.W., ed. *A Bibliography of Cricket.* London: Library Association, 1977.
Pavia, G.R. "An Analysis of Social Class of the 1972 Australian Olympic Team". *Australian Journal of Physical Education* 61 (September 1973).
—— "An Investigation into the Sociological Background of Successful South Australian Footballers". *Australian Journal of Physical Education* 63 (March 1974).
Pollard, Jack. *Ampol's Sporting Records.* Sydney, 1973.
—— *Six and Out: The Legend of Australian and New Zealand Cricket.* 4th ed. Sydney: Pollard, 1973.
Ramsden, Caroline. *Ladies in Racing.* London: Stanley Paul, 1973.
Robinson, Ray, *On Top Down Under: Australia's Cricket Captains.* Sydney: Cassell, 1975.
Sage, G.H., ed. *Sport and American Society.* Reading, Mass.: Addison-Wesley, 1970.
Scott, Jack. *The Athletic Revolution.* New York: Free Press, 1971.
Seymour, Harold E. *Baseball: The Golden Age.* New York: Oxford University Press, 1971.
Smith, M.B. "The Growth and Development of Popular Entertainment and Pastimes in the Lancashire Cotton Towns 1830-70". M.Litt. thesis, University of Lancaster, 1970.
Smith, R.A. *The Social History of the Bicycle.* New York: McGraw-Hill, 1972.
Summers, Anne. *Damned Whores and God's Police.* Ringwood, Vic.: Penguin, 1975.
Talamini, John T., and Page, Charles H., eds. *Sport and Society: An Anthology.* Boston: Little, Brown, 1973.
Thomas, K. "Work and Leisure in Pre-Industrial Society". *Past and Present* 29 (December 1964).
Thompson, E.P. "Time, Work-Discipline and Industrial Capitalism". *Past and Present* 38 (December 1967).
Thompson, Richard. *Race and Sport.* London: Oxford University Press, 1964.
—— *Retreat from Apartheid: New Zealand's Sporting Contacts with South Africa.* Wellington: Oxford University Press, 1975.
—— "Rugby and Race Relations: A New Zealand Controversy". *Journal of the Polynesian Society* 69, no. 3 (September 1960).
Topham, R.G. "The C.F.C. and Collingwood". BA Hons. thesis, University of Melbourne, 1974.
—— "The Stricken Magpie". *Meanjin* 2, 1975.
Tunis, J.R. *The American Way of Sport.* New York, 1958.
Vamplew, Wray. *The Turf: A Social and Economic History of Horse Racing.* London: Allen Lane, 1976.

Voigt, David Quentin. "Cash and Glory: The Commercialization of Major League Baseball as a Sports Spectacular, 1885-1892". DSS thesis, Syracuse University, 1962.

Walvin, James. *The People's Game: The Social History of British Football.* London: Arrow, 1975.

Webster, Capt. F.A.M. *Sports Buildings and Maintenance, Making, Management, Maintenance and Equipment.* London, 1940.

Westman, S.K. *Sport Physical Training and Womanhood.* London: Bailliére, 1939.

Wood, J.L. *Cycles: A Short History.* London, 1970.

Young, P.M. *A History of British Football.* London, 1973.